CONTESTED MEDITERRANEAN SPACES

Space and Place

Bodily, geographic, and architectural sites are embedded with cultural knowledge and social value. The Anthropology of Space and Place series provides ethnographically rich analyses of the cultural organization and meanings of these sites of space, architecture, landscape, and places of the body. Contributions to this series will examine the symbolic meanings of space and place, the cultural and historical processes involved in their construction and contestation, and how they are in dialogue with wider political, religious, social, and economic ideas, values and institutions.

CONTESTED MEDITERRANEAN SPACES

Ethnographic Essays in Honour of Charles Tilly

edited by

Maria Kousis
Tom Selwyn
David Clark

Berghahn Books
New York • Oxford

First published in 2011 by

Berghahn Books

www.berghahnbooks.com

Library of Congress Cataloging-in-Publication Data

Contested Mediterranean spaces : ethnographic essays in honour of Charles Tilly
/ edited by Maria Kousis, Tom Selwyn, and David Clark.
    p. cm. — (Space and place v.4)
    Includes bibliographical references and index.
    ISBN 978-0-85745-132-3 (hardback : alk. paper)
    1. Ethnology—Mediterranean Region. 2. Human geography—Mediterranean
Region. 3. Mediterranean Region—Social life and customs. 4. Tilly, Charles.
I. Kousis, Maria. II. Selwyn, Tom. III. Clark, David.
  GN588.C66 2011
  305.8009182'2—dc22

                                            2010051910

British Library Cataloguing in Publication Data

A catalogue record for this book is available from the British Library

Printed in the United States on acid-free paper.

ISBN: 978-0-85745-132-3 Hardback

❧ CONTENTS ❧

৹ FIGURES ৡ

❧ TABLES ☙

❧ ABBREVIATIONS ❦

ACNAT	Actions by the Community for Nature Conservation (EU/WWF)
AD	Alternativa Demokratika
AI	Amnesty International
ASG	Arnavutkoy Semt Girisimi (Arnavutkoy Citizens' Initiative)
ADAM	Association d'Anthropologie Méditerranéenne
AXH	AX Holdings
BL2000	Bethlehem 2000
CCHP	Centre for Cultural Heritage Preservation
CHP	Turkish Republican People's Party
CIZ	Citizens' Initiative of Zakynthos
DELTA	Development of Territorial Cultural Systems Project (EU)
DLH	Din L-Art Helwa
EC	European Commission
EGCR	Environmental Group of Citizens in Rethimnon
EIA	Environmental Impact Assessment
EIC	Ecological Initiative of Chania
EIS	Environment Impact Statement
ENGO	Environmental Non-Governmental Organisation
EOKA	Ethniki Organosis Kiprion Agoniston (Greek Cypriot Nationalist Movement)
ERDF	European Regional Development Fund
EURODAC	European Dactyloscopy
EUROMED	Euro-Mediterranean Programme for Cultural Heritage (EU)
ESF	European Social Fund
EU	European Union
EUCC	European Union for the Conservation of Coasts

EURONATUR	European Nature Heritage Fund
FAVP	Federacio d'Associacions de Veins de Palma (Federation of Neighbours' Associations of Palma)
FEERI	Federacion Espanola de Entidades Religiosas Islamicas (Spanish Federation of Islamic Religious Entities)
FOE	Friends of the Earth
FOEE	Friends of the Earth Europe
FOEI	Friends of the Earth International
FRONT	Front Kontra I-Golf Kors
ILO	Immigratio Liaison Officer
IBC	Instituto per I Beni Culturali (Institute for Cultural Heritage)
IDF	Israeli Defence Force
IMF	International Monetary Fund
JHA	Justice and Home Affairs
LA	Liberacion Andaluza
LF	Lebanese Forces
MA	NMPZ Management Agency
MAP	Mediterranean Action Plan (UN)
MEDA	Mesures d'Accompagnement (EU)
MEDASSET	Mediterranean Association to Save Sea Turtles
MEDCAMPUS	Programme of de-centralised university co-operation in Mediterranean region (EU)
MEDNET	Mediterranean Programme of FOE
MED-VOICES	Mediterranean Voices Programme (EU)
MEPA	Malta Environment and Planning Authority
MIGREUROP	Network for rights of migrants in Europe
NGO	Non-Governmental Organisation
NMPZ	National Marine Park of Zakynthos
NT	National Trust
NTO	National Tourism Organisation
Orrinotererra	Ecological Intervention for Mountainous Municipality of Makrys Gialos
PA	Planning Authority
PADICO	Palestine Development and Investment Company
PAGANINI	Participatory Governance and Institutional Innovation

PERI	Plan Especial de Reforma Interior
PGOU	Pla General d'Ordenacio Urbana
PNR	Passenger Name Record
PSEC	Palestine Securities and Equities Commission
PSP	Progressive Socialist Party (Druze)
PTIC	Palestine Tourism Investment Company
RAC	Regional Activity Centre (UN)
RAI	Royal Anthropological Institute
RMSU	Regional Management Support Unit
SAGE	Siggiewi Action Group for the Environment
SIS	Schengen Information System
SOAS	School of Oriental and African Studies
SOLIDERE	Societé libanaise pour le development et la reconstruction de la centre ville de Beyrouth
SSCN	Society for the Study and Conservation of Nature
SMAP	Sustainable Management of Natural Resources and Energy (EU)
SPA	Specially Protected Area (UN)
STPS	Sea Turtle Protection Society (ARCHELON)
TEMPUS	Trans-European Mobility Programme for University Studies (EU)
UCIDE	Union de Communidades Islamicas (Union of Islamic Communities in Spain)
UNEP	United Nations Environment Programme
UNESCO	United Nations Educational and Scientific Cultural Organisation
UNHCR	United Nations High Commissioner for Refugees
UNRWA	United Nations Relief and Works Agency
URBAN	Urban Community Inititiative
USAID	United States Agency for International Development
VIS	Visa Information System
YMCA	Young Men's Christian Association
YPEHODE	Ministry of Environment, Urban Planning and Public Works
Zghazwagh ghall-Ambjent	Young Environmentalists

♂ PREFACE ♀

The lineages of this volume go back partly to an international conference held at the University of Crete (Rethymno, 2003) and partly to the larger project that was one of the main sponsors of this conference, 'Mediterranean Voices: Oral History and Cultural Practices in Mediterranean Cities' (Med-Voices for short).

The Rethymno meeting served at least two functions. The first was to honour Charles Tilly for his contribution to the field of Mediterranean studies, in particular history and politics. The second was to encourage the growth of an informal academic network of mainly young scholars of the region. These latter consisted both of Tilly's former students and of participants in the Med-Voices project. The present volume complements another recent publication that flowed from the conference (Tilly, Franzosi and Kousis 2008).

Med-Voices was originally a three-year project, partly funded from 2002 until 2005 by the European Commission's EuropeAid programme and thereafter continuing with a more independent life of its own (see below). The project was coordinated from London by Julie Scott, Raoul Bianchi, Tom Selwyn and Jonathan Karkut, with invaluable periodic assistance from Brigitte Voland, in cooperation with a consortium of research units in thirteen Mediterranean cities.[1] The various aspects of the project generated the following distinctive outputs.

First of all, a large website/database (www.medvoices.org) was constructed to hold the visual and textual data gathered by each of the researchers in the partner cities. The site was structured with reference to seven themes: *spaces, living together, worship, work, objects, play, the person*. The rationale for choosing these as organizing themes was to provide a framework capable of shaping the way the data was to be researched and recorded and to provide an intellectual structure that would allow regional comparative work to take place. Secondly, Med-Voices has produced, and continues to produce, other publications including edited books, journal articles, films, exhibitions with catalogues, and reports (e.g. Radmilli and Selwyn 2005). Thirdly, the project has formed the basis of presentations at university seminars (for the most part in departments of social anthropology and education), conference panels and school sixth form audiences.

Med-Voices has been described in detail in a special edition of the *Journal of Mediterranean Studies* (2005) featuring a collection of essays by some of its participants.[2] As indicated above, the EC encourages those who take part in the projects it funds to design ways of continuing the work after its own grant has come to an end. To this end an association has been set up to look towards opportunities for future work and projects in the region.[3]

The contributors to the present collection of essays present fresh approaches to the study of contentious politics in the region. Mediterranean scholars themselves, they either reflect on concepts and methods related to Tilly's work, or point to alternative ways of looking at the topic through the lenses of ethnographic examinations of a variety of Mediterranean spaces. All views presented here are the authors' and do not represent those of the EC.

There are many people and institutions to thank for helping to make this volume possible. We would like again to thank Julie Scott and Jonathan Karkut (both at London Metropolitan University), Raoul Bianchi (University of East London) and Brigitte Voland for their continuous support in this long endeavour, as well as the University of Crete for its match funding of both conference and project, Rachel Radmilli of the University of Malta for her unflagging encouragement, and Tony Aquilina, Stephanie Borg and the rest of the team at Miranda (Malta). We are also grateful to Michael Herzfeld (Harvard University) and Javier Auyero (University of Texas at Austin) for their encouragement. Most of all we would like to thank all our contributors for their enthusiasm throughout this endeavour as well as Marion Berghahn, Ann Przyzycki, Melissa Spinelli and Jaime Taber at Berghahn Books for their generous support in the publication of this volume. In this connection we are sad to report that one of the contributors, Günhan Danışman, died before the volume was published.

Finally, what follows owes a great deal to the inspiration, encouragement and support of Charles Tilly himself, who died on 29 April 2008. We dedicate the volume to him.

Rethymno, December 2010
Maria Kousis, Tom Selwyn, David Clark

NOTES

1. Alexandria, Bethlehem, Beirut, Nicosia South, Nicosia North, Istanbul, Chania, Ancona, Valletta, Ciutat de Mallorca, Marseilles, Granada, Las Palmas.
2. A complete list of these may be obtained from j.karkut@londonmet.ac.uk
3. Details of the Mediterranean Voices Association and its ongoing work may be obtained from j.karkut@londonmet.ac.uk and the Mediterranean Voices Association: info@medvoices.org

REFERENCES

Radmilli, R. and T. Selwyn (guest eds). 2005. *Journal of Mediterranean Studies* 15(2): 'Turning Back to the Mediterranean: Anthropological Issues and the MED-VOICES Project'

Tilly, C., R. Franzosi and M. Kousis (guest eds). 2008. *American Behavioral Scientist*, special issue *Mediterranean Political Processes, 1400–2006*, Part I: *Historical Perspectives*, 51(10) and Part II: *Contemporary Perspectives*, 51(11).

❧ Introduction ❧

MARIA KOUSIS, TOM SELWYN AND DAVID CLARK

This Introduction has two aims, both shaped by the work of Charles Tilly. The first is to locate the collection of essays within a framework of overlapping spaces. These consist of the Mediterranean region itself, the European Union, the cities from which the ethnographies have come and the streets and neighbourhoods in which the individual persons described here live and work. The second is to suggest how the essays express the dynamics of social structures and processes within these spaces in terms of relationships between politics, capital and identity. What follows is divided into two parts reflecting these two aims.

Mediterranean Spaces

The Mediterranean Region

Tilly (2008, 2004: 229–232) argued that despite periodic historical and geographical expressions of provincialism, isolationism, nationalism and sub-nationalism, the Mediterranean region has always been one of the world's most cosmopolitan regions. (For us, cosmopolitanism does not necessarily stand in opposition to particularism but rather contains it within itself). Tilly identified three particular features of the region that have historically given rise to its cosmopolitanism. Firstly, it is home to clusters of intercontinental contacts and networks. Mediterranean networks of trade, for example, stretch deep into both Africa and Asia. Secondly, its islands, cities and coasts house a diverse population whose members are both divided and united by their attachments to the three great monotheistic religions of Judaism, Christianity and Islam. Thirdly, although repetitive attempts have been made by various powers to control the entirety of its borders – for the economic and political benefits that such control would bring – none has succeeded.

The opening essay of the collection, by Yiakoumaki, looks at the region as a whole whilst the majority of the remaining essays complement the work of the social historians and political sociologists that has appeared elsewhere (e.g. Tilly 2008) by offering a 'Braudelian tour' of particular places and spaces within the Mediterranean.

The European Union

Not surprisingly, the EU is the major player in the trade of goods and services to and from the Mediterranean partner countries. It is also the largest direct foreign investor, the region's main provider of financial assistance and funding, its main source of tourism and the first destination of migrants (European Commission 2005: 1). During a historical period in which Europe itself has witnessed substantial economic growth, extension of largely Western European social democratic political systems, the collapse of state socialism and consequent migration from south to north, there has also been a flourishing of multilateral Mediterranean partnerships between Europe and the non-European Mediterranean partner countries. Thus, in 1995, the EU and twelve southern and eastern Mediterranean countries[1] launched the Euro-Mediterranean Partnership[2] under the Barcelona Declaration requiring 'a strengthening of democracy and respect for human rights, sustainable and balanced economic and social development, measures to combat poverty and promotion of greater understanding between cultures'. More recent Euro-Mediterranean association agreements between the governments of Israel, Morocco, Tunisia, Jordan, Egypt, Algeria, Lebanon and the Palestine National Authority have concerned the three main areas included in the Barcelona Declaration: political dialogue, establishment of a free trade area and economic, financial, social and cultural cooperation. Critics have argued that attention has been paid mostly to those instruments related to the establishment of free trade areas, structural adjustments and security, and less to issues of economic and social rights (e.g. Martin, Byrne and Schade-Poulsen 2004).

The second essay of the collection, by Samatas, offers us a view (from the Mediterranean) of the European Union as a whole, the policies and agencies of which clearly play an important (if not principal) role in the majority of the rest of our essays. All of them refer in one way or another to the influence of the EU in fields that include policies concerned with urban renewal, regional economy, the environment, sociocultural frameworks and 'security'.

States

Although all the essays, except the first two, focus on cities and neighbourhoods, all also contain references to states and state policies. In particular,

Boissevain and Gatt examine state-level environmental political processes in Malta whilst the other essay with a specific focus on the politics of the environment, namely that by Kousis and Psarikidou, concentrates on two islands but also speaks of policies of the Greek state. Moreover Haugbolle's examination of the gentrification of Beirut clearly points readers towards broader aspects of the politics and economics of the Lebanese state.

Cities, Neighbourhoods and Individuals

Tilly argued that:

> Cities constitute our best laboratories for investigation of historical contingency – the way that social action in a given time and place constrains what will happen next there and in adjacent places, what will happen after that and so on through long strings of path-dependent processes. (1996: 715)

In Tilly's (1998) view one of the major problems in contemporary social science and history is the relationship between biography experience on the very small scale and larger social processes (involving, for example, trade, commercialization, capital accumulation, state formation and transformation). By linking such large processes with local life and considering the effects of time and space seriously, the field of urban studies (including urban history) is able to shed considerable light on all sorts of questions, including those of urban inequality, xenophobia and stable democracy (Tilly 1996: 715). Cities are spaces in which imaginative urban anthropology and the use of such conventional ethnographic tools as interviews, conversations and participant observation, may bring together theory, policy and personal experience (Tilly 1967). In this respect urban anthropology – particularly urban political ethnography – is a promising avenue of study (Tilly 2006).

The majority of the essays that follow offer politically oriented ethnographies within and across Mediterranean cities. Ten of the twelve present contributions are based on fieldwork and ethnographic research carried out under the aegis of the Med-Voices project (see preface to this volume). Some contributions (including those by Sansour Dabdoub and Zoughbi-Janineh, Clark, Danişman and Üstün, Morell and Franquesa, Haugbolle, and Selwyn) deal with conflicts related to urban planning and urban gentrification. Others focus more precisely on ethno-religious questions (Muslim/non-Muslim, Jewish/Christian, Jewish/Muslim, Palestinian/Israeli, Spanish/Arab) in the region's cities.

In summary, all the essays presented here deal with contentious politics (to use Tilly's best-known expression) and contested spaces in the Mediterranean at levels ranging from the overlapping regions of the Mediterranean and EU themselves to communities and neighbourhoods in Granada, Bologna, Malta, Istanbul, Beirut, Bethlehem, Ciutat de Mallorca and Chania as well as the two Greek islands of Zakynthos and Crete.

Politics, Capital and Identity

We may now approach our collection from another angle. Here the intention is to show that what the chapters have in common is a concern with a set of politico-economic and cultural dynamics that stem from the relationship between politics, capital and identity. We will begin by tracing how this concern flows directly from Tilly's own work.

On the Citizen

One of Tilly's starting points in the analysis of the contemporary world is the citizen him/herself. Tilly's citizen is one who lives in a world shaped by such geopolitical forces as globalization and (in the European and Mediterranean regions) the influence of the EU. He/she routinely interacts with new institutions at levels ranging from the local to the supranational and inhabits an increasingly fluid world in which the nature of citizenship and identity are undergoing fundamental transformations. Our essays follow Tilly in placing citizens at centre stage. The question is: what does this stage look like? Tilly's own approach to this question starts with critically reflecting on the nature of the politico-economic regimes in which citizens of the contemporary world live and work. He suggests (2004: 45–54) that regimes may be measured and compared with reference to three fundamental characteristics: *coercion, capital* and *commitment*. He uses these terms to apply respectively to the degree of coercive power a regime deploys against its citizens, the financial and legal structures associated with ownership and control over resources, and the various foundations upon which sociocultural and/or politico-economic solidarities rest (these being normally expressed in ethnic, religious, kinship, or other cultural ways, as well as in political and economic terms).

For present purposes we use a slightly amended version of this formulation and identify three of our own points of reference as *politics, capital* and *expressions/representations of identity*. We use these terms to apply respectively to political activities and discourse, the place of capital and the cultural/symbolic processes shaping the formation of identities. Using cases from different parts of the Mediterranean, the book thus seeks to examine the worlds of citizens caught up in the complex interrelations and interconnections between politics, capital and cultural processes in territorial fields that include region (and the world beyond), state and city/neighbourhood.

For the sake of clarity, we may take another passage from Tilly (with Hanagan) (1999: 5) to illustrate how our proposed framework fits. These authors argue that within the EU there are 'multiple political allegiances marked by fragmented sovereignty as a result of which cross-cutting jurisdictions are beginning to emerge'. Indeed, one of the questions that runs throughout our volume concerns the manner in which globalization and new regional alliances are influencing relationships between states, neighbourhoods and their citizens. As already noted above, whilst the boundaries and functions of states are being reconfigured, citizens increasingly interact with institutions and agencies from expanding geopolitical and economic parameters at local, regional, national and supranational levels.

Mediterranean and Euro-Med Citizens

The first three chapters are concerned with the two large and overlapping regions of Europe and the Mediterranean, within which all the chapters of the volume are located. Both Yiakoumaki and Samatas address issues that have to do with the nature of the regions themselves. Yiakoumaki's chapter examines the various meanings attached to concepts of Mediterraneanness and the symbolic importance of the region to EU strategic and policy-related rhetoric. The author is sceptical about notions that ascribe any sort of essentialist 'unity' to the Mediterranean as a region. Cultural connections between cities and states within the Mediterranean that EC-funded programmes such as Med-Voices are encouraged to celebrate – by way, for example, of the promotion of artistic productions that make a virtue of regionalism – are, she suggests, mainly window dressing for the bending of the Mediterranean to the political and economic interests of Europe. In this context the 'past' (associated with the idea of the Braudelian Mediterranean as an essentially unified region) may appear as a convenient source for 'legitimating the politics of the future'. The Barcelona Process, adopted following the 1995 conference in Barcelona between representatives of EU and North African countries and to which we have already alluded above, was launched under the banner of a Euro-Mediterranean Partnership. This was a partnership designed to establish 'economic and financial partnerships' between north and south, a Mediterranean 'free-trade area' and a 'common area of peace and partnership in social, cultural and human affairs'. Yiakoumaki observes that such measures as these (in which the essential unity of the Mediterranean served as a powerful ideological tool) grew directly out of the global economic recession of the early 1980s and the consequent need for the EU to develop the markets of the south, opening them up to foreign investment in order to revitalize its own economy.

In chapter 2, Samatas introduces us to a Europe that is driven by various 'security' agendas and as a result is increasingly becoming a 'fortress'. Focusing on the post-9/11 EU security agenda and the reinforcement of the Schengen Information System (SIS), he examines the various surveillance measures adopted by EU countries to restrict the entry of non-EU citizens into EU states and the impact this has on human rights and civil liberties. Whilst much of the discussion focuses on measures taken within EU states, the chapter also broaches the issue of buffer states that collaborate with EU countries in patrolling borders and seaways, especially along the North African coast, in order to further control and restrict illegal immigration into the EU. In this manner, the process of reconfiguring state and citizenship within Europe has implications for neighbouring states as well.

In her chapter, Kallimopoulou relates ethnomusicological representations of the 'Mediterranean' to broader Mediterranean discourses constructed in European academia and the commercial music market, linking them to dominant ideological paradigms of modernity such as that of nationalism. Her research is based on the Medi-Terra Music Festival in Crete, specifically organized in conjunction with the Med-Voices project, that brought together music and groups from the various regions of the Mediterranean – from Andalusia to the Balkans and Turkey to the Middle East. Members of many of the groups emphasized their own mixed cultural backgrounds and performed music that not only assigned a positive value to ideas of musical and cultural fusion but also placed their work within wider 'world music' traditions. The music and dance of the Palestinian group, however, stressed more local cultural affiliations whilst simultaneously attracting involvement and participation from the festival's cosmopolitan summer audience.

Taken together, these three chapters lead the reader to a position from which the Mediterranean appears as a region with a deeply ambivalent character. On the one hand it is presented rhetorically as a cultural cosmopolis (à la Tilly and much of the aims of the Med-Voices project described in the preface) in which, as in the Medi-Terra Festival, cultural styles are promoted that appear to blend and fuse. On the other hand (and having in mind, for example, the difficulties of people from the south of the region scaling the walls of the 'fortress' north) it appears as a geopolitical space divided into unequal parts within which categories of membership are distinguished from each other by markedly different access to human rights – including the right to travel easily throughout the region – and socioeconomic opportunities.

State, Capital and Resistance

The next three chapters are devoted to the relationships between political action and capital. Chapter 4, by Boissevain and Gatt, is concerned with the changing relationships between financial capital, the (Maltese) state and its citizens as the latter have exercised increasing political potency in their struggles against certain types of development projects over the past forty years. The authors observe that the networks of NGOs and the capitalist networks associated with the developments that the former oppose have in common the fact that they both are transnational. The chapter illustrates well how international capital and an internationally affiliated, but largely locally developed, civil society come face to face on the political stage of the Maltese state – and how the state itself is reconfigured in the process.

In chapter 5, Kousis and Psarikidou offer an exploratory and descriptive account of the ways in which environmental professional organizations and community activists have responded to *Caretta caretta* biodiversity concerns based on the EU Habitats Directive. More in Zakynthos and less in Crete, local small and medium-sized tourism enterprises and landowners have resisted the environmental protection legislation imported from Brussels that would curtail the economic (tourism) opportunities in the densest nesting beach of *Caretta caretta* in the Mediterranean. The essay does not focus so much on the conflict between the tourism-dependent local communities and the nonlocal actors who have been attempting to implement the directive in the islands of Zakynthos and Crete, as on the initiatives and resistance on the part of the environmental activists promoting sustainable development-oriented aims and practices through scientific and management initiatives.

Haugbolle, in his account in chapter 6 of neighbourhood distinctiveness in post–civil war Beirut, is also concerned with the state, although this time from the perspective of the Lebanese street. Here, partnerships between central government and private developers, coming together under the umbrella of the Solidere[3] company and driven by the late prime minister and main shareholder of the company, have initiated a wholesale redevelopment of downtown Beirut. Haugbolle reports that this redevelopment was 'presented by the company as a necessary *tabula rasa* on which to write a new and better chapter of Lebanese history' – one that sought to reconstitute the 'golden age' of the 1950s and 1960s, in which all sections of society, regardless of religious background, ethnicity or race, mingled together in the streets, markets, shops and cafés, worked harmoniously together and lived in ethnically mixed neighbourhoods. However, 'the initial process of clearing the area of any war remnants implied the destruction of whole neighbourhoods, including the old Ottoman *aswak* (markets)'. The Beirut of Solidere may have been presented as embodying the current aspirations for 'unity in diversity', but its critics have argued that the physical removal of much of the evidence of cultural diversity has done nothing of the kind.

Just beyond the city centre the realities of segregated and divided civic life can be seen in the posters, flags and graffiti all over the surfaces of the residential neighbourhoods. Logos and symbols associated with the different sectarian parties and identities mark out territorial boundaries and act as constant reminders of neighbourhood allegiances in the northern Maronite or southern Shiite suburbs. In the poorer neighbourhoods nearest the downtown area, many houses are still ruins, whilst shrines and monuments to dead fighters and dead leaders are further reminders of recent conflict. The state-sponsored message of harmonious coexistence clashes with the messages from the streets of the persistence of ethnic conflict and rivalries. Downtown Beirut asserts not so much Lebanese multiculturalism but the actual and symbolic power of international development capital. Haugbolle's chapter is a convincing examination of the relationship between cultural pluralism and international capital as articulated within the framework of political processes at state and neighbourhood levels.

Capital and Neighbourhood Governance

Although the scale and context are in many ways quite different, there are several continuities between the development processes described by Haugbolle for Beirut and by Sansour Dabdoub and Zoughbi-Janineh for Bethlehem. The authors of the seventh chapter trace the attempts by Bethlehem 2000, a para-state conservation association set up by the Palestinian National Authority in the mid 1990s to prepare for the millennium, to restore Star Street to something like its former prominence as one of the central arteries of the city. They describe how the combined processes of Israeli occupation (with the various checkpoints, barriers, road closures and diversions, and daily and nightly incursions by the occupying forces that define it), many former residents' outward migration from the city of Bethlehem (mainly as a result of the occupation) and a tourism industry that overwhelmingly stresses short bus trips from Jerusalem to the Church of the Nativity by tourists staying in Israel, had combined to empty the street of the traders whose small artisanal workshops and retail shops made up a historically significant part of the commercial life of the city.

For five years, and with considerable success, the architects and planners of Bethlehem 2000 worked to persuade some of the traders back to Star Street on the grounds that starting in 2000 the city would adopt a new tourism system whereby visitors would be dropped off at one end of the street and then walk down to the Church of the Nativity at the other end.

Good commercial opportunities, they argued, would flow from such an arrangement. Just before the millennium, however, the largest development company in Palestine – one of the few companies quoted on the Palestinian stock exchange – built a bus station near the church and made an agreement with the municipality that all tourist coaches were required to park there – and to pay the council for doing so. At a stroke the plans for Star Street fell apart. With few, if any, tourists walking along it, the traders packed up once more, and the opportunities for the planned restoration to contribute to the economic recovery of Bethlehem as a whole were lost.

In chapter 8 Morell and Franquesa look at the case of the Old City of Ciutat de Mallorca, focusing on the extent to which three particular neighbourhoods in the area have been, and are being, transformed on the basis of calculations by both municipal authorities and private investors about how to extract greater capital value through increased gentrification and commercialization. Their analysis points to the relative autonomy of the political sphere (in the sense that political processes are routinely distant from the experiences, needs and wishes of those who live and work in the neighbourhoods in question), the effects of globalization on the restructuring of urban space and the ways these impact on the generally upward political mobility of local leaders. The evidence shows that political brokers have exploited not only the built environment of the city, but its inhabitants as well.

Chapter 9 develops the theme of neighbourhood resistance in the face of the combined forces of the state and private capital. Danişman and Üstün address issues of the construction of a third bridge over the Bosphorus associated with overambitious transport plans out of keeping with local needs in Istanbul. Organized local community claims face a constant struggle, with occasional victories and reprieves, aiming to gain the long-term resolution (which would involve reconfiguration of the democratic and financial basis of the organization of the state) that is implicitly argued for by Boissevain and Gatt in the Maltese case. In the Istanbul and Mallorca cases it is clear that processes of commodification of neighbourhood spaces and the social relationships therein are given added impetus and indeed facilitated by the manner in which town planning at the local level is directed and encouraged by supranational and national directives and funding strategies.

Identities, Imaginations and Representations

The final three chapters in the volume are particularly concerned with questions of transforming identities. Thus the tenth chapter, by Rosón Lorente and Dietz, examines ethnicized inter-religious conflict in the El Albayzin quarter of Granada. On the one hand there are new converts to Islam, in-coming Muslim migrants and Spanish Islamophiles. On the other hand there are longer-term residents who wish to maintain a more Catholic and Christian approach to the province. The tension between these two cat-egories of people regularly comes ritually and ceremonially to the fore on the occasion of the anniversary of the 're-conquest' of Spain. The different camps, in opposition to one another, mark what is for one a 'glorious re-conquest' of Spain under the Christian monarchy and, for the other, the loss of the 'golden period of Andalusia' in which three faiths (Islam, Chris-tianity and Judaism) lived in harmony and prosperity.

Such ceremonies and counter-ceremonies must be understood not only in terms of divergent views of the past, but also in terms of divergent views of the present and in particular about where Andalusia should be position-ing itself in relation to the rest of Spain. The distinctiveness of Andalusia could be imagined in terms of a harmonious relationship between different ethnic or religious groups, then and now. But such distinctiveness could be forgone in favour of closer identification with a more unitary and in-deed more Catholic view of Spain. The ethnic and cultural antagonisms in Granada are clearly related to a politico-economic regional regime, framed in large measure by the EU itself, that exacerbates economic inequalities between the north and south banks of the sea (Bianchi 2005) and gives rise to the migratory movements upon which the political conservatives in the Albayzin Neighbourhood Association hang their localism and racism. Where does Mediterranean pluralism and EU openness go in this context? We will return to this issue and its implications later on.

Chapter 11, by Clark, examines the interplay between politics and ex-pressions of identity within the context of Jewish cultural heritage in Italy. The politics of heritage plays out both at the national level and at the very local level. Indeed, whilst enabling legislation at the national level has de-volved responsibility for maintaining Jewish material culture to the local level, much depends on how different political agenda and interest groups come together to formulate a joint course of action. In the case of Bologna, city centre regeneration issues, municipal cultural policies and regional heritage strategies favoured the establishment of a Jewish museum at the very moment that the city was preparing to become one of the European Cities of Culture in the year 2000. Yet, individual and Jewish communal initiatives also played a part in the decision to situate the museum in the old ghetto area of Bologna, thereby giving expression and symbolically re-affirming a Jewish presence in Bologna, a presence that had withstood the test of time despite many vicissitudes along the way.

Similarly in Ferrara, the decision to lend support to the establishment of a Jewish museum and to publicize a Jewish heritage trail in the city coincided with the designation of Ferrara as a world heritage site in 1995. Such support would not have been possible without the active involvement of a leading political broker who could straddle several social worlds, being actively involved in Jewish communal organization as well as municipal and regional heritage campaigns. Nevertheless, such ventures, in Bologna and Ferrara alike, also require the active support of local Jewish communities and activists, not all of whom, by any means, speak with one voice. Hence this chapter also examines the role of controversy and resistance and incorporates Foucault's notions of power as being diffuse and an integral part of all social interactions (Foucault 1980).

The twelfth chapter follows several of the thematic threads traced by Clark. Vardaki describes and analyses a multicultural festival in Crete, the first of its kind to take place on the island, and explores the interplay between cultural production and consumption. She examines local government's and local migrant groups' various motives for establishing the festival and explores the manner in which the festival was received by the media, local residents and those who took part in it. Based on the above, her analysis aims to understand and conceptualize transborder identities in light of the experiential dimensions of identity as well as the discursive role of place. She offers evidence of how the festival demonstrated that in Chania, immigrants can become part of the town's contemporary cultural scene. For the new immigrants themselves, home is no longer perceived as a fixed place.

The final chapter of the volume examines the case of a building in Bethlehem commonly known as Rachel's Tomb, a small shrine that the available records suggest has been the focus of Jewish/Muslim cooperation in a largely Christian municipal milieu throughout most of its history. Selwyn describes how the tomb has recently been surrounded by high concrete walls (part of the wider Israeli project of wall building in the Palestinian/Israeli borderlands), how the tomb has been administratively removed from Bethlehem and placed under the jurisdiction of the municipality of Jerusalem, how the neighbourhood around the tomb (11 per cent of municipal Bethlehem) has been economically and physically destroyed and how a large part of its Bethlehemite population has been 'cleansed' from the area.

The argument is advanced that here we have a particularly vivid example of the politics of identity at work. In the case of Rachel's Tomb this has to do with the way that Jewish identity in the region is rhetorically articulated by 'settlers' and their followers in order to argue for the inevitability of 'separation' between Israelis and Palestinians, and the impossibility of continuing the tradition of sharing a building between members of more than one faith. Selwyn also observes that the politics of religious separation in this case rely on a very particular interpretation of the biblical story of Rachel. This clearly fits well with wider economic and political interests that take us straight back to the images of a 'fortress' and the concrete and metaphorical walls that stand between Israeli and Palestinian, Jew and Arab, north and south of the Mediterranean and, in a larger sense, between 'us' and 'them'.

Conclusion

All of the chapters in this book deal with the manner in which particular Mediterranean spaces (at regional, state and neighbourhood levels) are being reconfigured in the light of struggles over rights, resources and identities. Political processes driven from the 'top' (of state and municipal political hierarchies, for example) and processes of resistance from the 'bottom' (in the shape of environmental movements, popular artistic and decorative events and expressions, for example) are described in such a way as to challenge any simple assumption about the nature and constitution of political power in the region. Our authors have approached their field sites from the viewpoint of an intellectual tradition generated by Charles Tilly and others – a tradition that we might term in shorthand the political economy of cultural geography. From this viewpoint the contested reworking and renegotiation of Mediterranean spaces and political landscapes becomes a matter not only of the activities and rhetorical/bureaucratic announcements of state or EU authorities, but also of the increasingly potent agency of a variety of other actors and institutions. These include environmental activists in Malta, cultural entrepreneurs in Crete, producers of posters and graffiti in Beirut, and globally affiliated cross-border social and political interest groups mobilizing in the streets and communities of Ciutat de Mallorca, Bethlehem, Ferrara and Istanbul, and from there across the region and beyond.

NOTES

1. http://ec.europa.eu/comm/external_relations/euromed/index.htm.
2. http://europa.eu.int/comm/external_relations/euromed/bd.htm.
3. Acronym for Societé Libanaise pour le développement et la reconstruction de la centre ville de Beyrouth.

REFERENCES

Bianchi, R. 2005. 'Euro-Med Heritage: Culture, Capital and Trade Liberalisation: Implications for the Mediterranean City', *Journal of Mediterranean Studies*, 15(2): 283–319.

European Commission. 2005. *Communication from the Commission to the Council and the European Parliament*, 'Tenth Anniversary of the Euro-Mediterranean Partnership: A Work Program to Meet the Challenges of the Next Five Years: External Affairs Euro-Mediterranean Partnership'. Retrieved on Feb. 2, 2007 from http://ec.europa.eu/comm/external_relations/euromed/bd.htm.

Foucault, M. 1980. *Power/Knowledge.* Hemel Hempstead: Harvester Wheatsheaf.

Hanagan, M. and Tilly, C. 1999. *Extending Citizenship, Reconfiguring States.* Lanham, MD: Rowman and Littlefield Publishers.

Martin, I., I. Byrne and M. Schade-Poulsen. 2004. 'Economic and Social Rights in the Euro-Mediterranean Partnership: The Missing Link?' *Mediterranean Politics* 9(3): 307–318.

Tilly, C. 1967. 'Anthropology on the Town', *Habitat* 10: 20–25.

Tilly, C. 1996. "What Good is Urban History", *Journal of Urban History,* 22: 702–719.

Tilly, C. 1998. *Durable Inequality.* Berkeley: University of California Press.

Tilly, C. 2004. *Contention and Democracy in Europe, 1650–2000.* Cambridge: Cambridge University Press.

Tilly, C. 2006. 'Afterword: Political Ethnography as Art and Science', *Qualitative Sociology,* 29: 409–412.

Tilly, C. 2008. 'A General Introduction to the Special Issue: Mediterranean Political Processes in C. Tilly, R. Franzosi and M. Kousis (guest eds.) Comparative-Historical Perspective; Part I: Historical Perspectives; Part II: Contemporary Perspectives', *American Behavioral Scientist,* 51(10): 1467–1471.

Part 1

❧ ◆ ☙

Recovering the Mediterranean?

Chapter 1

On Bureaucratic Essentialism

Constructing the Mediterranean in European Union Institutions

VASSILIKI YIAKOUMAKI

Introduction

The reemergence of the concept of the 'Mediterranean' in anthropological research reawakens memories of the essentialism of the 'culture area' but also raises questions pertaining to the legitimacy of this concept in contemporary research. This seeming return warrants examination in the broad politico-economic and historical context of European Union institutions and politics, a main locus of production of the Mediterranean discourse today. Drawing on research experience in an EU-funded programme on the Mediterranean, in this chapter I provide not an ethnographic analysis of material from the field, but rather an account of historical and geopolitical conditions allowing for the emergence of the 'Mediterraneanism' in question during the last couple of decades. In other words, I provide an account of the conditions generating the political necessity for adopting the 'Mediterranean' as a working concept. This is a crucial task for understanding what happens when seemingly essentialist concepts are redeployed and become institutionally binding, and for producing awareness of the historical/political contexts in which anthropological projects emerge today.

The concept of the Mediterranean has generated much debate among anthropologists in the context of reflecting on the 'culture area'. In this chapter I discuss the Mediterranean in the context of its deployment as a term in the discourse of policy makers in political/bureaucratic institutions of the European Union (EU) from the mid 1990s onwards, with an eye to the impact it can have, as such, on anthropological inquiry and ethnographic research. I draw on experience gained in the research programme Mediterranean Voices, funded by the European Commission, for which I have conducted extensive research – an experience that I share with other contributors to this volume. Therefore I wish to pinpoint the reemergence of the Mediterranean not solely because the use of the concept in official political discourse today evokes the culture area, thus making it an intriguing issue for anthropological reflection, but also because anthropological research is currently being generated and funded as a result, thereby creating an opportunity for its emergence in political institutions today.

More specifically, I am not concerned here with discussing ethnographic material from our research project mentioned above, or with methodological issues that have emerged in the process. That is, I am not concerned with the particular ethnography per se as an anthropologically valuable endeavour. Rather, I discuss the moment of 'turning back to the Mediterranean'[1] from the point of view of institutions, that is, of official actors promoting a certain definition of the Mediterranean as culture area. I consider it politically important to view our overall project as product of specific politics and socioeconomic circumstances at a significant historical moment in Europe. In other words, I am concerned with policy-making institutions, in this case with EU administrative institutions, as loci of production of a certain notion of 'cultural unity'.

Why ought one to become concerned with this administrative bureaucracy in order to talk about anthropology? In conducting research for the Mediterranean Voices project (our partner-project was located in the city of Chania, in Crete, Greece) and having to remain somehow faithful to the idea of a 'Mediterranean culture', I often had the feeling of an intellectual déjà vu in regard to speaking of the Mediterranean. Hence I became curious about the emergence of such a discourse in EU policy-making institutions, as well as about why it is emerging particularly in this present historical moment, i.e. the last couple of decades. Specifically, the use of the term connotes a certain cultural unity of the Mediterranean region, whilst also being compatible with a Mediterranean nostalgia known in existing literary traditions. Anthropologists have developed a knee-jerk reaction to the idea of a Mediterranean anthropology, as they are critical of the essentialism of the culture area and the geopolitics surrounding the construction of this culture area – one may recall the Mediterranean ethnographies of the 1960s and 1970s, and the subsequent critical debates on Mediterraneanism.[2] Undoubtedly, it is a concept identified with academic parochialism. Is the present moment therefore the return of a cultural essentialism? A bureaucratic essentialism?

In order to provide an answer, one needs to trace a certain genealogy of the term Mediterranean within the policy-making institutions that generate the research in question. The value of such a venture is conducive to understanding research as a product of specific historical and political circumstances. The process towards such an understanding makes an eth-nographer more aware politically, and by this I mean more aware of his/her role in research funded by political/administrative institutions as well as the potential his/her ethnography holds for engaging in the realities of the societies he/she is working in. As anthropologists we are aware that 'area' terms such as the 'Middle East', 'Latin America', 'South-east Asia' or 'the Balkans' are not neutral but are shaped by power relations in given political circumstances, and that they may essentialize and imply sweeping assump-tions about cultures with geographical proximity. However, they are not to be discarded as such but to be utilized with awareness of their history and their political underpinnings.

In what follows, I offer an account of the 'return' of the Mediterranean by placing the re-emergence of the concept in a broader politico-economic and historical context. Therefore this chapter addresses issues of histori-cal and political contextualization of anthropological research, rather than of anthropological interpretation in the strict sense of the word. In this process, I draw on the 'Mediterranean Voices: Oral History and Cultural Practice in Mediterranean Cities' programme, both as an example of how the above return is realized in the discourse of policy makers, and as an example of contemporary research funded by political/administrative institutions.

Speaking of the 'Mediterranean' (Once More...)

By 'return' or 're'-emergence, I am referring to the articulation of a dis-course of a 'Mediterranean' (or also 'Euro-Mediterranean') culture, or cul-tural 'heritage', which emerged in the mid 1990s in EU institutions. I draw my examples based on a three-year research experience on the European Commission programme 'Mediterranean Voices: Oral History and Cul-tural Practice in Mediterranean Cities', a recently completed project of EU-funded research on (and in) the Mediterranean. With this I wish to suggest, primarily, that this moment is not a revival of the agenda of Mediterra-neanism as anthropologists know it, but it is mainly about political and economic agendas pertaining to European integration processes during the last couple of decades.

Since the mid 1990s a number of research programmes have been funded by the EU under the broader programme Euromed Heritage (I and II), focus-ing on what has been called the 'Euro-Mediterranean' cultures and heritage as part of EU policy on the Mediterranean region, which I elaborate below. Mediterranean Voices, an ethnographic research project on Mediterranean 'urban heritage', is one such example. The project comprised thirteen partner projects across the Mediterranean, North and South, which meant in practice that fieldwork was done on thirteen Mediterranean cities: Alexandria, Ancona, Beirut, Bethlehem, Chania (Crete), Ciutat de Mallorca, Granada, Istanbul, Las Palmas de Gran Canaria, Marseilles, Nicosia North, Nicosia South and Valletta. Work was based on a partnership with a number of different institutions, such as universities and NGOs.[3] The stated objective of the proposed project was 'to collect oral histories and memories of residents living in historic urban neighbourhoods' (www.med-voices .org). This was an audio-visual project, based on the use of digital technologies for the purpose of creating audiovisual products (a website/database, ethnographic films) and in situ events (conferences, exhibitions, festivals) on Mediterranean oral histories and urban spaces.

It was in conducting an ethnography for such an undertaking that I became concerned with the recent geopolitical emergence of a particular type of Mediterraneanism, i.e. the emergence, within the framework of EU policy-making institutions, of a demand for research that claims the existence of a certain kind of cultural unity of the Mediterranean world. The programme was largely an applied one, meaning that our research products were intended to contribute to what is known as 'urban heritage management and policy' in Mediterranean countries by empowering local actors to participate in policy decisions, thus creating 'regional stakeholder networks' according to the priorities of Euromed Heritage programmes. These priorities have to do with seeking forms of sustainable development in European cities or urban spaces today.

This very material, practical and pragmatic aspect of such programmes is rhetorically framed by a representation of a Mediterranean world as united by common threads of history. While reminiscent of a Braudelian Mediterranean, this representation is often evocative of an essentialist, romantic approach to the region. To be more specific, the rhetoric of the Mediterranean, as articulated in the discourse of EU policy-making actors funding such research, appears to contribute to a renewed construction of the 'culture area'. This rhetoric may affect or shape in varying ways the discourse of the recipients/beneficiaries of such programmes (namely, academic researchers) carrying out the research. The nuances of such a rhetoric depend on authorship, i.e. on the degree of merger between the discourses of the actors involved – administrative or academic, sponsor or recipient.

The process of (re)constructing the Mediterranean can be traced in different discursive moments. One main set of examples is the discourse of the bureaucratic/administrative actor involved, in this case, the institution assigning the research, i.e. the European Commission through its different directorates. As one may discern, this is the case of an administration fostering the articulation of a discourse on culture: a discourse that may sound less 'refined' and 'sophisticated' to anthropological ears by virtue of the fact that it constructs a Mediterranean essence. I quote, for instance, the purported duty to 'preserve and better manage Mediterranean heritage', 'to increase the capacity of Mediterranean countries to manage and develop their cultural heritage' and the objective of 'turning the care and conservation of the Mediterranean's past into a cornerstone of its future', as stated in European Commission publications on the subject (European Commission/RMSU 2004: 4). Elsewhere, I quote statements on the duty for 'promotion of awareness and knowledge of the Mediterranean cultural heritage'; on the focus of research activities 'on the common physical and historical aspects of the region's heritage, so as to epitomize the relations among the cultures of different territories and populations'; or assertions that 'the Euro-Mediterranean partners have become more aware of their common culture, of the importance of their cultural identity and of the wealth of their respective cultural heritages.' In the official call for applications, the summary of the research objectives stated:

> the cultural heritage of the Mediterranean basin, beyond its local diversities and specificity, reflects the powerful links that unite Europe and the southern shores of the Mediterranean. The ultimate objective of the programme is to establish the idea of a common Euro-Mediterranean heritage that incorporates different traditions and customs and highlights the visible and invisible links between them.[4] (European Commission 2000: 3–5)

Another main set of examples comprises the more 'sensitive' (in terms of their theoretical and intellectual engagement) texts of the ethnographers undertaking the research. In the case of the Mediterranean Voices project, the ethnographers, who are located in various academic institutions or NGOs, speak of the Mediterranean in language that often departs from the 'administrative' example of policy makers. In a different manner, the ethnographers also contribute to a construction of the Mediterranean as culture area, albeit with a narrative that intends to be more historically informed. The difference in such texts is the perceptible presence of the anthropologist's awareness that he/she is institutionally bound to use 'area' concepts, yet also trained to be sceptical vis-à-vis their theoretical implications. For instance, as the collective statement of our project declares, our ethnographies in Mediterranean Voices aim 'to promote an awareness of the intangible cultural heritage of Mediterranean urban landscapes' by collecting

> the diverse, yet often fragile, fabric of memories and relationships which help to shape the meaning and character of Mediterranean urban quar-

ters. The cities and neighbourhoods which form part of the consortium and arenas of activity, are not intended to be in any way representative of a Mediterranean urban 'archetype'. However, they do share a number of traits or 'cultures of urbanism', typical of Mediterranean urban quarters and environments, for example, the dense co-presence of an ethnically and socially-mixed population. In addition, these attributes cannot be understood without reference to the trans-Mediterranean ties of trade and mobility which have historically nourished these fluid and cosmopolitan urban social ecologies. (www.med-voices.org)

In acknowledging the different authorship – the anthropologist on the one hand and on the other the policy maker – one may also see an inevitable affinity between the two kinds of texts/discourses when it comes to speaking of the Mediterranean. Both kinds of texts are produced under the aegis of the European Commission, although certainly the anthropologist maintains a degree of autonomy in terms of what the final product says.

On this note, it is worth identifying the inherent interplay between the frame of mind of the anthropologist-researcher who, while able to criticize essentialisms (the 'Mediterranean'), also has a duty to remain faithful to the European Commission's objectives. Judging from the Mediterranean Voices experience gained in the field, one may argue that this tension is not only inherent in the realization of such projects, but also can be a creative source. By this I mean that the commitment to taking the concept of the Mediterranean as point of reference does not necessarily entail that the project find itself confined within essentialist straps, hence sacrificing its anthropological values. Let me mention here our project's emphasis on the perspective of the local informant in the carrying out of fieldwork in the Mediterranean urban neighbourhood: 'neighbourhood-based interactions and experiences which are played out in and through story-telling, personal recollections of historic events, everyday social interactions and cultural practices' (www.medvoices.org) constitute the core of the data collected.

I wish to prevent the impression of a bipolar approach, which identifies the policy-making actor with absence of intellectual rigor, and the academic with more intellectual sophistication. Rather, what I wish to stress is that, inevitably, the two types of actors, i.e. the bureaucratic/administrative and the academic, find themselves making use of this concept in common, by virtue of the fact that the venture in question is more subject to imperatives pertaining to EU policy, and less to intellectual imperatives and sensibilities of the academics and/or specialists to be appointed for the research.

However, the above examples are merely indicative, as the present analysis is not intended to focus on the issue of the relationship between the bureaucratic and the intellectual. Such a relationship is crucial in these projects and, as such, it constitutes a topic deserving a separate analysis; for this reason, it is analysed in other stages and outputs of the writing process pertaining to this research.[5] Rather, the priority here is to highlight the issue of the historical and geopolitical conditions allowing for the emergence of the 'Mediterraneanism' in question during the last couple of decades – in other words, to focus on the conditions creating the need to adopt the 'Mediterranean' as a working concept.

A Political-historical Framing for the 'Mediterraneanism' of the 1990s

I shall now outline processes and conjunctures of events governing the emergence of this discourse in EU institutions today,[6] in order to clarify the place of social research in this emergence. The discourse of the Mediterranean, as adopted in EU institutions and policy during the 1990s, is articulated in a historical context in which the EU is undergoing change as a political and geographical entity and redefining itself as such. Specifically, this historical moment is marked by significant events and processes, such as the dissolution of the 'Eastern bloc', the European enlargement, increasing immigration particularly from Southern Mediterranean (i.e. Arab-African) countries towards the European Mediterranean and more recent concerns for European security issues and a European foreign policy. The emergence of the discourse of the Mediterranean as a unified area marks a new period in the relationship between the EU and the region of the Southern Mediterranean and/or Arab Mediterranean countries as a result of the above historical moment. It is perceived as a 'partnership', which means an all-inclusive approach to the relationship between the two sides. Prior to this period, the relationship between the (then) European Community (EC) and the Mediterranean region can be mainly summed up as close trade relations.

Europe and the Mediterranean: A History of 'Unfulfilled' Promises

The idea that the EC should have a coherent Mediterranean policy was first expressed in the early 1970s but seems to have been hampered or continually deferred until the mid 1990s. Originally it meant inclusion of the whole Mediterranean region, i.e. both the European South and the southern Mediterranean littoral. However, as the European South (Greece, Spain, Portugal) gradually became integrated into the EC during the 1980s, the Mediterranean policy acquired a different sense, to mean Europe's relations with the Mediterranean South. This meant specifically the Arab-

African countries, otherwise referred to as the non-members, or the Third Mediterranean Countries.

The nature of the EC's relations with the Mediterranean Arab-African countries did not change significantly (that is, beyond trade agreements) until the early 1980s, when the Community began to re-evaluate this relationship with the aim of forging a more wide-ranging and solid connection. The EC initiated an opening to these countries,[7] which seemed necessary for the Community's own economic revitalization – given the economic recession globally and the rising unemployment in Europe. The EC formulated its initiative as necessary to promote 'development' in the 'Third World', with the precondition that these countries (i.e. the Third Mediterranean Countries) 'restructure' their economies and consolidate 'democratic governments'.

Renewed attempts towards the implementation of a Mediterranean policy took place in the early 1990s,[8] whereby the Mediterranean began to be viewed as a unified space. However, it was only in 1995, with the Barcelona Process, that a Mediterranean policy was put into practice more firmly and comprehensively, as we shall see below. Until this period, therefore, Europe's repeatedly pronounced desire to have a Mediterranean policy did not appear to be fully applicable, or was impeded for various reasons; hence the Third Mediterranean Countries remained a second priority all along. Europe's approach has been criticized as inadequate as well as ambivalent, while blame has also been placed on the Mediterranean non-member countries for their 'resistance' to applying the anticipated changes. One may safely say that crucial political, economic and social events – both within Europe and in the region of the Mediterranean non-members – caused this process to appear constantly hindered.

Concerning the events within the European geopolitical space, the European Community's enlargement in the 1980s, and mainly the emergence of 'Eastern Europe' in the 1990s, were major reasons for rendering Mediterranean policy a secondary issue on the European agenda. Specifically, after 1989 the EC was faced with the end of the Cold War, a power vacuum in the former 'Eastern bloc' and the need for political control and stabilization of this part of Europe. As an outcome of this historical moment, the prospect of the (fifth) European enlargement (realized recently with the integration of a number of new member states from Central and Eastern Europe) became a priority for Europe – by now known as the European Union.

In the course of this enlargement a new tension became perceptible in Europe, a tension caused by two opposing forces within the EU pushing at once towards the Centre-East and towards the South. Specifically, the shift of the existing centre of gravity towards the Central and Eastern European states meant shifting European priorities, with which the long-overdue agenda of a European Mediterranean policy would now have to compete. Furthermore, the new reality exacerbated already existing tensions between the European North and European South within the Union,[9] as well as between the Northern Mediterranean and the (non-European) Southern Mediterranean. Hence the new reality was translated for Mediterranean countries (both north and south) into a continuing lack of attention, alongside increasing competition from the prospective member-states of 'Eastern Europe'.

As far as the region of the Mediterranean non-members is concerned, a number of long-standing yet intensified processes have also played a role in thwarting a solid partnership with the EU. One major impediment has been the lack of political and economic stability in the region. Southern Mediterranean economies have slowed since the 1980s due to a combination of factors such as oil prices, population increase, increased borrowing and debt, and reduced interest in private investment in the region. Population increase (otherwise referred to as 'demographic growth') in these countries has meant increasing unemployment and has triggered immigration from the 'Middle East' and Arab-African countries to the more prosperous European Mediterranean (Spain, Italy, France, etc.) during the last couple of decades. Not only have these events, such as immigration, been incompatible with the prospect of economic reforms and democratization of the Southern Mediterranean region, but they have also been alarming events with immense social and economic impact for the EU over the last couple of decades.

More recently, the emerging competitiveness of Central and Eastern European states, which are becoming capitalist economies within the new state of affairs, and the opening of Asian economies such as China have created new and cheaper labour markets and played a role in the waning of the Mediterranean non-members' economies. This redirection eastwards has also been a factor in rendering the Third Mediterranean Countries of lesser importance for the European agenda.

For a more complete picture, one needs to also consider the unstable political climate within the Arab Mediterranean world, intensified in light of issues such as the Palestinian Question. However, increasingly crucial for Europe are what are known as the 'security issues' associated with terrorism and with the rise of 'Islamic' movements. Although emerging at the supranational level, they are inextricably linked with the socio-political and economic situation of the Arab countries and the web of their relations, regionally and with the superpowers. Moreover, the existing balance of superpower presence is shifting in the region of the Middle East. With the end of the Cold War and the withdrawal of Soviet Union from the stage, control over these Arab Mediterranean countries has become more imperative because of the dominating presence of the United States in the region today. Therefore, the end of the Cold War generates issues not only of a new security environment (the 'threat' does not come from the 'East' any more but from the 'South'), but also of competing presence in the region.

In mapping the above events it becomes possible to comprehend why the issue of the 'Mediterranean' appeared indefinitely deferred, despite the long-standing and continued European interests in the region. Thus the EU's purported ambivalence vis-à-vis the adoption of a Euro-Mediterranean policy reflects the shifting priorities within the European space (the 'eastwards' direction) that render the Mediterranean markets less attractive. On the other hand, Europe must continue to rely on the Arab Mediterranean countries (not strictly for the energy resources but overall, because they remain significant for Europe as post-colonies) while at the same time coping with the political anxiety of immigration and security. Therefore investment on the Mediterranean appears, if not as a political desire, then as an inevitable and inescapable step.

Thus the new realities dictate a shift of attention towards the Mediterranean, for reasons of European enlargement pressures, of maintaining control over the Southern Mediterranean and of planning a common foreign and security policy in Europe. In order to manage such hot-button issues as, e.g., the influx of immigrants in Europe, it is necessary to adopt a Euro-Mediterranean policy that could conceive new forms of cooperation aimed at increasing the 'competitiveness' of Third Mediterranean Countries and encouraging 'foreign investments' – as put in the standard economic terms adopted. According to this logic, this would not be achieved with single measures but with a more comprehensive approach.

The Barcelona Process

It is in this context that the 'Mediterranean' (re-)emerges in the political discourse of European institutions – in other words, attention to the South has become timely again, and Europe (including the EU Mediterranean countries) is more willing to play the card of Mediterranean unity and to refashion its old relationship with the rest of the Mediterranean. The renewed entry of the Mediterranean onto the EU political agenda in the mid 1990s has been realized not merely through economic aid but through a more inclusive relationship. Ethnographic research finds a place here as a feature of the 'cultural' chapter of this relationship.

Specifically, it is with the Barcelona Process that the shift to the Mediterranean becomes a more comprehensive political commitment for both sides. In the Barcelona Conference in 1995 the EU launched what is known as the Euro-Mediterranean Partnership, an entity with a large number of

Mediterranean partners that are non-members.[10] This policy is allegedly the first of its kind promoting cooperation between 'Europe' and the 'Mediterranean', with a stated goal to reduce the gap between the neighbours to the North and South of the Mediterranean. As evident in the Barcelona Declaration, the three basic axes of the Euro-Mediterranean cooperation sum up the main demands of all former European (albeit incomplete) efforts to establish a Euro-Mediterranean policy: establishment of 'a common area of peace and stability'; establishment of 'economic and financial partnership', including the establishment of 'a free-trade area' between the EU and its Mediterranean partners accompanied by substantial financial support;[11] and establishment of 'partnership in the social, cultural and human affairs'.[12]

It is the third axis of the Barcelona Process, i.e. the cultural chapter, that becomes more directly relevant to our questions as it advocates 'cultural heritage', thus involving the role of social research and having direct relevance to anthropological inquiry. Accordingly, by promoting the 'understanding between cultures and exchanges between civil societies', the partnership aspires to promote sustainable forms of development in the non-member countries.[13]

To serve these purposes, Barcelona launched the Euromed Heritage Programme,[14] the EC's regional programme 'aiming at the preservation and development of the Euro-Mediterranean cultural heritage' via the funding of various research projects – such as the ethnographic Mediterranean Voices, which I draw on in this chapter. The rhetoric of cultural unity is manifest in the general objective of Euromed Heritage, as in the example below:

> The cultural heritage has been identified as a priority field of action … It is a tangible sign of exchange processes between different cultures. The cultural heritage of the Mediterranean basin, beyond its local diversities and specificity, reflects the powerful links that unite Europe and the southern shores of the Mediterranean. The ultimate objective of the programme is to establish the idea of a common Euro-Mediterranean heritage that incorporates different traditions and customs and highlights the visible and invisible links between them. The cultural heritage should thus become a tool for a policy of openness, tolerance, peace and stability in the region (European Commission 2000: 4).

Therefore the discourse of the Mediterranean and the stated promotion of a Mediterranean 'cultural heritage', institutionalized and articulated from the mid 1990s onwards, is part of a broader European investment at a specific historical conjuncture.[15] It is in this context that the administrative/bureaucratic encounters the academic: the anthropologist hired to conduct research in this region finds him/herself making a tacit and binding agreement to accept the Mediterranean as a working concept, being aware of its contested nature. This tension, as also mentioned earlier, can be a very productive opportunity for anthropological reflection. It is crucial to be able to view the emergence of the 'Mediterranean' in its complexity, i.e. not plainly as a political/economic and bureaucratic venture devoid of theoretical considerations, but as a potential for constructive anthropological encounters and applied research. Essentially this position means that the anthropologist is conscious of the relationship between politics and research, aware that his/her research project is a product of specific political and economic circumstances.

On the Place of Social Research in the
EU Institutional Structure: A Small Illustration

To complete my brief mapping of the geopolitical moment in question, I provide a simplified illustration of an institutional structure within which research is placed, once more using Mediterranean Voices as my example. Specifically, it is through the EuropeAid Office[16] that EU development cooperation with different countries worldwide is achieved. EuropeAid is a directorate of the European Commission set up to manage Commission funding of the so-called management of external aid, or 'external assistance', in relation to these countries. These countries are categorized in terms of regions, and one such region is the so-called Southern Mediterranean and Middle East Countries. Under EuropeAid, it is the MEDA[17] programme that manages cooperation with countries of this particular region. It is at this point that this institutional structure connects with the Barcelona Process. The MEDA programmes are conceived as instruments for the establishment of the so-called free trade area, and MEDA is reportedly the main financial instrument for the implementation of the Euro-Mediterranean Partnership, initiated in Barcelona and assisting the 'reform of economic and social structures in the Mediterranean partner countries'.[18]

One of the main regional activities of MEDA II (which ended in 2006), has been Euromed Heritage, discussed in the previous section, a regional programme specifically focused on the 'Euro-Mediterranean cultural heritage'. Mediterranean Voices – one of the various Euromed Heritage II projects active as of 2002 – is a research programme with anthropological orientation.

My aim in illustrating the above institutional structure, as well as the overall route towards the emergence of the Mediterranean in EU institutional discourse, is neither to serve archival purposes, nor to venture into the field of political science. Rather, it is to attempt to identify processes in which a theoretical concept becomes adopted by a policy-making institu-

European Commission
▼
EuropeAid Office
▼
MEDA[17] Programme (I and II)
▼
Euromed Heritage (I and II)
▼
Mediterranean Voices Programme

Figure 1.1. Illustration of an institutional structure: the place of "Mediterranean Voices" in the larger picture of EU research.

tion/administrative entity and, at the same time, the political and economic framework and network of mechanisms supporting it. Political analysts today hesitate to characterize the Barcelona Process and the Euro-Mediterranean policy at large as successful, fearing that the South Mediterranean will continue to have a low priority on the European agenda in terms of the momentum of its economic integration. Regardless of the future outcome of this European initiative, which at any rate is beyond the competence of this analysis, it is crucial for an anthropologist to be able to acquire a more complete understanding of the overall institutional framework within which he/she is placed, and hence of the conditions producing the discursive universe governing his/her research – in this case, the 'Mediterranean', with all its likely ideological repercussions.

In this process, the anthropologist is enabled to make sense of his/her place as a social scientist in the political processes of his/her project's making. In effect, he/she can make sense of the conditions shaping the conceptual tools used and can therefore strategically utilize them to the benefit of the research and the local society studied. The degree to which such a politically informed consciousness can be formed, and hence the social value of the research, may be judged from the actual research output. Such output is either in the form of processed ethnographic material accessible to all types of public (see, e.g., the Mediterranean Voices website) or in the form of anthropological reflections as they appear in professional academic publications (see e.g. note 5 below).

Conclusion

In this chapter I embarked on the mapping of a geopolitical moment that shapes the 're'-emergence of the concept of the Mediterranean in EU institutional discourse and the ways in which it evokes the culture area, thus warranting anthropological reflection. In this process, I identified a historical moment in the mid 1990s when the discourse of Euro-Mediterranean cultural unity began to be articulated systematically. I argued that the vision of a Mediterranean world and the promotion of what might seem a Mediterranean quintessence, in the designing and carrying out of EU-funded programmes, need to be viewed as part of a broader European political investment.

For the EU, the 'Mediterranean' and the 'Euro-Mediterranean cultural heritage' emerged in the 1990s, in light of the political urgency of a long-overdue Euro-Mediterranean partnership addressing political, economic and social relations between the EU and the Mediterranean region. As the (so far) most comprehensive partnership between the two sides, this was predominantly a European attempt to manage the state of affairs following the end of the Cold War: the European enlargement pressures, immigration pressures and, secondarily, security issues pertaining to the role of the Mediterranean region during the last couple of decades.

The discourse of Mediterranean unity has been part and parcel of this European effort. I examined the emergence of the concept of the Mediterranean not merely because it is used in official political rhetoric, but also because it has been a contested issue in anthropological literature and presently shapes ethnographic research as funded by European institutions during the above-described political moment.

As anthropologists, we need to be able to contextualize our role in research, so as not to be disconnected from the social and political conditions that produce it. My aim in mapping this geopolitical moment was to address the need to be conscious of genealogies: it is essential for a researcher/social scientist to be aware of the historical conjunctures, institutional framework and institutional constraints within which he/she is working, and the conditions producing the discursive universe within which he/she finds him/herself communicating. Otherwise any anthropological endeavour runs the risk of consuming itself in ahistorical and apolitical analyses.

In compiling the above account, which by no means professes to be exhaustive, I aimed to contribute to an understanding of what happens when seemingly essentialist concepts, such as the 'Mediterranean', are redeployed and become institutionally binding. In this process I intended to shed light on the complexity of the relationship between the academic and the bureaucratic, while at the same time reflecting on the creative and socially sensitive potentials of what may seem to be conformist institutional frameworks.

With the re-emergence of the Mediterranean on the EU political agenda, the Mediterranean is becoming a constitutive element in the EU's effort to play a certain role in the global economy. Thus what may at times seem like a gaze back to the past is not merely cultural essentialism but rather a deeply political act. It is a legitimization of a politics for the future. In short, the historical-political contexts in which our projects and our concepts emerge have a crucial impact on the ethnographies we write. Understanding them helps us better understand what our role as social actors is, 'what goes on in the field', and what each social reality we delve into is about.

NOTES

1. I am borrowing the phrasing from our final conference in the Mediterranean Voices Programme (Alexandria, 2005), which had the same title.
2. For examples of this literature, see e.g. Peristiany (1965), *Anthropological Quarterly* (1963); Pitt-Rivers (1963); Boissevain (1979); Gilmore (1982); Herzfeld (1980, 1984); *Critique of Anthropology* (1986).
3. The partner institutions were, respectively: Bibliotheca Alexandrina (Alexandria), University of Bologna, American University of Beirut, Centre for Cultural Heritage Preservation (Bethlehem, Palestine), University of Crete (Rethymno Campus), University of the Balearic Islands (Palma de Mallorca), University of Granada, Tarih Vakfi-Economic and Social History Foundation of Turkey (Istanbul), University of Las Palmas de Gran Canaria, Association d'Anthropologie Méditerranéenne (ADAM) (Aix-en-Provence), Youth Center Union (Nicosia North, Northern Cyprus), Intercollege (Nicosia South, Republic of Cyprus), University of Malta. The project was coordinated by London Metropolitan University, the International Institute for Culture Tourism and Development.
4. I must note here that social scientists are not absent from the committees conceiving and approving of such research for the European Commission. However, the end result is a text inevitably shaped by EU policy imperatives, thus produced within the institutional framework of an administrative and bureaucratic entity.
5. As an example of reflection on such a tension, see e.g. Yiakoumaki (2007).
6. There are various primary sources one may consult for the course of these events, such as the *Official Journal of the European Communities*. For analytical approaches on Euro-Mediterranean policy, one may consult e.g. the Council of Europe series on the subject (such as Council of Europe 1997). See also e.g. Xenakis and Chryssochoou 2001; Pierros et al. 1999; Jünemann 2004; Attina and Stavridis 2001; Panebianco 2003; Pollacco 2006.
7. This took place within the then existing framework of Europe's Global Mediterranean Policy.
8. Known as the Redirected (or Renovated) Mediterranean Policy.
9. There is a history of unequal dependence between the European North and the European South, which has meant an alleged bias towards North-Central European norms of development. Most of the economically vulnerable areas tended to be in the south of the Union, namely, Greece, the Mezzogiorno,

Spain and Portugal – which for that reason happened to be the more dissatis-
fied areas of the Union, until recently.

10. At the time of launching, the partnership had a majority of Mediterranean
non-members. With the 2004 enlargement, the proportion changed. Today it
comprises 35 members: 25 EU member states and 10 Mediterranean partners
(Morocco, Algeria, Tunisia, Egypt, Israel, Jordan, the Palestinian Authority,
Lebanon, Syria and Turkey).

11. 'The South and East Mediterranean and the Middle East is an area of vital strategic importance to the European Union, which both the EU Council and the European Commission have identified as key external relations
priority for the EU. The aim of the Euro-Mediterranean Partnership is to
turn the Mediterranean basin into an area of dialogue, exchange and cooperation guaranteeing peace, stability and prosperity; strengthen the political dialogue, development of economic and financial co-operation, social,
cultural and human dimension and by 2010 establish a free-trade area. It
makes economic transition and free trade the central issue of the EU financial co-operation with the Mediterranean region' (see http://europa.eu.int/
comm/europeaid/projects/med/foreword_en.htm, or, e.g., http://europa.eu
.int/comm/external_relations/med_mideast/intro).

12. See the Barcelona Declaration at http://ec.europa.eu/comm/external_relations
/euromed/bd.htm, or http://www.euromedheritage.net/en/euromedheritage/
objectives.htm

13. 'As an aspect of sustainable development, the cultural heritage must be integrated into national and multinational strategies for economic planning, regional organisation and tourism. ... It must be considered a component of economic
policies, and an attractive target for private and public investment' (European
Commission 2000: 7). Elsewhere, 'cultural heritage as a high priority field of
action, due to the richness and needs of this domain, its visibility for a broad
public and its effects on cultural tourism and creation of employment' (http://
europa.eu.int/comm/europeaid/projects/med/regional/heritage_en.htm).

14. http://www.euromedheritage.net

15. See e.g. http://europa.eu.int/comm/europeaid/projects/med/foreword_en.htm,
or http://europa.eu.int/comm/external_relations/med_mideast/intro

16. http://europa.eu.int/comm/europeaid

17. Mesures d'accompagnement.

18. http://europa.eu.int/comm/europeaid/projects/med/foreward_en.htm

REFERENCES

Anthropological Quarterly. 1963. 'Europe and Its Cultures' (Special Issue), vol.
36(3).

Attina, F. and S. Stavridis (eds). 2001. *The Barcelona Process and Euro-Mediterranean Issues from Stuttgart to Marseille.* Milan: Giuffre.

Boissevain, J. 1979. 'Towards a Social Anthropology of the Mediterranean', *Current
Anthropology* 20(1): 81–93.

Council of Europe. 1997. *The Challenges Facing European Society with the Approach of the Year 2000: Strategies for the Sustainable Development of European States in the Mediterranean Basin.* Volume on European regional planning, no 59. Council of Europe Publishing.

Critique of Anthropology. 1986. 6(2) and 7(2).

European Commission 2000. Euromed Heritage II, Guidelines for Applicants, Budget Line B7-4100. (Printed document, also available at the EU website, http://europa.eu.int)

European Commission/RMSU (Regional Management Support Unit). 2004. *Euro-Mediterranean Partnership, Euromed Heritage II: Projects and Partners.* Brussels: European Commission, EuropeAid Cooperation Office.

Gilmore, D. 1982. 'Anthropology of the Mediterranean Area', *Annual Review of Anthropology* 11: 175–205.

Herzfeld, M. 1980. 'Honour and Shame: Problems in the Comparative Analysis of Moral Systems', *Man* 15b(2): 339–351.

Herzfeld, M. 1984. 'The Horns of the Mediterraneanist Dilemma', *American Ethnologist* 11(3): 439–454.

Jünemann, A. (ed.). 2004. *Euro-Mediterranean Relations After September 11: International, Regional, and Domestic Dynamics.* London: Frank Cass.

Panebianco, S. (ed.). 2003. *A New Euro-Mediterranean Cultural Identity.* London: Frank Cass.

Peristiany, J.G. (ed.). 1965. *Honour and Shame: The Values of Mediterranean Society.* London: Weidenfeld and Nicholson.

Pierros, F. et al. 1999. *Bridges and Barriers: The European Union's Mediterranean Policy, 1961–1998.* Aldershot: Ashgate.

Pitt-Rivers, J.A. (ed.). 1963. *Mediterranean Countrymen: Essays in the Social Anthropology of the Mediterranean.* Paris: Mouton & Co.

Pollacco, C. 2006. *The Mediterranean: The European Union's 'Near Abroad'.* Malta: Agenda.

Xenakis, D.K. and D.N. Chryssochoou. 2001. *Europe in Change: The Emerging Euro-Mediterranean System.* Manchester: Manchester University Press.

Yiakoumaki, V. 2007. 'Archiving "Heritage", Reconstructing The "Area": Conducting Audio-Visual Ethnography In EU-Sponsored Research', in Sarah Pink (ed.), *Visual Interventions: Applied Visual Anthropology.* Oxford: Berghahn Books.

List of Electronic References
(Final Retrieval for all sites in February 2007)

http://europa.eu.int/comm/europeaid/projects/med/foreword_en.htm http://europa.eu.int/comm/external_relations/med_mideast/intro

http://ec.europa.eu/comm/external_relations/euromed/bd.htm http://www.euromedheritage.net/en/euromedheritage/objectives.htm

http://europa.eu.int/comm/europeaid/projects/med/regional/heritage_en.htm

http://www.euromedheritage.net

http://europa.eu.int/comm/europeaid/projects/med/foreword_en.htm

http://europa.eu.int/comm/external_relations/med_mideast/intro
http://europa.eu.int/comm/europeaid
http://europa.eu.int/comm/europeaid/projects/med/foreward_en.htm
http://europa.eu.int
www.medvoices.org

Chapter 2

European 'Securitization' Policies and the Southern 'Fortress-Europe'

MINAS SAMATAS

This chapter presents a socio-political assessment of the 'securitization' policies of the European Union (EU) and their impact on immigration, human rights and civil liberties in the EU and especially in Southern Europe. We focus upon the post-9/11 EU security agenda and the reinforcement of the Schengen Information System (SIS) in building a 'fortress-Europe.' Documented evidence is provided, especially from Southern Europe (Greece, Italy, France, Spain and Portugal). 'Securitization' logic and practice are examined in relation to social issues like immigration and anti-globalization protests, which are perceived as security threats. The decentralization of 'fortress-Europe' in non-EU Mediterranean states is also explored in terms of *buffer states* protecting the EU from transborder threats of terrorism and migration. Real and perceived threats are taken into consideration to assess the current predomination of 'fortress-Europe' versus an inclusive, secure and open-minded approach that would allow for an active civil society.

Introduction: 'Fortress-Europe'

In the post–Cold War era, and long before 9/11, terrorism had been changing the human rights landscape across the world (Alston 1999; Gilbert 1994; Peers 1999). However, especially after 9/11, the 'war on terror' has caused gross abuse of human rights as well as a general undermining of international law (ICHR 2002; Hohm and Newman 2003; Lyon 2003; Schutz 2003; Sidel 2004). The tragic terrorist events in the United States and then in Turkey, Spain and lately in the UK have caused panic in public opinion and have been used by anxious political leaders to promote 'security above all' other priorities in the Western world. Yet, they are also used by the security industry to promote their market interests. Like the Cold War, the 'war on terror', first in the United States and then in the EU, is ultimately a war against freedoms and civil liberties, promoting 'securitization', i.e. the security logic in all policies reinforcing the democratic deficit at the national and European level (Waever et al. 1993).

If one were to suggest that before 9/11 there were some trends towards a 'fortress Europe', (den Boer and Wallace 1996), thereafter the evidence points even more strongly towards such a process (Leone 2003). Ultimately, the EU, from a community of democratic states based on pluralism, human rights, civil liberties and the rule of law, is transformed into a 'fortress Europe', particularly fortified against immigrants and refugees from underdeveloped countries. Moreover, in regard to its own citizens the EU is increasingly following a panoptic road to an Orwellian '1984' (Bunyan 2002). Fortress policies are particularly adopted by the EU's southern states in their effort to combat illegal immigration from Asia and Africa. Anti-terrorist and anti-immigration policies undermine the civil liberties and fundamental rights of all who live in Europe (Schutz 2003).

In fact, in the wake of the terrorist attack in Madrid, the 2004 EU summit of prime ministers in Brussels produced the Declaration on Combating Terrorism, which contains several draconian measures curtailing civil liberties and human rights (Council of the EU 2004). According to Amnesty International, 'the EU is not succeeding in putting human rights at the heart of its policies, disregarding the growing recognition that the various "wars" on terror and illegal immigration can only be won in the long term through a strong and consistent "war" on third world poverty, human rights, and a democratic approach' (AI 2004: 2).

The Western world and the EU have begun to retreat from ideas of multiculturalism and openness. On the one hand, xenophobic fears and attitudes foster draconian proposals for restrictions on immigrants and refugees; on the other, anti-democratic tendencies encourage provisions for mass surveillance and restriction of free movement for certain active EU citizens and NGOs. Constitutional safeguards are removed, and more power is gathered into the executive and other technocratic bodies at the national and EU level. This prompts the question: '[B]y placing EU member states on a permanent war footing against the "other", against those considered as outcasts, how long will it be before every EU citizen becomes the "other"?' (Upton 2004).

It is important to analyse the EU 'securitization' logic and practice, which perceives all social issues, especially immigration and even anti-globalization protests, as EU security threats (Waever 1996; Huysmans 1995; Geddes 2000). Long before and especially since 9/11, the reinforcement of the Schengen Information System (SIS) and the new EU security agenda clearly reflect a securitization mentality and practice that transform social issues as security issues (Waever et al. 1993). In our study, real and perceived threats, as well as various economic and political interests, are taken into consideration to assess whether an exclusivist, authoritarian 'fortress-Europe' or an inclusive, secure and democratic Europe will finally prevail.

The Theoretical Debate on Security and 'Securitization'

The definition of security depends upon the geographical and temporal context in which it is used. The concept of security, an elusive and slippery term, has come to include a wider range of issues connected with the well-being of society, in addition to more traditional ideas of state security (Manitakis and Takis 2004). What constitutes security for the average person? Physical safety? Safety of home? Safety of food (no genetically modified products, for example)? But security can also mean the right to freedom of expression, freedom to read and write, research, explore ideas, publish, email, talk, assemble, discuss, debate, inquire, lobby, petition and protest. Thus the meaning of personal, human security is not confined to the safety of national, state boundaries, which usually tends to predominate (ICLMG 2004: 34). Security has to be understood as a social construct, i.e. a product of social practices in a particular special and temporal context, and it is determined by the interests of big states, of security industry ruling elites and mass media. Real and perceived threats affect that security definition in each case (Huysmans 1995, 2000; McSweeney 1999; Guerra 1997). According to Waever et al. (1993), in the post–Cold War era emphasis shifted from the security of nation-states to human safety and from military defence to human security. That means that safety from chronic threats such as hunger, disease and repression, relating to the quality of life, comes first, to be followed by military defence and national security. Moreover, questions of 'human security', including economic, environmental and societal security, must predominate over pure state, military and defence issues (UN Development Program 1994: chap. 2). In brief, there is a contrast between the 'human security approach' and the traditional 'state-based approach'. The primacy of human rights – including economic, social and civil rights – is what distinguishes the human security approach from the state-based approach (Kaldor 2005).

Taken together, the data show that EU policies consider immigration to be a real security threat greater than any other, such as organized crime. In the past ten years immigration has become an issue of 'high politics' in Europe. Eurocrats, national governments and some population segments have increasingly perceived it as an economic, cultural and political threat. Meanwhile, there is a consistent failure to perceive immigration as a beneficial phenomenon for the EU and host societies.[1] Instead of an 'open-society' approach, 'fortress' mentalities predominate, which misread the complexity of the immigration issue and opt in general for the demonization and criminalization of clandestine immigration.[2] This is the 'securitization' approach to immigration, which involves the social construction, formulation and implementation of anti-immigration policies and practices that place the greatest emphasis on the security of the state, even at the cost of human rights and the civil liberties (Weiner 1995; Huysmans 2000; Geddes 2000).

In fact the EU had shown its anti-immigration preoccupations long before 9/11, relating immigration to threats posed by transnational criminality, terrorism, drug trafficking, etc. For example, Article K.1 of the Justice and Home Affairs (JHA) Pillar directly associates transnational criminality with immigration by constructing 'crimes of arrival' (Webber 1995) and a 'security continuum' (Andersen and Eliassen 1996). Unauthorized immigrants are viewed as clandestine, illegal and criminal, and are equated with members of criminal organizations, terrorists and drug traffickers. It is not only immigrants who have unlawfully entered the EU that are viewed as criminals: even legal immigrants are viewed as potential criminals (Spencer 1995; Mitsilegas 1997, 2002).

The Schengen Treaty Is Building a Dangerous Fortress Europe

The Schengen Treaty officially represents an attempt to achieve four fundamental freedoms concerning movements of persons, goods, capital and services. It is of particular importance for the free movement of persons as it removes internal controls and transfers them to the EU external borders. The Schengen passport-free zone is thus a testing ground for an EU without frontiers, through which EU citizens can move freely, provided for by the EEC treaty, the single Act and Treaty on European Union (Maas 2005). The Schengen Information System (SIS) was conceived in the mid 1980s to 'compensate' for the removal of internal borders between France, Germany, Holland, Luxembourg and the Netherlands. It was agreed at the time that their police, intelligence, immigration and customs services would be able to 'alert' each other about people refused admission (immigration offenders or security risks); people wanted for arrest, extradition or testimony in court; fugitives; and persons to be placed under surveillance, as well as notification about stolen objects (vehicles, works of art, identity documents, etc.). So it was that the SIS went online in March 1995 with the five original Schengen signatory states participating (*Statewatch News Online, 2005*).

By March 2003 the SIS, now under the auspices of the EU, covered thirteen of the fifteen EU member states, plus Norway and Iceland. This generated records on 877,655 people, a further 386,402 aliases and more than 15 million objects. EU officials estimate that there are 125,000 access terminals to the SIS. Under finalized proposals, access to the SIS is to be extended to Europol (Hayes 2002), Eurojust, national prosecutors and vehicle licensing authorities (Boettchter 2000; Van Buuren 2003; Samatas 2003a).

Nevertheless, the implementation of the SIS has been very uneven. While in 2003 as many as 778,886 people registered as aliens were refused entry in the Schengen Information System, Italy and Germany topped the list, accounting for 77 per cent of the total number of records. As Statewatch points out: 'Germany has registered all failed applicants for asylum; and Italy too is registering unwelcome immigrants en masse. In doing so they are effectively banning all those they register from the entire Schengen territory ... although they have not committed any criminal offence.'[3]

Table 2.1. Article 96** Alerts in the SIS, as of 1 February 2003

*Italy	*335,306*
Germany	267,884
*Greece	*58,619*
*France	*52,383*
*Spain	*10,882*
*Portugal	*1,744*
Austria	33,732
Sweden	4,454
Finland	2,727
Norway	863
Luxembourg	406
Belgium	367
Denmark	147
Iceland	10
Total	**778, 886**

Source: The statistics in this table were collated by the Schengen Joint Supervisory Authority and cited in *Statewatch News Online,* March 2006 (http://www.statewatch.org/news/2005/apr/08SISart96.htm)

*Southern European States

**Article 96 is the category under which Schengen states register 'illegal aliens' who are to be denied access to Schengen territory on immigration, public order or national security grounds. The Schengen member states are encouraged to register 'illegal aliens that pose a threat to public order or national security and safety or who have been the subject of a deportation, removal or expulsion measure ... accompanied by a prohibition on entry or, where appropriate, residence'. Yet a check on 16 February 2006 found that 503 citizens from the EU and associated countries (Iceland, Norway and Switzerland) have been wrongly classified under Article 96.[4]

Having studied the implementation of the Schengen Treaty in Greece (Samatas 1997, 2003a, 2003b), we can argue that the Greek Schengen case reflects wider implications all over the EU, especially on the security issue. For instance, in Greece following other Schengen member states' requests for stricter controls, the Greek SIS databank on persons who are not allowed to enter Greece and the EU increased significantly after 2003. Due to the Athens 2004 Olympics, Greece alone had registered 64,717 persons refused entry in June 2004; however, the total number of non-EU people refused entry to Greece and therefore to the EU in 2004 was 778,000, according to the full SIS databank (*Eleftherotypia*, 18 June 2004; Samatas 2003b).

The strengthening of a comprehensive system of internal surveillance, combined with the tightening of strict external border controls, reinforces the process of securitization in 'Schengenland' over human rights and civil liberties. As both Greek and independent organizations' data prove, the SIS has substantially shifted from freedom of movement to control of movement, reflecting national and supranational fears of migration, regarded as being on the same level as crime and terrorism (AI 2004; Leone 2003; Peers 1999; Samatas 2003a; Schutz 2003).

If the real aim of the Schengen Information System is the free movement of people and goods, and the protection of the EU against organized crime, then its serious implementation problems and negative implications call for more openness and accountability. Member states and civil society need to cooperate to avert any authoritarian tendency (Meijers et al. 1991; Van Lancker 1996; Van Buuren 2003).

Cementing 'Fortress Europe' and the U.S. Connection

The EU in coordination with the United States has designed several security projects and systems, such as the 'second-generation' Schengen Information System (SIS II), the new Visa Information System (VIS) and the Passenger Name Record (PNR), to extend the 'counterterrorism' net. These systems will be used for speculative surveillance, general intelligence gathering and 'fishing expeditions', but more importantly, individual records will increasingly result in coercive sanctions, such as bans on travel, the refusal of visa or asylum applications, the refusal of admission to a country at external borders, detention pending extradition or even deportation (Mathiesen 1999; Heyter 2004). Moreover, the massive sharing of data between the EU, the U.S. and other wealthy nations could provide for a kind of informal 'mutual recognition' of these sanctions, where a (potentially arbitrary) decision taken by one country is then enforced by all the others (Guild and Niessen 1996; Katrougalos 1995; Sitaropoulos 1992).

The impact of 9/11 on the Schengen Information System became obvious with the introduction of SIS II. This second-generation system will allow the United Kingdom and Ireland and the ten accession states to participate in the SIS – and, as expected, new security functions are planned. These include the addition of biometric identification data (photographs and fingerprints); new categories of 'terrorist suspects' and 'violent troublemakers' (who are to be banned from travelling to demonstrations or football matches); and the linking of individual records. A second database, the Visa Information System (VIS), will contain the extensive personal information supplied by people from around the world in an estimated 20 million visa applications to the EU member states every year. Like SIS II, VIS will contain biometric identification data.[5] As Statewatch argues:

> SIS II and VIS must be seen in a wider context. Firstly, there are global plans, promoted by the US and the UK in various intergovernmental fora, to introduce biometrics in all travel documents and the databases of the issuing authorities. Secondly, the EU has agreed to US demands for European airlines to provide data on EU citizens despite the absence of an adequate data protection framework in the US, but more importantly, has proposed its own PNR (Passenger Name Record) scheme.[6]

Taken together, SIS II, VIS and PNR will result in the surveillance of the movements of everyone in the EU – citizens, legal resident third-country nationals, visa entrants and irregular migrants – and the storage of their personal data on an unprecedented scale.[7] Muslims, Arabs, migrants, and refugees from underdeveloped countries will suffer disproportionately from these measures (Lavenex 2001). In the longer term, EU-U.S. security cooperation heralds a global identification system, the global surveillance of movement and a global police information system, where there is no place of 'free movement' and privacy (Hayes 2004).[8]

Furthermore, Schengen III, or the Prüm Treaty, signed on 25 May 2005 by the original Schengen group of Austria, Belgium, France, Germany, Luxembourg, Spain and the Netherlands, and later by Italy, seeks to establish an infrastructure to step up cross-border cooperation, particularly to combat terrorism, cross-border crime and illegal immigration.[9]

Following the 'Schengen Cooperation' model, eight powerful EU states agreed on stronger cooperation outside the formal structures of the EU, intending to transfer the treaty's rules, elaborated on a bilateral level, to the level of the EU. Schengen III regulates new practices (some of which, like the deployment of air marshals, are unprecedented in some countries), decreeing that they must be developed with a view to implementing a high degree of information exchange between national police forces, not limited to terrorism or serious crime. It requires contracting parties to establish DNA profile databases that the other contracting parties will be able to check on request for the purpose of prosecuting criminal activity. The parties must also be able to run automatic comparisons of fingerprints in partner countries' fingerprint databases, when the individual in question is identified, for either the prosecution or 'prevention' of criminal activity. It also allows for the 'cooperation and the exchange of personal data in relation to political demonstrations and other mass events and to prevent terrorist attacks, regulates the deployment of air marshals ("security escorts") on commercial flights and of immigration liaison officers (ILOs) in countries of origin or transit, establishing national contact points to coordinate the activity of ILOs and authorises the carrying out of joint deportations... This will lead to preventive detention, detention or refusal of entry at the border' (http://www.statewatch.org/news/2005/jul/17schengen-III.htm).

This new treaty legalizes joint deportation action, such as that of 13 September 2004, when the German Bundesgrenzschutz organized, with the help of Belgian and Swiss authorities, the 'repatriation' of seventeen African asylum-seekers on a chartered plane from Hamburg, whereupon the asylum seekers were escorted by seventy officers of the border guard (http://www.sosf.ch/blog/2004/09/asyl-asylsuchende-aus-der-schweiz-ber.html).

The Decentralization of 'Fortress Europe'

The EU creates a circle of neighbouring friends, such as the southern Mediterranean states of Algeria, Egypt, Israel, Jordan, Lebanon, Libya, Morocco, Palestine, Syria and Tunisia. These act as 'buffer states' to protect the EU from transborder threats of terrorism and migration. These buffer states are subjected to political and economic pressures to adopt EU standards in the control of migration and crime. In effect the EU has tried to decentralize fortress Europe to secure its own borders with the creation of buffer states in central Eastern Europe, most of which have joined the EU since May 2004, as well as new neighbours in the Mediterranean South. In addition, the EU strengthens its external borders through high-tech 'smart' borders, moving from voluntary repatriation to forced repatriation. The EU has adopted the U.K. government's proposal to create 'safe havens,' i.e. migrant and refugee camps in neighbour states such as Ukraine, or in regions of origin, e.g. West Africa. Through such practices, the EU wishes to remove national-level procedures and responsibility for refugee and asylum-seekers. Further, the EU insists that more and more non-EU countries sign up to readmission obligations with very little in return (Lavenex 2001; Heyter 2004).

The whole concept is based on the EU Strategy Paper on Migration and Asylum Policy (9809/98) of July 1998, which proposed a model of concentric circles of migrant policy that could replace that of fortress Europe. This is to be seen in the context of a 'global approach' by the EU and should incorporate all the main regions of origin of immigrants. The strategy paper suggests that economic aid should depend on visa questions and guarantees of readmission. Further, there need to be 'information campaigns' targeted at potential immigrants that clearly communicate information about immigration management measures. In other words, the paper recommends setting measures in place that would stop people entering the EU and remove them from the EU if necessary. Ever since, the EU's anti-immigration policy also includes the privatization of border controls, airline liaison officers, a special deportation class in airlines, fingerprinting the Third World European Dactyloscopy (EURODAC), the drastic reduction of granting asylum and much more. As a result, this 'global approach' to migration control, proposed in the notorious 1998 strategy paper is now a central tenet of EU policy. The shadowy world of liaison officers posted to Third World countries has been given an EU legal basis, and the policy of using aid and trade to secure readmission agreements under the Lomé Convention is being extended to more general 'migration management clauses' (Geddes 2000: 105–107; Samatas 2003b).

EU financial assistance is not going to the development of 'Third World' countries to eradicate the reasons for immigration; instead it expands the establishment of 'reception or detention centres' for illegal immigrants and offshore 'processing centres' for asylum applicants (Hayter 2004). Although in 1999 the EU resolved to end asylum policies based on detention, denial and deterrence, the next five years showed these promises to be false; instead an even more sophisticated framework was developed for the registration, surveillance and expulsion of immigrants and refugees. Meanwhile, fortress Europe is now cemented by a plethora of repressive measures such as border militarization, anti-asylum laws and practices, detention and deportation policies, carrier sanctions, etc. In addition, the EU's buffer-state policy extends its fortress to global control (Hayes 2004).

Yet, three new issues have now emerged. First, there are calls for 'offshore protection' and protection in the region of origin, rather than at destination. Second, faced with a demand for both highly skilled and unskilled immigrants to do the work EU citizens are unable or unwilling to do, some call, with a racist tone, for restrictions on their temporary and regulated entry. Finally, data collected by the EU on visa and asylum applicants and 'illegal' migrants are being shared with the U.S., Canada, Australia and other nations under the guise of tackling terrorism (Hayes 2004; Van Buuren 2003; Privacy International 2004).

The Fatal Reality of Fortress Europe

A growing fatal reality haunts fortress Europe: hundreds of refugee deaths. Over 3,800 deaths in the decade from 1993 to 2003 were documented by UNITED, a European network of 560 anti-racist groups and refugee organizations against racism that has monitored refugee deaths since 1993 (http://www.united.non-profit.nl/pdfs/listofdeaths). By June 2006 this statistic had increased to 7,182 deaths, including refugees who drowned in the Mediterranean Sea and the Strait of Gibraltar, suffocated in trucks and committed suicide in Europe's detention centres (http://www.statewatch .org/news/2006/jun/05united-address-book.htm).

According to the latest UNITED documented list, announced on January 20, 2011 at least 14,921 people have died since 1988 along the European frontiers. Among them 6,469 were missing in the sea. In the Mediterranean sea, and through the Atlantic Ocean towards Spain, 10,925 migrants died. In the Sicily channel 4,183 people died along the routes from Libya, Egypt and Tunisia to Malta and Italy, including 3,059 missing; 138 other people drowned sailing from Algeria to Sardinia. Along the routes from Mauritania, Morocco and Algeria towards Spain through the Gibraltar strait or off the Canary islands, at least 4,507 people died, including 2,302 who were missing. In addition, 1.355 people died in the Aegean Sea between Turkey and Greece – but also between Egypt and Greece – including 824 missing, and 603 people who died in the Adriatic Sea, between Albania, Montenegro and Italy, including 220 missing.[10]

UNITED has also criticized the U.K.'s proposal for EU 'Transit Processing Centres' located outside the EU, potentially in Ukraine, Romania or Bulgaria – such centres are now being built inside the changing EU external borders, to be used as 'zones of protection.' Human rights organizations like Amnesty International and Human Rights Watch call such centres 'unlawful and unworkable' and argue that they drive even more refugees underground. According to UNITED,

> Instead Europe should turn to policies that address the causes for flight. Global social injustice and world-wide armed conflicts make people leave everything behind and risk their lives. If we do not take care that the global political and socio-economic situation gets better, we cannot realistically expect people to stay in situations that we ourselves would find unbearable. Our commitment to human rights demands us to see refugees as human beings with individual rights and needs. (http://www .unitedagainstracism.org)

On 11 November 2003, the European Commission produced its draft regulation on the establishment of 'a European Agency for the Management of Operational Co-operation at the External Borders' (European Commission 2003: 687, 11.11.03. ref 1), which will continue to develop outside of any meaningful democratic control. It suggests that 'Member States should endeavour to apply all existing international instruments for the prevention and punishment of illegal immigration by sea, while ensuring the safety of individuals and compliance with human rights provisions' (Statewatch analysis, 2003).

The next sections will examine some of the EU securitization measures and policies as they are being implemented in Greece, France, Italy, Spain and the Mediterranean.

Greece

Greece was among the few countries that have actually recorded a major increase in the number of asylum requests. According to the Ministry of Public Order, 9,050 asylum applications were registered by the Greek authorities in 2005, compared with 4,469 asylum seekers the previous year. Thanks to United Nations High Commissioner for Refugees UNHCR information campaigns for refugees in Greece, several articles in the national press have accentuated a number of refugee protection issues that need to be addressed. These included the low number of persons who obtain asylum (only 0.84 per cent of applicants in 2005), the limited reception capacity (less than 900 places compared to the 9,050 asylum applications registered in 2005) and the lack of measures for the protection of unaccompanied children and other vulnerable groups (*Kathimerini*, 17 February 2006; *Avgi*, 20 February 2006; *Ta Nea*, 21 February 2006).

In 2006, the Greek state appealed a court decision to provide pecuniary compensation of 12,000 euros to a man from Bangladesh who was illegally detained by the authorities for one whole year, under cramped conditions. The state argued that since irregular migrants are responsible for the increasing crime rate, and for the sake of public order, degrading detention conditions should not constitute a serious offence against humanity (Ta Nea, 28 February 2006; Rizospastis, 1 March 2006; Apogevmatini, 2 March 2006). Following a report by the Greek ombudsman condemning the appalling conditions under which aliens are held in various police stations in Greece, the Supreme Court issued a circular saying that all aliens who either have served their sentence or are on conditional release should remain in prison until they are deported, and not be transferred to the detention facilities of police stations (Statewatch News Online, March 2006). In 2010 Greece has become the favoured port for entry for most illegal pouring into the EU, especially after Greece's newly de-mined, north-eastern flank. The deployment of a small EU FRONTEX rapid border intervention team along the border with Turkey was proved insufficient; hence, the Greek socialist government has recently announced that it plans to build a razor-wire fence along the border. It will be equipped with sonar systems and thermal sensors and be modelled along the lines of similar "walls" in Spain, Lithuania and France.[11]

France

The Council of Europe Human Rights Commissioner presented a damning report in relation to his visit to France in September 2005, criticizing the legal system, detention conditions, the lack of prosecution of abuses committed by members of the police and generally the treatment of members of ethnic minorities. Recent developments in immigration and asylum policy have meant that the stricter understanding of asylum now prevailing in France is likely to undermine the rights of genuine asylum seekers. A number of irregularities are noted in relation to detention in 'waiting zones', the conditions of asylum applicants awaiting the outcome of their applications and the list of 'safe' countries (allowing applications from nationals of these countries to be systematically refused) that has been adopted by French asylum authorities.[12]

Italy and Spain

Italian journalists could not enter the Centres for Temporary Stay and Assistance, Italy's detention centres for foreigners, on 23 March 2006. In Spain, on Saturday 24 June 2006, over fifty activists from different European countries involved in a protest in the Zona Franca in Barcelona, the Second Caravan for Freedom of Movement, were arrested as they occupied the site of a future detention centre for foreigners (http://www.statewatch .org/news/2006/jun/06-detention-protest.htm).

According to Peio Aierbe, the Spanish media have misrepresented events at the Spanish-Moroccan border fences at the enclaves of Ceuta and Mellila, presenting them as medieval assaults when what the migrants (whose numbers were vastly exaggerated) actually were doing was jumping a border fence in considerable numbers. Moreover, it was the migrants who were on the receiving end of the violence that took place – many were shot to death (PeioAierbe at http://www.statewatch.org/news/2006/jul/06rabat.htm). The first anniversary of the shooting of the immigrants – 7 October 2006 – has been called a transnational day of action against migration controls.

Fortress-Europe is also reinforced by EU Mediterranean joint patrols to stop migrants from Africa. Such patrols started in 2003, when the first pioneering joint maritime surveillance scheme was formed, but failed. Boats from five EU member states patrolled the Mediterranean from Algeciras to Palermo between 28 January and 8 February 2003 as a prototype for a future European border police force to guard Europe's southern seaboard against illegal immigration. Yet, it foundered due to the lack of a common language; moreover, it failed to stop a single person, even though over that period some 300 people completed the hazardous crossing from North Africa to Andalusia (*The Independent,* 11 March 2003).

Despite this initial failure and excess expenditures of 1.2 million euros, Spain now wants Brussels to increase its contribution to the second phase from 60 per cent to 80 per cent, and in the process extend surveillance to Atlantic waters between the Western Sahara and the Canary Islands, using aircraft to monitor large expanses of sea (Statewatch article, http://database.statewatch.org/protected/article.asp?aid=664).

A Mediterranean Fortress Policy

The Ministers of the Interior of the G5 countries (France, Italy, Spain, Germany and the U.K.) met in July 2005 in Evian, where they agreed to develop the following 'fortress-Mediterranean policy' proposals to combat immigration by sea from Africa: EU joint grouped flights for the repatriation of irregular immigrants; EU and Mediterranean cooperation in repatriation; joint patrols in the Mediterranean; joint analysis of migration flows from Sub-Saharan Africa; joint investigation teams at the departure point for immigrants. Recognizing also the importance of the European Border Agency in the coordinated EU fight against illegal immigration, the ministers reaffirmed their commitment to ensuring the agency has a positive early effect and is able to begin its operational work as soon as possible. They also decided on the implementation of strengthened controls at the internal borders of the European area (*Statewatch News Online,* 2005).

In addition, an EU-African ministerial conference on immigration, held in July 2006 in Rabat, Morocco, highlighted the dramatic consequences that cooperation in this field is causing on the ground in North African countries. As Claire Rodier, president of the Migreurop network, has pointed out, the notion of 'illegal emigration' that is being touted by the EU and forced – via the adoption of draconian legislation to counter such emigration, among other things – upon African countries in exchange for funding, should be banished.[13]

Concluding Remarks: What Kind of Europe?

If security is a social construct, the question remains: who poses the threat, who is threatened and who is to take action to eliminate that threat? Which threat is real and which is imaginary? Hence, who is the real enemy of the EU? Is the EU threatened collectively by immigration? Is the proposed anti-terrorist policy efficient enough, or just a fortress against immigration and civil liberties? And if it is, why should the EU, as a security actor, take extraordinary action, even going against human rights and democracy to survive (Guerra 1997; Mitsilegas 1997; Samatas 2003a, 2003b)?

Numerous economic and political interests have invested in the building of the fortress Europe – to protect the EU from whom? Nobody will disagree about the necessity of an EU fortress against organized crime, drug dealers, human trafficking, corruption and terrorism. However, a fortress Europe against desperate immigrants and refugees at a time when an aging Europe can absorb them (see note 4), and an 'Orwellian' EU that considers everyone a suspect, especially political demonstrators and activists, raise many questions about what kind of Europe we want. Terrorism and illegal immigration are serious problems indeed, but at issue is whether such problems can be effectively treated by 'wars' and a European fortress against human rights and democracy (Leone 2003).

So who are the power actors and the interest groups behind that fortress Europe? Aside from the post-9/11 impact and the influence of the U.S., there is a 'pro–fortress Europe coalition' characterized by the following:

- Neoliberal governments and policies that favour privatization of internal security and the decrease of the welfare state;
- Nationalist and populist parties and politicians who seek votes by promising zero immigrants;
- Security officials and practitioners, like border guards, immigration and custom officers, etc., who might lose their status and jobs as a result of the abolition of the internal borders;
- Law enforcement agencies that demand the surveillance of everyone's movements (Lyon 2003);
- U.S., British and other high-tech security corporations, which with the end of the Cold War are looking for new markets, propagating panoptic surveillance systems as a panacea for social problems (Norris and Armstrong 1999);
- Conservative nationalists with mass media connections and property rights who favour the privatization of internal security (Buzan 1991; McSweeney 1999; Geddes 2000).

Representatives from most of the above groups and categories are staffing the operational bodies that propose and promote EU security policy (Geddes 2000; Samatas 2003b). Concrete evidence for this is provided by the aforementioned Evian 2005 meeting of the G5 Ministers of the Interior, where it was agreed to develop the 'fortress-Mediterranean policy' against immigration by sea from Africa.

Counter to the 'pro–fortress Europe coalition' is a growing 'pro–people's Europe coalition' comprised of not only leftist parties and unions but also grassroots movements, as well as many NGOs. These include Human Rights Watch, Statewatch, EU migrants Forum, European Citizens Action Service, Starting Line Group, United Justice, Amnesty International, Privacy International and others (Geddes 2000). All these, and thousands of other NGOs around the world, form a coalition of resistance to securitization and fortress logic at the local, national, regional and global level, adopting the solidarity principle and defending human rights, democracy and liberties.

The inhumane conditions in migrant holding centres located all over the EU and especially in the Southern states, combined with the violent reaction of authorities against civil society groups that criticize the use of these facilities, have given impetus to a European campaign and an appeal to all EU citizens to shut down these detention centres in Europe. The campaign started in March 2006, when police violently stopped journalists from visiting Italy's Centres for Temporary Stay and Assistance. The campaign was intensified the arrests in June 2006 of fifty protesters from the Second Caravan for Freedom of Movement in Spain who sought to occupy the Zona Franca in Barcelona, which was earmarked as a future detention centre for foreigners. As the appeal points out:

> In the twenty-five Member States, there are 178 holding centres, while more have been built in candidate or neighbouring countries. The conditions in migrant holding-centres are very similar, sometimes even worse, than those in prisons. Following visits to holding centres, NGOs, international agencies, parliamentary delegations and journalists have denounced the iniquity, inhumanity and degradation of these places, where human rights and fundamental freedoms are often violated and violence used against migrants. (http://www.no-fortress-europe.eu/showPage.jsp and http://www.statewatch.org/news/2006/jun/06-detention-protest.htm)

Two worlds are clashing in the EU: the pro– and no–fortress-Europe. The pro–fortress-Europe side includes the power holders and policy makers; the no–fortress-Europe side is made up of civil society groups that are excluded from the decision-making process and whose members are considered troublemakers by the securitarians, who accuse them of being radicals who have sympathy or links with terrorists, and hence suspects who have to be watched. This clash reflects the democratic deficit at the national and EU level (Chryssochoou 1998; Chryssochoou et al. 1998;

Warleigh 2003). Nevertheless, and because of this deficit, European and global civil society must watch the watchers and fight for an open but safe Europe and a better and safer world, promoting peace, democracy, justice, human rights, fair trade and sustainable development, and eliminating the inequalities gap and injustice between North and South that produce insecurity, wars and terrorism.

Despite the evidence provided in this chapter that a fortress-Europe is firmly entrenched, thanks to the pro-fortress coalition we should not regard it as inevitable. European integration is still an open bargaining process in which EU citizens are often ignored and permanent alien residents largely excluded. However, as the French and Dutch people have shown at the last referendums for the ratification of the EU constitutional treaty, we are still in the process of debating and discussing what kind of Europe we would like to have.

NOTES

I thank the Statewatch Group for their significant contribution to this chapter (completed in 2006) via the material offered at www.statewatch.org.

1. According to the European Commission (2002), there were 13 million third-country aliens in the EU, i.e. 3.5 per cent of the EU population. The European Commission used this report to show that even if the flow of immigrants doubled, the EU social security systems could still afford it.
2. Melossi's research (2003), published in the journal *Punishment and Society*, shows a big overrepresentation of foreigners in European prisons.
3. *Statewatch News Online*, March 2005. Retrieved on March 10, 2008 from http://www.statewatch.org/news/2005/apr/08SISart96.htm
4. On 1 February 2003 there were a total of 1,266,142 records relating to persons in the SIS. Of this total, 390,368 related to aliases. Of the 875,774 remaining records, 89 per cent are article 96 alerts. Statewatch article: RefNo# 26999.
5. In September 2004 the European Commission signed a €40 million contract with a consortium of IT specialists to build two sprawling new EU law enforcement databases, SIS II and VIS, which will provide EU law enforcement agencies with a powerful apparatus for surveillance and control. This was scheduled to go online early in 2007. Statewatch, news online, February. 23, 2004. Retrieved on March 12, 2008 from http://www.statewatch.org/news/2004/feb/23Aeu-plan-security.htm
6. Statewatch, news online, February. 23, 2004. Retrieved on March 12, 2008 from http://www.statewatch.org/news/2004/feb/23Aeu-plan-security.htm
7. John Lettice (2004) has explained how the 'current enthusiasm for profiling, the idea of being able to identify possible threats from people who aren't known, and have no record, absolutely requires broad data capture, use and retention. Of course we've got to compile records on people who're innocent

– otherwise, how could we confirm they're innocent? And anyway, innocent people have nothing to hide. Or they soon won't have…'.
8. Statewatch News Online, March 2005. Retrieved on March 10, 2008 from http://www.statewatch.org/news/2005/apr/08SISart96.htm
9. Statewatch News Online, July 2006. Retrieved on April 2, 2008 from http://www.statewatch.org/news/2006 /jul/06rabat.htm
10. www.unitedagainstracism.org/pdfs/listofdeaths.pdf. Retrieved on Jan. 30, 2011
11. Retrieved on February 7, 2011 from http://www.guardian.co.uk/world/2011/feb/06/fortress-europe-greece-migrant-surge
12. Statewatch News Online, July 2006. Retrieved on April 2, 2008 from http://www.statewatch.org/news/2006 /jul/06rabat.htm
13. Statewatch News Online, July 2006. Retrieved on April 2, 2008 from http://www.statewatch.org/news/2006 /jul/06rabat.htm

References

Alston, P. (ed.). 1999. *The EU and Human Rights.* Oxford: Oxford University Press.
AI (Amnesty International). 2004. *International Report: Recommendations to Ireland's EU Presidency,* January 2004.
Andersen, S. and K. Eliassen (eds). 1996. *The European Union: How Democratic Is It?* London: Sage.
den Boer, M. and W. Wallace. 1996. 'Justice and Home Affairs: Integration through Incrementalism', in H. Wallace and W. Wallace (eds), *Policy-Making in the European Union,* 4th ed. Oxford: Oxford University Press.
Boettchter, D. 2000. 'The Impossibility of Schengen', *OJPCR Online Journal* 3.1, March.
Bunyan, T. 2002. 'The War on Freedom and Democracy: An Analysis of the Effects on Civil Liberties and Democratic Culture in the EU', *Statewatch* publication, September.
Bunyan, T. 2005. *Countering Civil Rights.* Nottingham: Spokesman Books.
Buzan, B. 1991. 'New Patterns of Global Security in the 21st Century', *International Affairs* 67(3): 431–457.
Chryssochoou, D. 1998 *Democracy in the European Union.* London: I.B. Tauris
Chryssochoou, D. et al. 1998. 'European Democracy, Parliamentary Decline and the Democratic Deficit of the EU', *Journal of Legislative Studies* 4(3): 108–128.
Council of the EU. 2004. *Declaration on Combating Terrorism,* Doc. no. 7486, Rev 4, 25 March 2004 and 9048/04, 19 May 2004 (www.eu2004.ie/template/news.asp).
European Commission. 2002. *Social Europe Report.* May.
European Commission. 2003. Management of Operational Co-operation if the External Borders. EC 687, 11.11.03.
Geddes, A. 2000. *Immigration and European Integration: Towards Fortress Europe? Manchester:* Manchester University Press.
Gilbert, P. 1994. *Terrorism, Security and Nationality.* London: Routledge.

Guerra, S. 1997. 'International Migration in the Mediterranean', paper presented at conference on 'Non-military Aspects of Security in Southern Europe'. Santorini, 19–21 September.

Guild, E. and J. Niessen. 1996. *The Developing Immigration and Asylum Policies of the EU*. The Hague: Kluwer Law International.

Hayes, B. 2002. 'The Activities and Development of Europol: Towards an Unaccountable "FBI" in Europe'. London: Statewatch.

Hayes, B. 2004. 'Implementing the Amsterdam Treaty: Cementing Fortress Europe'. *Statewatch Bulletin* 14(2).

Hayter, T. 2004. *Open Borders: The Case against Immigration Controls*. London: Pluto Press.

Hohm, C. F. and O. Newman. 2003. *Migration, Terrorism and Human Rights*. Thousand Oaks: Pine Forge Press.

Huysmans, J. 1995. 'Migrants as a Security Problem: Dangers of "Securitizing" Societal Issues', in R. Miles and D. Threnhardt (eds), *Migration and European Integration*. London: Pinter.

Huysmans, J. 2000. 'The European Union and the Securitization of Migration', *Journal of Common Market Studies* 38(5): 751–777.

ICHR (Inter-American Committee on Human Rights). 2002. *Report on Terrorism and Human Rights*. 1 June. Retrieved on 22 March 2006 from www.cidh.oas .org/terrorism

ICLMG (International Civil Liberties Monitoring Group). 2004. *Anti-Terrorism and the Security Agenda*. Ottawa, 17 February. Retrieved on 25 March 2006 from www.interpares.ca/en/publications/pdf/ILLM6

Kaldor, M. 2005. 'What Is Human Security?' in D. Heldet al. (eds), *Debating Globalization*. Cambridge: Polity Press.

Katrougalos, G. 1995. 'The Rights of Foreigners and Immigrants in Europe: Recent Trends', *Web Journal of Current Legal Issues* 5.

Lavenex, S. 2001. *The Europeanization of Refugee Policies: Between Human Rights and Internal Security*. Aldershot: Ashgate.

Leone, R.C. 2003. *The War on Our Freedoms: Civil Liberties in an Age of Terrorism*. New York: A Century Foundation Book.

Lettice, J. 2004. 'Got a Ticket? Get a Record', *The Register*, 3 February.

Lyon, D. 2003. *Surveillance After September 11: Themes for the 21st Century*. London: Polity.

Maas, W. 2005. 'Freedom of Movement inside "Fortress Europe"', in E. Zureik and M. Salter (eds), *Global Surveillance and Policing: Borders, Security, Identity*. Devon: Willan Publishing

Manitakis A. and A. Takis (eds). 2004. *Terrorism and Rights: From State Security to Law Insecurity* (in Greek). Athens: Savalas.

Mathiesen, T. 1999. *On Globalisation of Control: Towards an Integrated Surveillance System in Europe*. London: Statewatch.

McSweeney, B. 1999. *Security Identity and Interests: A Sociology of International Relations*. Cambridge: Cambridge University Press.

Meijers, H. et al. 1991. *Schengen: Internationalisation of Central Chapters of the Law on Aliens, Refugees, Security and the Police*. Amsterdam: Kluwer.

Melossi, D. 2003. 'In a Peaceful Life: Migration and the Crime of Modernity in Europe/Italy', *Punishment and Society* 5(4): 371–397.

Mitsilegas, V. 1997. 'Dangerous Liaisons: Transnational Crime and Immigration in the Construction of European Security Identity', paper presented at the conference 'Non-military Aspects of Security in Southern Europe.' Santorini, Greece, 19–21 September 1997.

Mitsilegas, V. 2002 'The Implementation of the EU acquis on Illegal Immigration by the Candidate Countries of Central and Eastern Europe', *Journal of Ethnic and Migration Studies* 28(4): 665–682.

Norris, C. and G. Armstrong. 1999. *The Maximum Surveillance Society: The Rise of CCTV.* Oxford: Berg.

Peers, S. 1999. 'Human Rights and the Third Pillar', in P. Alston (ed.), *The EU and Human Rights.* Oxford: Oxford University Press.

Privacy International. 2004. 'Condemnation of EU Data Sharing with US', 1 February. Online at http://www.privacyinternational.org/article.shtml?cmd[347] =x-347-72181)

Samatas, M. 1997. "The Schengen Surveyland ': The inclusionary and exclusionary impact of the Schengen Agreement vis-a-vis a pan-European Union of People" paper presented at the Conference of the European Sociological Association "20th Century Europe: Inclusions / Exclusions, panel: "Migration and Fortress Europe" Essex University , U.K. 27–30 Aug.

Samatas, M. 2003a. Greece in the 'Schengenland': Blessing or Anathema for Citizens and Strangers' Rights?' *Journal of Ethnic and Migration Studies,* Jan.– March, 29(1): 141–156.

Samatas, M. 2003b. 'Security, Freedom, and Democracy under the Schengen Agreement' (in Greek), *Greek Political Science Review* 22.

Schutz, W.F. 2003. *Tainted Legacy: 9/11 and the Ruin of Human Rights.* New York: Thunder's Mouth Press/Nation Books.

Sidel, M. 2004. *More Secure, Less Free? Antiterrorism Policy and Civil Liberties after September 11.* Ann Arbor: The University of Michigan Press.

Sitaropoulos, N. 1992. 'The New Legal Framework of Alien Immigration in Greece: A Draconian Contribution to Europe's Unification', *Immigration and Nationality Law and Practice* 6: 89–96

Spencer, M. 1995. *States of Injustice: A Guide to Human Rights and Civil Liberties in the EU.* London: Pluto Press.

Statewatch analysis 2003 Cover-up! Proposed Regulation on European Border Guard hides unaccountable, operational bodies Retrieved on March 10, 2010 from http://www.statewatch.org/news/2003/nov/10euborders.htm

Statewatch News Online, 2005, March. Retrieved on March 10, 2008 from http:// www.statewatch.org/news/2005/apr/08SISart96.htm

Statewatch News Online, July 2005 Retrieved on March 10, 2008 http://database .statewatch.org/protected/article.asp?aid=26599

UN Development Program. 1994. *Human Development Report 1994.* Oxford: Oxford University Press.

Upton, J. 2004. 'An Authoritarian State is in the Process of Construction', *The Guardian,* 23 February.

Van Buuren, J. 2003. 'The Network of the Schengen System' (in Greek), *Le Monde* in *Sunday Eleftherotypia*, 6 April.

Van Lancker, A. 1996. 'Transparency and Accountability of Schengen', in H. Wallace and W. Wallace (eds), *Policy-Making in the European Union*, 4th ed. Oxford: Oxford University Press.

Waever, O. 1996. 'European Security Identities', *Journal of Common Market Studies* 34(1): 103–132.

Waever, O. et al. 1993. *Identity, Migration, and the New Security Agenda in Europe.* London: Pinter Publishers.

Warleigh, A. 2003. *Democracy in the EU.* London: Sage.

Webber, F. 1995. *Crimes of Arrival: Immigrants and Asylum-seekers in the New Europe.* London: Statewatch.

Weiner, M. 1995. *The Global Migration Crisis: Challenges to States and to Human Rights.* New York: Harper Collins.

Chapter 3

Locating the Mediterranean in Music

The Medi-Terra Music Festival

ELENI KALLIMOPOULOU

Music travels across real and imaginary borders. Across the Mediterranean, a variety of traditions have intertwined over the centuries and continue to carry the traces of their encounters. Music encodes the complexity of cultural interaction and provides a field where this can be fruitfully studied. As a non-verbal type of cultural practice and expression, it is an immediate and therefore powerful means of constructing identities, memories and the experience of place and space. Among the peoples of the Mediterranean, music serves to forge national and regional loyalties; at the same time it may provide the opportunity for international exchange and for raising public awareness of interlaced cultural histories.

The Medi-Terra Festival was set up with the idea of highlighting aspects of the composite cultural make-up of the Mediterranean. The music of the groups featured suggests not just the wide diversity of musical idioms and traditions of the region, but also a plurality of ways in which these may be re-worked to enact different senses of identity and locality.

—Med-Voices flyer

Cultural Representation

In his discussion of the making of ethnographic texts, James Clifford stresses the embeddedness of power relations in any act of cultural representation. Ethnographies are seen as complex, plural cultural accounts, as hierarchical arrangements of discourses, inherently partial and enmeshed in dynamics of difference and power. The crucial task of placing them within larger contexts of power inequality necessitates – also – a specification of discourses, identifying who speaks/writes, when and where, with or to whom, and under what institutional and historical constraints (Clifford 1986). In what follows, I wish to consider the Medi-Terra Music Festival conducted in Crete in 2005 in the context of the Med-Voices research programme as such an ethnographic text. My interest is in probing the particular cultural narratives in the Medi-Terra representation and the ideas of the Mediterranean that it put forward. Viewing the festival as the point of intersection of various hierarchical paradigms, I examine comparatively the Med-Voices' general aims, my own ethnomusicological perspective in setting up the festival and the outlooks of the four groups who participated as well as the audience, which partook productively in the generation of musical meaning. At a second level, I relate these to broader Mediterranean discourses as they have been constructed in European academia and in the commercial music market as well as by dominant ideological paradigms of the modern period – especially that of nationalism.

Central to the representations was my own involvement as an observer/ participant in charge of selecting the groups and setting up the festival. To query the cultural poetics of the festival is thus first of all to embark on a reflexive analysis of the causes – and results – of my own power-broking activities. These activities entailed choices that were by no means ideologically neutral; in fact, they prove in retrospect to be quite revealing and often inconsistent.

Three of the groups I selected drew upon traditional material, which they reformulated in a contemporary language. This seemed to me to achieve a dual goal: on the one hand it suggested an overview of Mediterranean idioms, while on the other hand it put forward local musical visions, presenting the particular groups' own ideas and experience of locality. Choosing groups that composed their own music appeared to be a way of resisting exoticism in the festival representation. They might describe their musical credo as follows: we are as 'modern' as you; we are not 'authentic' insiders to these musical traditions, instead we are drawing from them and from all our other musical stimuli to express who we are, and what is important to us. In this sense the groups countered, in my eyes, stereotypical images about the Mediterranean with their own ideas of who they are and what they do.

At the same time, in order to give an idea of the diversity of musical styles of the peoples of the Mediterranean, I focused on regions where prolonged and documented interaction had taken place in the past. I accordingly chose groups whose musical activity seemed to fit onto this earlier cultural/geographical map. Although this was framed in the festival's texts by reference to the 'plurality of ways in which [musical idioms and traditions of the region] may be re-worked to enact different senses of identity and locality', individual groups were nevertheless subsequently 'read' as drawing largely from this Mediterranean musical fund. But the notion of reading the music of contemporary groups on the basis of earlier cultural configurations is quite problematic; moreover, as will be suggested further down, not all groups would find it fully relevant.

Although I tried to avoid producing exoticizing texts, the groups I chose would fit quite well the profile of world music groups (described below). This meant excluding other groups that could make equally valid claims to Mediterranean-ness, but that would not be 'hip' and therefore marketable in a world music context. But the criterion of what sells better among contemporary non-specialized ethnically mixed audiences, and thus what sort of groups were more likely to enhance the output of the regional exhibition (discussed below), does not alone provide an adequate explanation for my choice. More tellingly, perhaps, all the groups I selected are acoustic, another point that suggests the festival recalled the notion of an old, traditional, 'authentic' Mediterranean. Further, genres such as rock and pop were completely absent. I somehow took it for granted that the best way for a festival to present music of the Mediterranean would be through groups exploring traditional idioms/instruments/styles, even if in a contemporary, creative way.[1]

These choices suggest an essentialization on my part of the Mediterranean and a reification of culture, an underlying assumption that there is some Mediterranean essence to be found inherent in traditional music that would be eliminated by overt technological mediation or by expressive styles originating in the West. Upon reflection, I wonder to what extent this reasoning did not in effect perpetuate stereotypical notions both of the Mediterranean and of what constitutes tradition. More importantly perhaps, would my readings correspond to the groups' own understanding of their music? And if not, which are the implications in terms of power relations?

This self-critique is quite revealing – all the more so since it comes from a U.K.-trained ethnomusicologist whose Greek origin makes her a cultural insider and who perceives herself to be sensitive to issues of misrepresentation and cultural stereotyping and domination. Whilst trying to conform to what I thought the festival concept was, in reality I was reproducing inward-looking stereotypes about the culture I consider myself to be part of. At the same time this suggests not only the pervasiveness of such stereotyping, but also, in Said's words, that 'no production of knowledge in the human sciences can ever ignore or disclaim its author's involvement as a human subject in his own circumstances' (2003: 11). It is only in retrospect that I can engage with the work in a more critical fashion.

The Medi-Terra Music Festival

The Medi-Terra Music Festival was organized as the Regional Exhibition of the University of Crete, regional partner in the research programme Mediterranean Voices: Oral History and Cultural Practice in Mediterranean Cities. The main aim of the regional exhibition, which took place at the end of the programme's three-year duration, was to publicize its on-the-ground activities and main outputs. Giving it the form of a music festival was therefore an obvious choice, as music tends to draw larger audiences than exhibitions, seminars or talks generally do. Moreover, a music festival could potentially attract a variety of target groups, including locals, members of the economic immigrant communities and European and other tourists, which a more 'intellectual' event might not. The festival was conducted in partnership with the municipalities of Chania, Rethymno and Heraklio, which maximized the project's geographical reach, while their financial contribution to the budget allocated for the regional exhibition helped in 'supporting' an exceptionally large number of groups and concerts. As researcher ethnomusicologist employed by the University of Crete to set up and carry out the regional exhibition, I had a wide variety of tasks. These ranged from budget allocation and project proposal, shaping the music festival in terms of its general contour and selecting the groups, to more administrative tasks such as organizing the groups' transport and accommodation and accompanying them during their stay. I worked in close collaboration with the head of the Cretan team, and my choices were subject to approval by the University of Crete and the coordinating team, and ultimately – in their broad lines – the EU Commission.

The main concern in shaping the festival was to give it a theme in line with the Med-Voices programme's content, but also to translate in musical terms the main objective it set, namely, 'to enhance knowledge and awareness of the cosmopolitan oral heritage of the Mediterranean region as a means of demonstrating the link between oral and built heritage, as well as the deep-rooted cultural ties between different Mediterranean populations.'[2] Foregrounding the notion of the Mediterranean as geographical umbrella and unifying theme was thus an obvious and rather un-interrogated decision, underlined also by the name chosen for the festival: *Medi-Terra, Music across Lands*.

In further specifying its content, I relied on two principal criteria. First, I looked at the idea of regions in which cultural interaction has been historically a prominent feature and has resulted in the formation of distinct musical idioms. Although a series of practical considerations related to size, cost and accessibility of individual groups made it impossible to represent all such main regions, the four groups chosen drew upon styles more or less corresponding to some principal regions of this cultural map of the Mediterranean. These included Andalusian Spain (L'Ham de Foc); the Balkans and Turkey (Balkan Journey); commercial and migratory routes between South and North (Dounia); and the Arab Middle East (Artas). Secondly, I selected groups that explored specifically intercultural musical aspects by combining a variety of idioms related to these cultural regions. These two criteria were also central to the way that the groups were (re)presented in the festival's written texts (programme notes, brochures, news bulletins):

> [L'Ham de Foc's] ... vibrant musical explorations draw from the historical past of the Iberian Peninsula, where the Arab, Christian and Jewish cultures intersected, and also from continuing research into a number of other traditions, including the Eastern Mediterranean and Crete.

> [Balkan Journey] ... explore the deep-rooted cultural affinities across Turkey, Greece, and the Balkans.

> Dounia perform traditional songs of the Middle East as well as original compositions, evoking the historical proximity of Sicily and the Arab world and being inspired by various traditions from around the world. (Medi-Terra Programme Notes 2005)

With respect to the second criterion, Artas formed an exception. The other three groups all seem to cross regional musical boundaries, either by deliberately pursuing a variously defined musical hybridity in terms of their inputs (L'Ham de Foc, Dounia) or by playing music from diverse regions, even if their renditions are framed by notions of faithfulness to the source (Balkan Journey). This is corroborated also by the answers they gave to a questionnaire prepared for them (see below). Artas, on the other hand, perform the music, songs and dances of their locale, Artas village. They sing and play the music that accompanies *Debka*, the traditional Palestinian dance, while their version – despite some similarities with that of other regions – is peculiar to their own region. The songs are in the Palestinian dialect of the specific area, as opposed to modern standard or classical Arabic. They typically perform in the context of life cycle events and celebrations (weddings, etc.) as well as in festivals in Artas and the vicinities. This was quite evident also in the way they structured their performance for the Medi-Terra festival. It emulated a wedding, a task necessitating the recruitment of members of the audience to stand as the bride and as the newlyweds' kin and friends. The event ended with a long procession of people walking around the square of Agios Minas and dancing.

But the group was arguably at a distance from the other three groups in terms of general outlook as well as of music. Unlike Artas, whose members are all drawn from the local community and perform as amateurs, the members of the other groups are professional musicians whose music is their main occupation. Moreover, these three groups have an international-ist outlook, as is also suggested by their promotion strategies and/or their audiences and CD distribution. L'Ham de Foc and Balkan Journey have eth-nically mixed audiences and distribute both nationally and abroad;[3] Dounia distributes only nationally but like the other two seems geared towards the international commercial world music scene, as is evident in their web-site presentation style – an English version is also included. On the other hand, Artas, short for Artas Folklore Troupe, do not have their own web-site featuring them as an artistic/music group. They are affiliated with the Artas Folklore Center and are featured on its website[4] as a side project. In fact, it was the Bethlehem-based Med-Voices team working with the Artas Folklore Centre who proposed that we include the group in the festival in the first place, and were it not for this fortunate coincidence it would have been quite hard to find out about them. Further, it was partly owing to the mediation of the Med-Voices team, who acted as interpreters between us and Artas and assisted in the difficult task of acquiring visas, that the group could finally come.

The liminalities that Artas thus seem to encapsulate in relation to the festival offer a quite revealing point from which to view its cultural po-etics both at a micro-level (distinct meanings that it generated) but also within the broader contemporary European landscape of musical practice and discourse. To begin with, their case raises important questions about who has access to European funding institutions and to the commercial world music circuit at large. Despite variations and differences, one may convincingly argue that the majority of groups who usually feature in inter-national festivals have at their disposal not just specific technical resources (website, communication, language, etc.) but, importantly, also the cultural resources, and by this I refer specifically to *knowledge* of how to shape and present their work, how to channel it and to whom. Possessing the cultural capital to market their work is directly linked to issues of power relations, and it is thus not surprising to note correspondences in terms of the geog-raphy of the Mediterranean.

More often than not, groups featured are from – or at least based in – the European Mediterranean. Even, that is, those North African styles that are popular in Europe today have found their way and been filtered through a specifically European aesthetic. Algerian *Rai* is a typical example, but a similar case can be made for Arab musicians who participate in Southern European groups. Artists originating from countries of the Southern or Eastern Mediterranean who reside in countries of the Northern Mediterra-nean function thus as cultural brokers, mediating between 'us' and 'them';

while the same counts for European Mediterranean groups whose music variously incorporates aspects of North African and/or Arab idioms. This would suggest that the European Mediterranean, being ambiguously both familiar and exotic, is thus easier for Northern/Western European audiences to assimilate and consume as a cultural Other. In the musical setting of world music festivals and the like, it is such ambiguities that are especially current, whereas styles deemed completely foreign – in this case from the 'exotic' or 'oriental' North Africa and the Eastern Mediterranean[5] – are less easy to accommodate.

Upon reflection, the question of accessibility (in practical and musical terms) impinged significantly on my own planning. Finding a group from North Africa proved especially hard, given the time and resources available: the few ones that turned up in an Internet search were difficult to contact or prohibitively large to bring, while arranging for visas, etc. would push our organizational resources to their limit. In the end I resorted to choosing groups from the European Mediterranean that variously encompassed also North African/Arab elements in their music. But this consequently meant foregrounding hybridity, so that in effect the festival may be seen as having in many ways showcased a major world music theme.

The flagging of hybridity appears in fact to be a widespread feature of international world music festivals today. One look at how artists/groups venerated on the European world music scene are represented by its producers and critics suffices to make the point: groups are celebrated for mixing different cultures, sounds, instruments. Often the groups themselves are an iconic microcosm of this mixture in terms of the ethnic origin of their members; often the bicultural background (ethnically or musically) of an artist, too, is stressed. Indeed, world music concerts are stereotypically cast as musical encounters in which artists/groups coming from different traditions – the more unlikely the combination the better – are brought together on stage, their performance being often assessed on the basis of whether or not they manage to gel.

At the same time, the extent to which groups possessing cultural capital are able to appropriate this discourse to represent and sell themselves is quite remarkable. As far as the Mediterranean region is concerned, a look at groups typically identified as symbols of Mediterranean-ness suffices to make the point. Radio Tarifa, a Spain-based group twice nominated for the BBC Radio 3 World Music Awards, describes itself on its website as follows:

> Distancing itself from all forms of musical purism in their choice of timbres and treatment of melodies, the group mixes arrangements of traditional compositions with their own original works. They use instruments

which were played in Ancient Egypt (*ney:* a cane flute), and others from classical Greek and Roman times (Mediterranean instruments such as the wooden oboe or harmonium), combining them with modern instruments like the saxophone or electric bass guitar. The resultant music is both familiar and exotic.[6]

A more recent example is Israeli singer Yasmin Levy, twice nominated for the same awards and revered by the musical press for creating a cross-breed of Flamenco and Sephardic cultures:

> I am proud to combine the two cultures of Ladino and flamenco, while mixing in Middle Eastern influences. I am embarking on a 500 years old musical journey, taking Ladino to Andalusia and mixing it with flamenco, the style that still bears the musical memories of the old Moorish and Jewish-Spanish world with the sound of the Arab world. In a way it is a 'musical reconciliation' of history.[7]

This is human agency at work: groups use the rules of a dominant discourse to negotiate their social, political, cultural position in specific historical contexts of asymmetrical power relations.[8] There are, however, some other implications here, which I wish to consider briefly.

The representation of the Mediterranean, especially during the Romantic era, as the marginal Other where European civilization traces its roots entailed a process not dissimilar from the one described by Said (2003). One can thus legitimately speak of 'Mediterraneanism' (Herzfeld 1999)[9] as the construction of knowledge about, and thereby constitution of, the Mediterranean by its North/Western European neighbours as their contemporary, living past. The choice of acoustic groups or the framing of the festival in terms of notions of tradition and cultural regions – even if some groups composed their own music – points in a way to the salience of such representations of the Mediterranean as natural, old, etc. But cultural stereotyping along Mediterraneanist lines could potentially be countered here through Mediterranean groups such as the ones described above, who are able to successfully articulate their own notions and voices. If nothing else, then, the examples discussed here show that significant ground has been covered in the course of time: they suggest today's much more composite picture, where locals too have a formative role in the ways in which the Mediterranean is sold.

One could thus reverse the perspective and interrogate notions of (Europe and) the Mediterranean by asking how the Mediterranean is defining itself, how it produces notions of Self and how these relate to a European Other and/or Self.[10] But here there is clearly also another issue at stake that brings me back – via a different path – to the question of cultural capital and asymmetrical power within the Mediterranean: which voices in particular do international institutions and/or networks such as the world music market empower? Who gets to be the vocal insider, and to voice the insiders' vision? In other words, it is clear that not all Mediterranean groups, peoples, and regions have equal access to representation: in the cases discussed here, for instance, why is it Spanish and/or Jewish people who get to define the 'Arab' and its place in the Mediterranean? As citizens of Northern Mediterranean states, we can also more easily afford to travel and interact with 'people' of the remote corners of the Mediterranean (or other Others), or study their music and cultures: here there are obvious parallels to Said's discussion about the interconnection between knowledge and power (2003: esp. 4–28).

It is clear that L'Ham de Foc and Dounia – and, though less so, Balkan Journey – fit fairly well the profile of empowered insiders. But where does this leave Artas? Performed outside its normal live cultural context, or outside the context of staged festivals, their music might arguably acquire folkloristic resonances simply by evoking – in presentation if not in ideology – the style of state-staged troupes.[11] Ironically, Artas are perhaps the most rooted, traditional group of all, yet it seems that for world music audiences and producers hybridity has come to stand precisely as a new authenticity. What are its implications?

Considered from an anthropological/ethnographic perspective, the strong regional focus of a group like Artas seems to somehow conjure up the survivalist outlook that characterized the discipline especially in earlier times: the idea of cultural survivals treated as cases of arrested development. Herzfeld sees this doctrine as the anthropological contemporary of systematic nationalism (1999: 9–10). Strangely enough, groups like Artas can somehow speak to the aspirations of these two historically opposed doctrines (ibid.: 64), the anthropological doctrine of cultural survivals and the nationalist folkloric one, while at the same time it is doubtful that they would identify themselves in ideological terms with either, and especially not the former.[12] This is by no means to criticize the programme for its largely anthropological approach; on the contrary, Med-Voices seems to have been committed precisely to empowering such groups.[13] It does point out quite eloquently, though, the perplexities in the identity of a discipline that 'rejects Exoticism (the sensationalizing of cultural difference) but nevertheless paradoxically pursues the study of cultural *otherness*' (Herzfeld 1999: 2–3).

The irony here would not be lost to the perceptive eye: a group that I, as an ethnomusicologist, would most likely not have chosen, made it to the festival through the intervention of the local team of a largely anthropologically oriented research programme. In the context of the festival, the group appears arguably a bit outmoded and prosaic in its folkloric content and format; therefore, one might expect that it would have embodied the essentialized, exoticized Other, representing the outsider's look into the region rather than ways in which insiders would choose to be seen by and relate to outsiders. Yet, this group was arguably the most political of all. Their insistent claim upon preserving their local culture, language and way of life cannot be considered separately from the Palestine issue and Israeli policy on the ground, which renders it deeply real and contemporary. There were instances when the artistic glaze of the festival was ruptured to reveal the hard realities of life in Palestine: during their stay, a member of the group made insistent appeals to the Cretan Med-Voices team to mediate for the acquisition of a visa for someone needing medical treatment not available at home. Presenting their musical instruments to the audience, *ud* and *darbukka* player Mahmoud Abu-Kamal pointed out that on their way to Crete the Israeli police had torn the *rababa*'s skin while searching for explosives.

In such instances, reality seems to call into question claims about music being a universal language with the power to unite: music is not just about connecting but also about separating, and the history of the region is one of tension, difference and struggle as much as it is one of communication and exchange. But narratives of friction are rarely present in the world music circuit; they are rather resolved through hybridity, the symbolic overcoming of musical difference, which in turn signals our respect for other cultures: expectedly, it is the music of other people that is transformed in our musical terms, rather than the other way around.

Not surprisingly, perhaps, Artas were warmly received: a long procession was formed as people spontaneously responded to their call to reconstruct a Palestinian wedding (Figures 3.1 and 3.2). In fact, this was arguably one of the highlights of the festival in terms of audience participation: in an impromptu act circumventing the prescribed concert format, Artas and audience performed their cultural intimacy as insiders partaking in a common Mediterranean culture.

For the concerts in the square of Agios Minas, at the very centre of Heraklio, no fees were charged and there was also the option of sitting in the square's coffee places and *meze* bars. This meant that along with world music fans, the audience held people who do not fit the profile of the typical world music concert-goer. Thus, besides Cretan students and non-Cretan Greek students studying in Crete, and a few tourists, mainly Europeans, the concerts attracted a large number of locals, children, families and elders from the district as well as passers-by. Present were also members of the Palestinian community of Crete (economic migrants and students) and Balkan economic migrant communities.

Responsiveness to the group was not unrelated to the popular feeling of support and solidarity that the Palestinian cause raises in Crete and in Greece generally. Modern Greek identity has been symbolically construed on the basis of a duality: Eastern/Byzantine and Western/Hellenic.[14] Aspects of the Greek Oriental past, which have been systematically suppressed by the Greek state, have consistently resurfaced in different forms and shapes.[15] Like the Eastern aspect of Greek identity, the Mediterranean, too, often serves as a symbolic opposition by which Greeks seek to distinguish themselves from Western/Northern Europeans.[16] What is more, the marginal place to which Greece has been relegated in the modern period by its European allies[17] is perhaps one of the reasons to account for the popular feeling of solidarity with the Arab people and generally all those seen as oppressed by U.S. and Western European imperialist policies. Cretan identity[18] could be seen as an intensified albeit micrographic version of Greek identity in this respect: here, one can also note a combination of intense localism on the one hand, and on the other a love of independence and a rebellious history against outside oppressors.

But the warm reception of the Palestinian group was about more than political principle. It was arguably also an expression of cultural proximity. To the elderly women literally wrapped up in the reconstruction of the wedding, the dressing of the bride and the various stages of the event that they were trying to decode would most likely not be cultural exotica but a pertinent theme of their own experience, too (Figure 3.3).

▲ **Figures 3.1 and 3.2.** Artas Folklore Troupe and audience reconstruct a traditional wedding.

◀ **Figure 3.3.** Other members of the audience prefer to watch...

My discussion so far has looked at some of the main assumptions under-pinning the festival's representation, focusing among other things on the ethnomusicologist's role. In this section I turn to the views of the groups as expressed in the questionnaire I handed out to them upon completion of the festival, asking especially: how do the groups describe their music? Do they use terms such as 'Mediterranean', 'Balkan', etc. to speak of themselves? Which are the identities they articulate? Are they at one or in tension with the cultural paradigm that the festival put forward?

Ethnomusicologists interested in elucidating the interrelationship be-tween music and identity have consistently pointed out how notions of identity can be fruitfully studied in music: 'Music constructs our sense of identity', thus allowing us 'to place ourselves in imaginative cultural nar-ratives' (Frith 1996: 124). Defining our Selves always entails defining our-selves in relation to Others. In his discussion of the musical construction of place Stokes notes that 'music is socially meaningful not entirely but largely because it provides means by which people recognize identities and places, and the boundaries which separate them'. He then stresses the im-portance of turning 'from questions directed towards defining the essential and "authentic" traces of identity "in" music ... to the questions of how mu-sic is used by social actors in specific local situations to erect boundaries, to maintain distinctions between us and them' (1994: 5–6). In the context of nation building, difference is conceived against external national Others or against marginal internal Others, and its construction is often a top-down, centre-periphery project. But difference may also take regional content and serve to separate us from others and to articulate our experience of place. As Cohen convincingly argues with regard to the discourses surrounding the notion of an identifiable Liverpool Sound, the construction of a Liv-erpool Sound contrasted with Manchester and London 'is revealed as a political strategy, a resource through which relations of power at local, re-gional, national and international levels can be addressed'; 'the notion of a local sound ... does reflect the desire to symbolically assert difference and a sense of local identity' (1994: 117, 129).

Here I am also interested in the regional identities that the groups vari-ously put forward, with a view to noting correspondences and/or discrepan-cies with 'Mediterraneanist' (unifying) outlooks and nationalist (separating along national lines) outlooks. On the basis of the following discussion it can be said that although in many respects the groups' self-perceptions are close to the festival representation, in certain cases they are quite disjunct. For instance, while some of the groups might consider what they do, broadly defined, as being within the frames of tradition (Balkan Journey), others would not necessarily describe themselves as traditional (L'Ham de Foc,

Dounia). This bears out my initial suggestion that a degree of straitjacketing took place in terms of how the groups were represented.

More importantly perhaps, a look at the individual groups reveals a plurality of outlooks and of senses of locality and identity, whose elucidation would need intensely localized ethnographies (beyond the limits of this study, sadly). According to the L'Ham de Foc musician Efrén López:

> We compose ourselves the music we play using material, instruments and elements of modal music, ranging from Western medieval music to North African, Greek, Turkish, Afghan, etc, music. We also play some traditional instrumental pieces (Bulgarian, Occitanian, etc).[19]

L'Ham de Foc compose their own music and arrange also some traditional melodies. Their repertoire is mainly vocal, and much importance is given to the lyrics (written by Mara Aranda, the singer), which are in Catalan. Asked which term would best define their music, Efrén answered: Eastern; Mediterranean; and contemporary modal music. Asked what other types of music their music is close to, he responded: neo-medieval; and neo-traditional Greek and Turkish music.

The emphasis on the language suggests that regional identity is strongly asserted – possibly against an all-unifying national Spanish fabric. At the same time the term 'Mediterranean' seems to be meaningful to the group in terms of their broader cultural affiliations, while an appeal seems to be made also to a common historical past and to the pan-Eastern *makam* tradition. Efrén also stressed that in L'Ham de Foc they compose their own music, putting together creatively all the things they play and like, so that they do not consider themselves to be a traditional group.[20]

Muammer Ketencoğlu of Balkan Journey described what they do as 'pure traditional Balkan music with minimum contemporary approach' and added:

> The music [of Balkan Journey] is contemporary acoustic folk music. ... Our repertoire consists of only traditional music sung in various Balkan languages such as Bulgarian, Macedonian, Albanian, Serbian, Romanian, Greek, Turkish, Roma, Croatian.

Balkan Journey play traditional instrumental and vocal melodies from all over the Balkans, arranged by Muammer Ketencoğlu, the group leader. They are quite emphatic about the use of electronic instruments, or about newly composed repertoire: 'It is against our conception. We want to carry only folk music to stage.' Asked which term would best define their music, Ketencoğlu replied: Balkan: 'All the music traditions which lived and still live in the Balkans regardless of region and nation have the same importance and value to us.' Asked what other types of music their music is close to, he mentioned the Old Yugoslavian State Folk Ensemble, 'which represented the variety and colourfulness of the Balkan territory. From the contemporary groups, we may say we're close to ... many other folk music groups which play folk music in various languages and cultures.'

In interviews – and in their general presentation – Balkan Journey stress the role that music can play in bringing together, instead of separating, Balkan peoples in the face of individual nationalist policies. Occasionally, when performing in Turkey they have encountered problems with right-wing extremist groups. It is thus reasonable to say that the group treats the Balkans as an area where extended musical interaction has taken place, also putting forward the notion of solidarity of the Balkan peoples based on cultural closeness.

Vincenzo Gangi and Giovanni Arena, group members of Dounia, compose their own music while also arranging some popular Middle Eastern songs. The lyrics are written by Palestinian singer Faisal Taher in classical Arabic or sometimes in Palestinian colloquial, while the group 'sometimes use other languages like Spanish, French and Portuguese, or rather Brazilian, for short parts of the songs.'[21] Faisal's themes are generally about love, 'but also including a love for his land, for peace, etc.' Asked to describe their music, the group's drummer Riccardo Gerbino used the term world music but pointed out that it is not properly world music, as it is strictly acoustic and has no electronics or samplings. Asked what other types of music their music is close to, he answered: 'our music is influenced by a lot of different types of music, pop and Latin American music, like Brazilian music for example, but with the lyrics and, above all, Faisal's voice and particularly way of singing, our music keeps an original colour, I don't know like who or like what.' Interestingly, as Riccardo pointed out, they do not see their music as having peculiarly local – Italian or Sicilian – characteristics. Here there is a clear inconsistency between the group's own perception of their music and the way it was represented in the festival. Further, the notion of the Mediterranean does not seem to be particularly relevant to their outlook.

They also place a lot of emphasis on Faisal Taher's Palestinian origin, pointing out how that is really important to their experience: 'not only in musical terms, but for all its other implications. We are not a political band, but we sing for Palestine, like for human rights, against war.' What seems to emerge here, besides an internationalist outlook, is also a quite political identity conceived in terms of a stress on multiculturalism and on opposition to discrimination or racism against economic migrants to Italy.[22]

Artas, in their questionnaire,[23] gave a detailed description of their local music – which, having been largely reproduced above, will not be repeated here. Artas play popular Palestinian songs sung in religious contexts (Ramadan, the return of pilgrims from Mecca) and other occasions (weddings). Asked which term would best define their music, they spoke of Palestinian music that expresses the joys and sorrows of the Palestinian people. Asked what other types of music their music is close to, they responded: old Arab music.

Concluding Remarks

The present chapter makes no claim to comprehensiveness. The topic merits an examination in greater depth than has been possible here. One would especially need to look in detail at audience reception and at individual groups and the specific geographical and sociopolitical contexts within which they operate, as well as broaden the scope to look at centralizing discourses such as those of ethnomusicology, the commercial market and even the EU in the context of policy-making.

Nevertheless, this brief discussion has, I hope, offered some revealing insights, especially as concerns the role of scholars in the (re)production of cultural difference. If nothing else, by making an ethnographic problem of itself ethnomusicology – as Herzfeld notes about anthropology – 'may offer pragmatic insight into the social worlds that it examines and to which it belongs' (1999: x). This chapter may be construed as an attempt at least to recognize some of the ideological work at play during the festival, and there is a certain irony here in the fact that it is I who come to analyse, in retrospect, the nature of my own decisions and the consequences that followed from them.

In memory of Aytunç Nevzat Matraci, clarinet player and member of Balkan Journey.

ACKNOWLEDGEMENTS

I am indebted to Owen Wright and Federico Spinetti for commenting insightfully on earlier versions of this chapter. I would also like to thank Maria Kousis for her continuous trust and support.

NOTES

1. Original plans to include an accredited Arab composer whose work traverses both Arab and classical Western fields did not materialize, but even this deviation would have been towards a genre that again merges Western with Arab/Mediterranean. This in turn raises the issue of the ethnicization of European

classical music as a Western music to which non-Westerners' contributions are often assessed in terms of the local or 'exotic' elements that they bring into it from their own countries of origin.

2. Med-Voices official proposal to the EU.

3. Thus, besides Spain, L'Ham de Foc distribute in Germany, France, the U.K., Japan, Greece and Holland; they also perform abroad quite a lot, while their main audiences are in Germany and the Catalan region of Spain. Balkan Journey distribute mainly in Turkey but also in parts of Europe and the U.S.

4. Artas Folklore Center: http://www.geocities.com/artas_heritage/Articles.html (accessed February 2007). See also: http://www.geocities.com/paltournews/ptn11artasfestival2.html (accessed February 2007).

5. See also Herzfeld 1999.

6. Radio Tarifa, official website (accessed February 2007).

7. Yasmin Levy, official website (accessed February 2007).

8. See esp. Turino 1993: 8–13.

9. The term is modelled on Said's 'Orientalism' (2003) as a sub-discourse that – in Herzfeld's words (1999: 64) – suggests 'the reification of a zone of cultural difference through the ideologically motivated representation of otherness'.

10. Further down I discuss the groups' own self-perceptions and outlooks as these were expressed in the questionnaire.

11. The collapse of multicultural and – more recently – colonial empires was followed by intensive cultural activity on the part of nascent nation-states around the Mediterranean seeking to define themselves both in opposition to neighbouring nations and in proximity to the West, the centre of economic and military power and thus of an idealized culture. In the field of music this process entailed the selective fusion of indigenous elements as markers of an authentic national essence with Western elements, and was significantly aided by the parallel emergence of folkloric studies (see Herzfeld 1999). Ethnomusicology has made an important contribution to the study of the phenomenon of musical nationalism, in the form of both theoretically oriented studies (Turino 2000; Stokes 1994; Rice 1994; Askew 2002) and case studies (for the Mediterranean region, some are Davis 2002; Slobin 1996; Stokes 1992; Tekelioğlu 1996; El-Shawan 1980, 1984; Racy 1982; Regev 1996). More recent trends (ascendancy of the free market economy, technological developments and intensification of intercultural contact) have arguably not caused the nationalist paradigm's pertinence to wane but have rather interacted with it and reconfigured it in new ways.

12. Fabian (1983) has convincingly shown how anthropology relegates its object in a time other than the present, thus denying it coevalness; a similar case can be made about nationalist folklore studies (see e.g. Danforth 1984).

13. One of the principal concerns of the Med-Voices programme has been to provide structures/forums in order to redress cases of long-term unequal access to power. The programme's principal aims are outlined thus: 'to work collectively within a network of partners in order to carry out the research; secondly, to interrogate the basis of the Euro-Mediterranean's 'common heritage' from an

ethnographic and oral history perspective; thirdly, to challenge the customary emphasis given to 'monumental' heritage and to emphasize its relationship to intangible cultural heritage; fourthly, to promote an awareness of cosmopolitan and multi-ethnic aspects of Mediterranean urban cultural heritage; and finally, to further understanding and encourage respect for pluralism, tolerance and peaceful co-existence between the many peoples who inhabit the Mediterranean urban environments.' (http://www.medvoices.org/pages/introduction .aspx, accessed March 2008)

14. See Herzfeld (1999: 41), who interestingly also adds the categories Mediterranean and European to this two-partite schema (180).

15. To name a few: *café aman* (turn of the nineteenth century); Greek shadow theatre (first half of the twentieth century) and rebetika (Interwar period); *laiko* (popular song) of the 1950s and 1960s, which incorporated Indian melodies; the *tsifteteli* (belly dance) craze after the military dictatorship (1967–1974); and more recently the *paradosiaká* revival, in the context of which the Ottoman Greek legacy was largely reinstituted as part of the official musical canon (see Kallimopoulou 2009).

16. Crete in particular is often represented as the Mediterranean crossroads par excellence, situated between three continents (Europe, Africa, Asia).

17. According to Herzfeld (1999), the Turkish-derived elements in Greek culture marked the failure of modern Greece to live up to each idealized classical image. The ambivalence of Greeks towards their Western allies is also grounded in the sense of betrayal caused by the latter's failure to intervene in the face of the military regime and events in Cyprus.

18. For a discussion of Cretan musical identity see Dawe 1999.

19. Efrén López: poly-instrumentalist and the main composer and arranger in L'Ham de Foc.

20. Efrén López. Personal interview 2005.

21. All answers to the questionnaire were given by percussionist Riccardo Gerbino.

22. On Dounia see also Plastino 2005.

23. I am particularly indebted to Leyla Zuaiter, advisor to the Arab Educational Institute's Genealogy/Family History Project, Artas Folklore Centre and to Fadi Sanad, director of Artas Folklore Center, for assisting with the translation of the questionnaire from English into Arabic and vice versa.

References

Askew, K. 2002. *Performing the Nation: Swahili Music and Cultural Politics in Tanzania*. Chicago and London: University of Chicago Press.

Clifford, J. 1986. 'Introduction: Partial Truths', in J. Clifford and G.E. Marcus (eds), *Writing Culture: The Poetics and Politics of Ethnography*. Berkeley and Los Angeles: University of California Press.

Cohen, S. 1994. 'Identity, Place and the "Liverpool Sound"', in M. Stokes (ed.), *Identity, Ethnicity and Music: The Musical Construction of Place*. Oxford: Berg.

Danforth, L.M. 1984. 'The Ideological Context of the Search for Continuities in Greek Culture', *Journal of Modern Greek Studies* 2(1): 53–87.

Davis, R. 2002. 'Patronage and Policy in Tunisian Art Music', *The Garland Encyclopedia of World Music* 6: 505–513.

Dawe, K. 1999. 'Minotaurs or Musonauts? "World Music" and Cretan Music', *Popular Music* 18(2): 209–225.

El-Shawan, S.A. 1980. 'The Socio-Political Context of al-musika al-arabiyyah in Cairo, Egypt: Policies, Patronage, Institutions, and Musical Change (1927–1977)', *Asian Music* Symposium on Art Music in Muslim Nations 12(1): 86–128.

El-Shawan, S.A. 1984. 'Traditional Arab Music Ensembles in Egypt since 1967: The Continuity of Tradition within a Contemporary Framework?' *Ethnomusicology* 28(2): 271–288.

Fabian, J. 1983. *Time and the Other: How Anthropology Makes Its Object.* New York: Columbia University Press.

Frith, S. 1996. 'Music and Identity', in Stuart Hall and Paul du Gay (eds), *Questions of Cultural Identity.* London: Sage.

Herzfeld, M. 1999 [1987]. *Anthropology through the Looking-Glass: Critical Ethnography in the Margins of Europe.* Cambridge: Cambridge University Press.

Kallimopoulou, E. 2009. *Paradosiaká: Music, Meaning and Identity in Modern Greece.* Aldershot: Ashgate.

Medi-Terra Programme Notes 2005. Music festival 'Medi-Terra: Music Across Lands' in Rethymno, Chania and Heraklion. Mediterranean Voices, DG Europe-Aid, University of Crete, September.

Plastino, G. 2005. 'Open Textures: On Mediterranean Music', in D. Cooper and K. Dawe (eds), *The Mediterranean in Music: Critical Perspectives, Common Concerns, Cultural Differences.* Lanham, MD, Toronto, and Oxford: The Scarecrow Press.

Racy, A.J. 1982. 'Musical Aesthetics in Present-Day Cairo', *Ethnomusicology* 26(3): 391–406.

Regev, M. 1996. 'Musica Mizrakhit, Israeli Rock and National Culture in Israel', *Popular Music* 15(3), Middle East Issue: 275–284.

Rice, T. 1994. *May It Fill Your Soul: Experiencing Bulgarian Music.* Chicago: Chicago Press.

Said, E.W. 2003 [1978]. *Orientalism.* London: Penguin Books.

Slobin, M. (ed.) 1996. *Retuning Culture. Musical Changes in Central and Eastern Europe.* Durham and London: Duke University Press.

Stokes, M. 1992. *The Arabesk Debate: Music and Musicians in Modern Turkey.* Oxford: Clarendon Press.

Stokes, M. 1994. 'Introduction', in Martin Stokes (ed.), *Ethnicity, Identity and Music: The Musical Construction of Place.* Oxford: Berg.

Tekelioğlu, O. 1996. 'The Rise of a Spontaneous Synthesis: the Historical Background of Turkish Popular Music', *Middle Eastern Studies* 32(2): 194–215.

Turino, T. 1993. *Moving Away from Silence: Music of the Peruvian Altiplano and the Experience of Urban Migration.* Chicago: University of Chicago Press.

Turino, T. 2000. *Nationalists, Cosmopolitans and Popular Music in Zimbabwe.* Chicago: University of Chicago Press.

Websites (all websites were accessed in February 2007)

Med-Voices: http://www.medvoices.org
Dounia: http://www.dounia.it/english/home.php (accessed in March 2011)
L'Ham de Foc: http://www.lhamdefoc.com/
Balkan Journey: http://www.muammerketencoglu.com/home/page/9 (accessed in March 2011)
Artas Folklore Center: http://www.geocities.com/artas_heritage/Articles.html
On Artas Folklore Center see also:
　http://www.geocities.com/paltournews/ptn11artasfestival2.html.
　http://www.palestine-family.net/index.php?nav=223-222
　http://www.geocities.com/artas_heritage/
Yasmin Levy: http://www.yasminlevy.net/
Radio Tarifa: http://www.radiotarifa.com/

Part 2

❖ ◆ ❖

State, Capital and Resistance

Chapter 4

Spaces of War, Spaces of Memory

Popular Expressions of Politics in Postwar Beirut

SUNE HAUGBOLLE

In 2005, Lebanon returned to international attention after a seemingly un-eventful period of political and social reconstruction. In order to explain the political and social transition that Lebanon has witnessed since 2005, we must turn to that very 'uneventful' period between the end of the civil war in 1990 and the death of former Prime Minister Rafiq al-Hariri in 2005. The social transformations of postwar Lebanon and the legacy of its civil war had an important impact on the transformations in political alignment that allowed a broad opposition to be formed against the regime in the fall of 2004.

Social transformations cannot be approached through a reading of il-lustrious events like elections, demonstrations and speeches alone. They happen in the lived spaces of daily life and inform the ongoing negotiations of national identity that shape social and cultural boundaries between sects and classes. Based on material collected in the summer of 2003 as part of the Mediterranean Voices project, this chapter leaves national and regional power-politics aside and takes a look at contentious politics in postwar Lebanon from a street level. In Beirut's residential neighbourhoods, po-litical posters, monuments and graffiti express sympathy with particular political ideas and the leaders who represent them and represented 'the street' during the civil war. This ever-changing urban text reads as a ver-sion of Lebanese society and history quite different from that presented by the state-related reconstruction company Solidere in downtown Beirut. By tracing the changing nature of Beirut's spaces, from spaces of war to spaces of memory, I argue that the urban realm can be seen as an alterna-tive public sphere in which the dictum of a 'reconciled' Lebanese society is turned on its head. The contentious legacy of the civil war is expressed, lived and negotiated in this realm without the inhibitions of a national pan-optic public.

Sectarianism and Nationalism in Lebanon

Lebanon's present political system dates back to 1943, when the country gained independence from France. In that year, clan-leaders, political thinkers and influential businessmen, mainly from Lebanon's two leading sects, the Maronite Christians and the Sunni Muslims, came together to formulate the unwritten National Pact, which stipulated a consensus of power sharing among Lebanon's sixteen religious communities. The vague formulations of the National Pact said more about the difficulties of uniting the two main ideologies of Lebanon's elites – Arabism and Lebanonism – than they did about the social make-up of its people. To the extent that the architects of the National Pact can be described as sociologists in their own right, they were employing a vertical analysis, stressing cultural and ethnic stratifications. Lebanon to them was first and last a country of cultural groups, of sixteen different sects. 'La diversité est notre destin', claimed the foremost nationalist ideologue Michel Chiha, who did not see unity and diversity as mutually contradictory. He envisioned Lebanon as a plurality of sects, whose very syncretism makes up its unique national character. This was a distinctly urban ideology that reflected Beirut's 'plural society in which communities, still different on the level of inherited religious loyalties and intimate family ties, co-existed within a common framework' (Hourani 1976: 38). Political pluralism was perfectly suited to be the political manifestation of this idea, so in order to regulate their relationship with each other peacefully and democratically, the sects were made to engage in a system of power-sharing through proportionate representation. Multiconfessional assemblies had their roots in the *mutasarrifiyya* period before the First World War, but unlike the governorate of Mount Lebanon from 1860–1918, the Republic of Lebanon in 1943 included a sizable number of Shiite Muslims. In accordance with a national census from 1932, each group was allocated a specific number of seats in parliament, and each of the large confessions was given the privilege of specific important positions. The titles of president and general of the national army were reserved for the Maronites, prime minister for the Sunnis and speaker of the parliament for the Shiites (Firro 2003: 15–70).

The advantage of choosing a consociational political system was to hold together an exceptionally composite nation state by transferring local, sectarian power structures to the parliamentary setting. However, such a transformation also had disadvantages. Patron-client relations between leading families and their respective constituency secured the passing down of political power from father to son. The state became a medium for securing favours and working for local, often sectarian, interests, rather than for the common good. Perhaps more distressing, consociationalism as a system has not furthered social change in Lebanon. Many Lebanese and outside observers before the war, like Samir Khalaf, believed that Lebanon was a 'society in transition from a kin-centred, traditional type of social organization to one based on rationality, specialization and freedom of association' (Khalaf 1969: 147). The 1950s, 1960s and early 1970s were golden years for the Lebanese economy, and there was widespread optimism about the ability of the consociational system to ride off the storms of intercommunitarian contentions that arose in times of regional instability. Those hopes were later thwarted, first by the civil war, which brought out every possible antithesis to national unity and civic patriotism, and second by the postwar period, where the strictly nationalist rhetoric of the political leaders was repeatedly undermined by fraud, favouritism and sectarian bickering, despite a clearly stated intention to work towards the opposite.

On an ideological level, there is a schism between *ta'ifiya* and *wataniya* – between sectarianism and nationalism – inherent in the political system (Makdisi 1996). The National Pact was a consensus, but it was also designed to cover the fact that the Lebanese have very divergent concepts of the national character of their country. The Muslim side of the population has always conceived of Lebanon as an Arab country, with the latent connotation 'Arab Muslim', and therefore a country that, as a given, should align itself with the Arab world and support the Palestinian cause. The Christian communities and particularly the Maronites have traditionally had a more particular view of Lebanon. To them Lebanon is a 'rose among thorns', the historical refuge for Christians and other persecuted minorities in the Middle East, such as the Shiites and the Druze (Salibi 1988). Furthermore, they see Lebanon's destiny closely tied to Europe and to Western civilization. Indeed, they claim, Lebanon has a historical mission to be 'the doormat of Europe' and 'the lighthouse of the Middle East': to establish the link between East and West and set an example for the Arab and Muslim world in enlightenment, progress and coexistence. After independence, these different visions of Lebanese nationalism became embodied in political parties closely connected to leading families of the respective sects: the Chamouns, the Jumayils and the Karamis, to name a few. Thus, the new parliamentary setting brought the different views out in the open and into the realm of political debate.

Questions of Lebanon's national character were closely related to the short civil war in 1958. President Camille Chamoun refused to align himself with Egypt's President Nasser and his movement for pan-Arab unity. The population as well as the political establishment split in two over the question, and for several months the country was on the brink of serious civil conflict. This 'small civil war' could be seen as a prelude to the series of civil wars that ravaged the country from 1975 to 1990. Again, the question of alignment was the major contention, although more complex social problems played in as well. On a purely political level, the civil war in 1975 broke out over the question of the right of Palestinian groups to attack Israel from Lebanon. The Christian parties and their leaders asserted the right to defend Lebanese sovereignty against the Palestinian 'state in the state'. The opposite party, the so-called National Movement led by the Druze socialist leader Kamal Jumblatt, was pro-Palestinian, and largely Muslim, but also anti-sectarian. However, the anti-sectarian socialist aspect of the National Movement was curtailed after the assassination of Jumblatt in 1977. Syrian intervention and growing Israeli involvement with the invasions in 1978 and 1982 changed the form of conflict. This is not the place to trace the whole conflict and the twists and turns of the involved parties in Lebanon and beyond. Important to note here is that deep-rooted historical-ideological questions played a role in fuelling the conflict, and that these questions were represented by political parties, which before and during the war transformed themselves into militias. In short, regional conflict destabilized the consociational system and gave way to sectarian mobilization around ideologies of 'romantic ethno-nationalism' (Johnson 2001: 228), which led to the breakdown of the consensus of coexistence between Lebanon's sects.

One of the results of the war was the failure of any ethno-nationalistic project of partition or supremacy. At the same time, the socialist, anti-sectarian vision for Lebanon suffered defeat too. Instead, the postwar system has attempted to restore and revive coexistence around the principles of prewar Lebanon. In order to defend the ethos of the National Pact, the postwar leaders, many of whom were militia leaders or otherwise implicated in politics during the war, have had to practice a curious reading of history. Because they see it as their mission to defend the viability of consociationalism, they have had to explain the war in terms other than those of a sectarian war. The war, so the standard explanation goes, was a 'war of the others', of Israelis, Arabs and Americans who manipulated the Lebanese and made them fight other people's conflicts on their own soil (Tueni 1985). The episodes in the war that were expressively sectarian and linked to the sectarian political system have been left in the dark in official forms of national memory, such as national schoolbooks, political discourse and the reconstruction of downtown Beirut. Curiously, an overarching ethos of anti-sectarianism thus coexists with the continuing sectarian foundation of state and society. In this climate the nature of politics is such that in order to obtain legitimacy, politicians have to publicly state their nationalist credentials and their will to work against sectarianism, but in order to obtain and maintain power, they have to act according to the logic of sectarianism (Haugbolle 2005).

This dilemma is to a large extent the product of the difficult transition from war to peace. Lebanon came out of the war with a number of political problems unresolved. The Ta'if Accord, formulated, signed and imposed in 1989 through foreign mediation, was a compromise to end fighting and return to a political status quo under Syrian hegemony. On the regional level, postwar Lebanon was caught between an ongoing war in the South and an elusive regional peace. These obstacles to true sovereignty weakened an already weak state and induced it to resort to the instruments of its security. The strengthening of the state apparatus became a primary occupation under the reigns of presidents Elias Hrawi (1990–1998) and Emile Lahoud (1998–). However, the security, which a strong state and a strong military brought about, also brought dissent and political frustration to new heights, particularly in the Christian parties, who, if anyone, were losers in the civil war. While the incorporation of militias into the post-Ta'if system encompassed all major Muslim and Druze fractions, the major Christian group, the Lebanese Forces, was ostracized and in 1994 completely banned. Intimidation of its followers played into a growing sense of defeat and exclusion in the Christian communities, dubbed *al-ihbat al-masihi* (the Christian disenchantment), and prompted an ever-larger number of Christians to emigrate. In conclusion, the remake of the political system did not succeed in reconciling the major population groups on either a political or a popular level. Instead, as a report from 2001 on national reconciliation in Lebanon by the Council for the Advancement of Arab-British Understanding concludes, the principal requisites of democracy and civil peace, namely participation and national reconciliation, have been hindered by unresolved political issues stemming from the war.[2]

Spaces of War

The first rule of Prime Minister Rafiq al-Hariri (1992–1998) has been dubbed 'the age of physical reconstruction', with a stress on 'physical' (Sarkis and Rowe 1998: 12). In this period people focused on recovering from the chaos of civil war, and ethical issues were given second priority. For the dazed Lebanese population it was the future, *al-mustaqbal* as the platform for Hariri's multiple projects were dubbed, that counted, not the past. The centrepiece of the physical reconstruction efforts was reconstruction of downtown Beirut. This area had served as the 'beating heart of the nation' before the war, in the multiple sense of meeting place, trading place and monumental and administrative hub of Lebanon. Historically, this area was Beirut until the late Ottoman period, when economic and administrative expansion and the succeeding need for suburban neighbourhoods to fit the bourgeoning bourgeoisie expanded the city's boundaries beyond the city walls to include new suburbs like Basta and Ashraffiyeh. These suburbs with time became integrated neighbourhoods, often but not solely inhab-ited along communitarian lines. At the outbreak of the war in 1975 the layout of Beirut was characterized by a division between a mainly Christian East Beirut and a mainly Muslim West Beirut, with confessionally mixed areas like the Hamra, Ras Beirut and 'Ain Mraise districts in West Beirut and the downtown area to soften the equation.

The war exacerbated this geography of communitarian divisions. As Jorge Silvetti has explained, such violent and abrupt splits in the social and physical fabric of a city due to civil strife have their own spatial logic: 'In order to claim control over the new territory, combating factions rapidly establish lines of demarcation to delineate their area of control. These in-stantaneous borders are not haphazard. They tend to trace boundaries that may have been socially, ethnically or religiously present, but not necessarily physically marked in the fabric of the city.' (Silvetti 1998: 242). In Beirut, daily intimidation and retaliation increasingly polarized the population socially and spatially, and whole communities were displaced as formerly mixed neighbourhoods morphed into homogeneous sectarian entities. The 'two years' war' of 1975–76, which more than any other sequel to the civil war was marred by sectarian strife, created most of the homogeneous zones which are still in place. In this process, the conception of private and public space was inverted, or even perverted. The intimate spaces of 'base-ments, rooftops and strategic openings in private homes became part of the logistics of combat' (Khalaf 2002: 249). Former meeting places became dangerous barriers to cross, whereas before the war they had served as spaces of linkage between communities. Perhaps most ironically, national symbols such as the National Museum, the *Mathaf,* and the former 'buffer zone' per se downtown, became permanent war zones and among the most ravaged parts of the city. Coexistence was practically blotted out, and the downtown became a no-man's-land.

Postwar Beirut inherited this divided urban space, and since the govern-ment made virtually no efforts to reconcile divisions and reestablish the mixed nature of residential Beirut, the sectarian enclaves are still in place. The downtown area, whose corporate planners have sold it as a reborn pub-lic meeting place, is a lot of different things to different people, but prior to February 2005 it could hardly have been described as the throbbing heart of the nation. The social space of Beirut in the early 2000s resembled more the space of the wartime city than that of the prewar city. As a result of the war, 'what was previously a monocentric city became transformed to a multicentric configuration, even if this shift was not planned' (Silvetti 1998: 246). On such a background of unreconciled political, social and communitarian grievances, naked ruins by themselves do not facilitate the creation of a shared sense of national memory and identity. Rather, it would seem, they exacerbate the spatial division of Beirut today along sectarian lines. In spite of efforts to cover up the holes and scars, Beirut still entails a physical map of reminders to those who, like the author Jean Makdisi, lived through the war. In her war memories *Beirut Fragments* from 1990 she writes:

> The streets of Beirut, even those that are relatively intact, provide a shifting landscape of memories and sorrow. Whenever I walk by one house, for instance, I remember with fresh pain my friend who lived in it and who was killed one night years ago. At a street corner, I remember when the shell landed and killed the mother of my son's friend. By another house, I think of the family that was kidnapped and has not been heard of since, and by yet another, I remember the friend who left the country and never came back. Each of these physical landmarks, and many others like them, are milestones in my inner journey of pain. Memories wash over the map and layers of time alter its shadings. (Makdisi 1990: 77–78)

The ruins function as potential 'memory triggers' for those who inhabit their adjacency, not necessarily as immanently painful as evoked by Makdisi in 1990 – after all, time does heal some wounds – but more likely as internalized, domesticated memories. The social histories of the different neighbourhoods are deeply embedded in the war experience. Therefore, social construction of memory continues to evolve in a way that fits daily needs. In the commercial heart of Beirut, a different picture emerges.

Solidere

Because of its former status as a mediating space for the Lebanese, the reconstruction of Beirut's downtown in and by itself attained a symbolic meaning. The Lebanese were to rise from the ashes as one united people: what better effort to epitomize this reunification than the grand project of rebuilding the downtown? The project has been conducted by Solidere (Societé libanaise pour le développement et la reconstruction de la centre ville de Beyrouth), a private company whose main shareholder, Rafiq al-Hariri, conceived of the overall plan and directed the efforts. As an essential part of the new political regime, Hariri was able to mobilize public resources for private sector endeavours by coupling the state to the huge economic machinery of Solidere. In this way the downtown emerged as an impressive physical manifestation of Lebanese officialdom's version of Lebanon's past, present and future.

Much of the research on Solidere has converged on the way in which the project has re-created or obliterated the connection to the past.[3] Since 1991, this research has run parallel with a heated debate among the Lebanese public. The critics of Solidere can be divided into two broad categories: critics of the actual transformation of urban space, and critics of the public discourse of Solidere and the representation of national identity that it entails. A wide range of public intellectuals has participated in the debate, some in defence of Hariri but most as voices of dissent. Some felt that the far-reaching demolition of old buildings that took place between 1990 and 1994 was an unhealthy expurgation of the past. Presented by the company as a necessary tabula rasa on which to write a new and better chapter of Lebanese history, the initial process of clearing the area of any war remnants in fact implied the destruction of whole neighbourhoods, including the old Ottoman *as-waq* (markets), which could have been saved. Squatters who had taken residence in the ruined and not-so-ruined buildings were dealt with briskly. In that sense, Solidere's self-portrayal as a reconstruction project on the base of wartime destruction assumes destruction to have ended with the war, whereas in fact most of the destruction happened after the war at the hands, or rather at the bulldozers, of Solidere (Hanssen and Genberg 2001: 236).

Two different geographical imaginations of Beirut were on the table in the conception of Hariri's Solidere project (Denoeux 1998; Smid 1999). Early plans toyed with the idea of a 'Hong Kong of the Middle East', a vision of Beirut as a piece of the Gulf in the Levant. Although the bank sector certainly has its place in the economic order of the downtown, the finished design alludes to a more historically wholesome vision of a 'Paris of the Middle East', in which the restoration of the old buildings and the construction of new ones, in the prewar style, serve as symbols of a peaceful coexistence reinstalled (Khalaf and Khoury 1993; Sarkis and Rowe 1998).[4] The nostalgia imbued in *Faransa* (France), as some Lebanese sarcastically call the downtown, has drawn criticism from people who point to the amnesic gap left by missing references to the war and an overriding tendency in Lebanon to attach rosy memories to Beirut before the war. A more clearheaded historical perspective would suggest that it was in fact the social and political reality of the much praised and longed-for *Beyrouth d'avant guerre* that brought about the war. Reproducing the past in this sense means reproducing its errors. In the words of one of the staunchest critics of Solidere, the architect Jad Tabet: 'The project [Solidere] thus played a therapeutic role by founding the city on a sort of salvation-like amnesia that would protect it against the old ghosts which caused its destruction ... The selective memory that wants to cleanse the past and polish it in order to transform it by simple real estate speculation, is playing with fire; by wanting to repress at any price, it risks causing a tragic return to the repressed' (Tabet 2002: 68).

In short, Solidere's downtown does not suffer from amnesia, but from selective memory. Partly as a result of such criticism, the past has been incorporated in different ways. On one side, a Phoenician past not unlike that operationalized by the Maronite elites at the onset of the first republic in the 1920s was fabricated to constitute the backbone of the reinvented identity of Beirut and Lebanon, and to gloss over the sectarian reality of both politics and society in postwar Lebanon (Nagel 2000: 224). Phoenician and Roman ruins discovered during the reconstruction have been incorporated into the urban fabric. The Phoenician imagery was a versatile way to symbolize the sought-for continuity of the Lebanese people and convince corporate investors, tourists and the Lebanese themselves of the historical continuity of the nation. Therefore it seems fitting that the slogan of Solidere, 'Beirut – ancient city for the future', comfortably leaves out the present and the overhanging past, or to be precise, the war and its repercussions.

On the other hand, the Ottoman-French style architecture, the antiquity shops and the restaurants downtown all lean heavily on nostalgia for the early modern period and the so-called Golden Age of Beirut in the 1950s and 1960s. Nostalgia is a widespread trend in all of postwar Lebanon that the actors involved with the reconstruction project have merely seized upon and made use of because of its obvious marketing potential (Misk 1999). Nostalgia is a way of connecting a difficult past with a bearable perspective of one's present self and of the future and therefore inevitably involves a reenchantment of the disenchanted. By remembering former selves in a favourable light, the present becomes merely a temporary crisis before the circularity of existence enforces itself and reinstalls the past conditions (Davis 1979). In Beirut, this mechanism can be observed in the way that many of the social functions that made the downtown a 'throbbing heart' before the war – such as the bus station, cinemas and popular marketplace – have been taken out of the context. In their stead is a commodified reconstruction alluding to the past lived-life in a rather self-conscious way. Whether this self-consciousness produces the élan or the élan produces the self-consciousness is difficult to say. The fact is that the un–self-conscious *milieu de mémoire* with its popular street life from before the war has been replaced by a stale representation, rather than a reflection of the Lebanese in all their social diversity. This representation, whose framework is set and arranged by Solidere, reflects amnesia more clearly than any other phenomenon in postwar Lebanon. The war happened downtown if anywhere, but it is there if anywhere that the war today has been rendered invisible.

The difficulties of incorporating the civil war into an optimistic, forward-looking master narrative have undermined history at the expense of culture in postwar Lebanon. Or to be more precise, political history has been replaced by cultural history in an attempt to conjure up a new nationalism for Lebanon that truly lives up to the words of the national anthem: *'kulluna lil-watan'* ('we all belong to the nation') (Hanssen and Genberg 2001: 259). Instead of focusing on the politics of religion that divide, state and society in postwar Lebanon have been preoccupied with *turath* (heritage) and shared culture such as food, music and folkdance. Where prewar nationalism was essentially built on a history of emancipatory postcolonial optimism, postwar nationalism is forced to build itself on culture in place of a politically unheroic past. Commodified by commercial actors such as Solidere, this 'culture of culture' has tended towards escapism without any historical depth. This in turn has emptied culture of its social functions. Downtown Beirut is an amalgam of such decontextualized history-as-culture-cum-kitsch overridden with international luxury consumer goods. Although this production of urban space has been driven in large part by the private sector, it is also closely linked to the political regime. By associating itself with a reborn, reconciled Lebanese identity based on the premise of a 'new old' and fundamentally open city, the regime lends itself an air of legitimacy, which contrasts with political reality.

Spaces of Memory

Moving out of Solidere's downtown to the still ruined and underprivileged neighbourhoods of Basta and Bashura in West Beirut, or in the more affluent Ashraffiya in East Beirut, one will come across stories, jokes, posters, graffiti and even ceremonies that would never appear in the national public. These neighbourhoods of multicentric postwar Beirut with their distinctly sectarian boundaries are realms of 'cultural intimacy' (Herzfeld 2005) where the slick images of Solidere's downtown do not apply. In Basta, Bashura and Ashraffiya, symbols referring to the war and the memory of the war can be freely observed. Whereas the reconstruction of Downtown Beirut has been explored from every possible angle, and the suburbs, al-Dahiya, have been studied with a view to the development of alternative social structures and local government, and as the locus of the Shiite party Hizbollah (Harb 2003), social transformations in residential Beirut have hardly received any attention. The following is a contribution to filling this gap and adding to our understanding of the transformation of urban space in postwar Beirut.

Symbols referring to the war function as cultural markers and dividers between different neighbourhoods in Beirut. All of Beirut's inhabitant groups have richly varied ways of expressing their cultural, religious and political beliefs. Moving through the streets of Beirut, it is hard to escape the posters, flags and writings that dot the streets and buildings. Some symbols have been arranged consciously with the purpose of marking off a certain space for inhabitants. Other discernible symbols are less conscious parts of daily life. Graffiti, posters and the emblems of political parties sprayed onto houses and ruins are subtle – or less subtle – reminders, for the people who inhabit the space and the people who pass through it alike, of the cultural, religious, political, ideological world view that holds sway over this particular part of the city, and the interpretation of the war that this world view entails. Residents also carry around other more loosely connected symbols as emblems of allegiance. Stickers on the windscreens of cars, crosses, Korans and Shiite swords worn around the neck, and more vague cultural codes such as clothes (veils, hats, *jallabiyas*), language, or other forms of social conduct distinguish their owner. Of course, not all Beirut's inhabitants care to be recognized and categorized so easily, but the phenomenon is real enough, in Lebanon and elsewhere. 'Posters of the body' transport the private space beyond the safe haven of the neighbourhood into the public, making the difference, or privacy, recognizable. In Beirut, such cultural distinctions are also political distinctions. Sectarian parties such as the Druze PSP, the Maronite Kata'ib and the Shiite Amal, whose logos and symbols are omnipresent in public space, represent cultural and religious difference.

Territorialisation thus goes beyond the strict sense of territory as a confined geographical space. Inside the city's quarters, the production of space establishes the sectarian identity of the neighbourhood or street in question. The very need to territorialize, in turn, should be understood in the context of Lebanese history and urban history of Beirut in particular. The parties and groups that fought in the civil war and today vie for influence in the urban space all originated as social movements or local group mobilizations in the 1940s, 1950s and 1960s. During the 1960s, movements like Kata'ib and Amal started to claim an increasing influence over, respectively, the northern Maronite and the southern Shiite suburbs of Beirut. Territorial markers were used to delineate the different territories. This 'decentralization by force' partly came about as a result of declining state control over security, education and welfare under presidents Charles Helou (1964–1970) and Suleiman Franjieh (1970–1976). When Beirut descended into violence in 1975 the phenomenon of territorialisation moved from the suburbs into the formerly 'liberal', 'open', 'mixed' areas closer to the city centre. Long years of incessant war, destruction of the habitats, population displacement, belligerent propaganda and separation did away with the former openness of 'liberal Beirut' so famed before 1975. Ras Beirut, Hamra, Ain al-Mraise, Ashraffiya, Bashura: these were all neighbourhoods that, to varying degrees and in varying ways, used to be meeting places for Beirutis of different descent and orientation in life. Thirteen years of civil peace have not managed to bring these areas back to their former state, and in 2003 most of them remained the rather uniform zones that the war years made them.

Accordingly, it is here that the persistence of divergent interpretations of the war is most evident. In Ashraffiya, which was the locus of the Christian militia the Lebanese Forces (LF), posters of the former leader Bashir Jumayil and other dead leaders like Dany Chamoun, Elie Hobeiqa, or the ostracized Samir Ja'ja' and General Aoun are abundant. Graffiti going back to the war merge with newer symbols. One note sprayed on a wall in seeping red paint reads 'Aoun will return'. Another handwritten note decrees: 'One East/ Christian area/ will remain One/ intruders out', and a particularly popular formula simply states: *'Bashir hay fina'* (Bashir lives within us). Monuments and shrines consecrate the memory of dead fighters of the LF and the Kata'ib militias. Most notably, the central square in Ashraffiya, Sassine Square, is adorned with a larger-than-life monument to Bashir Jumayil, which was erected in the last part of the war but never taken down after the war ended. Most everyone who comes and goes in Ashraffiya will pass by Bashir Jumayil's pointed finger at least once a day. Of course it is possible to overestimate the importance of such symbols. Accustomed to their presence, some Lebanese see right through them or shrug their shoulders. Still, the totality of belligerent propaganda creates a discourse of consent and cultural and political distinction, which is upheld by the memory of an unfinished war, or at best a war with an unfair end to it. The symbolic meaning reaches back in time and connects the present feeling of marginalization and resistance against Syrian hegemony to the struggle in the war.

On the other side of the former dividing line between East and West Beirut, in Basta and Bashura, one finds an equally sectarian space. The streets here are crammed with public edifices of their inhabitants' identity. Large signs promising the followers of Amal the immediate liberation of *al-Quds* (Jerusalem), smaller posters of Nasserist, Arabist and Islamic parties, and here and there on the walls a graffito or a print honouring Islamic leaders or the local (Sunni Muslim) football team, al-Ansar. On every second wall Amal logos are displayed, in the green and black colours of the Shiites. The neighbourhoods of Basta and Bashura are visibly poorer than Ashraffiya. Before the war, they were home to a thriving middle-class population of mixed, albeit predominantly Sunni Muslim, orientation. During the war, though, the Christian population was displaced and much of the economic activity stopped, never to resume once the war had ended. In these neighbourhoods the hardship of postwar Lebanon has taken its toll, and most young people dream of emigrating to Canada or Europe. In contrast to Ashraffiya and the nearby downtown, many houses are still completely ruined.

Here, the memory of the war forms part of everyday life. In and around the ruins of a church in Bashura, not more than fifty metres from the shining facades of Solidere's downtown, families of Shiite squatters from Southern Lebanon have made their home in dilapidated buildings. There is a direct line between the events of the war and the living conditions of these people. And should they allow themselves to forget the war, symbols of sectarian allegiance fill the walls and streets around them. On one particularly ruined building in Bashura, just across the street from Ashraffiya, big black letters spell out 'Amal hata al-maut' (Amal until Death). Further south, in Basta, large colourful wall paintings celebrate the Islamic resistance, and street banners and signs of martyrs set up by Hizbollah leave passers-by in no doubt about the identity of these streets. Graffiti merge with propaganda to create a territory sharply contrasted to that of Ashraffiya, which represents the very territory that fighters from Palestinian militias, Amal, Hizbollah and leftist groups fought against for most of the war.

Unity in Diversity

This chapter has examined the different transformations of spaces of war into spaces of memory in postwar Beirut. It finds that a sanitized nostalgic discourse void of contentious memory has been constructed by a mix of commercial and state actors in the rebuilt heart of Beirut, whereas unreconciled memories normally protected by cultural intimacy and guardedness produced by the war are expressed and negotiated more organically by political propaganda and graffiti in residential areas. The juxtaposition between official and lived space suggests two conclusions about Lebanese politics in the years before the Independence Intifada in 2005. First, the negotiation of the past happened differently in closed and open spaces. The official discourse aimed to construct a wholesome image of the Lebanese nation in which an unfiltered rendition of the civil war and of the real nature of sectarian politics in Lebanon had no place. The popular construction, on the other hand, mirrored social reality in Lebanon, where awareness of differing opinions did not necessarily mean acceptance or reverence of 'the Other'. Self-righteous memories of the war, symbolized by political parties and their dead leaders, persisted and were expressed publicly. The public visibility of cultural difference and political contentions in the urban space of the capital constituted a daily negotiation of the real content of the questions that politicians were afraid to address head-on. In the public sphere of postwar Lebanon, sectarianism was often the unspoken but open secret, the elephant in the living room, whereas in the public space the writing was on the wall: the contentions that led to the civil war are still very much alive today.

These conclusions bear a specific resonance in the light of the very public and spatial nature of the Independence Intifada. The week-long sit-ins, demonstrations and concerts between February and April 2005 that transformed the downtown from commercial nostalgia to something like the Paris Commune were clearly a protest against the killing of Hariri. But they also marked a change in the way the Lebanese use urban space. The demonstrators – members of sectarian parties, pro-Americans, anti-Americans and unattached civilians of the silent majority alike – finally made their voices heard in public, in public space, in multiple colours and multiple shapes. This inevitably entailed a certain 'censoring' of sectarian symbols, but even the call of political leaders to restrict banners and slogans to national symbols could not detract from the impression that the demonstrations had shown the possibility of unity in diversity. What emerged was a vision of Lebanon as a multiple, often divided nation, but a nation – a public, no less – in which open dialogue and open recognition of difference, rather than guarded mistrust and empty commitments to national unity, are possible. In that sense, the slogan *al-Haqiqa* (the Truth) was both a call for a new political culture that dares to resist political violence, and a call for a reconstituted public sphere of dialogue, acceptance of otherness and political participation. The Independence Intifada may have been a fleeting moment, but it shows that 'unity in diversity' is possible in Lebanon.

Notes

1. I use this expression coined by Samir Kassir rather than 'the Arab Spring' (which never happened) or 'the Cedar Revolution' (which falsely implies complete national backing).
2. Report by Karen Abi-Ezzi. www.caabu.org
3. In the following I rely in particular on Hanssen and Genberg (2001); Makdisi (1997); Nagel (2000, 2002).
4. For an up-to-date assessment of the project, see http://www.lebanon.com/construction.

References

Davis, F. 1979 *Yearning for Yesterday: A Sociology of Nostalgia*. New York: Free Press.

Denoeux, G. 1998. 'Hariri's Lebanon: Singapore of the Middle East or Sanaa of the Levant?' MERIP (6):158–173.

Firro, M.K. 2003. *Inventing Lebanon: Nationalism and the State under the Mandate*. London and New York: I.B. Tauris.

Hanssen, J.-P. and D. Genberg. 2001. 'Beirut in Memoriam', in: A. Neuwirth and A. Pflitsch (eds), *Crisis and Memory in Islamic Societes.* Beirut and Würzberg: Ergon.

Harb, M. 2003. 'La *dahiye* de Beyrouth: parcours d'une stigmatisation urbaine, consolidation d'un territoire politique', *Genèses* 51: 70–91.

Haugbolle, S. 2005. 'Public and Private Memory of the Lebanese Civil War', *Comparative Studies of South Asia, Africa, and the Middle East* 25(1): 191–203.

Herzfeld, M. 2005. *Cultural Intimacy: Social Poetics in the Nation-state.* 2nd ed. New York and London: Routledge.

Hourani, A. 1976. 'Ideologies of the Mountain and the City', in: R. Owen (ed.), *Essays on the Crisis in Lebanon.* London: Ithaca Press.

Johnson, M. 2001. *All Honorable Men: The Social Origins of War in Lebanon.* Oxford, London, New York: I.B. Tauris; New York: Center for Lebanese Studies; distributed in the United States and Canada by St. Martin's Press.

Khalaf, S. 1969. 'Basic Social Trends in Lebanon', in S. Khalaf (ed.), *Cultural Resources in Lebanon.* Beirut: Beirut College for Women.

Khalaf, S. 2002. *Civil and Uncivil Violence in Lebanon: A History of the Internationalization of Communal Conflict.* New York: Columbia University Press.

Makdisi, J.S. 1990. *Beirut Fragments: A War Memoir.* New York: Persea Books.

Khalaf, S. and P.S. Khoury. 1993. *Recovering Beirut: Urban Design and Postwar Reconstruction.* Social, Economic and Political Studies of the Middle East/*Études sociales, économiques et politiques du Moyen Orient 47.* Leiden: Brill.

Makdisi, S. 1997. 'Laying Claim to Beirut: Urban Narratives and Spatial Identity in the Age of Solidere', *Critical Inquiry* 23: 661–705.

Makdisi, S. 1997. 'Reconstructing History in Central Beirut', *MERIP* (203): 23–30.

Makdisi, S. 1996. 'Reconstructing the Nation-State: The Modernity of Sectarianism in Lebanon', *Middle East Report* 200: 23–26, 30.

Misk, Z.N. 1999. *Heritage Organisations in Beirut: Institutionalization of Nostalgia.* Beirut: American University of Beirut.

Nagel, C. 2000. 'Ethnic Conflict and Urban Redevelopment in Downtown Beirut', *Growth and Change* 3: 211–234.

Nagel, C. 2002. 'Reconstructing Space, Re-creating Memory: Sectarian Politics and Urban Development in Postwar Beirut', *Political Geography* 21 (5): 717–725.

Salibi, K. 1988. *A House of Many Mansions.* London: I.B. Tauris.

Sarkis, H. and P. Rowe (eds). 1998. *Projecting Beirut: Episodes in the Construction and Reconstruction of a Modern City.* Munich: Prestel.

Silvetti, Jorge. 1998. 'Beirut and the Facts of Myth', in H. Sarkis and P. Rowe (eds.), *Projecting Beirut: Episodes in the Construction and Reconstruction of a Modern City.* Munich: Prestel.

Smid, H. 1999. 'Solidère, das globale Projekt: Wiederaufbau im Beiruter Stadtzentrum', *INAMO* (20): 9–14.

Tabet, Jad. 2002. 'Des pierres dans la mémoire', in: J. Tabet (ed.), *Beyrouth, La Brulûre des rêves.* Paris: Autrement.

Tueni, G. 1985. *Une guerre pour les autres.* Paris: J.C. Lattes.

∾ Chapter 5 ∾

Environmentalists in Malta

The Growing Voice of Civil Society

JEREMY BOISSEVAIN AND CAROLINE GATT

Our chapter is dedicated to the memory of Julian Manduca, one of the pioneers of the Maltese environmental movement. Long the coordinator of Moviment ghall-Ambient-Friends of the Earth (Malta), he devoted his life to defending Malta's environment. He died suddenly, at the age of 46, on 17th May 2005

In 1964, civil society in newly independent Malta was relatively mute, cowed for centuries by fear of, and obedience to, various colonial rulers, the powerful Roman Catholic Church and, since independence, a highly centralized government. Within four decades Maltese environmentalists succeeded in giving a strong voice to the islands' 'civil society', a diffuse term that has been defined as 'that segment of society that interacts with the state, influences the state and yet is distinct from the state' (Chazan 1992: 281 in Fisher 1997: 487). This study explores how they accomplished this, looking at new trends, patterns and prospects for the environmental movement in Malta.

Anthropologists and Environmentalists

In 1999 in two different review articles both Peter Brosius (1999) and Arturo Escobar (1999) identify environmental movements as rich sites for anthropological enquiry. However, the anthropological literature addressing this area is still relatively sparse. We find it strange that given their engagement with grass-roots research, anthropologists have apparently been uninterested, at least until very recently, in seriously examining environmentalist activity. Others have also noted this apparent lack of interest among anthropologists (Milton 1993: ix; Berglund 1998: 4; Però 2005: 336); political scientists, geographers and sociologists, in contrast, have been extremely busy in the field since the 1980s, as the bibliographies in Doyle and `McEachern (1998) and Carter (2001) clearly demonstrate.

There appear to be at least five reasons for the lack of anthropological engagement with environmentalism. First, as Kay Milton has indicated, some anthropologists are uneasy about the possibility of research into environmentalism being 'applied' and thus contributing to cultural change (1993: 13). This is not a hesitation we share. Second, the funding constraints of the new audit culture favour the recruitment of 'safe' anthropologists unlikely to be interested in oppositional movements such as environmentalism (Lindisfarne 2004: 2). Third, the groups, organizations and social movements involved in environmental activism are popularly categorized as civil society, a notion whose wide application makes it so theoretically and empirically problematic 'that most anthropologists hitherto have ignored it' (Hann 1996: 1). It seems as though the diffuseness of the term has caused this field of research to be overlooked together with the term.

Fourth, much grass-roots environmentalist action is directed at NIMBY (Not in My Back Yard) developments by loose coalitions that disband when, for better or worse, the issues they have addressed are resolved. The significance of such apparently temporary coalitions tends to go unnoticed because of the relatively short period anthropologists spend in the field. This prevents them from observing that many of the same people regroup later with others to form new coalitions to contest new environmental challenges. The relevance of such networks, quasi-groups and patterns of political engagement were also overlooked by the structural-functionalists of the previous generation, who were chiefly interested in delineating enduring, ordered structural patterns (but see Wolf 1966; Mayer 1966; Boissevain 1968, 1974).

Fifth, at roughly the same time that environmentalist action seriously began to increase, theoretical interest in political anthropology, once a core subject of study and research, began to have trouble maintaining its identity as a subdiscipline (Hann 1996: 22). In fact, it has all but disappeared. Studies of big men, patronage, factionalism, coalitions, stratagems and spoils, rebellion and class conflict, which saw their heyday in the 1960s and 1970s, made way in the 1980s and 1990s for postmodern interest in globalization, deconstruction, reflexivity, interpretation and, especially, discourse. Environmentalist action is, if nothing else, intensely political. Politics is concerned with the ways persons and groups compete to influence the outcome of disputes and community decisions in accordance with their own interests (Mair 1962: 10). They do this by resorting to various means to gain and exert power. As we shall see below, besides political rhetoric, these means include demonstrations, petitions, threats to withhold votes from politicians, threats of physical violence and other means of coercion, financial 'gifts', family connections and so on. These are political dimensions that tend to be ignored, due to the 'questionable assumptions that grow out of anthropology's "linguistic turn" about the *pre-eminent importance of discursive competence over all other kinds of power differentials*' (Edelman 2002: 114, emphasis added).

In the light of the recent trends in anthropology within which studies of environmental activism are situated, this chapter aims to contribute to the growing ethnographic literature on environmental practices by documenting particular cases as well as providing an analysis of some political and theoretical concerns. As Anderson and Berglund succinctly put it, this account cannot be anything but partial (in both senses) (2003: 15). We aim to convey a sense of political action and interactions in Malta through the environmental nongovernmental organizations (ENGOs) described and the particular issues outlined.

The academic and fieldwork milieus of environmental activism and development, including tourism, are closely interrelated. Therefore a closer cooperation between these two areas can provide the theoretical and empirical grist needed to enrich anthropological research. A case in point is a study by Berglund (1998) that explores the distribution of privilege in relation to ecopolitics and demonstrates how a focus on political anthropology can incorporate multiple voices and processes of meaning formation advanced by recent theoretical trends in anthropology (see for example Fox and Starn 1997; Berglund 1998; Anderson and Berglund 2003). We address these issues within the wider context of Maltese politics and history.

Malta

The Maltese archipelago is minute, covering only 315 square kilometres. Malta, the largest island, is twenty-seven kilometres long and just over fourteen wide, roughly the size of the Channel Island of Jersey or the Dutch island of Schouwen-Duiveland. Gozo is only fourteen by eight kilometres. Finally, Comino, which lies in the channel separating the two larger islands, covers less than two square kilometres. The islands are oriented along a northwest-southeast axis. From 250-metre cliffs on the southwest coast, Malta's hilly terrain descends to an accessible foreshore on the eastern side. Most of the tourist and industrial development has taken place along this foreshore. With a population approaching 400,000 and 1.1 million tourists visiting annually, Malta is the most densely populated state in Europe. Awareness of this density and the small geographic scale is basic to understanding the environmental problems that face Malta. Maltese is a distinct language based on a Semitic morphology and syntax, drawing on romance languages for its alphabet and for some of its vocabulary. English is widely understood and in middle-class areas like Sliema the inhabitants are likely to be fluently bilingual, but it is rarely used in the villages.

The developments in Malta are similar to those that have occurred all along all along the Mediterranean since the 1960s (Kousis 2001; Selwyn 2004). Rising affluence, fuelled by the tourist boom, enabled people living in the traditional cramped accommodation in towns and village centres to build their own houses. New housing developments sprouted around towns and villages. The tourist industry required massive accommodation. Hotels and cheap apartment complexes mushroomed in disorderly fashion along the north-eastern shore in Mellieha, St. Paul's Bay, Bugibba, St. Julian's, Sliema and Marsascala (Figure 5.1). From the mid 1970s onwards, Malta has been caught up in a frenetic building boom and has become 'a building site on heat'.[1] The building boom not only encroached on scarce agricultural land but has quite literally consumed much of the countryside. New quarries, concrete ready-mix batching plants, many of them illegal, and uncontrolled illegal dumping of building debris have eaten away or covered vast areas of the country's limited terrain. Malta's clientelistic political culture facilitated the award of building permits to political clients, thus furthering rampant abusive building and subverting the enforcement of building regulations (also see Mallia 1994: 700–702).

Population pressure, tourism and affluence intensified existing water, energy and waste disposal problems, requiring the construction of desali-

Figure 5.1. Changing coastal landscape in Malta. Photograph: Marc Morell

nation units, a new power station and a giant landfill, nicknamed 'Mount Maghtab'. All are located on the coast. Desalination consumes almost one fifth of the island's electricity output; meanwhile, the power station emits toxic fumes. Noxious smoke from 'Mount Maghtab' affects four downwind villages and an adjacent hotel; the landfill also leaches toxic effluent into the aquifer and foreshore. Eighty-six per cent of sewage is discharged un-treated into the sea (Moviment ghall-Ambjent 1997; Mallia 2000).

The revised Tourism Master Plan of 1989 targeted 'quality' and 'cultural' tourists (Horwath and Horwath 1989). The government touted luxury ho-tels, urged visits to the countryside in winter and spring, and promoted diving and golf. The new policy actively commercialized Malta's natural, social and cultural landscape. The government and planners ignored the impact that the increased appropriation of the environment, especially for luxury accommodation, might have on public opinion (see also Ioan-nides and Holcomb 2001). Not surprisingly, the new policy increased the destruction of the environment and hampered access to the countryside. This in turn escalated the tension between nongovernmental organizations (NGOs) and local action groups on the one hand, and construction entre-preneurs and government planners on the other.

Politics

For over two thousand years the Maltese islands were dominated by a pro-gression of foreign rulers. Malta gained independence from Britain in 1964. The islands' social and political life is dominated by the extreme rivalry between the two dominant parties, the Nationalist Party and the Malta La-bour Party, which divide the country almost equally. The Nationalist Party, traditionally the party of the clergy, professional classes and farmers, has a Christian Democratic signature. It governed from 1964 to 1971, from 1987 to 1996 and from 1997 to the present. Generally open to the voice of civil society and tolerant of NGOs, it strongly supported Malta's membership of the European Union, which it joined in 2004. The Malta Labour Party traditionally favoured industrial workers and the less well off. During its tenure of government between 1971 and 1987 it became increasingly auto-cratic and dealt harshly with NGO criticism. It was opposed to Malta join-ing the EU. Both parties favour industrial development, foreign investment and tourism. In the late 1980s young political and environmental activists formed a new party, Alternattiva Demokratika (AD). Though represented on several village councils, it is not yet represented in Malta's parliament due to the country's peculiar electoral system.[2] While paying lip service to the environment, the government has not taken firm action to enforce the existing laws protecting the country's monumental heritage and land-scape (Mallia 1994, 2000; Boissevain 2001; Bramwell 2003). The political culture of nepotism, patronage and political clientelism, the pervasiveness and intensity of which are a function of the country's small scale, popula-tion density and strong family ties, are largely responsible for this failure (Baldacchino 1997; Boissevain 1974, 2001: 292–293).

The Environmental Lobby

The Maltese attitude to landscape is ambivalent (Boissevain 2001). Until the late 1950s, few people lived in the countryside. Farmers usually returned to the villages at night. As in other Mediterranean countries, the countryside was considered dangerous, uncivilized and uncouth. Residence in the vil-lage centre conferred prestige, for built-up landscape was associated with 'civilisation' (Silverman 1975). Middle-class inhabitants of the towns looked down upon villagers, who in turn looked down on peasants. Except for hunters and farmers, Maltese showed little interest in the countryside. Af-ter the mid 1980s, public aversion to the countryside began to abate. More people slowly ventured forth, in part influenced by the interest in the coun-try's nature shown by expatriate settlers and tourists, and began to explore remote country lanes on weekends in their newly acquired cars.

Such environmental sensitivity as exists in Malta did not develop through the activity of government or political parties but through the efforts of non-governmental organizations (see also Mallia 1994: 686). It evolved slowly. In this Malta followed a pattern noted by Robin Grove-White (1993: 20), who observed that 'almost all of the most significant environmental issues, global or domestic, were crystallized first not by governments responding to or using "science", but by poorly resourced NGOs and sundry individual environmentalists'.

During the 1970s environmentalists were concerned mainly with pro-tecting monuments, flora and fauna (Mallia 1994). As noted, they rarely held public demonstrations because of the Labour government's hostility to criticism by NGOs. By the mid 1980s targets and tactics began to change. Younger, more radical activists, some of whom had worked with environ-mental groups abroad, were prepared to engage in physical action. The in-creasing activity of the environmental NGOs and growing public criticism of abusive building placed environmental issues on the political agendas of both parties in the run-up to the 1987 general election. Following the defeat of the Labour government, ENGO activity and lobbying increased, oblig-ing the new Nationalist government to honour its electioneering promises to pay serious attention to the environment. By 1992 Malta finally had a

Structure Plan (1990), an Environment Protection Act (1991) and a Development Planning Act (1992) providing for a Planning Authority to administer and enforce the relevant legislation (Mallia 1994; Boissevain and Theuma 1998)

On many occasions ENGOs and grass-roots movements clashed with private entrepreneurs and the government over environmental issues (see below). ENGOs increasingly worked together, thereby developing a new sense of solidarity and, in some cases, fusion. In 1998 some of the most active environmentalists established Alternattiva Demokratika – the Green Party. In August 2003 the Archbishop of Malta established a Diocesan Commission on the Environment, which supported the activity of the ENGOs by distributing literature and prayer cards, in Maltese, dealing with environmental issues throughout the diocese. Hitherto, ENGOs had mainly used the English-language media to target the public. The commission reached a much wider audience. In 2004 Malta became a member of the European Union and subject to its plethora of environmental regulations, some of which the government had already been obliged to implement in order to qualify for membership.

The ENGOs and some other NGOs formed Nature Group, a loose coalition that currently represents the environmental lobby in negotiations with the government representatives, para-statal agencies such as the Malta Environment and Planning Authority (MEPA) or WasteServ, and the refuse disposal agency. The Nature Group is a consolidation of Friends of the Earth (Malta), AD, Nature Trust, Bird Life Malta, among others, and grassroots organizations (such as the farmers' association during the Verdala Golf Course campaign). Although the Nature Group is not a formal or structured federation, the ENGOs mentioned communicate regularly via email to plan who will attend meetings with government representatives, prepare and issue press releases and organize demonstrations in its name. The ENGOs that participate in this Nature Group increase their activity depending on the relevance of the issue to their aims and values and depending on the perceived gravity of the issue. New organizations join the Nature Group from time to time. The formation of the Nature Group in no way points to a merger between the different ENGOs. Each regularly issues separate press releases, even when, or especially when, they are not in agreement with the majority opinion of the Nature Group.

Some NGO Profiles

There are around twenty NGOs in Malta that are in some sense concerned with the environment. The four most active are Friends of the Earth (Malta),

Nature Trust, Graffitti and Din L-Art Helwa.[3] These ENGOs all roughly follow two lines of activity: implementing projects that are designed, planned
and realized according to the organizations' different aims and principles,
and acting as environmental stewards by reacting to issues that arise and
inciting public discussion about these issues in order to pressure the government and/or the developers. Besides these structured ENGOs, there
are many grass-roots action groups that campaign against specific issues.
As noted, these groups disband when the issues they have addressed are
resolved. Later, many of the same people regroup with others to form new
alliances to combat new assaults on the environment.

Moviment ghall-Ambjent/Friends of the Earth (Malta)

Moviment ghall-Ambjent/Friends of the Earth (Malta) (henceforth FoE
Malta), formerly 'Zghazagh ghall-Ambjent' (Young Environmentalists), has
been active since 1985. In 1991 Moviment ghall-Ambjent became part of
Friends of the Earth International (FoEI), a federation that includes groups
from over seventy countries. FoE (Malta) is also linked to the Friends of the
Earth Europe network (FoEE), which places it in direct contact with FoE
member organizations in thirty-one European countries. It is a key member of FoE's Mediterranean Programme (MedNet). This links it with FoE
local organizations in Croatia, Cyprus, France, Italy, Spain and Tunisia. The
aim of the movement is to achieve sustainability that is informed by 'deep'
ecological values. FoE (Malta) concentrates on issues of climate change,
land use, energy, pollution, waste and the threats posed by tourism. It has
organized conferences and meetings to achieve higher environmental standards in the tourist industry. FoE Malta does not have an organized membership base. It has an executive committee of about ten members most of
whom were in Zghazagh ghall-Ambjent. All have university backgrounds.

The work of FoE Malta is based on email. Two volunteers dedicate many
hours a week dealing with it. Core members discuss plans via an email forum. FoE campaigns work first through articles, letters to the editor, press
releases and information posted on its website and email shots. They are
outspoken. The organization's experts prepare technical reports on campaign issues for media and relevant authorities. Finally, they take active
direct measures that include online petitions or help those organized by
other groups. FoE has organized demonstrations in the past and actively
cooperates with the demonstrations of other NGOs. It has no ongoing
projects for which it must solicit local funds, thus preserving its freedom
to criticize. However, it has run a number of projects funded by EU programmes, such as the 'Sustainable Hotels' document published in 2000;
Community Centres for Sustainable Living, a community project that ran

from 2002 until 2005; and New European Citizens, a media project involving all ten of the new accession countries in 2004. FoE (Malta) is a member of several government boards, including the National Commission on Sustainable Development, the Eco Contribution Committee, the Malta EU Steering Committee and the Nature Group.

Nature Trust Malta

Nature Trust's (NT) main focus is the conservation of Malta's nature by means of promoting environmental awareness, managing areas of natural and scientific interest, and lobbying for effective environmental legislation. NT was established in 1999 following the merger between the Society for the Study and Conservation of Nature (SSCN), founded in 1962, Arbor, founded 1983, Verde, founded 1997 and, in 2001, Marine Life Care Group.

NT has a formal organizational structure. Its president is an IT executive for a para-statal agency. NT has an executive committee, each of whose five senior members is responsible for a subcommittee of active members. Executive members communicate mostly by email and receive and send many emails daily. Face-to-face executive meetings occur monthly unless there are pressing issues. The subcommittees meet more often. There are regular social gatherings that most of the executive members attend. Some core groups meet several times a week.

NT manages four nature reserves, one of which is an afforestation project run by a part-time employee. It runs a public education programme via press releases, published articles, an email newsletter, a regular illustrated publication on the country's natural environment, *Archipelago*, and a quarterly printed newsletter, *Il-Kampanja*, in which some items are in Maltese. All the other publications are in English. It is responsible for a carefully researched, often outspoken monthly column in a Sunday newspaper, though it does not advertise its involvement to avoid jeopardizing relations with government. It has also organized educational activities for adults and children for many years; most notably the education and youth committees jointly offer a course for Skola Sajf, the government's summer school programme, which has been running for many years.

The executive committee reviews proposals submitted to MEPA and EIAs (Environmental Impact Assessments), and prepares critical scientific reports. NT does not organize and until recently rarely participated in demonstrations. More radical groups consider it an accommodating organization that participates only nominally in the Nature Group and the various 'Fronts' that preceded it. For each contentious issue NT normally issues few official press releases, and it typically avoids open conflict with authorities. The primary concern of the majority of the core members is the professionalization of the organization. It is achieving this through several large projects funded by the European Union and United Nations. However, even within NT there are different approaches, and some members of the core group have not only increased their participation in demonstrations and the Nature Group email discussions, but are often the organizers and the catalysts for action.

Core members recruit new members from the university and junior college or the schools. Most of the dozen or so core members began as university students and remained active members after graduation. NT is represented on some fifteen local and a number of international committees and boards. The latter include WWF (privileged partner), the Environmental Network of New EU Accession Countries (coordinator), the Mediterranean Information Centre, Medforum and Foundation for Environmental Education (Malta coordinator), Youth Environment Europe (chair) and European Environmental Bureau.

Moviment Graffitti

Founded in 1994 by a handful of university students, Graffitti is the most radical of the Maltese NGOs. It was once associated with the Malta Communist Party, with which it shared headquarters, active members and some joint activities. After a factional split in 2000, the activities of the group became more clearly focused on freedom and social justice issues.

Its loose organization is based on weekly open meetings where decisions are taken by a variable group of around fifteen people. There is no official executive body. Attendance depends upon personal interest in the local and international current affairs to be discussed. Long-standing members take leading roles in these. Only the treasurer is elected. During press conferences and public appearances active new members are often foregrounded. Members and non-members contribute to an online forum.

Graffitti engages in annual and ad hoc campaigns characterized by what they define as two forms of activity: direct action through demonstrations, and ideological action via articles, press releases and letters to the editor in both English and Maltese. Internet discussions supplement ideological action by presenting different points of view. Graffitti is linked by email to many radical NGOs abroad and relays their petitions and news to its own constituents.

Due to past controversial clashes with the authorities, Graffitti now publicly supports only the campaigns with which the concerned local community agrees. For example, Graffitti did not publicly join the Mnajdra landfill campaign discussed below. Several of the most active founding members now work for government and the media and no longer participate or openly support the movement. New members are recruited via Graffitti's branches in the junior college and university. Although a mixed public attend the open meetings, junior college and university student members are the active participants in the online forum.

Din L-Art Helwa

Din L-Art Helwa (DLH), which translates as This Fair Land, was founded in 1965 to safeguard the nation's historic and natural environment. It functions as the National Trust of Malta, restoring historic sites on behalf of the state, the church and private owners, and maintaining and managing these sites. It seeks to stimulate an awareness of heritage and environmental matters through its educational activities. These include excursions, public lectures and presentations in the press of heritage and environmental issues. It publishes a quarterly illustrated magazine, *Vigilo,* and a newsletter. It has also published a number of booklets about the monuments it has restored, a CD-ROM and a video. All its lectures and publications are in English.

DLH has a formal organizational structure presided over by an executive president, a leading local businessman presently beginning his five-year term of office. A five-person executive team and a twelve-member council assist him. All are prominent members of Maltese society. DLH has a large paid membership that includes many expatriates, and financial support from some sixty-five corporate sponsors. Its fundraising events include dinners and musical events, the best known of which is its annual International Music Festival in a medieval chapel it restored. To date DLH has restored eighteen historic monuments. All have commercial sponsors and are managed with the help of DLH volunteers. In some cases the public is charged a small entrance fee.

DLH is very cautious. As a rule it does not participate in demonstrations or sign petitions. After careful study of EIAs it may openly endorse a controversial campaign. Like NT, it has built up good relations with government over the years. It is very careful not to tread on sensitive influential toes, some of which may belong to its own highly respected members, who can provide channels useful for lobbying policy goals. Its executive carefully scrutinizes building and development proposals it receives as a member of the Nature Group. Following the Mnajdra landfills issue, described below, DLH is explicitly including environmental concerns that go beyond the built environment into their agenda. Because DLH is now widely respected for its solid achievements, it has of late been more openly critical. The outgoing president recently used robust language to castigate architects and successive governments that had 'condoned their ugly work since the country's independence' (Scicluna 2000). The new president took a leading role in Nature Group discussions and especially by acting as a mediator between government representatives and the Nature Group in recent anti–golf course campaigns.

Din L-Art Helwa has reciprocal membership with the National Trust of England, Wales and Northern Ireland, the National Trust for Scotland, the Barbados National Trust, the National Trust of Australia, the Gelderland Trust for Historic Houses and the Gelderland 'Nature Trust'. It is also a member of Icomos-Malta, the European Network of National Heritage Organisations and Europa Nostra.

Defending the Environment:
Confrontation, Campaigns and Conflict

The first environmental campaign waged in Malta was Din l-Art Helwa's successful move in 1966, via discreet correspondence between its president, Judge Caruana Curren, and the prime minister's office, to limit the height of the Excelsior Hotel then being built against Valletta's bastions. The environmental voice of civil society then was very modest, respectful and decidedly Anglophone. But by the mid 1980s the lobby's targets and tactics were changing.

The first public demonstrations by Maltese environmentalists were organized by all NGOs on the UN World Environment Day, 5 June 1984. Then, as now, the NGOs were divided over the desirability of public demonstrations, especially since the Labour government (1971–1987) had condoned harsh attacks by its supporters on those who criticized it.[4] Nonetheless, though the official representatives of SSCN and The Malta Ornithological Society (MOS) abstained, green activists paraded in Valletta. They carried banners with green-painted messages calling for the protection of the environment. The demo passed without incident. This was in part because it was not specifically directed against policies of the Labour government. In part it was also because Labour spectators mistook the green banners as support for Libya, at the time a political ally of the government.

Encouraged by the success of the 1984 demo, the newly formed Zghazagh ghall-Ambient (Young Environmentalists) organized a demonstration in November 1985. The demo now had a clear target: the rampant development of beach concessions and uncontrolled building activity. This time the demonstrators were severely mauled. While police looked on, Labour activists, mobilized by a constituency aide of the minister of public works, ripped up banners and beat up demonstrators. Those injured included a woman who was whipped with a bicycle chain. The unexpected attack received wide press coverage. It served to put the Zghazagh ghall-Ambjent 'on the map', according to the late veteran demonstrator Julian Manduca. The Labour prime minister ordered the police to investigate the matter.[5] The attack and ensuing publicity created a sense of solidarity and determination among those who had demonstrated.

During 1986 and 1987 Zghazagh ghall-Ambjent unsuccessfully campaigned against an illegally built tarmac plant; it also sought to stem the massive allocation of government building plots.[6] The environment was beginning to become a public issue, albeit not a very important one. As noted, it figured in the run-up to the 1987 election.

Following the election Zghazagh ghall-Ambjent targeted plans of the new Nationalist government to erect a second power station. The site chosen was the scenic Delemara Peninsula overlooking Marsaxlokk, quite literally on the doorstep of former Labour Prime Minister Dom Mintoff's country hideaway. In spite of NGO efforts to keep the issue neutral, it became a contest between the two parties. Not withstanding the environmentalists' detailed scientific briefs, camp-ins and the pinpointing of viable alternative sites, the power station was built as planned. The campaign had demonstrated to the public, like nothing before, that environmentalists were prepared to oppose major government projects. It was becoming a well-coordinated pressure group.

The 1990s were turbulent and formative years for the ENGOs. The number and scale of confrontations increased. Some of the most notable encounters are discussed below.

The Gozo Air Strip

In 1995 Alternattiva Demokratika, Moviment ghall-Ambient and Graffitti vigorously opposed the proposal of the Maltese Armed Forces to construct a light aircraft landing strip in Gozo. The Nationalist government backed the proposal. The NGOs presented a joint position paper to the Planning Authority (PA) demonstrating that the proposal was against the Structure Plan and violated the agricultural environment. The NGOs organized one of the best-attended demonstrations held in Gozo. The Labour party opposed the project and shelved it when it was re-elected the following year (Boissevain and Sammut 1996), but every now and again it gives a sign of life.

The Hilton Extension

In 1995 the Spinola Development Co. Ltd submitted final plans to the PA to redevelop the Hilton Hotel in St Julian's.[7] The project involved a new 300-bed hotel, 250 luxury apartments, a sixteen-story business tower, the excavation of a marina and the construction of a breakwater. In well-documented briefs and press announcements, Alternattiva Demokratika, SSNC, Moviment ghall-Ambjent/Friends of the Earth, Graffitti and a local residents' action group united to argue that the marina excavation would destroy a unique fortification and pollute nearby sea grass meadows and several popular swimming areas. The Environmental Impact Statement (EIS) failed to examine the project's socioeconomic consequences: the public would be denied access to sections of the foreshore, and the project would subject locals to five years of extreme inconvenience. The NGOs organized a press campaign and numerous demonstrations. Despite these arguments, the Planning Authority Board, on which both Nationalist and Labour parties were represented, approved the project in June 1996. Four months later there was a change of government. The newly elected Labour Party had indicated that the NGOs' allegations would be looked into. When nothing happened, NGOs acted again. Activists, mainly Graffitti members, of the newly formed Front Kontra l-Hilton held a week-long hunger strike in January 1998 in front of the prime minister's office. The new Labour prime minister then authorized the ombudsman to look into the affair and allowed the Front Kontra l-Hilton to examine the Planning Authority's Hilton files.

The ombudsman concluded that whereas no illegalities had been committed, the government had taken bad administrative decisions 'without due consideration to the national interest' (Ombudsman 1997: 13). The Planning Authority rejected the Front Kontra l-Hilton's scathing, detailed report on the files as 'simplistic', and the developers dismissed the group as a 'handful of undemocratic fundamentalists' (Front Kontra l-Hilton, 1997a, 1997b; Planning Authority 1997).

Nonetheless, the Front Kontra l-Hilton's analysis (Front Kontra l-Hilton 1997a) had clearly demonstrated the degree of cooperation, even intimacy, between the PA experts and the developer. This was perhaps not surprising, as they had been working together on the project for years. Still, it was instructive to read that the director of planning had asked his staff to check the draft text of a letter to be sent by the developer's architect to the PA on the Outline Application (1997a: 7); to discover that the developer's legal advisor was also the legal advisor of the Planning Authority (although the PA maintained it had not consulted him on the Hilton project [Planning Authority 1997: 32]); to note that the director of planning had persuaded the director of museums to overrule the Museum Department's previous 'strong objection' to breaching the listed monumental entrenchment so that the marina could be built (Front Kontra l-Hilton 1997a.: 8); and to learn that the developer had added a personal note to a fax (of 22 January 1996, and thus well after the approval of the Outline Application) sent to the PA case officer handling the project (who at the time was chairman of the Fundraising Committee of the Malta Hospice Movement): 'Dear Chris, I gladly enclose a donation of LM 2,000 for the Hospice movement which is so close to your heart. George' (1997a: 7–8; Boissevain and Theuma 1998: 111).

Although the efforts of the NGOs were defeated and the Hilton re-opened in 2000 with a 21-story tower, the NGOs achieved a good deal. Their campaign exposed the way powerful developers operated, displayed the government's weakness in dealing with powerful developers and demonstrated what could be achieved by coordinated nonviolent action. They put both the Planning Authority and the developers on notice that they would be monitored and that irregularities would be attacked.

The Munxar Leisure Complex

Around the same time, another confrontation concerned an Italian-Maltese project to develop a huge leisure complex at Munxar Point.[8] In contrast to the Hilton case, opposition to this project was successful. Munxar Point is located alongside St. Thomas Bay on Malta's east coast. The location had so far been spared the garish developments that have scarred most of the northern coastline. It is a favourite bathing, picnicking and hunting area for inhabitants from inland villages, many of whom had small sheds and boathouses along the foreshore. Opposition to the project began within days of the submission of the formal development application, in November 1995. Alerted by FoE Malta and a local councillor, the *Malta Independent* announced the proposed development with an article headlined 'Tourist village plans for Marsascala Beauty spot' (26 November 1995). A week later a popular local priest wrote an emotional letter pleading for the preservation of the Munxar area. He then set up an action group to fight the application. In four months their activities generated over a hundred articles and letters to the press and a petition with 10,700 signatures. The environmental NGOs and the two opposition parties, the Malta Labour Party and the green Alternattiva Demokratika, supported them. Faced with this massive opposition, the consortium withdrew its application in March 1996.

Tuna Farming

Between 1998 and 2002 ENGOs and AD waged a hard-fought but unsuccessful campaign against Azzopardi Fisheries' proposal to the Planning Authority to establish a tuna farming operation.[9] The scheme involved setting up giant tuna pens close to the Maltese coast. Its object was to catch small tuna, fatten them and ship them by air to the insatiable Japanese market. This potentially lucrative scheme involved well-connected local financial interests and, ultimately, those of Korea, Japan, Spain and Croatia. The campaigners argued that the project threatened colonies of rare sea birds and sea grass and would affect the livelihood of local fishermen; it would also pollute nearby bathing areas and diving zones, thus seriously affecting the tourist industry. In the course of the campaign Maltese and Spanish, Croatian and Sicilian fishermen clashed at sea, shots were fired at Maltese fishing boats and Spanish spotter planes, and Sicilian and Maltese fishermen exchanged blows on shore. Through AD contacts with the European Federation of Green Parties, the disputes were placed before the Italian, Spanish and European parliaments. Though the ENGOs' joint submissions and that of the fishermen's cooperative slightly delayed the expansion of tuna farming in Malta, they were defeated. By 2002 four of the thirteen tuna farms in the Mediterranean were located in Maltese waters.[10]

The Verdala Golf Course

In 1994, AX Holding purchased the bankrupt Verdala Hotel and promptly applied to the Planning Authority for permission to build an annex with thirty-six luxury apartments and to construct an adjacent golf course with a clubhouse on land just below the hotel.[11] The application triggered a ferocious ten-year debate between AX Holdings (AXH) and the tourist industry on the one hand, and some twenty groups united under the umbrella of the Front Kontra l-Golf Kors (the Front) on the other.[12]

AXH argued that the golf course would enhance the environment, create employment and boost quality tourism. The land would be landscaped and include vineyards that farmers displaced by the project could tend. The opposition claimed that the island was too small to accommodate a second golf course, that over 100 full- and part-time farmers would be displaced, and that the projected golf course contravened Structure Plan policy, would deplete the already limited water supply and would pollute the aquifer with its necessary pesticides, herbicides and fertilizers. Their strongest argument was that the transfer by government of former church land contravened the conditions of the contract transferring church land to the Malta government.[13] The campaign was long, bitter and active. The Front organized several demonstrations in Valletta. Front members toured the proposed golf course site. The general secretary of the European Federations of Green Parties, an AD member, lobbied European members of parliament. Foreign NGOs, briefed by Maltese NGOs, criticized the Verdala project in the Maltese press. FoE Malta sent copies of a carefully argued dossier condemning the AXH proposal to key persons in Brussels and Malta. The Front together with the Progressive Farmers Union developed plans for an organic centre adjacent to the proposed golf course site. AXH contracted Regent International Hotels, a subsidiary of Carlson Hospitality

Worldwide (USA) to manage the hotel. Carlson agreed to assume a 50 per cent stake in the eventual golf course. Alternattiva Demokratika warned the CEO of Carlson against doing business with AXH. AD informed the European Federation of Green Parties, the United States Green Party and the Global Greens of Carlson's questionable business practices in Malta. AXH and AD threatened each other with lawsuits.

All the while, the number of NGOs supporting the Front increased. The Front organized an email petition to the prime minister, and ninety-two farmers sent an anti–golf course petition to the Holy See, the president of Malta, the archbishop and the papal nuncio. AXH sent a fifteen-page document to the highest civil and ecclesiastical authorities. The Malta Labour Party came out against the Verdala project. The Nationalist minister for tourism advocated two more golf courses and a Formula One track for Malta, arguing, 'The environment is not the be all and end all of everything.' Local councils of nearby towns Zebbug and Siggiewi opposed the project as did, later and more reluctantly, neighbouring Rabat, which anticipated hotel and golf clients.

The archbishop, long under pressure from the University Chaplaincy and the Jesuits to take a stand on the golf course, climbed off the fence in 2002 and in a pastoral letter openly called for '[d]ue respect for the nation's natural and environmental heritage', proclaiming: 'It must never be that, in spite of laws, there are those who, in one way or other, destroy or cause irresponsible damage to creation, nature and the natural environment' (Mons. Mercieca 2002, emphasis added). This was a powerful message to a devout citizenry.

The Front presented the PA with a fifty-page technical critique of the AXH Environmental Impact Statement. On 22 July the PA held a public hearing on the EIS at which AXH's foreign consultants presented their EIS report. But they did so in English, which caused an uproar since most of the affected farmers spoke little if any English. The meeting was turbulent and inconclusive. FoE Malta wrote a blistering attack on the mismanaged EIS hearing.

Finally, after dithering for two years, the Planning Authority Board on 9 September 2004 unanimously turned down the Verdala golf course proposal on the formal grounds that could have been applied years before. Malta's environmentalists had won their longest and most fiercely fought battle to arouse the public's environmental conscience. The stunned AXH chairman appealed the decision, but the issue, so far, has not re-emerged.

The Mnajdra Landfill

The Mnajdra landfill campaign was a landmark demonstration of the power that civil society in Malta has achieved since independence. For the first time, a grass-roots movement directly confronted and defeated the Maltese government. The Malta government, in order to qualify for EU membership, was forced to address the problem of the Mount Maghtab landfill. The cabinet decided to open interim landfills in two quarries the Polidano Brothers had been obliged to close because they endangered the Mnajdra and Hagar Qim Neolithic temple complex, a World Heritage site near Siggiewi. A group of concerned citizens from Siggiewi, including some who had fought off a cement factory in 1999, rallied around the nonconformist Nationalist MP who had helped scupper the cement factory and decided to try to stop the project. They formed the action group SAGE (The Siggiewi Action Group for the Environment) and launched a campaign. While concerned about possible damage to the temples, local villagers were particularly worried that the toxic seepage from the proposed landfill would pollute the local aquifer and their favourite swimming area at Ghar Lapsi, and also that the stench and dust generated by the procession of refuse-laden trucks grinding through the area would affect their health.

They were soon supported by FoE Malta, Heritage Malta, Alternattiva Demokratika and later the Qrendi Local Council. The government planned to have the landfills operational by August 2003. Throughout the summer NGOs called for a delay until the results of the EIA requested by MEPA were made public. In October 2003 SAGE presented a petition of over 10,000 signatures against the Mnajdra landfills to the Maltese parliament. In December 2003 WasteServ Ltd, the government authority responsible for national waste management, called a public hearing to discuss the EIA it had commissioned, which had been made available before the meeting. FoE Malta and the Diocesan Environment Commission prepared detailed critical reactions to it. The public hearing was well attended by NGOs, grass-roots activists and journalists. After hearing the NGOs' technical criticism, the audience rejected the EIA. In January 2004, on the initiative of the AD candidate for the European elections and secretary of the European Green Party, the European Parliamentary committee on Health and the Environment endorsed a motion expressing concern about the Mnajdra landfills proposal.

The Nationalist-dominated local council of Siggiewi, whose mayor is a member of the National Commission for Sustainable Development, did not participate in the debate. Din L-Art Helwa, normally deeply concerned with World Heritage site issues, also sat on the fence during the entire debate; neither wanted to challenge the proposal of the Nationalist cabinet.

With the resignation of the prime minister in February 2004, attention focused on the Nationalist Party's internal election of a new prime minister. There was heavy lobbying for the candidate who would agree to drop the Mnajdra landfill project. In March the new prime minister took office, and until May public and NGO interest focused on the country's EU accession. This was followed in June by the European Parliamentary elections. Then, in June 2004, less than a year after the Mnajdra landfill project became public, the new prime minister announced that the project had been withdrawn and that the new interim landfill was to be sited within the current landfill site at Maghtab.

Discussion

The cases show that detailed planning procedures do not guarantee protection to the environment. While operating within the legal framework, lease conditions may be altered to benefit developers, government officers can be persuaded to approve destruction of monuments and expert opinion can be suppressed. The Hilton and Verdala golf course hearings were rituals staged to persuade the public that the decisions taken were based on expert advice, that they incorporated the voice of 'the citizens' and that they conformed to planning and environmental protocols. The patent carelessness of both AX Holdings and MEPA in failing to realize the importance of presenting the argument for the golf course and acceptance of the EIS to the affected farmers in a language they could understand demonstrates how little importance they attached to the hearing. Adrian Peace, who examined a planning sequence in rural Ireland, borrowing a term from E.P. Thompson (1978), quite rightly called such public hearings 'modern theatres of control' (Peace 1993: 20). Similarly, Simone Abram concluded that Norwegian local government planning processes were best understood as 'ritual practices and as forms for disciplining participants' behaviour and expectations' (2002: 32). It suggests that ostensibly independent planning authorities are prepared to approve questionable projects and condone infringements that are backed by important political and economic interests.

The network of ENGOs has succeeded in sensitizing elements of civil society. If in the 1960s environmentalists were dismissed as 'harmless lunatics' (Boissevain and Theuma 1998: 114) and more recently as communists and undemocratic fundamentalists, they are steadily gaining respect and stature in the public eye. Gradually they are engendering an approach to the country's environmental heritage as valuable and beautiful. This changing attitude can be observed in the types of representations of the environment in the media and in increased participation in the ENGOs' educational, social and political activities. Through campaigns, demonstrations and increasingly sophisticated use of the local media – five dailies, six weeklies, five television and twenty-seven radio stations – they have succeeded in keeping environmental issues before the public.

Like the rise and fall in support of environmental campaigns that Berglund encountered in East Germany (1998), the types and intensity of participation of the ENGO activists in Malta is characterized by fast-changing peaks and troughs. Furthermore, types and intensity of political action is a constant dialectic between ENGOs, developers and the various agencies of the state. This activity is creating an ever more vocal civil society. The constant, politically nonpartisan vigilance of the NGOs and their documented exposure of the political and economic elite's manipulation of the environment for political and personal gain are emboldening citizens to speak out. They now dare to sign their names to strong letters and petitions voicing their disgust with the visual and physical pollution of their country. Two or three decades ago critical letter writers remained anonymous. Public voice was then muted by the belief in what might be called 'the hierarchy of infallibility'. This belief combines fear of established authorities with a passive acceptance of their decisions and, above all, avoidance of open confrontation. It is a world view inculcated by the unquestioning obedience exacted by both the Roman Catholic Church and the various colonial regimes that for centuries dominated Malta (Boissevain 1990) and, more recently, by the unwavering loyalty demanded and enforced by each of the two dominant political parties.

Finally, through their expanding personal and organizational networks, environmental NGOs and individual environmentalists are slowly gaining some influence on environmental policy and decision making at the local and national levels. They are now beginning to be accepted on government boards and committees dealing with environment-related issues. The level of awareness that the environmental NGOs has raised was such that in a national synod organized by the Diocese in 2003, the Catholic Church in Malta was called to take a clear, educated stand on environmental issues.

Many leading environmental activists became members of Alternattiva Demokratika. In the fourteen years of its existence, Malta's third party has gradually shifted its focus from environmental radicalism to pragmatic green political activism and social justice. The Brussels-based AD secretary of the European Green Party regularly brought local issues to the attention of the Commission and the European Parliament.

The freedom of association that the concerted activity of the ENGOs over time has encouraged cannot be ignored. However, it would be equally misrepresentative to portray the ENGOs as a uniform section of Maltese society with equal access to resources, prestige and spheres of social action. The alliance of ENGOs in the Nature Group has the effect of glossing over the difference in the aims and strategies, the position of the members in Maltese society and the social groups with whom the different ENGOs mainly interact. Overestimating the power of the ENGOs as equal reinforces the state's self-legitimizing discourse of decentralization and inclusion of dissident voices. It is indisputable, however, that participation in ENGOs is seen as a direct conflict of interest with government employment. Most activists who take jobs in the civil service or in para-statal agencies resign or tone down their activism upon or shortly after being hired. Furthermore, government constantly proposes or supports new developments that are contrary to the principles of environmental sustainability advocated by the ENGOs. Even the power of the church's Environment Commission should not be overestimated.

For example, during recent campaigns against two more proposed golf courses, a key political figure warned the chairman of the church's Environment Commission by telephone not to get involved in matters that did not concern the church directly. Unlike the Verdala golf course issue, where a direct misuse of the church's land justified the church's involvement, participation in the more recent anti–golf course campaigns was motivated more directly by environmentalist ideology. The church's Environment Commission withdrew its official support of the campaigns and began research into the effects of fireworks on health. It is important to note that the chairman of the Environment Commission is a prominent academic. Though the University of Malta is constitutionally independent, it is closely tied to government via its governing body, funding and social relations. This underlines the tightly woven mesh of social relations that underpins most environmentalist activism. As such the distinction between NGO activists, academics, entrepreneurs/developers and government representatives is not clear-cut. It is complicated by the fact that many key individuals fulfil multiple roles as well as engage in reciprocal ties with people in these different spheres. Economic and social power of the dominant group still seems to determine the major changes of land use.

Nonetheless, while in the past most people were reluctant to express an opinion, fearing reprisals, they now engage in political activity with less fear of repercussion. The growing activity of grass-roots groups is an indicator of increased political activity in spheres of society not traditionally active in politics. If environmental activism thus far has had only limited impact on specific developments, that does not mean that it is not contributing to wider changes in society (Berglund 1998: 73). The environmental movement in fact has had a substantial impact on wider Maltese society:

- It helped sensitize the public to the importance of the environment.
- It has placed the environment firmly on the national political agenda.
- It has greatly strengthened the voice of civil society.
- It has, modestly, influenced environmental policy.
- It has obtained limited political legitimacy and representation.

- It is training a new political elite.
- It is directly challenging the traditional clientelistic system of decision-making.
- It brought the archbishop and through him the Maltese Church into the environmentalist fold.
- It is successfully challenging the right of the state to commodify local culture and environment without adequate consultation.
- It is slowly creating alternative political (green) space between the two dominant parties.
- It is creating a healthy mistrust of politicians and the 'expert' opinion of scientists and economists commissioned by developers to work on environmental impact studies.

Malta's new membership of the European Union is already providing environmentalists with more political leverage and opportunities. Studies of the political role of environmental NGOs in Spain, Portugal and Italy demonstrate that the EU relies on NGOs for information on the adherence and implementation of environmental regulations (Aguilar Fernandez 2001: 273; Jiménez 2001: 240; Pridham 2001: 386). The European Union provides 'new space for the self-organisation of people by providing a space beyond the nation' (Eder 2001: 49).

Patterns and Prospects

Particular patterns emerge from our study of the activities of organizations actively involved with environmental affairs in Malta, all of which are in some way engaged with contexts beyond the borders of the nation-state. Pressure for change does not come from the Maltese government. Because of the way the Maltese government is bound up with local interest groups and clientelistic networks, it has been reactive rather than proactive regarding environmental policy. The pressure for change has come from outside, from the UN, EU and international ENGOs, and from below, from local ENGOs and grass-roots action groups.

There are two types of civil action at work in the scenarios we examined above. On the one hand there are temporary grass-roots groups that form in reaction to particular issues that directly affect their locality. On the other, there are the more or less structured ENGOs that throughout the year promote their own agendas, which at times coincide with those of the international organizations or networks of which they form part.[14] The activity of the grass-roots groups is often triggered or reinforced by the support of the formal NGOs – as was the case with the Munxar resort and the Mnajdra landfill issues. The grass-roots groups mobilize local networks to achieve their aims, for example when collecting signatures for petitions. The ENGOs, besides mobilizing each other, often activate outside resources by tapping into their international networks. This international dimension strengthens their legitimacy in the eyes of the general public, which gives them more clout to influence state policy and helps them rally grass-roots groups (Gatt 2001: 37). In addition to this, both grass-roots groups and structured ENGOs employ the discourse of globalization to influence the local situation. The central message conveyed is that by protecting the local, the Maltese help protect global heritage, but if they fail to protect the local they detract from the global.

In this sense local movements utilize articulated knowledge of global and local as part of their ideological strategies (Choy 2005: 6). For example, all NGOs involved in the landfill dispute used the same rhetorical tool – namely, that the installation of a landfill in the vicinity of the Mnajdra temples, a World Heritage site, would jeopardize the legacy of the world's future generations. Environmental activists, steadily becoming established as legitimate experts about the 'environment' (Gatt 2001: 73), ably entwine global and local notions in their discourse.

Furthermore, Castells, who maintains that the nation-state is weakened by its increasing inability to sustain the welfare state (1997: 254), predicts that international ENGOs are increasingly taking over the role of safe-guarding the global 'quality of life', further invalidating the power of the state (1997: 268; see also Eder 2001: 49). Our empirical material suggests that these predictions are largely correct and that access to resources outside the nation-state strengthens the position of activists struggling to have their values taken seriously by government. However, while such access simultaneously reducing the power of the state, certain historical factors show that this statement needs to be qualified.

The distinction between state and nongovernmental organizations is not always clear. Different organizations use transnational networks in very different ways, and some not at all. We saw that DLH and NT have considerable contact with transnational networks and employ them to increase their legitimacy and status in Malta in order to be able to influence environmental policy. Expatriates were among the founding members of both DLH and NT, and many of their members are part of the dominant social group. Their international influence, especially British influence (see list of affiliations above), in Malta is closely related to the country's colonial history.

FoE Malta and Graffitti, founded by university students during the 1980s, deploy their links to international nongovernmental organizations differently than DLH and NT. FoE Malta and Graffitti have been the most radical groups and have not become established as part of the elite as have DLH and NT. Graffitti organizes very theatrical demonstrations to support international anti-capitalist events advocated by members of their international networks. These have often ended with police involvement. Although creating a space for expression, Graffitti has become isolated as an extremist group, tolerated as a student group but incompatible with regular salaried employment or serious political action. FoE Malta use their international contacts in yet another way: they cooperated with the former AD executive, who until recently was the secretary of the European Green Party in Brussels. They use channels offered by FoE International, or approach other international organizations directly, in order to pressure the Maltese government in relation to specific projects.

It would be a misrepresentation to imply that the transnational networks of Maltese ENGOs intrinsically weaken the nation-state because of their transnational character. The ENGOs we discussed above have long had widespread connections with people and groups abroad. In most cases these links – primarily to Italy, Britain, the U.S., Canada and Australia – predate Malta's independence in 1964. For DLH's restoration work, NT's pedagogical programmes and FoE Malta's community research projects each NGO made use of its international connections, not to challenge the Maltese government but for technical support, funding and motivating participants. They used their transnational networks, in cooperation with state agencies, to fund, organize and manage projects. It could be argued, therefore, that far from weakening the state, the use the NGOs made of their transnational networks strengthened the state by helping it to fulfil its tasks of caring for the social and physical environment of its citizens. Yet some of the transnational linkages they employed were the very same ones used to pressure the government to abandon the Verdala golf course and the Mnajdra landfills projects. In brief, ENGOs use their transnational networks to protect and improve the quality of life of Maltese citizens by successfully challenging the state as well as by cooperating with it.

In conclusion, there is more than a family resemblance between the campaigns of international environmental NGOs battling giant corporations (Monbiot 2000, 2004) and the combat waged by Maltese environmental campaigners. Just as Maltese capitalists form alliances with multinational corporations – such as Hilton International, Carlson Hospitality Worldwide and Japanese and Spanish tuna fishing magnates – to further their local projects, so local ENGOs seek transnational help – from fellow European Green Parties, from Italian, Swiss, British and German NGOs, and even from the Holy See – to block these projects. The political arena involves interconnections that move beyond the borders of the nation-state. Local environmentalist networks are linked to different transnational networks that, in their turn, form an intrinsic part of other global movements such as the global anti-capitalist social forum and conservationist environmentalism. In view of this, two things have changed. These are the utilization of older networks in relation to a clearly imagined 'nation-state', and the greater access to these and newer networks coupled with a wider participation in this form of collective action. Where in the past translocal connections were the reserve of particular social groups, they now are more widely accessible. More importantly, people from diverse social backgrounds are less afraid and thus more likely to utilize these, thereby strengthening the voice of civil society.

Acknowledgements

The first version of this discussion was presented to the workshop on A New Climate for Green Social Movements, at the 7th Nordic Environmental Social Science Research Conference, Göteborg University. We are grateful to conference participants Asa Boholm, Michelle Shipworth, Johanna Alkan-Olsson and Daniel Berlin for their helpful comments. We also thank Maria Kousis, who gave us very valuable suggestions, as did Andrew Whitehouse and Sophie Elixhauser.

Finally, we would like to express our gratitude to the environmental activists with whom we engaged during the past years, and particularly the late Julian Manduca, one of the pioneers of the Maltese environmental movement, to whose memory our chapter is dedicated.

Notes

1. Quoted from the London West End production *Straight and Narrow!* in Richard England (1998).
2. Malta uses the system of proportional representation with single transferable vote. This requires a candidate to amass around 3,400 personal votes in order to be elected in one of the 13 five-member constituencies. So far, no parliamentary AD candidate has been elected. In the 2003 national election AD received only 0.7 per cent of the total votes, while in the 2004 European parliamentary elections, the AD candidate for one of the country's five seats, though not elected, received almost 10 per cent of the total votes. In Malta's patronage dominated, winner-take-all system, voters are reluctant to back a party perceived as having little chance of entering the national parliament and thus of rewarding its supporters. The European parliament is a very different political arena.
3. This chapter was written between 2005 and 2006. Attesting to the fast-changing situation of civil society in Malta, three more groups should be counted amongst the most active ENGOs. These are Flimkien Ghall-Ambjent Ahjar (FAA – Together for a better Environment), the Gaia Foundation and the Ramblers Association.

4. For example, in November 1977 Labour supporters physically and verbally attacked lecturers, students and guests at a university graduation ceremony. In October 1979 they wrecked and then burnt the premises of the *Times* (of Malta) and vandalized the private residence of the leader of the opposition. In September 1984 they attacked and damaged the law courts in Valletta and sakked the archbishop's curia, situated opposite police headquarters. The police, present on all these occasions, seemed unable to bring the culprits to book (Boissevain 1993: 154).

5. After a change of government and many court appearances, nine of the attakkers were finally sentenced and fined in March 1991.

6. The campaign questioned the sense of distributing 12,000 new building plots, given that 19 per cent of the country's housing stock was unoccupied. In 2005 the problem was still not resolved and now 20 per cent of the housing stock is still unoccupied.

7. For a more detailed account of the Hilton conflict see Boissevain and Theuma (1998) and Briguglio (1998).

8. For more about the Munxar encounter see Boissevain and Sammut (1996) and Boissevain (2004: 243–247).

9. The NGOs involved were Din l-Art Helwa, Nature Trust/Marine Life Care Group, ECO Foundation, FoE Malta and the Biological Conservation Research Foundation.

10. About the tuna farming campaign see Boissevain (2004: 246–254).

11. For more details on the Verdala golf course campaign see Boissevain (2003: 102–110); Retrieved on August 3, 2002 from http://www.nogolfmalta.cjb.net/

12. In February 2004 the Front Kontra l-Golf Kors was made up of the Progressive Farmers Union, FoE Malta, Moviment Graffitti, Alternattiva Demokratika, Inizjamed, Move Organization, Zminijitna, Alternattiva Demokratika Zghazagh, International Animal Rescue, Azzjoni Pozittiva (A+), Vegetarian Society, Pembroke Residents Association and Nature Trust, Ghaqda Zghazagh tax-Xelluq. It was supported by the University Chaplaincy, Malta Organic Agriculture Movement, Kopin, Farmers' Central Co-Operative Society, Front Insalvaw Wied Garnaw and Third World Group. Retrieved on February 5, 2004 from http://www.nogolfmalta.cjb.net/

13. Ecclesiastical Entities [Properties] Act 1992 : "*To provide for the implementation of the Agreement signed on the 28th day of November, 1991, between the Holy See and Malta relative to the transfer to the State of such immovable property in Malta as is not required by the Catholic Church for pastoral purposes and on the determination of certain issues pertaining to the relations between the Church and the State as regards matters of patrimony.* (12th June, 1992)*"* Retrieved on February 12, 2011 from: https://quality-mitts.gov.mt/secureb/mjha/DownloadDocument.aspx?app=lom&itemid=3279

14. The general structure and strategy of ENGOs that Brosius (1999: 284) noted also holds for those in Malta. There are 'radical' ones, which concentrate more on direct action and tend to be non-hierarchical (FoE Malta and Graffitti), and 'mainstream' groups, which are hierarchical, emphasize cooperative institu-

tional solutions and establish good working relationships with elites (NT and DLH).

REFERENCES

Abram, S. 2002. 'Planning and Public-making in Municipal Government', *Focaal* 40: 21–34.

Aguilar Fernandez, S. 2001. 'Is Spanish Environmental Policy Becoming More Participatory? Institutional Building Versus Participation', in K. Eder and M. Kousis (eds), *Environmental Politics in Southern Europe: Actors, Institutions and Discourses in a Europeanizing Society.* Dordrecht, Boston and London: Kluwer Academic Publishers.

Anderson, D. G. and E. Berglund (eds). 2003. *Ethnographies of Conservation: Environmentalism and the Distribution of Privilege.* New York and Oxford: Berghahn Books.

Baldacchino, G. 1997. *Global Tourism and Informal Labour Relations: The Small Scale Syndrome at Work.* London: Mansell.

Berglund, E.K. 1998. *Knowing Nature, Knowing Science: An Ethnography of Local Environmental Activism.* Cambridge: The White Horse Press.

Boissevain, J. 1968. 'The Place of Non-Groups in the Social Sciences', *Man* (N.S) 3: 542–556.

Boissevain, J. 1974. *Friends of Friends: Networks, Manipulators and Coalitions.* Oxford: Basil Blackwell.

Boissevain, J. 1990 [1969]. 'Why Do the Maltese Ask So Few Questions?' *Education* (Malta) 3(4): 16–18.

Boissevain, J. 1993 [1965]. *Saints and Fireworks: Religion and Politics in Rural Malta.* 2nd ed. Valletta: Progress Press.

Boissevain, J. 2001. 'Contesting Maltese Landscapes', *Journal of Mediterranean Studies* 11(2): 277–296.

Boissevain, J. 2003. 'Confronting the Tourist Industry in Malta', in R. Mursic and I. Weber (eds), *Mediterranean Ethnological Summer School*, vol. 5: *Piran 2001 and 2002.* Ljubljana: Department of Ethnology and Cultural Anthropology, University of Ljubljana.

Boissevain, J. 2004. 'Hotels, Tuna Pens and Civil Society: Contesting the Foreshore in Malta', in J. Boissevain and T. Selwyn (eds), *Contesting the Foreshore: Tourism, Society, and Politics on the Foreshore.* Amsterdam: University of Amsterdam Press.

Boissevain, J. and N. Sammut. 1996. 'Contested Space: Tourism, Heritage and Identity in Malta', unpublished paper presented at the Biennial EASA Conference, Barcelona, July.

Boissevain, J. and N. Theuma. 1998. 'Contested Space: Planners, Tourists, Developers and Environmentalists in Malta', in S. Abram and J. Waldren (eds), *Anthropological Perspectives on Local Development.* London: Routledge.

Bramwell, B. 2003. 'Maltese Responses to Tourism', *Annals of Tourism Research,* 30: 581–605.

Briguglio, M. 1998. 'State Power: Hiltonopoly', unpublished B.A. Honours dissertation, Department of Sociology, University of Malta.

Brosius, J.P. 1999. 'Analyses and Interventions: Anthropological Engagements with Environmentalism', *Current Anthropology* 40: 277–309.

Carter, N. 2001. *The Politics of the Environment: Ideas, Activism, Policy.* UK, USA, Australia, Spain and South Africa: Cambridge University Press.

Castells, M. 1997. *The Power of Identity.* Oxford: Blackwell Publishers Ltd.

Chazan, N. 1992. 'Africa's Democratic Challenge', *World Policy Journal* 9: 279–307.

Choy, T. 2005. 'Articulated Knowledges: Environmental Forms after Universality's Demise', *American Anthropologist* 107: 5–18.

Development Planning Act (Act No. I of 1992). 1992. Valletta: Department of Information.

Doyle, T. and D. McEachern (eds). 1998. *Environmental Politics.* London: Routledge.

Edelman, M. 2002. 'Toward an Anthropology of Some New Internationalisms: Small Farmers in Global Resistance Movements', *Focaal* 40: 103–122.

Eder, K. 2001. 'Sustainability as a Discursive Device for Mobilizing European Publics: Beyond the North-South Divide', in K. Eder and M. Kousis (eds), *Environmental Politics in Southern Europe: Actors, Institutions and Discourses in a Europeanizing Society.* Dordrecht, Boston and London: Kluwer Academic Publishers.

England, R. 1998. 'Dos, Don'ts and Dogmas', Building and Architectural Supplement, *The Sunday Times (Malta)*, 1 November.

Environment Protection Act (Act No. V of 1991). 1991. Valletta: Department of Information.

Escobar, A. 1999. 'After Nature: Steps to an Antiessentialist Political Ecology', *Current Anthropology* 40(1): 1–30.

Fisher, W.F. 1997. 'Doing Good? The Politics and Antipolitics of NGO Practices', *Annual Review of Anthropology* 26: 439–464.

Fox, R.G. and O. Starn. 1997. *Between Resistance and Revolution: Cultural Politics and Social Revolution.* New Brunswick and London: Rutgers University Press.

Front Kontra l-Hilton. 1997a. *Report on the Files Relating to the Granting of Planning Permission to Spinola Development Co. Ltd. for the Hilton Project.* Malta: Front Kontra l- Hilton.

Front Kontra l-Hilton. 1997b. *Reply to the Planning Authority's Comments on Our Report of 23rd March 1997 Regarding Planning Permission Given to Spinola Development Co. Ltd. for the Hilton Project.* Malta: Front Kontra l-Hilton.

Gatt, C. 2001. *Environmentalism in the Maltese Context: The Case of Nature Trust,* unpublished B.A. Honours dissertation, Mediterranean Institute, University of Malta.

Grove-White, R. 1993. 'Environmentalism: A New Moral Discourse for Technological Society', in K. Milton (ed.), *Environmentalism: The View from Anthropology.* London and NewYork: Routledge.

Hann, C. 1996. 'Introduction: Political Society and Civil Anthropology', in C. Hann and E. Dunn (eds), *Civil Society: Challenging Western Models.* London and New York: Routledge.

Horwath and Horwath. 1989. *The Maltese Islands Tourism Development Plan.* London: Horwarth and Horwath (UK) Ltd.

Ioannides, D. and B. Holcomb. 2001. 'Raising the Stakes: Implications of Up Market Tourism Policies in Cyprus and Malta', in D. Ioannides, Y. Apostolopoulos and S. Sonmez (eds), *Mediterranean Islands and Sustainable Tourism Development: Practices, Management and Policies.* London: Continuum.

Jiménez, M. 'Sustainable Development and Participation of Environmental NGOs in Spanish Environmental Policy: The Case of Industrial Waste Policy', in K. Eder and M. Kousis (eds), *Environmental Politics in Southern Europe: Actors, Institutions and Discourses in a Europeanizing Society.* London: Kluwer Academic Publishers.

Kousis, M. 2001. 'Tourism and the Environment in Corsica, Sardinia, Sicily and Crete', in D. Ioannides, Y. Apostolopoulos and S.Sonmez (eds), *Mediterranean Islands and Sustainable Tourism Development.* London: Continuum.

Lindisfarne, N. 2004. 'Another World is Possible', *Anthropology Today* 20(2): 1–3.

Mair, L. 1962. *Primitive Government.* Harmondsworth: Penguin Books.

Mallia, E.A. 1994. 'Land Use: An Account of Environmental Stewardship', in R.G. Sultana and G. Baldacchino (eds), *Maltese Society: A Sociological Inquiry.* Malta: Mireva.

Mallia, E.A. 2000. 'The Environment: Prospects for the Millennium', in C. Vella (ed.), *The Maltese Islands on the Move: A Mosaic of Contributions Marking Malta's Entry into the 21st Century.* Valletta: Central Office of Statistics.

Mayer, A. 1966. 'The Significance of Quasi-Groups in the Study of Complex Societies', in M. Banton (ed.), *The Social Anthropology of Complex Societies.* London: Tavistock Publications.

Merceica, Joseph (Mons.), 'Duty to Safeguard Environment', Pastoral Letter, The Times of Malta, 11th August 2002.

Milton, K. 1993. 'Introduction: Environmentalism and Anthropology', in K. Milton (ed.), *Environmentalism: The View from Anthropology.* London: Routledge.

Monbiot, G. 2000. *The Captive State: The Corporate Takeover of Britain.* London: Macmillan.

Monbiot, G. 2004. 'Jump on our Bandwagon', *The Guardian*, 6 April, 1.

Moviment ghall-Ambjent – Friends of the Earth Malta. 1997. *Towards Sustainable Europe. Sustainable Malta: A Discussion Paper.* Valletta: Moviment ghall-Ambjent.

Ombudsman. 1997. *Land Development by Spinola Development Co. Ltd. (The Hilton Project).* Report on Case No. 1398. Malta: Office of the Ombudsman.

Peace, A. 1993. 'Environmental Protest, Bureaucratic Closure: The Politics of Discourse in Rural Ireland', in K. Milton (ed.), *Environmentalism: The View from Anthropology.* London and New York: Routledge.

Però, D. 2005. 'Engaging Power: Recent Approaches to the Study of Political Practices', *Social Anthropology* 13(3): 331–338.

Planning Authority. 1997. *Hilton Redevelopment Project: Response to Report from 'Front Kontra Hilton'.* Malta: Planning Authority.

Pridham, G. 2001. 'Tourism Policy and Sustainability in Italy, Spain and Greece: A Comparative Politics Perspective', in K. Eder and M. Kousis (eds), *Environ-*

mental Politics in Southern Europe: Actors, Institutions and Discourses in a Europeanizing Society. Dordrecht, Boston and London: Kluwer Academic Publishers.

Scicluna, M. 2000. 'Halting the Uglification of Malta', *Vigilo* 26 (October): 4–5.

Selwyn, T. 2004. 'Privatising the Mediterranean Coastline', in J. Boissevain and T. Selwyn (eds), *Contesting the Foreshore: Tourism, Society, and Politics on the Foreshore.* Amsterdam: University of Amsterdam Press.

Silverman, S. 1978. *Three Bells for Civilization: The Life of an Italian Hilltown.* New York: Columbia University Press.

Structure Plan for the Maltese Islands. 1990. Draft Final Written Statement and Key Diagram. Valletta: Ministry for Development and Infrastructure.

Thompson, E.P. 1978. 'Folklore, Anthropology and Social History', *The Indian Historical Review* 3(2): 247–266.

Wolf, E.R. 1966. 'Kinship, Friendship and Patron-Client Relations in Complex Societies', in M. Banton (ed.), *The Social Anthropology of Complex Societies.* London: Tavistock Publications.

⊰ Chapter 6 ⊱

Science and Community based Environmental Activism, Mediterranean Coastal Biodiversity and the EU

The Caretta caretta *Case in Greece*

MARIA KOUSIS AND KATERINA PSARIKIDOU

Introduction

The aim of this chapter is to explore and describe Mediterranean coastal biodiversity governance issues concerning the endangered sea turtle *Caretta caretta* in the coastal communities of Zakynthos and Crete. Participatory governance is visible in the aims, practices, actions and collaborations of the major environmental and science oriented NGOs Archelon, WWF-Greece, Medasset and Greenpeace, as well as local NGOs and citizen environmental groups, especially since the adoption of the EU Habitats Directive.[1]

The most serious problems faced by Mediterranean coastal and marine resources are environmental ones (Huber et al. 2003). Local environmental conflicts related to the protection of coastal and marine ecosystems amounted to more than one quarter of all such protests in Greece, Spain and Portugal (Kousis 2004a). Mediterranean coastal zones, the prime tourist destination of the world, have experienced drastic changes due to the rapid development of tourism as a major industry in the past few decades (Boissevain and Selwyn 2004; Kousis 2004a). Environmental organizations and local groups are taking actions to inhibit and improve the 'de-Mediterraneanization' of traditional 'unspoilt' Mediterranean regions (Selwyn 2000) through scientific initiatives, sustainable management and action organizing.

Tourism's negative environmental impacts on Mediterranean coastal regions have altered the dynamics in the use of local natural resources, especially for the closed island ecosystems, which constitute important contributors to biodiversity (Briguglio and Briguglio 1996; Psarikidou 2006). Tourism-related activities in Zakynthos and Crete, as on other Mediterranean islands, have had negative impacts on wild life and local natural resources (Kousis 2000; Psarikidou 2005; Kousis and Psarikidou 2006; Psarikidou 2008). Coastal and tourism-related biodiversity concerns have been a major focus of earlier (Grenon and Batisse 1989) and more recent (Guillaume and Comeau 2005) projections on sustainable Mediterranean futures.

Following UN objectives, sustainable development strategies for the Mediterranean include the promotion of a balanced development in coastal zone management, the prevention of marine and land pollution, the elimination of operational pollution by 2025, stopping marine and coastal biodiversity loss, and the development of sustainable fisheries and aquaculture. Based on the description of these strategies, the definition and understanding of sustainable development follows a science-led, technocratic approach, while sustainable development policies are translated into scientific applications and environmental conservation. Under the auspices of the UN Environment Programme (UNEP), the Mediterranean Action Plan (MAP) (2006) stresses the need to develop territorial prospective approaches involving state, economic and civil society actors in order to promote territory-specific sustainable development.

At the same time, by their very nature, Mediterranean biodiversity concerns extend beyond the local level. Thus, another important prerequisite for a sustainable Mediterranean future is the strengthening of multilateral and bilateral regional cooperation (UNEP/MAP 2006). In the case of marine turtles, UNEP/MAP conservation activities include (UNEP/MAP 2006) a monitoring programme for Mediterranean nesting sites, collaboration with environmental, science-oriented conservation NGOs and government agencies, information dissemination, as well as scientific studies and international meetings.

According to UNEP/MAP's Plan Bleu, one of the six sustainability objectives for the entire Mediterranean center on the conservation and sustainable management of the natural and cultural heritage of additional 4,000 km of coastline up to 2025, so as to preserve functional ecosystems and a quality environment for local populations and sustainable tourism. Tourism policies could limit negative ecosystem impacts and offer sustainable alternatives to urban, rural and coastal development (UNEP/MAP 2006).

With peaks in June and July, the sea turtle nesting season on Mediterranean coasts largely coincides with the tourist season, posing severe threats to turtle sustainability. These coasts, which host millions of tourists every summer, are of vital significance for the survival of the loggerhead sea turtle since their biological circle is completed there – through nest construction, egg laying, hatching and hatchling racing towards the sea following the reflection of the starlight. Out of the 110 eggs of a nest, only 35–50 eggs succeed in producing hatchlings, and even a much smaller number of newborns reach adulthood.[2]

Three of the seven species of sea turtles in the world are found in the Mediterranean, but only the loggerhead sea turtle nests in Greece. *Caretta caretta*'s main nesting sites are also found in Turkey and Cyprus, followed by substantial yet non-quantified ones in Libya and a few nests in Egypt, Israel, Italy, Syria, Lebanon, Tunisia and Spain (Margaritoulis 2005: 923).[3] Loggerheads tagged in Greece have been recovered in Italian, Tunisian and Libyan waters (Archelon 2005).

Laganas Bay in Zakynthos hosts the largest nesting concentration of *Caretta caretta* in the Mediterranean, i.e. an average annual number of 1,293.7 nests (based on a nineteen-year study), representing 42.4 per cent of the total nesting effort in Greece and 25.7 per cent of the total nesting effort in the Mediterranean (Margaritoulis 2005: 923). Since the 1980s, persistent efforts by environmental activists and organizations, especially Archelon, WWF-Greece and Medasset, eventually led to the establishment of the National Marine Park of Zakynthos (NMPZ). Important nesting sites also exist in the Bays of Chania, Messara and Rethymno in Crete, where the establishment of a national marine park has yet to become an issue. According to the international treaties of Ramsar and Barcelona, the National Ministry of Environment in Greece is obliged to accept the habitats of *Caretta caretta* as protected areas, since Greece is considered among the only remaining habitats of *Caretta caretta* (Ministry of Foreign Affairs 2004).

The aim of this chapter is to provide an exploratory and descriptive account of how environmental science-oriented conservation NGOs have responded to *Caretta caretta* biodiversity concerns with reference to the Habitats Directive. Specifically it addresses the ways in which they have attempted to promote sustainable development-oriented aims and practices through their scientific and sustainable management contributions, as well as through resource building and action-organizing initiatives. The presentation is based on information drawn from websites of environmental NGOs and other civil society groups as well as from interviews with involved actors in Athens, Zakynthos and Crete. The data derive from two EC-funded projects, primarily Participatory Governance and Institutional Innovation (EC, DGXII), and to a limited extent Mediterranean Voices (Euromed Heritage II, EuropeAid).

Science-oriented Environmental Activism
in the Mediterranean

Charles Tilly's definition of a social movement is useful to students of the environmental movement. He portrays social movements as sustained challenges to power holders in the name of interested populations – which in contemporary times appear as professional movements, 'ad hoc' community-based and specialized movements, or communitarian, unspecialized movements – giving rise to a new community (Tilly 1994: 7, 18).[4] These types of social movement entities are reflected in the three forms of the environmental movement: the formal environmental movement organizations; the grassroots, community-based environmental groups or initiatives; and the radical, highly committed ecological groups (Kousis 1999). Movement participants, whether they take direct or indirect action, in general call for power holders to take crucial measures to address their claim and redress the situation (Tilly 1994).

After the consolidation of the new democracies in Southern Europe (Gunther, Puhle and Diamandouros 1995), the 1980s saw a significant rise in the number of environmental organizations (Kousis and Dimopoulou 2000; Gil Nave 2001; Figueiredo, Fidelis and da Rosa Pirez 2001; Jimenez 2005), analogous to the development that had already taken place in Italy (Diani 1995). By the second half of the 1990s, Southern European environmental organizations were flourishing (della Porta and Andretta 2000; Karamichas 2003). The changes that took place on the environmental political scene also brought changes in the opportunities for the development of the environmental movement. In the case of those Southern European countries that were late entrants into the EU, the incorporation of EU environmental policies also meant rapid institutionalization of the already expeditious growth of environmental associations (Kousis 2004b).

Whereas in the 1980s environmental NGOs were scarcely involved in environmental policy-making circles, this situation changed significantly in the 1990s. Relations between environmental NGOs and the state became more cooperative and less confrontational. Environmental organizations were increasingly involved in collaboration schemes facilitated by EU environmental policies (Eder and Kousis 2001). The incorporation of EU environmental laws by member states provided formal ENGO legitimation while simultaneously enhancing the institutionalization and deradicalization of these organizations (Kousis, della Porta and Jimenez 2008). Influenced by these developments, professional, science-oriented, conservation ENGOs have adopted sustainable development alternatives and mobilized their expertise to seize the economic opportunities offered in the wider context of international and national economic policies targeting sustainability objectives (Kousis 2010). These new science-oriented organizations reflect the emergence of a culture of environmental research oriented professional activists (Frickel 2004), who often combine social roles and expert knowledge that were previously separated (Jamison 2006).

The need for compliance with EU environmental legislation has fostered the financial and organizational support of large ENGOs by EU as well as national agencies. The provision of funding by national or international bodies, individuals and businesses, among other factors, is considered of vital importance for the survival, development and success of professional ENGOs (Kousis 2004b). In Greece, ENGOs have sought contributions from the Ministry of the Environment, Urban Planning and Public Works (YPE-HODE), its support, or its assistance in dealing with local problems, such as those in Zakynthos concerning the protection of *Caretta caretta*, a threatened species. During the 1990s ENGOs played a decisive role in handling local and national issues, participating in various committees related to the entrepreneurial programmes of the second and third Community Structural Funds and in the management of protected areas (Kousis 2004b).

The environmental groups and organizations that emerged in the 1980s in Greece have steadily worked towards mobilizing public opinion, disseminating information to the public, increasing public participation and building social capacity to deal with emerging challenges. In order to sustain their status they seek to create and strengthen their ties with resource-rich groups, such as fund providers (individuals, businesses, national and international bodies), state and governmental agencies, other nonprofit groups, media groups, local government, schools, the church, private enterprises and the public (Kousis, Petropoulou and Dimopoulou, 2001). Even though environmental NGOs in Greece engage in a wide-ranging field of actions, they especially focus on environmental education initiatives, while their scientific, conservation and animal welfare interests supersede most other issues (Kousis and Dimopoulou, 2000). These professional NGOs maintain their contacts and collaborations in the related scientific and conservation networks (national, regional and global), as well as in the local community itself (Diani 1995; Pridham 2001).

The case of *Caretta caretta* in Zakynthos and Crete

In his ethnographic account of the conflict over the conservation of *Caretta caretta* in Zakynthos, Theodossopoulos (2003) offers a refined view of local livelihood issues in relation to the threatened species, not focusing nevertheless on the involved environmental groups. This chapter centres on environmentalist claims and practices, which view human activities as the most significant threats to the endangered species.

Eighty years ago, the *Caretta caretta* population numbered over 50,000 with nesting sites in many Mediterranean countries (e.g. Italy, France, Israel), but rapid tourism development in the last few decades appears to have been a major cause of a dramatic drop to fewer than 4,000 (WWF-Greece 2008). Given the inadequacy of government structures to respond to conservation needs, the scientific community through professional environmental NGOs has been of vital importance in promoting conservation and sustainable development objectives and initiatives. Professional NGOs actively involved in scientific actions have become key actors in sustaining these practices at a national level, supported by the state. In the past three decades, their members were influenced by the new "conservation biology" which was established as a biological subdiscipline applying the systematic research methodology of population ecology and genetics to conservation issues (Haila et al. 2007: 12). In contrast, local environmental activists arrive later to participate in the protection of *Caretta caretta,* undertaking different type of activities, such as community organizing, letters of complaints, or confrontational actions.

For almost three decades, the conservation of *Caretta caretta,* primarily in the tourism-developed Laganas Bay in Zakynthos, has been a Greek governance problem at the local, national and EU levels (Haila et al. 2007; Psarikidou 2005, 2008a). Failure of implementation tied to local economy, development, culture and ownership rights intensified the problem between local family entrepreneurs/landowners and conservationists in the 1980s (Psarikidou 2006, 2008b). These conflicts increased even more in 1990 with the establishment of an urban control zone for nature protection, the precursor to the National Marine Park of Zakynthos, by YPEHODE. The implementation of the 1992 EU Habitats Directive created new reasons for tensions between environmental NGOs and state agencies at the national level, under the EU's economic and political shadow.

As late as 1998, EC Habitats Directive 92/43 was transposed into Greek law, providing a strong base for environmental protection of the species. Following pressure from Greek NGOs and recommendations by the Council of Europe, NMPZ was established in 1999. Similar legislature has not been in effect for other nesting areas. NMPZ's Management Authority, the first in Greece, started operating in 1999 – thirteen years after its creation via presidential decree, most likely under the threat of EU sanctions (Andreou 2004: 5). In 2001 the European Court of Justice indicted Greece for not adhering to the directive and in 2002 it ruled that Greece had failed to fulfil its EC obligations (case c-103/00). The crucial role of the state is visible in the failure to fund NMPZ in 2004, which led to the creation of serious problems in Laganas Bay (Haila et al. 2007).

For the important *Caretta caretta* nesting sites in Crete, controversy comparable to that in Zakynthos has not developed, even though since 1994 a variety of smaller-scale local actions and protests have been carried out mostly in Chania, and less often in Rethymno (Kousis, Petropoulou and Dimopoulou 2001). More recently, local community and international groups have identified a tentative plan to construct a huge transit harbour in the Bay of Messara as a new potential threat to the loggerhead turtle population in Crete (Ecological Intervention of Heraklion, 2006a).

Three professional environmental NGOs stand out as promoters of *Caretta caretta* protection in Greece: Archelon, WWF-Greece and Medasset. All three are partners of the United Nations Environment Programme/ Mediterranean Action Plan (UNEP/MAP) and collaborate with Mediterranean-based groups in order to promote an effective plan for the protection of the endangered sea turtle. Archelon, the Sea Turtle Protection Society (STPS) of Greece, was founded in 1983 with the aim of studying and protecting the endangered species. Through various projects (some co-funded by the European Commission), it has carried out scientific work on all potential nesting beaches in Greece (hosting the largest nesting population of loggerhead turtles in the Mediterranean). Besides being a partner of UNEP/MAP, it is a member of the European Union for the Conservation of the Coasts (EUCC). Members of Archelon participate in the Marine Turtle Specialist Group of the International Union for Conservation of Nature (IUCN) and contribute to the formulation of the international strategy for the conservation of sea turtles (Archelon 2008).

The World Wildlife Fund started its collaborations with IUCN and UNEP in the 1980s. In 1998, it published recommendations for a new approach to conserving the Mediterranean's turtles through a number of urgent measures to reduce mortality of adult and sub-adult turtles. In 1994, WWF-Greece purchased 32.7 ha of land surrounding Sekania Beach (site of 500–1,000 nests, one of the highest recorded nesting densities for this species worldwide) as part of the ACNAT EU/WWF-Greece Integrated Ionian Project (Panda 2008).[5]

The Mediterranean Association to Save the Sea Turtles (Medasset) was founded in 1988, aiming to work for the conservation of sea turtles and their habitats throughout the Mediterranean. Since 1988 the organization has been a partner to UNEP/MAP and a permanent observer-member of the standing committee of the Convention on the Conservation of European Wildlife and Natural Habitats (Bern Convention). It presents annual assessments of major nesting areas, such as Akyatan, Dalyan, Kazanli, Patara and Samandag in Turkey, Akamas in Cyprus and Zakynthos and Kefalonia in Greece, to the standing committee of the Bern Convention at the Council of Europe. Medasset has also operated a research programme in Lebanon, investigating the nesting activity on the beaches of El Mansouri (Medasset 2006a).

Community based environmental NGOs and citizens' environmental initiatives in the islands of Zakynthos and Crete have also been directly involved in the protection of the species. The Citizens' Initiative of Zakynthos (CIZ)[6] and the Ecological Initiative of Chania (EIC) constitute two of the most powerful local environmental NGOs. Greenpeace and the Ornithological Association, as well as other local environmental activist groups, have not been as directly involved in the *Caretta caretta* conservation efforts, compared to those mentioned above.

Table 6.1 depicts the Sources, Offences and Impacts linked to *Caretta caretta* protection efforts. Using content analysis techniques related to those applied in studies of environmental activism (see Kousis 1999), threats to *Caretta caretta* were coded for Table 6.1 as they appear on websites, in interviews and in other related sources. They were sorted into sources (or ecosystem disruptive activities), offences and impacts threatening the survival of *Caretta caretta.* Ten major sources or activities of ecosystem use or intervention are shown, as identified by the activists. They include tourism expansion and construction activities, as well as the existence of obstacles such as lights, beach furniture, coastal traffic, marine traffic, waste and fishing activities. As given in Table 6.1, specific sources or their combinations can lead to one or more diverse eco-disturbing offences, which in turn produce a variety of subsequent impacts on the species' survival. A summary of the repertoire of sources, offences and impacts is presented in the table below – where the categories in each column do not necessarily correspond to the categories of the same-number, in the other two columns.

The sources create coastal, sea and noise pollution, beach shrinkage, disorientation of the turtles, sand erosion and compaction, and the disorganization of the local ecosystem. The offences in turn negatively impact the ecosystem, the nesting beaches and nests themselves, the health of the turtles (e.g. poisoning) and the population of the species.

The environmental activist discourse that developed over the past few decades reflects the aims and practices of the involved professional organizations and community-associated groups. With an overall aim to protect the endangered species and the ecosystem, activist discourse specifically centres on: (a) protection against sea turtle population reduction, (b) protection of nests from human threat, pollution and erosion, (c) limitation of hatchling mortality, (d) preservation of the area and habitat restoration and (e) restoration of coastal ecosystems. The key contributions of this discourse are: scientific and sustainable management practices, and resource

Table 6.1. Sources, Offences and Impacts related to the *Caretta caretta* Case, According to Environmental Activist Claims

Source of the problem	Eco-disturbing offences linked to sources	Impacts on sea turtle survival due to offences
1. Tourism expansion and its development	1. dramatic beach shrinking	1. decrease in nesting beaches
2. Construction of	2. coastal pollution	2. decrease in number of nests
a. buildings (hotels, taverns, bars)	3. sand compactness and erosion	3. adverse impact on the incubation of the nests and the bearing
b. new accessible roads		
3. Lights shining on the beaches	4. decrease in sand temperature	4. poisoning due to waste in the sea (e.g. plastics)
4. Beach Objects/Ostacles (umbrellas, sea mattresses)	5. noise pollution	5. death by speed boats or fishing
5. Human presence on the beaches and subsequently:	6. coastal & marine pollution	
a. heavily used beach paths	7. difficulties in accessing the back of the beach	6. injuries by fishermen, fishing or speed boats
b. sand castles and vehicle tracks	8. 'light pollution' causing dis-orientation of both females and hatchling sea turtles	7. drowning due to by-catch in fishing gear
c. planting of shade trees		
6. Vehicular traffic in Coastal Areas		8. decrease in sea turtle population
7. Fishing	9. disturbances	
a. fishing methods (nets, inappropriate tools)	a. of the balance of gases	9. destruction of biodiversity
b. products (turtle-meat, turtle- accessories)	b. on their absorption by the eggs	10. threat to endangered species
8. Marine Traffic	10. disorganisation of the ecosystem	
a. fishing boats		
b. speed boats		
10. Waste:		
a. coastal		
b. marine		
(e.g. petrol, chemical substances, plastic bags)		

Source: The data used in Tables 6.1, 6.2, 6.3, and 6.4 derive from the EC, DGXII funded project Participatory Governance and Institutional Innovation (PAGANINI, Contract No. CIT2-CT-2004-505791).[7]

building and action organizing. The sections to follow offer a detailed account based on the experience from Zakynthos and Crete.

Scientific and Sustainable Management Contributions

Since the 1980s, Archelon and WWF-Greece have been the two professional environmental organizations actively engaged in addressing scientific objectives related to the protection of *Caretta caretta* in the islands of Zakynthos and Crete. With an ultimate aim of securing the conservation and protection of the species, they have made significant efforts to enhance and diffuse relevant scientific knowledge. In doing so, from the 1980s to the present, they proceeded to an array of scientific practices and organized scientific meetings for the dissemination and exchange of knowledge and strategies. These environmental NGOs have been key actors in carrying out relevant research activities – such as monitoring and mapping of nesting areas, monitoring and tagging of the species movements – as well as establishing rescue centres for injured turtles. In securing the long-term protection and monitoring of the turtles, they also engaged in activities related to the safeguarding of the protected areas as well as to the construction of permanent and seasonal stations within and outside those zones.

Archelon's monitoring activities for more than two decades, point to the central and critical role it plays at the national level in the scientific work concerning *Caretta caretta*. The first systematic recording of *Caretta caretta* nests was initiated in 1977 by Dimitrios Margaritoulis, a scientist who came to Zakynthos on holiday and a few years later co-founded Archelon. He 'discovered the first turtle nesting areas on Zakynthos and turned to American expertise, to the Hellenic Society for the Protection of Nature as well as to the National Ministry's Council for Environment, Urban Planning and Public Works for help' (Interview 8-4; Warren and Antonopoulou 1990: 19). A nationwide survey during the 1980s identified the areas of densest nesting and led to the establishment of permanent monitoring and nest conservation projects in the six most important areas. These are located on the island of Zakynthos, on Kiparissia and Lakonikos in the Peloponnese, and on the beaches of Rethymno, Chania and Messara on the island of Crete (Irvine, Margaritoulis and Arapis 1999: 49). Thus, Archelon has been the basic surveyor of *Caretta caretta* in Zakynthos, and since 1984 of the rest of the turtle's nesting areas in Greece. This is usually carried out through research projects that include tagging the nesting females at the nesting areas, or assignments.

Scientists participate in NGOs either as staff or as external collaborators. Recognizing their contribution, the Greek government included them in the

Natura 2000 Committee. With a 25-year presence on the island, Archelon was assigned the responsibility of the annual surveys by the Management Agency of the NMPZ. Archelon has also been the most active professional organization in terms of monitoring nesting areas in Crete, where the first monitoring programme was implemented in 1993, in Rethymno. In addition, a public awareness programme was initiated with slide shows in major hotels, a portable kiosk and the use of the local tourist office as an information outlet. The scientific contribution of Archelon extends beyond monitoring activities and is marked by its collaborations with the global scientific community. This is illustrated in its leading initiative to organize and host the 26th International Mediterranean Sea Turtle Symposium, held in Crete, in April 2006 (Margaritoulis 2006).

The wider scientific community also aids in the diffusion of scientific knowledge to the wider public. They offer seminars, such as one on Protection of Sea Turtles held at the European Parliament in Brussels in November 2004. They also maintain close collaboration with local groups, like the Citizens' Initiative of Zakynthos, and members of the local scientific community (e.g. the Technological Institute of Ecology in Zakynthos), as well as with members of the national scientific community. Such links also include collaborative work with Dr Ioannis Pantis, professor of biology at the Aristotelian University of Thessaloniki and former president of the NMPZ Management Agency (MA) (Interview 12-4).

Sustainable management aims and practices are characteristic of a number of environmental organizations and groups in Zakynthos and Crete from the 1980s to the present, as seen in Table 6.2. On the basis of the data analysed, Archelon, WWF-Greece and Medasset are directly involved in sustainable management practices, while Greenpeace and the Ornithological Association are involved indirectly.

Archelon has collaborated with various ministries concerning sustainable management practices on *Caretta caretta* protection. These include collaborations with YPEHODE concerning ecosystems, the Ministry of Rural Development and Food regarding wildlife and endangered species protection, the Department of Fisheries on matters concerning fishing rights, the Ministry of Mercantile Marine on sea turtle rescues and the National Tourism Organisation (EOT) on tourism development at the local level (Interview 8-4). YPEHODE assigns managerial responsibility to the NMPZ MA, which in turn comes to an agreement with Archelon concerning the operation of the annual surveys; meanwhile, the Ministry of Rural Development and Food grants permission for the surveys. At the end of each nesting season Archelon sends reports of the scientific results to the MA and YPEHODE. The data are used as needed, especially in planning for the next nesting season (Interview 18-4).

Although Archelon has full responsibility of monitoring the NMPZ zone, it maintains close collaboration with WWF-Greece, one of the participants of the NMPZ MA, which assists in the implementation of the protective measures and the transfer of technical knowledge. WWF-Greece support of the promotion and the effective implementation of Archelon's awareness programme has been significant (Dimopoulos 1991). WWF-Greece's purchase of the Sekania nesting area was met with suspicion in a few popular newspapers, leading to a 'terrorist' attack (Fotiou 1998). Amongst WWF-Greece's scientifically informed products is a management plan (compiled in January 2001) specifically for the region of Sekania in Laganas Bay that adopts a holistic approach, considering climate and erosion conditions in the area of the National Marine Park of Zakynthos (Interview 4-4).

Confrontations with state officials however, did take place. For example, the WWF-Greece conservation manager has accused the minister of YPEHODE several times of failing to adopt a specific managerial and financial framework (Hadoulis 2005). Although local economic interests are at times resistant to WWF-Greece actions, the ENGO tries to maintain a cooperative relationship with many local actors, supporting complaints such as those concerning the existence of two-metre concrete columns in the coastal zone of Vasilikos (WWF-Greece 2005), or the construction of a large tourist-holiday village within the NMPZ (Euroturtle 2004).

Moving beyond national borders, Archelon is in close contact with EU agencies, as reflected in their financial support from LIFE Projects, which co-finances and directs one area of their activities. An example of a LIFE project concerns the establishment of a new Management Plan in Crete (1995–1997) aiming to ensure the viability of the beaches as nesting sites. The plan aimed to address the threats sea turtles were facing in the area, using techniques that can secure their coexistence with human activities. Its implementation included monitoring, nest protection through caging, relocating hatcheries and shading in order to prevent hatchling disorientation. Metal cages are located on top of the nests in order to protect them from accidental destruction by beach users. Nest shades are installed to prevent the disorientation of the turtles. There are also signs in three languages informing people about the aim of the project. This management plan, which proved successful, was designed to be implemented and enforced at very low cost, balancing the conservation needs for the sea turtles with the local need for sustainable tourist development (Archelon 2004a). Archelon also contributed to the establishment of the Sea Turtle Rescue Centre in Glyfada in June 1995, as well as that of a New Sea Turtle Rescue and Public Awareness Centre in July 2005 at Pagalochori (Rethymno, Crete), with the assistance of local municipalities. One of Archelon's stable sources of funding remains the sensitized public.

Table 6.2. Sustainable Management Aims and Practices Concerning *Caretta caretta* in Zakynthos and Crete and Environmental Activists/Bodies (1980s–2007)

Environmental Activists/Bodies	Sustainable Development Aims	Policies & Practices
Archelon WWF-Greece Medasset CIZ EIC Greenpeace Ornithologiki EGCR Orrinoterra NMPZ MA	1. Implementation of a specified model of sustainable development 2. Strategy for the conservation of sea turtles 3. Development and implementation of management plans 4. Upgrading of existing rehabitation facilities 5. Protection from extensive expansion of construction 6. Environmental Law abidance 7. Raising public awareness through educational programmes on sea turtles biology and human activities.	*Sustainable Physical Planning* 1. Creation of new and more extensive green zones 2. Purchase of new fields around the protected areas 3. Construction of small boardwalks to reduce sand erosion 4. Pilot sand dune restoration projects 5. Installation of nest shades to prevent disorientation 6. Assignment of blue flags 7. Participation in management agencies of protected areas 8. Appointment of scientists and researchers in related committees 9. Identification of the abuse of laws 10. Organisation of public awareness campaigns and educational programmes (for tourists, local entrepreneurs, local community and schoolchildren) *Implementation of Laws* 1. Multi-level activities to further the implementation of existing legislature 2. Seeking help from the EC to implement protective measures

Source: PAGANINI, as in Table 6.1 (based on related Internet sites and interviews)

In addition to its information related campaigns, one of Medasset's main objectives has been its collaboration with local fishermen on the one hand, and UNEP/MAP on the other (Venizelos and Corbett 2005). This is reflected in its educational efforts, including the publication of a Greek version of the Fishermen's Guide that was co-produced and funded by the Regional Activity Centre for Specially Protected Areas (RAC/SPA, UNEP/ MAP). The Greek Ministry of Rural Development and Food has also contributed to the expansion of this initiative. The guide contains simple, practical, illustrated advice enabling fishermen to deal with healthy, injured or dead sea turtles accidentally caught while fishing. Medasset is sympathetic to the fishermen's livelihood interests and criticizes the Greek government for its reluctance to provide compensation measures (Interview 11-4).

In addition to the professional organizations, two local environmental groups are also directly involved in sustainability practices concerning the sea turtle: the Citizens' Initiative of Zakynthos (CIZ) and the Ecological Initiative of Chania (EIC). A CIZ representative has actively supported sustainable management of the area, mainly through the media. CIZ criticized the Greek government for its reluctance to proceed to the implementation of protective measures:

> [T]he employees of the National Park, including the guards, are on strike, because they have not received their salaries from YPEHODE since June of 2004. NMPZ is funded by YPEHODE and co-funded by the 'LIFE Nature' project, which is currently frozen because the government is withholding its share of funds that make it operational. This situation makes things easier for all those who would like to make a profit from the lack of protective measures and leads to the consequent reign of chaos on the beaches. (Lalotis 2005)

CIZ emphasizes the central role of local authorities (e.g. municipalities, prefectures, port and police authorities) in achieving a successful implementation of the protective measures:

> The local community was negative towards national conservation policy given their vested interests in the area. The local authorities were obliged to follow because of their political power dependence on the electoral body. ... For this reason, I have turned to local authorities several times. ... I am also defending my environmental interests through press releases and my own radio programme at a local station. In general, our role is focused on criticism and accusations against every actor who adopts a negative attitude towards conservation strategies. On the other hand, we are trying to be in contact with all the environmentally sensitized members and bodies in our local community. (Interview 2-4)

With the support of YPEHODE in 2004, the EIC organized a project based on the clean-up of beaches in cooperation with NGOs such as the Italian NGO Legambiente, Mesogeios SOS (MEDSOS) and Archelon.

Environmental groups that are indirectly involved in sustainable practices related to *Caretta caretta* in Zakynthos and Crete include the *ecocrete* network and others. In contrast to Zakynthos, local interest groups, such as tourism family-entrepreneurs in Messara, are demanding the implementation of the Habitats Directive in order to avoid environmental deterioration caused by the possible construction of a mega transit harbour by foreign investors. Interestingly, thus far, locals do not appear to be as strongly supported by national professional NGOs as they are by regional and Northern European ones. Regional environmental groups have also recommended biological treatment facilities for the northern coast of Chania, given tourism activities, in order to avoid the negative impacts of waste on the local ecosystem (MEDSOS 2005).

Local environmental groups have strongly criticized Greek laws leading to the uncontrolled exploitation of coastal areas by hotel owners, tour operators, fishermen, industries, individual citizens and others, pointing out impacts on the local population and the endangered species conservation at the area (Ecological Initiative of Chania 2001). The Mountaineering Club of Rethymno, a Cretan environmental group, is seeking the implementation of EU's protective legislation:

> We have already sent the appropriate documents to the Prefecture, the Port Police, the Municipality, asking for the implementation of protective measures. They should seriously take into consideration that the specific area is protected by EU legislation... (Rethymniotika Nea 2005)

European agencies such as the European Parliament and European Courts, as well as EU legislation, in this case the Habitats Directive, have been referred to and regarded as strong potential allies by the concerned local groups. In this context, Ecological Intervention of Heraklion announced that:

> From a legal view, experts should immediately make a record of all legal infringements concerning the conservation of natural resources as well as those related to the environmental sustainability of large industrial projects within the European Union. (Ecological Intervention of Heraklion 2006a)

Scientists are expected to play an important role through their studies (Archelon 2004b), by providing the wider community with the knowledge needed to make informed decisions:

> The danger of an area-wide ecological catastrophe is obvious. Not only will the sea turtles *Caretta caretta* and their adjacent to the site nests be influ-

enced, but so will be many other flora and fauna in danger of extinction. At last, local and international biologists and environmentalists have begun to evaluate the expected size of the impacts and dangers which this huge investment will bring... (Ecological Intervention of Heraklion 2006b)

Resource Building and Action Organizing

The protection of *Caretta caretta* in Zakynthos and Crete has depended on the actions and resources of nine environmental organizations and groups from the 1980s to the present. They have sustained their efforts through resource building and action organizing. Table 6.3 and the presentation that follows reflect their related aims and practices.

Table 6.3. Environmental Activist Resource Building and Action Organizing Aims and Practices Concerning *Caretta caretta* in Zakynthos and Crete (1980s–2007)

Environmental Activists/Bodies	Aims	Policies/practices
	Sustaining Ties with Involved Groups to: 1. strengthen networks 2. increase public awareness (both local & tourist)	*Resource-Building* 1. campaigning for funding 2. attracting volunteers across the globe 3. collaborating with
ARCHELON WWF-GR MEDASSET CIZ EIC Greenpeace Ornithologiki EGCR Orrinoterra NMPZ MA	3. seek support from the public, tour operators, fishermen & local authorities 4. consider local needs (i.e. balance the needs of the species with those of the community)	• local authorities (municipalities, prefectures & port) • tourism entrepreneurs and tour operators • fishermen • media agencies • other NGOs
	Organizing Public Campaigns to: 1. pressure groups who oppose conservation measures 2. educate and promote environmental values (both local & tourist)	*Action-Organizing* 1. long-standing repertoire of mostly appeal and demonstrative actions* against government inaction for the establishment of park and species protection 2. special attention to environmental education actions

Source: PAGANINI, as in Table 6.1 (based on related Internet sites and interviews)
*Appeal and Demonstrative actions refer to softer actions forms such as complaints to authority, press conference, the collection of signatures, or demonstrations (Kousis, 1999).

A cooperative relationship between the most active environmental NGOs involved in *Caretta caretta* protection and the local community has been one of the goals that was earlier met with resistance but has been established in the later period (Theodossopoulos 2003).

Directly Involved Science-oriented Activists

As one of the major activist organizations, Archelon applies its scientific knowledge production to increase awareness through educational programmes. Educational material is publicized, public awareness campaigns are organized and seminars are offered to the public. For example, during 1988–1989, great progress was recorded thanks to its Awareness Programme, carried out through the information station at West Laganas. Archelon has been active in organizing public awareness campaigns for tourists, local people and local stakeholders, especially tour professionals and fishermen. Of vital importance for Archelon's sustainability are its volunteers, who number about 500 persons per year. Most of them are non-Greek university students from Northern countries; only 10–15 per cent are of Greek origin (Interview 6-4).

These programmes have been located and carried out at the entrances to the protected nesting beaches as well as at the West Laganas information station. Several educational projects, including educational materials directed at schoolchildren, teachers and the local community, slide/film shows at hotels (at least two per week) and informative signs, were set up by the prefecture, the Port Police Substation, the 'look-out stand', the natural hatchery and, more importantly, the STPS team. In 1994, STPS established contact with a student ecological group from the University of Crete at Rethymno, resulting in the organization of a new public awareness and beach clean-up programme. Cooperation with local managers, such as the manager of Rithymna Beach Hotel also proved positive (Ligdopoulou, Zohrer and Newbury 1994). EEC and WWF-Greece's cooperation and support for the programme's successful promotion has been noted by Archelon (Dimopoulos 1991).

In an attempt to increase tourist awareness, Archelon has cooperated with international tour operators and hotels such as Grecotel and Zante Park. Tourist entrepreneurs and STPS have been co-organizing presentations and animation programmes once per week (Interview 13-4). Public awareness programmes – including slide shows – have also been initiated in major hotels, and important information outlets have been established through the use of a portable kiosk and the tourist office. These pilot programmes are viewed by Grecotel as 'necessary for the harmonic symbiosis between turtles and tourists' (Interview 5-4).

Archelon also tries to communicate and collaborate with fishermen, whose economic viability is threatened by protection measures. According to an Archelon representative:

> Appropriate compensation and tax-free nets could offer a solution to the fishermen's case – thus, fishermen will also try to continue their activities in a sustainable manner and to avoid intense fishing techniques. (Interview 6-4)

A close collaboration has begun between Archelon and fishermen, aiming at the reduction of the mortality of adult turtles, as described by one fisherman:

> In the beginning, Mr. Margaritoulis and I formed a common struggle, aiming at the protection of different species living in the marine environment. We had both turned to the Minister of Environment, asking for intervention. ... There have been several times when I contacted the people in charge, to report injured turtles. (Interview 21-4)

In Crete, local authorities have also proved to be quite helpful, offering their support to the major activists, i.e. the STPS and the EIC. Although three regions in Crete have been proposed as sites of public awareness stations (Rethymno, Chania and Messara), local authorities appear reluctant to undertake the related responsibilities (Interview 6-4), fearing pressure from tourism entrepreneurs.

Municipalities differ in the ways they collaborate with environmental groups. In Crete, Archelon maintains contact with local NGOs such as the EIC, the Ecological Group of Sitia and the EGCR. They have also been in contact with Chania's Local Branch of primary and secondary schools, responsible for environmental education in the region. Archelon's environmental education activities include daily visits by schoolchildren to the Rescue Centre (almost 10,000 students visit the centre annually) (Medasset 2006a; Archelon 2008). The Prefecture of Zakynthos and the Municipality of Laganas have worked closely with Archelon, organizing public awareness programmes for students and creating the Awareness Station of Lithakia (Interview 19-4). The municipality has offered some accommodations (chemical toilets) and space as a way of supporting the volunteers' stay on the island (Interviews 18-4; 14-4).

Collaborations with the media are a necessary part of NGO activities and have been significant in publicizing Archelon's goals and aims. Signatures, lobbying and public protest emails have been widely used actions in the *Caretta caretta* case; e.g. those by WWF-Greece, the European Nature

Heritage Fund (Euronatur) and Medasset. Increasingly strong collaboration efforts between NGOs are noted, such as that of June 2006 (Medasset 2006b), expressed through the following letter of complaint to the European Commissioner:

> We urge the European Commission to seriously consider the present alarming situation in Zakynthos and to spare no effort in pressing the responsible Greek authorities to implement the ruling of the European Court of Justice and EC Directives to guarantee the ecological integrity of Daphne and the future of NMPZ. Our organisations will continue to act and lobby to protect this significant nesting beach and to ensure that international and national environmental legal framework is not undermined. (Archelon, Medasset and WWF-Greece 2007)

As an outgrowth of its public awareness campaign in Crete, in 1994 Archelon established contact with a newly formed student ecological group from the University of Crete at Rethymno and collaborated on public awareness and beach clean-up programmes. At the same time, it initiated contacts with local tourist accommodation managers, such as those at Rithymna Beach Hotel (Ligdopoulou, Zohrer and Newbury 1994).

WWF-Greece has taken an active part in raising public awareness about the endangered species across national borders, organizing protest campaigns against Greek government agencies through collection of signatures and emails, which in certain cases have reached the high number of 20,000 (Ecocrete 2006). For WWF-Greece, the mass media, especially local outlets, are of great importance for reaching out and maintaining contact with the local people. The organization has worked with several local and also national papers in order to inform the public and raise awareness (Interview 4-4); other types of media collaboration include the production of a radio programme at a local radio station (Interview 2-4). WWF-Greece has also participated in programmes organized by state and other agencies, such as those by the Hellenic Marine Environment Protection Association (HELMEPA), in collaboration with the Ministry of Education, the University of the Aegean, the EU, NMPZ and the Lithakia environmental education centre (HELMEPA, 2004). Many of WWF-Greece's actions take the form of educational projects carried out for school and public audiences. Its staff cooperates with the local fishermen, local police and Zakynthian groups (Interview 4-4).

Several ENGOs, including Archelon, Medasset and Euroturtle, have collaborated in organising a series of campaigns aiming at engaging local citizens via signature collection (Ecocrete 2006). Medasset has participated in a wide range of campaigns, complaints and ENGO reports, including the one sent to the EC that finally led to the European Court of Justice (ECJ) judgement of 31 January 2002. Medasset has also been actively involved in actions such as collection of signatures, press releases and public protest e-mails (Medasset 2004a; Medasset 2004b; WWF-Greece 2004). For example, in April 2005 the German environmental organization Euronatur and Medasset delivered a joint 17,000-signature petition and a letter to the Greek prime minister, expressing intense international and national concern, not only for the future of the NMPZ, but also for the rest of the twenty-six EC 'Natura 2000' designated protected areas in Greece. Yet, as pointed out by a Medasset representative, environmental organizations are not always able to form coalitions, possibly due to partial dependence on governmental and EU funding:

> Just very recently, some professional and EU funded NGOs realized the significance of a cooperation between them. Sometimes, they act as if given the monopoly of a specific protected area. (Interview 11-4)

Thus, although Medasset is not engaged in scientific surveys, it has a complementary role in organizing public awareness campaigns and educational projects with the collaboration of such members of the European scientific community as Max Kasparek, Ian Bright and Roger Holland (Interview 11-4). For example, in 2005 Medasset provided educational materials to 80 teachers and group leaders and 800 students from different parts of Greece. In early November 2005, it published an Environmental Education Kit for 6–12-year-old children, *The Mediterranean Sea: A Source of Life*, aiming to educate schoolchildren across the Mediterranean. The Hellenic Children's Museum and Kaleidoscope Publications, the Stavros S. Niarchos Foundation, the United Nations Environment Programme Mediterranean Action Plan (UNEP/MAP), the Regional Activities Centre for Specially Protected Areas (RAC/SPA) and the Prince of Wales Charitable Foundation have significantly contributed to this effort (Medasset 2005).

Local NGO and citizen group initiatives centre upon dissemination activities, which aim at informing Greek government agencies and local authorities through press releases, widespread publications, mass media reports, lobbying and participation in seminars. The CIZ maintains a key role in *Caretta caretta* conservation strategies through media dissemination, participation in EU and state programs as well as through protest campaigns against national and local governmental bodies. National NGO support plays a decisive role in their practices.

The EIC expressed their opposition towards the possible 'entitlement of some areas and beaches as private' (Ecological Initiative of Chania 2005). In this context, in December 2005 they issued a press release announcing:

'We, the local community representatives in Chania, demand the establishment of a national marine park at our NATURA coastal region, aiming at the wider environmental protection of local flora and fauna' (EIC 2005). They have also proceeded with specific accusations against the Minister of Mercantile Marine concerning tentative plans to transform part of the coastal zone of the Bay of Messara into a mega transit port for Chinese products.

The EIC publishes *Fourogatos,* an ecological newspaper focused on raising environmental consciousness by providing news and environmental education items on a variety of local and nonlocal environmental issues, including *Caretta caretta.* In an attempt to increase environmental education at the regional level, they have collaborated with the Environmental Group of Citizens in Rethymno and with an NGO in Athens, organizing a project on 'Volunteerism and Environment'. The latter included two seminars to educate volunteers, visits to the specific beaches and recognition of their specific problems (Ecological Initiative of Chania 2004a). They have also organized projects such as beach-cleaning, in collaboration with the Italian NGO Legambiente, Mesogeios SOS (MEDSOS), Archelon and YPEHODE.

In addition, EIC members keep a close and cooperative relation with the environmental educational departments in schools, in an attempt to attract volunteers from all social groups, especially primary school students. The Primary Education Office in the Prefecture of Chania, for example, played a decisive role in the resolution of environmental issues (Ecological Initiative of Chania 2004b). The EIC have also sought support from the Ministry of National Education and Religious Affairs.

Indirectly Involved Science-oriented and Community Activists

Greenpeace campaigns focus on marine pollution and criticize state agencies' failures to take appropriate measures (Greenpeace 2004). They also focus on the destructive impact of nets on marine flora and fauna. The Ornithological Association also shares in *Caretta caretta* concerns through a limited number of press releases focused on environmental and ecosystem preservation issues (e.g. Archelon et al. 2005). In a 2004 press release, for example, they exposed the non-implementation of protective measures ordered for the NMPZ (Elliniki Ornithologiki Etaireia 2004).

In Zakynthos, a variety of local associations, unions, groups and communities are indirectly involved in the environmental preservation efforts concerning *Caretta caretta.* These include the First Order of Sea-Scouts, the Association of Christian Youth (XEN), the Biological Beekeepers, the Cinema Society, the Rental Rooms Union, the Platyforos Association for Cultural Research and Development as well as others (Archelon 2005). Among them, the Zakynthian Association of Architects has expressed concerns, mostly focused on the aesthetic and recreational conditions of the regions included in the Marine Park territory (Interview 14-4). The unions of architects, engineers and teachers are also involved at the local level, in addition to groups and associations such as Dionysios Solomos, the Vougiateon in Athens, Artemis-Opitais and the Greek Drivers' Association in the region of Zakynthos who have provided their support (Archelon 2005).

As we have already seen in Tables 6.2 and 6.3, local environmental groups in Crete involve community based activists linked with the Cretan environmental NGO network (Archelon 2004b); they include The 'Environmental Group of Citizens in Rethymno', the 'Ecological Intervention of Heraklion', the 'Association for the Environmental Protection of Kokkinos Pyrgos' and the 'Ecological Intervention of Makris Gialos Mountainous Municipality' ('Oreinotera').

Local environmental groups and local community groups that support the conservation of Messara's ecosystems and the protection of Natura 2000 sites have expressed particular concern about the Memorandum of Collaboration for investment in the development, management and operation of a mega–transit harbour in the Bay of Messara, which was agreed between the Ministry of Mercantile Marine of Greece and the Ministry of Marine Affairs and Fishing of the Republic of Korea (Ecocrete 2006). In November 2005, the Independent Engineers of Eastern Crete (AMAK) warned Messara's communities that top-down plans for an international-markets oriented south port, which was rejected by the Ierapetra municipality's local groups,[8] will seriously threaten the wider area, including the protected sites of *Caretta caretta*'s nesting activities (AMAK 2005). Local, national and international press coverage (notably in the *Frankfurter Allgemeine Zeitung*) as well as Internet sites and blogs present the latest coverage, with frequent references to the Natura 2000 sites. Tourists from various parts of the world (e.g. Italy, Germany) voice their support for efforts to protect the local ecosystem to local tourism entrepreneurs, local authorities and local residents. Retired sailors with decades of first-hand knowledge of what such transit stations would mean for the local area, express their opposition. In general, ENGOs (e.g. WWF-Greece, Euronatur, Medasset) are key actors in the conflicts and collaborators with state agencies in actions such as collecting signatures and protest email campaigns.

The latest English version of the petitions circulating in the Internet[9] shows 7,270 signatures from citizens across the globe. The *Frankfurter Allgemeine Zeitung* reported that Euronatur[10] sent a letter of concern about the impacts on the local ecosystems and *Caretta caretta* to the Greek Ministries of Mercantile Marine, Tourism and YPEHODE. In December

2006, local groups, including tourism entrepreneurs, established a citizens' initiative (The Movement of the Citizen of Messara for the Environment 2010) aiming to protect the local environment and economy from the mega transit port project. They also considered approaching UNESCO and the European Court of Justice in search of assistance for their cause (Ecological Intervention of Heraklion 2006b). Alliances between local authorities, national and local NGOs, EU agencies, Greek government and related ministries, together with major tourism actors, play a central role in promoting sustainable tourism projects via the protection of *Caretta caretta* (Archelon 2004b). The current economic crisis is considered an immense challenge for the conservation of *Caretta caretta* nesting beaches for the island of Crete (Ertel 2010).

Conclusion

Governing biodiversity in the case of *Caretta caretta* and the Habitats Directive in Greece reflects the critical importance of science-oriented environmental activism and EU environmental policies in an enduring, multifaceted and intense conflict addressed through the collaborative efforts between professional ENGOs, an international supportive network and community based activists. This chapter offers evidence sustaining recent works concerning the changing role of public participation in the EU multi-level governance, as seen through the implementation of the Habitats Directive (Haila et al, 2007). It also follows previous work pointing to the economic opportunities offered to ENGOs in the context of sustainable development policies (Kousis 2004).

Supporting studies emphasizing the importance of scientific activism (e.g. Frickel 2004) our evidence offers a detailed account of the role played by a variety of science oriented environmental activists (Jamison 2006). Archelon and WWF-Greece, are the two professional NGOs dominating with their expertise, the monitoring, management and scientific contributions in protecting *Caretta caretta*. This science oriented environmental activism, adhering to sustainable development policies, led to biodiversity protection initiatives involving, (a) scientific monitoring and collaboration, (b) sustainable management and (c) resource building and action organizing.

Our evidence however also points to the significance of community based environmental activists (Kousis et al 2008). As in other Mediterranean societies, community based activists are vital to the successful conservation of their natural resources. They have done so in a more confrontational way – given local economic interests – but have also sustained efforts with minimal or nonexistent economic resources. Along with the professional community activists address and act on concerns related to sustainable development, law-based sustainability, local community cooperation efforts and consideration of local needs. Both types of activists, albeit in different ways, promote sustainable physical planning, the implementation of environmental legislation, resource mobilization and support building as well as educational and action-oriented practices.

Cooperation in these dimensions is essential and needs to be strengthened across Mediterranean coastal regions in order to slow down or inhibit the rapid degradation of local and regional ecosystems. Other coastal Mediterranean regions undergoing tourism development, that threatens the local ecosystem, could benefit from the experience presented in the chapter. As the case of *Caretta caretta* has shown, the endangered migratory species moves in boundless ways in order to secure its survival. Simultaneously, it depends on the quality of not only local ecosystems, but regional and global ones as well. This is reflected in the scientific, managerial and action-oriented practices of the involved activists, especially the professional organizations, which reach beyond national borders in order to improve their understanding and organizational efforts, and to address wider biodiversity concerns. The Mediterranean is an ideal case study for scholars working on environmental science-oriented activism and nature-society interactions. Future work needs to address transnational environmental cooperative efforts and salient environmental issues in relation to the precautionary principle and climate change, but simultaneously to the challenges of the recent economic and environmental crises.

NOTES

1. An earlier version of this chapter was presented at the international conference People and the Sea IV, 5–7 July 2007, at the Centre for Maritime Research, Amsterdam. We thank Nelson Graburn and Andrew Holden for their helpful comments in a subsequent presentation on October 2008 at the International Institute for Culture, Tourism and Development of London Metropolitan University. This chapter draws on research conducted in the context of the PAGANINI project (Participatory Governance and Institutional Innovation, www.paganini-project.net/), (EC, DGXII, CIT2-CT-2004-505791) as well as the EC, Euromed Heritage II project Mediterranean Voices: Oral History and Cultural Practice in Mediterranean Cities, www.medvoices.org/ (grant contract no. E8/AIDCO/2000/2095-05). Maria Kousis was the coordinator of the Greek teams in both projects. Katerina Psarikidou was the main researcher for PAGANINI's Work Package 4 on the Habitats Directive. We are grateful to Yrjö Haila (Work Package Leader) for his collaboration and to Jeremy Boissevain for his constructive comments.

2. Scientists estimate the number of the turtles that finally succeed in becoming adults at about ten from each nest.
3. Dimitris Margaritoulis, a marine turtle researcher and founder of Archelon, has been Regional Chair of IUCN, President of the International Sea Turtle Society and Chair of many scientific committees and events on sea turtles. He was honored by the Academy of Athens for his work.
4. Electoral competitions are excluded under this definition since parties do not challenge the system but work within it.
5. The 600 million drachmas for the land purchase came from this project and funds raised through a three year Pan-European campaign run by WWF-Greece.
6. Formerly the Zakynthian Ecological Movement.
7. Internet Sources used include:
   1. http://www.wwf.gr/caretta.htm
   2. http://www.archelon.gr/eng/biology.htm
   3. http://www.ornithologiki.gr/
   4. http://greenpeace.gr
   5. http://www.medasset.gr
   Interviews used: Interview 19-4, Interview 9-4, Interview 4-4, Interview 6-4, Interview 13-4,   Interview 10-4, Interview 11-4, Interview 5-4, Interview 14-4.
8. Ierapetra is located in the south-eastern part of Crete; see http://www.ierapetra.net/
9. http://www.petitiononline.com/forcrete/petition.html as of 13 February 2011.
10. Founded in 1987 by three German NGOs.

REFERENCES

AMAK. 2005. Independent Engineers of Eastern Crete, Ecocrete Press Release 29.11.05. Retrieved 17 June 2007 from http//www.ecocrete.gr/
Andreou, G. 2004. 'Multilevel Governance: Implementing the Habitats Directive in Greece', Organizing for EU Enlargement phase II, Occasional Paper-4.3-08.04. Athens: National and Capodistrian University of Athens. Retrieved 17 June 2007 from http://www.oeue.net/papers.asp
Archelon. 2004a. 'Biology', Retrieved 17 July 2007 from http://www.ARCHELON.gr/eng/biology.htm
Archelon. 2004b. 'Protection of Nesting activity in Crete, Nest Management'. Retrieved 15 December 2004 from http://www.ArchelonArchelonArchelon.gr/eng/habitat_crete.htm
Archelon. 2005. NMPZ: Zakynthians' Opinion. Press Release 27/08/2004 (in greek) Retrieved 18 December 2005 from http://www.ArchelonArchelon.gr
Archelon. 2008. 'Who we are'. Retrieved 1 February 2008 from http://www.Archelon.gr/eng/wois2.htm
Archelon, Medasset & WWF-Greece. 2006. Letter of Complaint. 25 June 2006. Retrieved 11 December 2006 from www.ecocrete.gr

Archelon, Hellenic Ornithological Society, Hellenic Society for the Protection of Nature, Hellenic Society for the Protection of Environment and Cultural Heritage, Mediterranean SOS Network MoM and WWF Greece. 2005. Report on the Status of the Protected Areas System in Greece. May 2005. *Ecocrete.* 14.06.05. Retrieved 15 December 2005 from www.ecocrete,gr

Boissevain, J. and T. Selwyn (eds). 2004. *Contesting the Foreshore: Tourism, Society, and Politics on the Coast.* Amsterdam: Amsterdam University Press.

Briguglio, L. and M. Briguglio. 1996. 'Sustainable Tourism in the Maltese Islands', in L. Briguglio, R. Butler, D. Harrison and W. Leal Filho (eds), *Sustainable Tourism in Islands and Small States: Case Studies.* London: Pinter, pp. 162–179.

della Porta, D. and M. Andretta. 2000. 'Environmental Movement Organisations and Political Representation in Italy', paper presented at the ECPR annual sessions (Environmental Movements in Comparative Perspective) 14–20 April.

Diani, M. 1995. *Green Networks: A Structural Analysis of the Italian Environmental Movement.* Edinburgh: Edinburgh University Press.

Dimopoulos, D. 1991. 'Zakynthos 1990: An Update on the Public Awareness Programme', *Marine Turtle Newsletter* 54: 21–23.

Ecocrete. 2006. Press Release 020906. Retrieved 11 December 2006 from http://www.ecocrete.gr

Ecological Initiative of Chania. 2001. *Ecocrete* Press Release 19.11.2001. Retrieved 11 December 2004 from www.ecocrete.gr

Ecological Initiative of Chania. 2004a. 'Volunteering Coastal Cleaning', Retrieved March 2 2005 from http://www.ecocrete.gr?index.php?option=com_content&task=view&id=519&Itemid=0

Ecological Initiative of Chania, 2004b. The EIC's actions during 2003, *Ecocrete* Press Release 020304. Retrieved 11 December 2004 from www.ecocrete.gr

Ecological Initiative of Chania. 2005. *Ecocrete* Press Release 02.03.2005. Retrieved 16 December 2006 from www.ecocrete.gr

Ecological Intervention of Heraklion. 2006a. Η σύσκεψη μεταξύ φορέων του Τυμπακίου, της Αγίας Γαλήνης και ξενοδόχων για το λιμάνι στη Μεσσαρά, "Άποψη του Νότου", 04.10.06, Retrieved 16 December 2006 from http://www.ecocrete.gr/index.php?option=com_content&task=view&id=2907&Itemid=0

Ecological Intervention of Heraklion. 2006b. Press Release 031006 Retrieved 16 December 2006 from http://www.ecocrete.gr/index.php?option=com_content&task=view&id=2908&Itemid=0

Eder, K. and M. Kousis (eds). 2001. *Environmental Politics in Southern Europe: Actors, Institutions and Discourses in a Europeanizing Society.* Dordrecht: Kluwer.

Ertel, M. 2010. 'Crete in the Crisis: An Island's Struggle to Save Its Soul' Der Spiegel Online International. August 26. Retrieved on February 13, 2011 from http://www.spiegel.de/international/europe/0,1518,713634,00.html

Euroturtle. 2004. 'Zakynthos National Marine Park Staff: No pay for 8 months', Press Release No 16 15.03.04. Retrieved 10 December 2004 from http://tofino.ex.ac.uk/euroturtle/medas/press_no16.htm

Elliniki Ornithologiki Etaireia. 2004. 'New Threat for the *Caretta caretta*', Press Release 17.05.04. Retrieved 13 December 2004 from http://www.ornothologiki.gr/gr/hos/dt/dt_17_05_04.htm

Figueiredo, E., T. Fidelis and A. da Rosa Pirez. 2000. 'Grassroots Environmental Action in Portugal (1974–1994)', in K. Eder and M. Kousis (eds), *Environmental Politics in Southern Europe: Actors, Institutions and Discourses in a Europeanizing Society.* Dordrecht: Kluwer, pp. 197–223.

Fotiou, A. 1998. 'Local Facets of Environmentalism: Actors, Sustainability and Tourism Policy in Southern Europe', in *International Conference on Environmental Movements, Discourses, and Policies in Southern Europe* (8–10 May 1998). Rethymno: Department of Sociology, University of Crete.

Frickel, S. 2004. 'JUST SCIENCE? Organizing Scientist Activism in the US Environmental Justice Movement', *Science as Culture*, 13 (4): 449–469.

Gil Nave, J. 2001. 'Environmental Politics in Portugal', in K. Eder and M. Kousis (eds), *Environmental Politics in Southern Europe: Actors, Institutions and Discourses in a Europeanizing Society.* Dordrecht: Kluwer, pp. 343–364.

Greenpeace. 2004. 'The Disaster of the Sea Environment, the Unpunishment of the Accountables and the Wrong Moves on Behalf of the Minister of Navigation', Retrieved 14 December 2004 from http://www.greenpeace.gr?shown.asp?id=280

Grenon, M. and M. Batisse (eds). 1989. *Futures for the Mediterranean Basin: The Blue Plan.* Oxford: Oxford University Press.

Guillame, B. and A. Comeau (eds). 2005. *A Sustainable Future for the Mediterranean: The Blue Plan's Environment and Development Outlook.* London: Earthscan.

Gunther, R., P.N. Diamantouros and H-J. Puhle (eds). 1995. *The Politics of Democratic Consolidation: Southern Europe In Comparative Perspective.* Baltimore: The Johns Hopkins University Press.

Hadoulis, J. 2005. 'State Holding Parks Hostage'. *Athens News.* 11 February 2005. Retrieved 5 December 2009 from http://www.athensnews.gr/old_issue/13117/12612?action=print

Haila, Y., M. Kousis, A. Jokinen, N. Nygren and K. Psarikidou. 2007. 'Final Report, Work Package 4. Building Trust through Public Participation: Learning from Conflicts over the Implementation of the Habitats Directive', *Participatory Governance and Institutional Innovation [PAGANINI]* Contract No. CIT2-CT-2004-505791. Retrieved 5 December 2009 from http://www.univie.ac.at/LSG/paganini/finals_pdf/WP4_FinalReport.pdf

HELMEPA. 2004 'Programs'. Retrieved 12 December 2004 from http://dim-lithak.zak.sch.gr?programmata.htm

Huber, M.E., R.A. Duce, J.M. Bewers, D. Insull, L. Jeftic and S. Keckes, on behalf of GESAMP and ACOPS. 2003. 'Priority Problems Facing the Global Marine and Coastal Environment and Recommended Approaches to their Solution', *Ocean and Coastal Management* 46(5): 479–485.

Irvine, C., D. Margaritoulis and T. Arapis. 1999. 'The Role of a Non-governmental Organisation in Sea Turtle Conservation and Management Planning in Greece', in H. Kalb and T. Wibbels (compilers) *Proceedings of the 19th Annual Symposium on Sea Turtle Conservation and Biology (2001)*, U.S. Dept. Commerce. NOAA Tech. Memo. NMFS-SEFSC-443, Miani, Florida, 2003 pp. 49–50.

Jamison, A. 2006. 'Social movements and science: Cultural appropriations of cognitive praxis', *Science as Culture*, 15(1): 45–59

Jiménez, M. 2005. *El impacto político de los movimientos sociales: Un estudio de la protesta ambiental en España* (The Political Impact of Social Movements: A Study of Environmental Protest in Spain). Colección Monografõas, 214. Madrid: CIS-Siglo XXI.

Kousis, M. 1999. 'Environmental Protest Cases: The City, the Countryside, and the Grassroots in Southern Europe'. *Mobilization*, 4(2): 223–238.

Kousis, M. 2000. 'Tourism and the Environment: A Social Movements Perspective', *Annals of Tourism Research*, 27(2): 468–489.

Kousis, M. 2004a. 'Marine and Coastal Issues in Local Environmental Conflict: Greece, Spain and Portugal', in J. Boissevain and T. Selwyn (eds), *Contesting the Foreshore: Tourism, Society and Politics on the Coast*. Amsterdam: Amsterdam University Press, pp.205–232.

Kousis, M. 2004b. 'Economic Opportunities and Threats in Contentious Environmental Politics: A View from the European South', *Theory and Society* 33: 393–415.

Kousis, M. 2010. 'New Challenges for 21st century Environmental Movements: Agricultural Biotechnology and Nanotechnology', in M. R., Redclift and G. Woodgate (eds) *The International Handbook of Environmental Sociology* (2nd edition), Cheltenham: Edward Elgar, pp. 226–244. http://www.e-elgar.co.uk/Bookentry_Main.lasso?id=13276

Kousis, M., D. Della Porta and M. Jiménez. 2008. 'Southern European Environmental Movements in Comparative Perspective' *American Behavioral Scientist*. Special issue Mediterranean Political Processes in Historical-Comparative Perspective, C. Tilly, R. Franzosi and M. Kousis (guest eds), volume 51(11): 1627–1647.

Kousis, M. and E. Dimopoulou. 2000. 'Environmental Movement Organizations in Greece: A Comparative Perspective', paper presented at the ECPR annual sessions *(Environmental Movements in Comparative Perspective)*, 14–20 April.

Kousis, M., E. Petropoulou and E. Dimopoulou. 2001. 'Local Environmental Politics in Urban and Rural Greece: A Study of North-Eastern Athens and the County of Chanea', paper presented at the 29th Joint Sessions of the European Consortium for Political Research (Local Environmental Politics), Grenoble, 6–11 April.

Kousis, M. and K. Psarikidou. 2006. 'Sustainability Narratives on *Caretta caretta*: Evidence from Zakynthos and Crete', in E. Manolas (ed.), *Proceedings of the International Conference Sustainable Management and Development of Mountainous and Island Areas*, Vol.1 Democritus University of Thrace, Heraklion, Crete, pp. 240–244.

Lalotis, N. 2005. 'The Greek Environmental Downfall Goes on'. *Raporto* Vol. 25 January 2005. Retrieved 17 June 2007 from http://www.ecocrete.gr/index.php?option=com_content&task=view&id=1041&Itemid=0

Ligdopoulou, T., M. Zohrer and N. Newbury. 1994. 'Sea Turtle Conservation Problems on Crete and the Need for Long-Term Planning', *Marine Turtle Newsletter* 64: 13–15.

Madden, C. 2004. 'MEPs urge Greece to save turtles of Zakynthos', page: A09, Athens News onLine, 02/07/2004. Retrieved on March 3, 2005 from http://www.athensnews.gr/athweb/nathens.print_unique?

Margaritoulis, D. 2001. 'The Status of Marine Turtles in the Mediterranean', in D. Margaritoulis and A. Demetropoulos (eds) *Proceedings, First Mediterranean Conference on Marine Turtles.* Barcelona Convention – Bern Convention – Bonn Convention (CMS). Nicosia, Cyprus(2003). 24-28 October 2001. pp. 51–61.

Margaritoulis, D. 2005. 'Nesting Activity and Reproductive Output of Loggerhead Sea Turtles, *Caretta caretta*, over 19 Seasons (1984–2002) at Laganas Bay, Zakynthos, Greece: The Largest Rookery in the Mediterranean', *Chelonian Conservation and Biology,* 4(4): 916–929.

Margaritoulis, D. 2006. 'The 26th International Symposium on Sea Turtle Biology and Conservation (Island of Crete, Greece, 3-8 April 2006) President's Report on the Symposium & ISTS Business', *Indian Ocean Turtle Newsletter,* Aug. vol. 4: 17–20.

Medasset. 2004a. '*Caretta caretta:* The Olympic Games' Loser', Press Release 21 June 2004 Retrieved on March 2 2005 from http://www.ecocrete.gr/index .php?option=content&task=view&id=595&Itemid=0 & Ecocrete.

Medasset. 2004b. 'Collection of signatures for the survival of the 27 management agencies for Greek under protection areas'. Press release 28/06/2004 (in Greek). Retrieved on March 2, 2005 from http://www.ecocrete.gr/index.php?option= content&task=view&id=608&Itemid=0 & Ecocrete.

Medasset. 2006a. Press Release. Retrieved 17 June 2007 from http://www.medasset .org/pdf/ZNMP_press_EN_05.06.06.pdf

Medasset. 2006b. 'About Medasset'. Retrieved 17 June 2007 from http://www .Medasset.org/med_about.htm

MEDSOS. 2005. 'Campaign for Voluntary Cleaning of Coastal Areas: Clean the Mediterranean 2005'. *Ecocrete.* Tuesday 22 February 2005. Retrieved 12 June 2007 from http://www.ecocrete.gr/index.php?option=com_content&task= view&id=1174&Itemid=0

Ministry of Foreign Affairs. 2004. 'Environmental Policy-Protection Measures'. Retrieved 17 June 2007 from http://www.mfa.gr/english/today/environment protection.html

Panda. 2008. 'Who we are'. Retrieved 12 June 2009 from http://www.panda.org /about_wwf/who_we_are/history/eighties/

Pridham, G. 2001. 'Tourism Policy and Sustainability in Italy, Spain and Greece', in K. Eder and M. Kousis (eds), *Environmental Politics in Southern Europe: Actors, Institutions and Discourses in a Europeanizing Society.* Dordrecht: Kluwer, pp. 365–392.

Psarikidou, K. 2005. 'Tourism, the Environmental Habitats Directive and *Caretta caretta* in Greece', in O. Iakovidou (ed.), *Mediterranean Tourism Beyond the Coastline: New Trends in Tourism and the Social Organisation of Space.* Thessaloniki: Ziti, pp. 449–521.

Psarikidou, K. 2006. 'Bioethics and Biodiversity: The *Caretta caretta* Case in Greece', MSc thesis (in Greek), Joint Postgraduate Programme in Bioethics, University of Crete at Rethymno.

Psarikidou, K. 2008a. 'Bioethics and Biodiversity: The *Caretta caretta* Case in Greece', *Bioethics Review* 1, Retrieved 11 December 2009 from http://www.bioethicsreview.uoc.gr/Vol1/Issue1/v1i1sa5_Psarikidou.pdf

Psarikidou, K. 2008b. 'Environmental Ethics and Biodiversity Policy in Tourism: The *Caretta caretta* Case in Greece', *TOURISMOS: An International Multidisciplinary Journal of Tourism,* 3(1): 153–168.

Rethymniotika Nea. 2005. Press Release 26.06.05. Retrieved 16 December 2005 from www.ecocrete.gr/

Selwyn, T. 2000. 'The De-Mediterraneanisation of the Mediterranean?' *Current Issues in Tourism* 3(3): 226–245.

The Movement of the Citizen of Messara for the Environment (2010) No Container Transshipment Hub in Timbaki. Retrieved on 30 September 2010 from http://www.no-container-port-in-timbaki.net/facts_en.php accessed

Theodossopoulos, D. 2003. *Troubles with Turtles: Cultural Understandings of the Environment on a Greek Island.* Oxford: Berghahn Books.

Tilly, C. 1994. 'Social Movements as Historically Specific Clusters of Political Performances', *Berkeley Journal of Sociology* 38: 1–30.

UN Environment Programme, Mediterranean Action Plan (UNEP/MAP). 2006. *A Sustainable Future for the Mediterranean: The Blue Plan's Environment and Development Outlook,* Executive Summary, July. SMAP, EuropeAid, Regional Activity Centre, Sophia Antipolis.

Venizelos, L. and K. Corbett. 2005. "Zakynthos Sea Turtle Odyssey – A Political Ball Game" *Marine Newsletter* No. 108: 10–12.

Warren, L.M. and E. Antonopoulou. 1990. 'The Conservation of Loggerhead Turtles in Zakynthos, Greece', *ORYX* 24(1): 15–22.

WWF-Greece. 2005. 'Endangered Species'. Retrieved 17 December 2005 from http://www.wwf.gr/index.php?option=com_content&view=category&layout=blog&id=138&Itemid=67

WWF-Greece. 2008. '*Caretta caretta*'. Retrieved 15 December 2008 from http://www.wwf.gr/index.php?option=content&task=view&id=185

WWF-Greece. 2004. "Greece accused by EC for the sea turtle once more? Political responsibilities for the chaos in Zakynthos". Press Release, 18.10.04 (in Greek). Retrieved on March 3, 2005 from http://www.ecocrete.gr/index.php?option=content&task=view&id=829&Itemid=085

List of Websites Used:

Archelon, www.archelon.gr , Final Retrieval on February 1, 2008

Athens News Online, www.athensnews.gr/, Final Retrieval on December 5, 2009

Bioethics Review, University of Crete, http://www.bioethicsreview.uoc.gr . Last Retrieval on December 11, 2009

Ecocrete, www.ecocrete.gr, Final Retrieval on June 17, 2007

EC PAGANINI Project, www.paganini-project.net/ , Final Retrieval on December 5, 2009

EC Euromed Heritage II project Mediterranean Voices: Oral History and Cultural Practice in Mediterranean Cities, www.medvoices.org/ , Final Retrieval on December 4, 2006

Elliniki Ornithologiki Etaireia, http://www.ornithologiki.gr/ Final Retrieval on December 13, 2004

Greenpeace Greece http://greenpeace.gr Final Retrieval on December 14, 2004

http://www.ierapetra.net/ . Final Retrieval on June 6, 2007

Medasset, http://www.Medasset.org/med_about.htm . Final Retrieval on June 17, 2007

Ministry of Foreign Affairs, http://www.mfa.gr/english/ Final Retrieval June 17, 2007

Organising for EU Enlargement, http://www.oeue.net/papers.asp Final Retrieval on June 17, 2007

Panda, http://www.panda.org/ . Final Retrieval June 12, 2009

Petition Online, www.petitiononline.com/ Final Retrieval January 22, 2007

Primary School of Lithakia, Zakynthos, http://dim-lithak.zak.sch.gr/ , Final Retrieval on December 12, 2004

University of Vienna, http://www.univie.ac.at, Final Retrieval on December 5, 2009

Virtual Victorians, http://tofino.ex.ac.uk/euroturtle/medas/press_no16.htm Final Retrieval on December 10, 2004

WWF-Greece, http://www.wwf.gr/ Final Retrieval on December 15, 2008

Part 3

❧ ◆ ❧

Capital and Neighbourhood Governance

Chapter 7

Contested Politics
of the Mediterranean

Star Street and the Struggle for Development
in Bethlehem

CAROL SANSOUR DABDOUB AND
CAROL ZOUGHBI-JANINEH

Introduction

Tourism in Bethlehem has long revolved around the Basilica of the Nativity, the birthplace of Christ. This connection to the nativity, and hence to Christmas festivities, has ensured Bethlehem's development as a tourist city. However, the importance placed upon the Nativity also presents a hindrance to the sustainability of the tourism industry of Bethlehem. In broad terms, it has meant that the bulk of tourism is seasonal, and that the visitor is interested in the basilica to the exclusion of any other available attraction. This problem has grown more acute over the past fifty or so years as Bethlehem has come under the occupation of a foreign power with its own political and territorial ambitions in the Bethlehem area.

The effects of occupation upon the daily lives of the citizens of Bethlehem are endless. From a tourism perspective, however, two points can be made: first, Bethlehem has no control over access from the outside world, which affects the marketing of tours and the supervision of tour operators, and second, the effective closure of Bethlehem discourages visitors from making extended stays in the city. The majority of tourists arrive in the city from Jerusalem on pre-sold coach tours that take them into the Church of the Nativity, with a possible visit to other proximate sites such as the Shepherds' Field or, more seldom, Solomon Pools. This is customarily followed by a meal and a visit to a local souvenir and gift shop.

The initial figures for Christmas 2005 show that between twenty-two and twenty-three thousand tourists visited the city for the festivities (Palestinian National Authority, Ministry of Tourism, 2005). This was lower than the projected figure of thirty thousand. Yet even if the final figure is somewhat higher, those visitors choosing to stay overnight in the city hotels numbered in the low thousands; moreover, hoteliers reported that in that year guests stayed at most two nights. By the evening of 26 December the city was once again deserted. These facts and figures are in line with the yearly trend: 90 per cent of visitors to Bethlehem do not stay overnight.

If Bethlehem is to develop a sustainable tourism industry that benefits the city in its entirety, it needs a strategic vision that fulfils two aims: (1) exercising more control over tours and tour operators; and (2) providing attractions that will ensure visitors' extended stay within the city. Over the past few years, a consensus has emerged that the first priority is to develop the old core of the city as a parallel attraction to the basilica. This strategic vision was reflected in the city of Bethlehem's application to the United Nations Educational and Scientific Cultural Organisation (UNESCO) for World Heritage status. The submission emphasized the basilica and the Old City as a single entity, with the city providing the architectural backdrop and cultural context for the church (Palestinian National Authority 2005). In this two-way relationship between church and city, the benefit to the tourist lies in the exploration of an ancient city and its people, its people being the living community that revolves around the church. The benefit to the city lies in the increased revenue generated from the tourist's extended stay.

It should be added that there is also a political benefit in encouraging visitors to enjoy extended stays in Bethlehem, as the visitors would be likely to learn more about the issues of occupation, gain a more complete understanding of the Palestinians and their way of life and act as ambassadors for Palestine on their return to their home countries. It would also help the Palestinians themselves feel that they can continue to have a connection with the wider world despite the blockade on their cities.

In this chapter we will try to present, with some detail, the powerful voices within Bethlehem who are opposed, in some measure, to the vision of a rejuvenated Old City core as a backdrop to the basilica. Yet a strategic vision does exist, and there have been two attempts to put this vision into practice, both focused on one site within the old city: Star Street. The ensuing pages will also explain why Star Street has been selected and how Star Street is used as a metaphor for discussing the political economy of the city. Having outlined the two attempts made to develop Star Street, we will argue that the focus on Star Street continues to make strategic sense and suggest ways in which any new plan for the street might ensure greater chances of success.

Star Street as a Location

For centuries before the beginning of the British Mandate in Palestine in 1917, the only entrance to Bethlehem was through the street known as Ras Fteis, which was officially named Star Street (Share' an-Nijmeh, in Arabic) around 1960. The name symbolizes the story of the star that led the Magi into Bethlehem to see the newborn Jesus Christ. During the British Mandate, when Hanna Miladeh was mayor of Bethlehem (1934–1935), a beacon (*Manarah,* in Arabic) was built at al-Manarah Square (formerly known as an-Nijmeh Intersection, the junction where Star Street and Paul VI Street meet), where it is believed that the Magi-leading star stopped. The beacon was pulled down in 1945 by the Bethlehem Municipality, which claimed that it hindered traffic. Even today, religious parades and funerary and wedding processions pass through this street on their way to the Church of the Nativity.

Star Street also represents the last stage of the pilgrimage trail from Jerusalem to Bethlehem, the route used by the patriarchs of the individual churches on their annual Christmas processions, known as the Patriarch Route. Christian pilgrimage to Bethlehem began within two hundred years after Christ's birth, and both popular tradition and church custom recognize Star Street as the historical entrance to Bethlehem, i.e. the road that brought the Holy Family into the city.

Not only is Star Street a pilgrimage route and historical entry point to Bethlehem; it is also a recognized part of Bethlehem's historic heritage. It contains much of the outstanding architecture and spacious charm of the Old City. These are mainly Ottoman-era mansions built of local stone in the traditional Levantine-Arabic style. These mansions have central, open courtyards that hold urban gardens overlooked by inner windows and balconies. Furthermore, the fact that until the early twentieth century Star Street was a commercial centre in Bethlehem for both locals and tourists gives it high potential for tourism development.

Families and Trades

It is believed that Star Street was first inhabited by the at-Tarajmeh clan, comprising the families of 'Abit, Abu al 'Arraj, Abu Fheileh, Abu Gheith, Abu Jaber, Abu Khalil, Batarseh, Dabdoub, Dahburah, Dawed, D'eik, Fleifel, Jabriyyeh, Mansour, Mickel, Rock, Sabat, Sara, Sabella, Suwwadi, Tabash, Tabbakh, Talamas and Tarud. According to Revault, Santelli and Weill-Rochant (1997: 14) at-Tarajmeh Quarter was established around the seventeenth century. At-Tarajmeh are believed to be the remnants of the crusaders, originally Italians, who married locals from Bethlehem and worked as interpreters or translators (*Tarajmeh*, in Arabic) for the Franciscan fathers as well as for the Italian pilgrims visiting the city.

It is believed that prior to the seventeenth century, the inhabitants of Star Street, like the rest of the citizens of Bethlehem, were originally farmers and stockbreeders. Abdullah Giacaman, in his book *History of Bethlehem*, describes the town centre of Bethlehem as crowded and dirty since most of the inhabitants there raised animals on the first floors of their houses to help them in agriculture (Abdullah Giacaman, 1994: 28). Later, however, many of the citizens of Bethlehem turned to artisanal production of olive wood and mother-of-pearl souvenirs, which they had learned from the Franciscan priests. At-Tarajmeh families pioneered this type of industry because of their close relationship with the Franciscans.

During the twentieth century, this active commercial centre of Bethlehem marked a decline in its bustling commercial activities, to the benefit of the newly emerging parts of Bethlehem. The situation on Star Street deteriorated more upon the outbreak of the first Intifada (uprising) in December 1987 and came to a total standstill at the beginning of the second Intifada in September 2000.

Of the eighty-six shops located on Star Street, fifty-three have been closed for the last five years; only thirty-three shops were open in November 2005.[1] Only a few of the shops are still owned by the descendants of original at-Tarajmeh families; a pertinent example would be the Abu Jaber family, which is still living in the street and owns around six stores, two of which are used as a grocery and the rest as storage space. Another example is the Sabat family, which still owns shops on the street, although they remain closed. The family no longer lives in the street but has moved to the outskirts of the city. Other at-Tarajmeh families reside abroad but still hold the proprietorship of shops on the street. The Abu al 'Arraj family, for instance, has a proxy in Bethlehem, Engineer Nader Saqqa; a proxy, customarily and officially, can develop full rights over the assets of the original owners.

Among the few shops open today are groceries, antique shops, carpentries, souvenir shops, barbershops, bakeries, boutiques, restaurants, etc. Most of these shops are owned by Assyrian or Muslim families from Bethlehem. The Latin Parish, the Assyrian Convent and the Melkite Church also own a number of shops on the street. Very few are still owned by at-Tarajmeh families.

At one time Star Street used to be the commercial centre for the whole of Bethlehem, but today few of its remaining shops attract shoppers other than the residents of the street. Two shops stand out: Abu Fouad fish and poultry shop, owned by Bethlehem resident Johnny Mbassaleh, and Fadi Boutique, owned by Khaled Bahnan, a Bethlehem Assyrian residing in the street. These two shops are relatively new, in contrast to that of Faraj Kasbari, a tailor originally from northern Palestine and a resident of Beit Jala, whose shop has been an amazing success story for many years, attracting customers from all over Bethlehem as well as its surrounding areas. The other shops, mostly small groceries, serve only the inhabitants of the street.

The remaining open shops on Star Street feature only a limited selection of goods. Moreover, whether clothes, souvenirs or other commodities, 80 per cent of the time the items were made someplace other than Palestine – most often China. A few of the souvenir stores offer a variety of local handmade products. Most of the items sold in the groceries are imported from different European or Arab countries or bought from Israel.

Transformation of Star Street in the Twentieth Century

Before the twentieth century, the village of Bethlehem was only about one kilometre long and half a kilometre wide, with two streets about four me-tres in width stretching westward from the Church of the Nativity. In those days the town was prevented from expanding by its location at 780 metres above sea level, surrounded by steep slopes to the east, north and south. The landscape surrounding Bethlehem was thriving with fields, olive groves and vineyards. 'It is believed that Bethlehem was originally founded on the plateau of the mountain which overlooks the Church of the Nativity from the northern side at the curve of the road stretching from Qos al-Zarrarah until the Assyrian Orthodox Church, that is between Star Street and the present market road' (El-Ali, 1991: 47).

In the second half of the nineteenth century, the Ottoman sultan gave permission to the European missionaries to establish institutions in the Holy Land. Many were established in Bethlehem, outside the crowded city centre to the northwest, southwest and southeast. By the end of the nine-teenth century, Bethlehem had started to expand gradually to the north and the west of the Church of the Nativity due to the construction of con-vents and missionary centres. Starting at the beginning of the twentieth century, the citizens of Bethlehem, especially those of the returning Dias-pora, were encouraged to build new houses in the fields surrounding these institutions. That was the start of the exodus from the city centre. People found it safer and healthier living near those establishments rather than in the crowded city centre. This is how Bethlehem expanded to include the western plateau around the College des Frères and the French Hospital (currently Bethlehem University and the Holy Family Hospital, respectively), the northern plateau around King David Hospital, and to the south Hindaza Mountain, al-Maslakh Street and As-Saf Street. At the time, the urban tissue of the city was focused along the expansion of three streets: Paul VI Street, al-Farahiyyeh Street and Star Street. Furthermore, the area between Paul VI Street (stretching west towards the Assyrian Church) and Star Street became the commercial centre of the town.

During the British Mandate in 1923, the first skeletal map of Bethlehem was formulated under the supervision of William Candell, director of the Urban Planning Unit. Among the recommendations presented with regard to city planning came the suggestion that because of the importance of Manger Square, vehicles should not enter it but instead drop people off at the intersection with the adjacent Beit Sahour area (Revault, Santelli and Weill-Rochant, 1997; Abdullah Giacaman, 2000). Some seventy years later, Bethlehem Municipality established a parking area for public and tourist transportation near this intersection. In 1999, in agreement with Bethlehem Municipality, the Diaspora-based Palestinian investment company Palestine Development and Investment Company Ltd (PADICO) built the current Bethlehem Central Bus Terminal, which also includes a shopping centre, on the exact location of the old municipal parking area.

Another recommendation presented by the Urban Planning Unit in 1923 was to establish a new exit road to Jerusalem in place of the fields and vineyards on the northern borders of the town. The renowned New Street, stretching from the northern side of Manger Square all the way to Rachel's Tomb, was constructed in 1926 and renamed Manger Street around 1980. Since 1940, buildings have been constructed on both sides of the street from Manger Square to Rachel's Tomb. By the mid twentieth century, Manger Street's thriving commercial activities had begun to rival those of Star Street, now mainly a residential area.

Today, and despite the pressure on housing in the Bethlehem district, Star Street has large, unused capacity, both residential and commercial. The reasons for this abundance are multiple. Firstly, the houses on the street are large and expensive in themselves as well as costly to renovate and modernize. Then, even as there has been an outward flight from the street, the current owners are reluctant to sell or lease their property, either for fear they will not obtain the commercial value of the property or will invite ownership disputes if they introduce tenants, or because they live abroad and cannot supervise contracts and agreements. This collapse of the residential area has had a direct impact on the commercial life of the street. Finally, the founding of Manger Street took traffic away from Star Street and led to the growth of retail outlets and restaurants away from the old route into the city.

The Social Transformation of Star Street

The social fabric of Bethlehem as a whole – from the seventeenth to nine-teenth centuries- made up of the clans of an-Najajreh, al-Farahieh, al-Anat-reh, al-Hreizat, al-Kawawseh, at-Tarajmeh, al-Fawaghreh – changed due to wars, immigration and emigration. At the beginning of the twentieth cen-tury a group of Assyrian families fleeing the genocide in Asia Minor sought refuge in Bethlehem. In 1927, the Church of the Virgin Mary belonging to the Assyrian congregation was founded on the ruins of old houses in the Manarah area bought by the Assyrian newcomers, mainly through the St. Afram Charitable Society (El-Ali, 1991:86). In 1948, *an-Nakba*[2] caused thousands of dispossessed Palestinian families to flee from the northern rural areas of historic Palestine and settle in and around Bethlehem. At the time the United Nations Relief and Works Agency (UNRWA) intervened to secure the well-being of these refugees. Three refugee camps with less-than-basic services were erected in Bethlehem. These refugees, who initially thought that this dispossession was a temporary one, eventually ended up realizing that unless they integrated into Bethlehem society they would not be able to provide for their families. And so it came that with time they became an integral and complementary part of the Bethlehem economic and social fabric. Similarly, some of at-Ta'amreh – a Muslim Bedouin tribe residing on the eastern slopes of Beit Sahour, east of Bethlehem – moved to the city and settled there, seeking more reliable sources of income away from their herd-raising community.

Concurrently, Bethlehem was going through an outbound wave of mi-gration. Upon joining World War I (1914–1918), the Ottoman Empire called on young Bethlehem men to join its army. The fear of being recruited pushed many of these men to abscond and go to other countries, chiefly in the Americas, leaving behind their families and properties. Bethlehem witnessed other waves of immigration to mainly Arab countries following the 1967 Six-Day War. This once more impacted on the constituents of the city's fabric. The hardship of the unstable political and economical realities of Bethlehem after the second half of the twentieth century caused many families of Bethlehem to leave for other countries in search of better living. Many Tarajmeh families, as in the case of other Bethlehem families, per-manently disappeared from the city; Abu al 'Arraj, Abu Gheith, Dahburah and Talamas are but a few. As Bethlehem was spreading out and expanding, many families like Dabdoub, Suwwadi, Rock, Batarseh and Jabriyyeh left at-Tarajmeh Quarter, Star Street today, to live on the outskirts of the city. Few Tarajmeh families still reside in Star Street (Sara, Abu Jaber and Tabash).

A further element in the Bethlehem fabric is the abundance of the mis-sionaries (mainly clergy) working in the different establishments that were founded around the city of the Nativity. These missionaries brought about a different set of social, religious and economic practices, adding to the already existing diversified ones. Today, Star Street is also inhabited by many Assyrian families, who are a religious community by nature and chose to reside in close proximity to their church. The street also embraces several Ta'amreh and other Muslim families, as well as the establishments of each of the Roman Orthodox Church (the Melkite Church), the Roman Catholic Church (the Rosary School, St. Joseph School, the Salesians) and the Assyrian Church (Virgin Mary Church). This is in addition to the descendants of the original inhabitants of the street, who are mainly Roman Catholic Christians.

External Forces Influencing Star Street

A Palestinian city, Bethlehem, like the rest of Palestine, has never truly fulfilled its ambition to act as a sovereign entity in control of its destiny. Throughout its recent history, Bethlehem was ruled by a succession of foreign conquerors including the Ottoman Empire, the British Mandate, Jordanian rule and the present Israeli occupation. On Star Street, the impact of the various ruling forces can be noticed in both the tangible and intangible heritage. For instance, Ottoman architecture is prominent on the street, yet the crosses that decorate the different entryways to the courtyards cannot be missed. Likewise, the mixed and inclusive social fabric (citizens descended from Bethlehem's oldest families, Palestinian refugees, Bedouins, international clergymen and women) is difficult to ignore. However, the major impact on Star Street comes from the Israeli occupation. The citizens of Bethlehem – subject to policies of apartheid and isolation, especially with the erection of a wall imprisoning the city – are living in a restricted environment with diminished social, cultural and commercial activities.

This situation has led many to become more conscious of the need to look for new means to enhance and protect their basic livelihoods. In search of a better and sustainable future many stakeholders (the municipality, church leaders, local NGOs and community leaders) started realizing that investing in tourism could be one of the few opportunities that are left for Bethlehem to survive. One of the most visible efforts to develop tourism was the creation of the Bethlehem 2000 Project. In the run-up to the millennium celebrations, the Palestinian National Authority (an administrative body formed as a result of the Oslo Accords) created a new entity, the Bethlehem 2000 Project (BL2000), as a development project for the Bethlehem district. BL2000 was charged with planning, managing and overseeing the works of regeneration of the Bethlehem district through funds provided by foreign donors.

BL2000's mandate required the project's involvement in most if not all sectors to ensure a comprehensive development strategy. However, and since the focus is on the Bethlehem district, a leading tourism destination in Palestine, tourism development was a priority on the BL2000 agenda: 'The development of tourism in Palestine is the overall long-term objective of the Bethlehem 2000 project. Principal among it priorities [sic], BL2000 endeavoured to expand the tourism product, upgrade the infrastructure, develop human resources and conduct a large-scale promotion campaign' (Bethlehem 2000 Project, 2002: 75).

In its tourism development plan, BL2000 had as its first long-term objective 'to extend the length of stay for day visitors by enhancing the range of activities and attractions within Bethlehem' (Bethlehem 2000 Project, 1998: 3). To do so BL2000 started allocating large investments to the infrastructure and rehabilitation works within the old city core, hence preserving the built heritage, improving the quality of life for the local community and attempting to attract tourism presence.

As the infrastructure and rehabilitation works were coming to an end, the BL2000 Private Sector Department, along with the Tourism and Events Departments, were drawing together a plan to regenerate the old city core, which would serve as a new tourism attraction, enriching and complementing the traditional offer: the basilica. The initial idea was to introduce the whole old city core – comprising Manger Square, Najajreh Street, Paul VI Street, Madbasseh Square, the Milk Grotto Street and Star Street – as the Bethlehem (Permanent) Christmas Market. In a concept paper presented by BL2000 to various donors, the Bethlehem Permanent Christmas Market project aimed at promoting entrepreneurship and business investment in quality arts, crafts, specialty food shops, coffee shops and restaurants; whilst artists' studios and artisan workshops would also be especially encouraged and assisted (Bethlehem 2000 Project, 1999). However, since the funds required to implement the Bethlehem (Permanent) Christmas Market were not forthcoming and time was running out, BL2000 opted to implement the idea of a Temporary Christmas Market on just one street of the old city core: Star Street.

The Focus on Star Street

The attempt to revive Star Street, and to revive it specifically as a tourism asset, is based on its heritage value as both a pilgrimage site and a site of architectural treasures. Not only does the street represent a route towards the basilica, but it is also a route into the old city – one that is more beautiful than much of the rest of the old city – that has the spare capacity to allow for new initiatives.

Christmas Market 1999

As the Spanish government provided funds to develop the external infrastructure of Star Street – including electricity, sewage and telephone lines – BL2000 focused its plans on creating a temporary Christmas Market on the street, starting 15 December 1999 and ending 6 January 2000. Unfortunately, the original long-term objective for a sustainable tourism offer had been minimized to a one-time, 23-day event.

As a first step, a survey was conducted to identify available stores, and owners (or acting owners) were encouraged to provide temporary leases for the duration of the market. Where retail property was made available, BL2000 intervened to renovate the interiors of the buildings, while the Spanish funds renovated the exteriors and covered services. In total BL2000 rehabilitated the interiors of twenty of the street's shops for use in the market. Contacts were made with arts and crafts unions, associations and individuals to ensure a supply of locally produced commodities in line with the celebrations, as well as to provide retail outlets for these goods. Craftsmen and women were also invited to participate in the market, as were performing groups. Over thirty shops (out of seventy-eight shops on the street) were open, providing a wide range of offerings from traditional Palestinian embroidery to Bedouin jewellery and traditional sweets.

Parallel to securing a quality venue and participation for the market, BL2000 worked closely with the Ministry of Tourism, Bethlehem Municipality, Bethlehem Chamber of Commerce, Bethlehem Police Department and most importantly, Star Street inhabitants, to ensure that there was an orchestrated effort to make the Christmas Market event a success. Likewise, BL2000 coordinated with and received the approval of the different local authorities (Municipality, Police Department and Ministry of Tourism) to create drop-off points at a number of periphery points leading to the old city. As Star Street is recessed from Manger Street and accessed by a ramp, BL2000 developed an area at the top of the ramp that included a roundabout so that coach tours could drop off tourists, turn around and continue to the newly-built Bethlehem Bus Terminal on Manger Street, close to the basilica. All parties, at least publicly, had agreed that it is essential to the revival of the old city core that all tourists coming to visit the basilica pass through the old city core first. Indeed, on the 4 June 1999, the Mayor of Bethlehem, Mr. Hanna Nasser, had issued a letter to the Bethlehem 2000 Project endorsing the dropping points and the regeneration of the Christmas Market.

At the same time, several intensive meetings with leading tour operators were held to ensure that they were aware of the new attraction in Bethlehem and to encourage them to include it on their Bethlehem itinerary.

It is worth mentioning that to many citizens of Bethlehem, the closer Bethlehem got to the year 2000 the further it was from being prepared. The construction projects took their toll on the city, for they lasted longer than expected, with little consideration for the inhabitants and the impact these projects had on the different aspects of their lives, mainly the commercial one. For over six months the city in its entirety was one big construction site generating animosity and scepticism among the citizens of Bethlehem. This situation was never addressed properly, and channels of communications between the general public and the official parties working on regenerating the city (mainly BL2000) were never established. Therefore, and after the infrastructure works were finished and BL2000 started implementing the different programmes within the community, BL2000, in the best scenarios, experienced weak partnerships filled with mistrust, as viewed by the citizens.

On a different level, BL2000 extended its hands to the tycoons of the Palestinian private sector in an attempt to get their interest in investing in Bethlehem, hence bringing about prosperity. Even these major role players in the Palestinian economy turned out to be a great disappointment. They viewed BL2000 and its activities as a simple, quick window of opportunity through which they would jump and reap quick profits. Sustainable and long-term community development through their potential contributions was not on their agenda.

Two days before the opening of the Christmas Market on Star Street, Bethlehem Municipality concluded an agreement with PADICO[3] whereby the bus terminal would be the first destination for all coaches entering the city, and that tourists must disembark at the said terminal and not at the dropping points. The agreement between the municipality and PADICO effectively destroyed the BL2000 initiative on Star Street. Since tourists were getting off at the bus station, in close proximity to Manger Square and the Basilica of the Nativity (and, indeed, were taken directly to the church), there was almost no possibility of tourists choosing to explore Star Street.

As the Christmas Market – along with its bright and lively decorations and music, its Christmas spirit, the excitement of overjoyed owners and shopkeepers anticipating a successful event – prepared to receive its celebrating tourists, no more than five coach buses dropped tourists at the roundabout at the entrance of Star Street. Even those tourists who had the chance to walk through the market were hurried down the street by their tour guides, with accompanying warning messages of impending pick-pocketing, violence and overpriced items. Five days into the market it was obvious that the high expectations both the organizers and the shopkeep-ers had had concerning the high turnover of tourists were nothing but an illusion. Before reaching closing day of the market, more than half of the participants had packed up and left the street with intense feelings of anger and deception. This was felt especially keenly as the majority of partici-pants, most of whom were small-sized, family-based entrepreneurs, had depended on bank loans to raise capital to enable them to participate in the Christmas Market. This dependence, the participants later felt, they could do without at a time when the financial risks they took were so high because of the promises that BL2000 gave but could not deliver. They were further burdened financially when the second Intifada broke out in September 2000 and the whole Palestinian economy came to a complete standstill.

In the beginning of the year 2001 and as the BL2000 project was coming to an end, the Centre for Cultural Heritage Preservation (CCHP), an inde-pendent public body, was founded as a continuation of the Cultural Heri-tage Unit within BL2000. Since its foundation, CCHP has been responsible for all activities related to cultural heritage preservation in the Bethlehem district.

Christmas Market 2005

With CCHP's mission to provide a sustainable mechanism for the pro-tection and management of cultural heritage resources in the Bethlehem district and to enhance awareness of cultural heritage in the public con-science, it was only a matter of time before CCHP would take interest in the development and revitalization of the old city core, including Star Street. Five years into the second Intifada, in mid 2005, CCHP decided to organize the second Christmas Market on Star Street, despite full awareness of the challenges that lay ahead, given that the whole outlook seemed bleak. The rates of unemployment were high as tourism in the city, which made up 80 per cent of Bethlehem's economy, had been in decline, losing an aggregate of 90 per cent of the market over the previous five years (Palestinian Na-tional Authority, 2005).

Unlike BL2000, CCHP decided to develop Star Street as a cultural route – the Patriarch Route – within its holistic approach towards cultural heri-tage development strategies. Those strategies could be summarized in four major categories: education and public awareness of the value of cultural heritage; physical works; training and research; and networking. CCHP had started implementing its strategies in the old core of Bethlehem long before the idea of another Christmas Market was introduced. The main project, focusing on developing the old core of Bethlehem, was executed by CCHP and through the Development of Territorial Cultural Systems Project (DELTA), within the EuroMed Heritage II Programme.

Similar to BL2000, CCHP had the long-term aim of developing Star Street and its Christmas Market as a viable, sustainable and integrated event within an overall plan for tourism development for the Bethlehem area. 'In the longer term, it would set the course for Bethlehem to become the gateway for Palestine and a member of the exclusive group of Christmas capitals in the world.'[4] Yet even though the revitalization of the street was a local vision and the plan implemented by a local body, it was very much dictated by the international donors, in this case the United States Agency for International Development (USAID). This was mainly felt in the lateness of the decision by USAID to commit its resources to the Christmas Market, leaving little space for the organizers (CCHP) to implement an effective and solid event; therefore development of the street occurred rapidly. Once again, and similar to what happened back in 1999, plans for the Christmas Market in 2005 were readjusted to fit the donors' agendas.

CCHP succeeded in engaging public and institutional participation by forming a steering committee. In addition to CCHP, the committee comprised Bethlehem Municipality, the International Centre of Bethlehem, the Catholic Parish of Bethlehem and the Bethlehem Peace Centre. The project demanded that a public awareness campaign be launched to foster local acceptance and to ensure public participation. As a result of the various meetings between CCHP and the residents of Star Street, a street association was created to liaise between the two parties to ensure a successful event. Preceding the signing of the agreement between CCHP and USAID to carry out a Christmas Market on Star Street, rehabilitation works[5]were executed on the street: cleaning the façades of buildings, repairing stone paving, repairing lighting fixtures and adding new ones where necessary, adding new signage and plantings and painting shop doors. Also as part of the preparations, an awareness campaign was carried out and a competition was organized for the three most beautifully decorated balconies and the three most creative shop-fronts.

The idea behind the Christmas Market was that a visitor could eat a snack or a meal, shop for gifts and attend entertainment performances, all in one place: Star Street between Catholic Action Club Square and al-Manarah Square. Thus, the organization of the Christmas Market included the reopening of some shops, the installation on Catholic Action Club Square of food and gift kiosks as well as a stage for cultural performances, and the preparation of a calendar of activities catering for both locals and visitors. The Christmas Market took place between 20 December and 27 December

2005 and opened for the public between 11:00 A.M. and 11:00 P.M. One of the main highlights of the week was the inauguration ceremony under the patronage of His Beatitude Patriarch Michel Sabbah, Latin Patriarch of Jerusalem. Other guests at the ceremony included Governor of the Bethlehem District Salah at-Ta'mari, Mayor of Bethlehem Dr. Victor Batarseh. All in attendance supported the idea behind the Christmas Market: revitalizing the economy and bringing new hope to Star Street. The Christmas Market presented a possible model of a community development project, as different organizations participated in implementing it to the benefit of the local community as a whole.

The twelve kiosks installed on Catholic Action Club Square were allocated to individuals and institutions selling foodstuffs, beverages and traditional handicrafts. Participants were chosen according to criteria set by the organizers that took into consideration the participants' products, offers and financial needs. Prior to the event a number of coordination meetings had taken place between the participants and the organizers, during which logistics, modalities of communications and suggestions were shared. CCHP restored some of the shops that were then readily available to serve the market, and the Latin Parish of Bethlehem offered two of its large unutilized shops to institutions and individuals selling traditional handicrafts. The *Anastas* family offered three unutilized shops to CCHP to hold an exhibition entitled 'Bethlehem: An Alternative Narrative'. The as-Sacca family offered a small unutilized shop to CCHP to be used as an Information Centre distributing calendars, brochures, books and maps of Bethlehem. Finally, the Palestinian Red Crescent Society in Bethlehem put four volunteers at the disposal of the market to help ensure the well-being of the participants and visitors.

Furthermore, and through its awareness campaign, CCHP encouraged several shop owners to reopen. One resident of the street used his shop as a fast food outlet for the market's duration, while another, Ms. Maha as-Sacca, opened her shop on a permanent basis as a branch of her existing Palestinian Heritage Centre at the main entrance of Bethlehem, selling traditional Palestinian embroidery. The Salem family, who reside and own a shop on the street, insisted on inaugurating their new Philadelphia Restaurant on the first day of the market. The restaurant is still open to this day. Two individual owners leased their shops for the market's duration to third parties wishing to sell handicrafts, jewellery and souvenir gifts. An interesting case is the al-Loussi calligraphy shop, which was turned into a gift shop exhibiting local women's embroidery and glassware. Al-Loussi and two other women now manage the shop.

The economic outcome was probably less satisfactory for some, but there were clear indications that some of the shops/kiosks sold very well. One of the vendors at the Young Men's Christian Association (YMCA) kiosk said: 'There should have been more coordination between the vendors in this event to decide on bringing a wider variety of attractive local produce. I did not sell much, but at least I participated in this initiative.'[6] A young woman from Bethlehem who sells handmade accessories and shawls said, on her visit to CCHP after the market's close: 'I sold very well during the Market, I even have a long list of special orders to deliver before the end of the season and I am thinking of finding myself a permanent shop on Star Street.'[7]

On the entertainment side, a number of groups were invited to perform during the Christmas Market. Some of them refused, as they would not be paid for their performance; only hospitality and transportation expenses could be covered for them. Fortunately, many groups from the Bethlehem and Ramallah areas were happy to participate in this local event. Some of the activities of the market were partly sponsored, as in the case with a couple of popular performing groups for children.

The social and economic impacts of future Christmas Markets could be substantial and of great significance. Not only does the market meet the public's demand to revitalize the street, but it also enhances the prospects for tourism and visitors' experience of the place and lays the ground for the development of Star Street as well as the old city core into a central tourism venue. The 2005 Christmas Market succeeded in generating a modest direct income to the shop owners established on the street and indirect income to the city as a whole. It proved to help promote a variety of local products from embroidery to food, activate the notion of street associations and provide an example of effective public participation in the planning and implementation of a project. The provision of amenities of a lasting nature through the rehabilitation work preceding the market itself was an attractive aspect of community investment leading to improved health, sanitation and amenities at the local level.

Nonetheless, and as has been noted, Star Street is at the farthest point from both Manger Square and the Bethlehem Bus Terminal. To a quite critical degree, it is inaccessible to all but the most informed and determined tourist. If the PADICO deal was an obstacle in 1999, it was a far greater impediment in 2005. The bus terminal revenue, while minimal, is generated solely by coaches using its facilities, which local government statutes require them to do. While the deal ensures that the bus terminal is the first disembarkation point, on the outward journey the coaches may make other stops – and indeed, tour operators' parking fees at the bus terminal are offset by payments derived from the local tourism industry. Local souvenir shops and restaurants have developed specialized businesses that depend solely upon servicing coach tours, which comprise 90 per cent of Bethlehem's visitors. By paying tour operators to place a particular restaurant or souvenir shop on the scheduled tour, the largest stakeholders in the local tourism industry have ensured the survival of their businesses.

The fees paid by local souvenir shops and restaurateurs to the coach operators come in different forms and include commission payments to tour guides and drivers. As previously happened in 1999, guides and drivers cautioned visitors to shop only at the approved outlets: the warnings were about price, or quality, but they also included warnings of the dangers presented by the city itself. The PADICO deal has thus become institutionalized within the local industry, exacerbating the central problem: the failure to broaden the appeal of the city and to encourage overnight visitors. There has always been a positive disincentive for local souvenir shops and restaurants to encourage visitors to explore the city. Today, that disincentive has grown – as was apparent at the 2005 Christmas Market.

Reflection

Emanuel de Kadt made a clear argument about managing impacts at the community level in tourism planning:

> [P]eople who enjoy, or suffer, the main impacts of such a project are those who live in the communities in the tourist destination (de Kadt 1979: 23). He goes on to argue that the issue of local community interests cannot, by itself, determine the desirability of a tourism project. However, if social impacts are taken into account and undue weight is not given to economic considerations, then local community interests are probably better promoted by slower development of widely dispersed, small-scale facilities than by massive integrated and concentrated ones (de Kadt 1979).

In a small project like the Christmas Market, community members can more easily develop and keep an interest; whilst the project is less likely to attract the attention of powerful outsiders who could use their influence with national or regional authorities to override local preferences or controls. As de Kadt suggests, the more an event is seen by its host community as emerging from within rather than being imposed on them, the greater that community's acceptance of the event will be.

In the case of Bethlehem, tourism is being developed within a weak local government, highly fragmented indigenous firms and poorly developed policies and skills. In addition there are powerful companies exercising oligopoly powers while having little long-term commitment to any particular local tourism system, as is evident in the PADICO bus terminal. Nor can one ignore the political and social impacts of donors who tend to exercise pressure on the receiving parties to impose their own agendas. In the case of Star Street, because the newly elected municipality included some Hamas[8] members, USAID opted to aid the implementation of the Christmas Market through other channels (mainly the CCHP), thereby ignoring the imperative role of the municipality.

Moreover, USAID interfered in all aspects of the implementation of the project, including who was hired, which organizations were chosen as partners, and what conditions partnerships were subject to – all to ensure its agenda of boycotting Bethlehem Municipality. The interference even went as far as the USAID not attending the inaugural event, where the mayor of Bethlehem made a speech, and refusing to have the name or logo of the municipality on any publication related to the project. Hence, the title 'The Committee for the Revitalization of the Old Core of Bethlehem' was reached as a compromise agreement satisfying all parties. Such an act has an immense impact on the local political and social structure. It undermines and weakens the development of an effective municipal institution in that case and in so doing enhances negative competition and loose networks among the various local organizations and groups.

A Vision for Star Street

Star Street remains the best first-step for the regeneration of the old city core through the city's primary industry: tourism. The only competitors are al-Fawaghra Street and Paul VI Street starting from al-Madbasseh Square, which bound the existing souk area. At present, these streets are overcrowded and contain far smaller properties, and hence are less flexible and represent more modest opportunities.

The most serious competition comes from al-Madbasseh Square: Paul VI Street extending from that square is more accessible to Manger Square and already contains tourism assets: the newly built International Centre of Bethlehem Dar Annadwa (a cultural complex of the Lutheran Church) and the Assyrian Orthodox Church further to the east, right on the main market's stairs. It is also a somewhat thriving street that is not solely geared around local shopping services (as al-Fawarghra Street and the souk area are). For instance, the International Centre of Bethlehem contains a restaurant, a bar and a gift shop, and the street has a number of jewellery shops and other exceptional souk shops (i.e. spice shops, bakers, antiquities, etc.). The problems with Star Street are its relative inaccessibility, made worse by the PADICO deal, and the fact that it currently contains no more tourism destinations than al-Madbasseh Square: Star Street has the Melkite Church – the church that can be described as Palestine's original, indigenous faith – and a single museum, the Salesian Church Nativity museum.

However, the chief attraction of Star Street is not that it possesses tourism destinations, but that it is one in itself: it is the route into the city taken by the Holy Family. Star Street also enjoys the reputation of being the pilgrimage entrance to the city, as well as the site for the traditional celebrations that surround Christmas pilgrimage. Star Street also has a special place in the city's life, as it is traditionally used for wedding and funeral processions.

But the fact is, Bethlehem's old city core has no tourism destination that in any way rivals the basilica – nor could any rival the birthplace of Christ, the sole reason for Bethlehem's fame. What Star Street represents is an opportunity: a near-blank canvas that could be turned into a tourist thoroughfare. A Bethlehem Ramble would rest upon the twofold heritage argument that Bethlehem most wishes to broadcast to the world: the intimate connection between the Church and the City, a two thousand–year-old heritage that survives because it is rooted in the community. The challenge lies in regenerating and sustaining this thoroughfare in the face of the real disincentives that stop the current tourists from visiting.

Several elements have to be factored in to achieve a sustainable and revived old city core. At the top of the priority list should be an intensive and focused consultation between the tourism industry players and local communities, organizations and institutions, so as to raise awareness of the benefits of the regeneration and resolve potential conflicts of interest. In short, the achievement would require a public-private tourism development initiative, with an integral part of the initiative focused on the local economy, since economic diversification could further stimulate economic growth in peripheral areas (Eber, 1992).

Further, the concept of a Christmas Market as a once-a-year event is a wasted opportunity: a Christmas Market should be year-round in the town that brought Christmas to the world. So that the name of Star Street might acquire more resonance, it is more than possible to create a decorative star theme for the street that can survive yearlong scrutiny, just as the decorative look of Paris's Metros, Spain's Cordoba or Miami's South Beach hotels have all withstood the test of time. Within this decorated street, and among its pilgrimage markings, certain stores can sell locally produced Christmas decorations year-round, as well as locally produced objects that relate to the Nativity and to the Christian faith in general. Better yet, the street could support workshops that produce traditional crafts, providing an arts-and-craft destination close to the centre of the city. Further the goal would be to open up the mansions along the street, so that it becomes a magnet for visitors interested in exploring the essence of the Palestinian way of life, in the past and present. In a similar fashion, the street could also support a boutique hotel, offering the quality of a five-star hotel but in a more intimate, central setting. However, to encourage investments of any size in the old city core, a scheme of incentives has to be introduced (i.e. tax-exempt status for the area, loan programmes and grants, technical assistance, etc).

It will also be necessary to rethink the street, not simply as a linear pilgrimage route, but as an entrance into the old city, so that hidden resources become woven into the fabric of the street and extended by even better signage and information points. Such resources include the Arab Women's Museum, the Centre for Cultural Heritage Preservation, the Melkite Church and back routes up to the souk and down to the bus terminal. In addition, appropriate plans, laws and regulations with regard to traffic, waste management, taxes, opening hours, safety, etc., ought to be well thought out and implemented to maximize rewards.

Last but not least, local and international tour operators have to be made aware of the potential of the old city core as a must-see destination paired with the basilica. Tour operators must be presented with an attractive package deal that is competitive and comprehensive in terms of quality and pricing. Supplementary information and promotional tools such as maps, leaflets, postcards, videotapes and so on have to be produced and distributed through such proper channels as tourism fairs (UNESCO, 1997). Ultimately, training curriculum for tour guides should not only emphasize the religious aspects of Bethlehem as a destination but also highlight the unique and rich cultural heritage it possesses, thus enriching the experience visitors get when visiting the old city core.

Conclusion

As mentioned, there is already a fragile consensus that Star Street presents the best first step to regenerating the old core of Bethlehem. The real issue is strengthening it. Those with most to fear from the regeneration of Star Street need to hear the argument that it would attract a different kind of tourist and would not weaken the already existing markets but rather anticipate future markets.

The issue for PADICO is double-edged: the financial health of al-Aqaria depends upon the bus terminal. Yet the Palestine Tourism Investment Company (PTIC), another PADICO subsidiary, has an interest in boosting Bethlehem's business and assuming ownership of tourism assets.[9] At present, PTIC's chief investment in Bethlehem is the Jacir Palace Intercontinental Hotel, but its portfolio could only be enhanced by building value in Bethlehem and creating new tourism assets.

The strategic vision exists. As the Palestinian Tourism Development Strategy, a document prepared by the Palestinian National Authority and the Palestinian Economic Council for Development and Reconstruction, states: 'Tourism growth in the Bethlehem area will depend on the development of a tourism system that enriches and diversifies the existing tourism product' (Palestinian Economic Council for Reconstruction, 2001). But political will has to be mustered to forge alliances across the public and private sectors to achieve this goal. In the end, this may prove a role for national government. We can hope. One of the attributes of nationhood is pride in heritage, which Palestine possesses despite its lack of, for instance, national museums (Chemonics International Inc. and Massar Associates et al. 1999). No spot in Palestine is as well placed as Star Street as the site for such a museum. And of all Palestine's cities, none provide as many potential visitors to a museum as Bethlehem and Jerusalem. Of these two, Bethlehem alone offers an opportunity to build a national museum immediately. The two cities share a single heritage, yet Bethlehem can still provide a celebration of Palestinian history – whereas a museum in Jerusalem will inevitably mourn for what has been destroyed.

NOTES

1. According to the Al-Jouthour Society (2005). The society was also concerned about the economy of the street and envisioned turning it into a mall, but the means were not found to implement this project.
2. 'The Catastrophe' – refers to the loss of Palestine to the Israelis in the 1948 war.
3. PADICO has a broad range of interests. It is active in telecommunications, tourism, real estate, housing, consumer electronics, industrial plastics and poultry farming, as well as developing and running industrial zones. It is also the majority shareholder of the Palestinian Securities and Equities Commission (PSEC), the Palestinian stock exchange supervised by the Palestinian Ministry of Finance. In short, PADICO is a public/private partnership active in all sections of the Palestinian economy, financed by private investors and banks. In addition PADICO is the chief engine for the use of investment funds from USAID, the World Bank and EU loans. As indicated on their website, PADICO's stated intention is to grow new businesses and, as they are floated, reduce its shareholding to under 50 per cent.

   Shortly after PADICO concluded its agreement with Bethlehem Municipality, it transferred the running of the bus terminal to a partially owned subsidiary, Al-Aqaria (51.8 per cent owned by PADICO). The chief reason for the failure of BL2000's attempt to revive Star Street was the agreement, neither expected nor accepted by the public, between the Bethlehem Municipality and PADICO. Although BL2000 was given the power of a ministry when it was first founded, certain weaknesses, both external and internal (as shown in the BL2000 presentation entitled 'Evaluation of Christmas Market 1999'), partially explain why it was blindsided by the PADICO deal. These weaknesses can be attributed to difficulties BL2000 faced in the revitalization of Star Street, such as the low number of participants (either shop owners or third-party tenants, because of the high risk these shop owners or tenants associated with the event altogether) in comparison to the actual existing shops, the high rental fees levied by BL2000 to third parties and the absence of other existing or planned attractions on the street. In addition, certain internal issues impeded achievement: the absence of adequate funding, the understaffing of the department of Tourism and Private Sector Development, the nonexistence of an awareness programme, poor publicity and the number of involved parties (BL 2000, Bethlehem Municipality, Ministry of Tourism, shop owners, tenants, PADICO), each seeking its own interest.

4. Oral Communication compiled by Christian Dabdoub Nasser, Head of Public Relations at CCHP.
5. Although Star Street had been extensively and conclusively rehabilitated in 1999, it suffered serious infrastructural damage in the recurring Israeli aggression on the city throughout the duration of the second Intifada.
6. YMCA vendor, oral communication.
7. Doris Hazboun used Dr. Suleiman al-Loussi's antiques shop to sell her wares. Usually she sold through a network of friends or in local events; she had never had her own shop. Oral communication.
8. Hamas, the Islamic Resistance Movement in Palestine, is viewed by the United States as a terrorist organization.
9. See http://www.padico.com, which, in its news and press releases section mentions a loan restructuring process for PTIC in connection with PTIC's ownership of the Intercontinental Hotel in Bethlehem (accessed 2/7/2011).

REFERENCES

Abdullah Giacaman, H. 1994. *A Tour in the History of the Holy Land, vol. 1: The New Entrance to Bethlehem.* Jerusalem: Modern Arab Press.

Abdullah Giacaman, H. 2000. *A Tour in the History of the Holy Land, vol. 4: A New Tour in the History of Bethlehem and Jerusalem.* Jerusalem: Modern Arab Press.

Al-Jouthour Society. 2005. *Statistics of the Current Shop Owners in Star Street.* Bethlehem: Al-Jouthour Society.

Bannoura, T. 1982. *The History of Bethlehem, Beit Jala, Beit Sahour 'Ephrata'.* Al-Ma'aref Print.

Bethlehem 2000 Project. 1998. *Sectoral Profile: Tourism Development.* Bethlehem: Bethlehem 2000 Project Authority.

Bethlehem 2000 Project. 1999. *The Bethlehem (permanent) Christmas Market.* Concept paper. Bethlehem: Bethlehem 2000 Project Authority.

Bethlehem 2000 Project. 2002. *Bethlehem 2000 Chronicle: The Story of a National Palestinian Development Project.* Bethlehem: Bethlehem 2000 Project Authority.

Centre for Cultural Heritage Preservation. 2005. Documents and Archives: Delta project, Emergency Master Plan, Christmas Market 2005. Bethlehem: CCHP.

Chemonics International Inc. and Massar Associates et al. 1999. *Palestinian Tourism Planning and Development Project.* Ramallah, Palestine: Palestinian Economic Council for Development and Reconstruction.

de Kadt, E. 1979. *Tourism: Passport to Development?* Oxford: Oxford University Press.

Eber, S. (ed). 1992. *Beyond the Green Horizon: Principles of Sustainable Tourism.* Discussion paper, World Wide Fund for Nature. Surrey: Panda House.

El-Ali, G. 1991. *Bethlehem: The Immortal Town.* Jerusalem: Emerezian Graphic Arts, trans. Dr Issa Massou.

Elliott, J. 1997. *Tourism: Politics and Public Sector Management.* London: Routledge.

Juha, I.W. 2004. *The Inscription of Palestinian Cultural and Natural Heritage Sites on the World Heritage List – Bethlehem as a Case Study,* master's thesis. Brandenburg University of Technology, Cottbus, Germany.

Lundberg, D.E., M.H. Stavenca and M. Krishnamoorthy. 1995. *Tourism Economics.* New York: Wiley.

Nasser, H. 1999. Letter dated 4 June from Bethlehem Municipality to the Bethlehem 2000 Project. Bethlehem: Centre for Cultural Heritage Preservation.

Negi, J. 1990. *Tourism Development and Resource Conservation. New Delhi: Metropolitan Publisher.*

Orbasli, A. 2000. *Tourists in Historic Towns: Urban Conservation and Heritage Management.* London: E and FN Spon.

Palestinian Economic Council for Development and Reconstruction. 2001. *Palestinian Tourism Development Strategy.* Palestinian Economic Council for Development and Reconstruction.

Palestinian National Authority. 2005. *Inventory of Cultural and Natural Heritage Sites of Potential Outstanding Universal Value in Palestine.* Palestinian National Authority Ministry of Tourism and Antiquities, Department of Antiquities and Cultural Heritage.

Raheb, M. and F. Strickert. 2000. *Bethlehem 2000: Past and Present.* Heidelberg, Germany: Palmyra.

Revault, P., S. Santelli and C. Weill-Rochant. 1997. *Maisons de Bethléem.* Paris: Maisonneuve & Larose.

Sansour Dabdoub, C. 2000. *Evaluation of the Christmas Market 2000.* Power Point presentation for Tourism Department of Bethlehem 2000 Project.

Shokeh, K. 2000. *History of Bethlehem During Ottoman Times 1517–1917: A Documentary and Historical Study.* Bethlehem.

UNESCO. 1997. *Emergency Action Plan for the Bethlehem Area.* UNESCO.

Williams, A.M. and G. Shaw. 1998. *Tourism & Economic Development: European Experiences, 3rd ed.* Chichester: Wileys.

Yeoman, I., M. Robertson, J. Ali-Knight, S. Drummond and U. McMahon-Beattie. 2004. *Festival and Events Management: An International Arts and Culture Perspective.* Oxford: Butterworth-Heinemann.

Web Resources

Arts and Business Council Inc., Cultural Tourism Initiative: www.artsandbusiness
.org/culturaltourism/guidelines.html

The Impact of Festivals on Cultural Tourism, Razaq Raj, The 2nd DeHaan Tourism Management Conference: www.nottingham.ac.uk/ttri/news/conference/
conference.html

Palestine Development and Investment Ltd.: http://www.padico.com

Oral Communication

Interview with Mr. Zahi Khoury, Board Member of Palestine Development and Investment Ltd. (PADICO), December 2005.

Christiane Dabdoub Nasser, Head of Public Awareness and International Relations at the Centre for Cultural Heritage Preservation, 2005.

YMCA vendor, YMCA kiosk on Catholic Action Square during the Christmas Market, 2005.

Miss Hazboun, vendor of handmade accessories and shawls at the Christmas Market, 2005.

Chapter 8

Contentious Politics in a Bosphorus Neighbourhood

Perspectives on Conflict and Solidarity during the Twentieth Century

H.H. GÜNHAN DANIŞMAN AND İSMAİL ÜSTÜN

A government proposal to construct a third bridge over the straits in Istanbul in 1998 resulted in the creation of a successful residents' association at Arnavutköy, a Bosphorus neighbourhood on the European side whose unique historic and social fabric would have been adversely affected by the project. Acts of civil disobedience by this impromptu NGO have until now successfully managed to prevent its realization. An oral history exercise initiated by the NGO in order to highlight the neighbourhood's long history and rich multiethnic social composition revealed that the threatening bridge proposal was only the latest in a long list of contentious policies imposed on the residents by the central or the municipal governments throughout the twentieth century. With their narratives, the residents have unfolded a story of not only tragic conflict but also substantial solidarity among members of different ethnic and religious groups, born of these political struggles.

Background

In November 1998 the State Highways Department of the Turkish Ministry of Public Works announced its intention to construct a third bridge across the Bosphorus that would run from the village of Kandilli on the Asian side through to Arnavutköy on the European shore. The residents of Arnavutköy immediately raised objections to the intended bridge on the grounds that the traditional social fabric of their multiethnic neighbourhood would be destroyed, its natural environment would irrevocably damaged and its unique cultural heritage, consisting of hundreds of listed historic buildings and monuments, would forever be lost. This response to the destructive challenge posed by the central government took the form of a civil disobedience group named the Arnavutköy's Citizens' Initiative (or ASG for Arnavutköy Semt Girişimi). This spontaneously created NGO has carried out demonstrations for the last few years with considerable success, apparently stopping the implementation of the project temporarily. The threat has not disappeared completely because announcements by government representatives, including Prime Minister Erdogan, continue to report the intent to realize the third bridge.

The bridge would be in violation of Turkish Law 2863 on The Protection of Cultural and Natural Assets, and the current Master Plan of Metropolitan Istanbul rejects a third bridge across the Bosphorus. In their fight against the project the members of ASG, while arguing for alternative and more effective public transport systems, such as a rail tunnel underneath the waterway and increased use of swift ferry boats between the two continents, have also realized that their major asset in this fight is the unique cultural heritage and rich urban fabric of their neighbourhood. To highlight the neighbourhood's history and its traditional social composition, ASG initiated an oral history project based on interviews conducted with the senior citizens of different ethnic groups of the neighbourhood (Danişman and Üstün 2000).[1] Following the recording of some initial narratives, it became apparent that the bridge project was only the latest in a long series of contentious politics from above that interfered with the lives of the citizens.

Earlier History of the Neighbourhood

Arnavutköy, or *Mega Revma* to its Greek Orthodox residents, means 'the Albanian Village'. The name is owed to Greek-speaking Albanians who were made to settle here in the second half of the fifteenth century by the Ottoman Sultan Mehmet II, who wished to employ them as stonemasons for reconstruction projects in his newly captured capital city. The earliest settlements in and around the Arnavutköy area date back to antiquity, according to archaeological evidence, and the original settlement used to be called Hestai. Later, during the Roman era and particularly from the fourth century onwards, it was called Promotu because of a villa built here by the consul Promotus. From the sixth century on, the name Anaplus was preferred over Promotu (Eyice 1976: 26–28).

The Roman village was famous because Emperor Constantine I (AD 337–361) had constructed a circular martyrium church here dedicated to the Archangel Michael, whose mosaic representation embellished a marbled courtyard surrounded by arcades. Historical evidence indicates that the Church of Hagios Michael was enlarged and its mosaic angel substantially restored by Emperor Justinian (527–565). Historians of later periods recorded that Anaplus Michaelion was in ruins following the Latin invasion of Constantinople during the Fourth Crusade, as well as due to the increasing raids by Ottoman Turks against the city in the late fourteenth and early fifteenth centuries (Kömürcüyan 1952: 272; Constantios 1846: 167). When the city was conquered by the Ottoman Sultan Mehmet II in 1453, he resettled the village with refugees from Albania, and later with Greek migrants from the Eastern Black Sea kingdom of Pontus when Trebizond was occupied by the Sultan in 1481 (İncicyan 1976: 115).

The history of the village during the sixteenth century is obscure because of limited documentary evidence; however, a number of travelogues by Ottoman travellers in the seventeenth century indicate that the village had grown to a settlement of around one thousand families, predominantly Orthodox Greeks plus a substantial community of Jewish residents (Çelebi 1971: 123–124). The neighbourhood became a fashionable suburb towards the end of the seventeenth century and the first half of the eighteenth century, when a large number of waterside mansions *(yalıs)* were built for wealthy Greek merchants and for some members of the Ottoman royalty (Koçu 1946: 1039).

It was not until the beginning of the nineteenth century that Muslim subjects of the empire began to settle in Arnavutköy in large numbers, which coincided with the Ottoman government's displeasure with Arnavutköy's Greek merchants, who were accused of aiding the Mora uprising (Koçu 1946: 1040). After the Greek independence, the Ottoman Sultan Mahmoud II confiscated the mansions and houses of the Greek merchants in Arnavutköy and turned them over to Jewish families brought over from the Jewish quarters within the walled city. This period also saw the construction of the village's first mosque and a police station in the neighbourhood. However, the Jews abandoned Arnavutköy in large numbers when 264 houses in the Jewish section of the neighbourhood were razed to the ground by a mysterious fire in 1887 (Ahmed Cevdet Paşa 1309/1891: 82).

Successive fires towards the end of the nineteenth century and during the first decade of the twentieth century caused a metamorphosis in the social and the physical composition of the neighbourhood. Sections of the village that burnt down were replanned with a criss-cross street pattern, while shapes of housing plots were remodelled to create terraced housing in place of the former plots with detached houses (Danışman 1999). The immediate result of this change was a corresponding increase in population figures of respective ethnic groups, while the establishment of regular ferry boat services increased the popularity of Arnavutköy as a favourite com-

Figure 8.1. A historic photograph of Arnavutköy showing the waterside mansions before the construction of the 'pyloned road' that drove a wedge between the residents and the sea.

Figure 8.2. The neighbourhood of Arnavutköy photographed from the middle of the Bosphorus, and threatened by the proposal to construct a third bridge.

muter suburb. A census carried out by the ferry company Şirket-i Hayriye, the results of which were published in the company yearbook (*Salname*) for 1912, indicated that there were 5,973 Orthodox Greeks in 975 house- holds and 493 Muslim Turks in 168 households, accompanied by smaller communities of Armenians and Jews (Artan 1993: 172–174).

This social profile was reversed completely by the end of the twentieth century owing to the series of contentious politics that have caused mas- sive migrations and population replacements. The 1999 General Election Register for the Arnavutköy election district, analysed in a recent study, has indicated that the ratio of the Muslim Turks is now 95 per cent, versus a ratio of 5 per cent for Orthodox Greeks (Danışman and Üstün 2000).

Twentieth-century Conflicts at Arnavutköy

The First World War brought the Ottoman Empire to an end and resulted in the occupation of Istanbul by the Allied Forces. The tragedy of the Great War instigated the first major wave of migrations in and out of the village:

> Karaman Greeks and Armenians came [to Arnavutköy] at first, during the Great War. They came following the massacres. You know the massacres were mutual and the cause. ... My dear father used to smoke a cigarette and narrate these stories to me. (Interview with R21)[1]

The Greek-Turkish War adversely affected the relationships among the eth- nic population of the city and caused many Christians to depart for Europe and America between 1914 and 1924 (Hirschon 2000: 54):

> During the Great War, people who had the means left for Europe, and then for America. (Interview with E11)

The Lausanne Peace Treaty of 1923, which also included the compulsory exchange of populations between Greece and Turkey, although technically exempting the 'established' residents of Istanbul, had its negative effects on Arnavutköy as well. This time the neighbourhood was on the receiving end, accepting migrants from the Black Sea area:

> Migrations from the Black Sea region started with the Exchange [of popu- lations between Greece and Turkey], more than 70 years ago. (Interview with R21)

> My father was born in Rize (on the Russian border along the Black Sea), and he migrated to Istanbul when he was 15. (Interview with T30)

The only criterion in determining the ethnic groups to be formally exchanged between Greece and Turkey was religion: factors such as language were completely ignored. Thus, Orthodox Greeks were exchanged with Sunni Muslims, leaving Catholic or Protestant Greeks exempt from deportation. On the other hand, Turkish-speaking Cilician Orthodox and Karamanlides were replaced by Greek-speaking Cretan Muslims. By 1928 over a million Anatolian Greeks (*Rum*) had been deported to Greece, while nearly half a million Muslims from Western Thrace had been sent to Turkey. Neither the Greek government nor the Turkish government had shown any willingness to consult the individuals as to whether they wanted to be subjected to this compulsory migration. At the beginning of the Second World War, the number of Greeks still resident in Istanbul was estimated at around 140,000 (Arı 2000; Pekin and Turan 2002).

The next traumatic contentious policy to affect the neighbourhood adversely was the notorious Wealth Tax Law of 1942, ostensibly levied against war profits but 'in reality [acting as a] thinly disguised penalty imposed on the non-Muslims' (Keyder 1999: 180). At the beginning of the war the Turkish government drafted over a million men into the army, thereby putting a heavy burden on the central budget. The government's intention to relieve this burden through a 'one-time only' wealth tax on incomes made during the inflation of the war period was, according to some researchers, in reality an attempt to transfer economic power from non-Muslim to Muslim businessmen (Ökte 1957: 217–227; Tezel 2001: 262). An article in the law closed off avenues for raising objections to the taxes that were to be levied, and the non-Muslim citizens of the republic were treated most unfairly: while they formed only 4 per cent of the total number of taxpayers in Istanbul, they were taxed at levels comprising 54 per cent of total revenues, and those unable to comply within the given period of time were made to join labour camps for payments in kind (Akar 2000: 71).

> There were many from Arnavutköy who couldn't pay the Wealth Tax and were sent to Ashkale for forced labour. Some couldn't return; they were unable to endure the strains. (Interview with E11)

Although Turkey was able to stay neutral during the Second World War, long stints of military service and scarcity of bread and other staple foods created more hardships. The labour shortage during the war prompted the Greek owners of the famous strawberry fields in Arnavutköy to draft young boys from the Black Sea region as migrant agricultural workers:

> When they first came, these boys looked hungry and dirty. Their employers first gave them a good bath and a scrub, and then new clothes to wear.

> ... They became part of the households. Later, when the Greek owners
> had to leave for Greece at short notice, these young men first became the
> keepers, and then the new owners of the strawberry fields and the houses
> of their employers. (Interview with R22)

After the war, Turkey began experimenting with the multi-party system,
and the Democratic Party was able to enter the parliament in opposition
following the general elections of 1946. The political power of the Republican People's Party (CHP) was waning, and the general elections on 14 May
1950 marked a turning point for the regime, with the Democrats winning
a big majority in the parliament and several members of parliament being elected from non-Muslim communities. The new liberal political at-
mosphere proved short-lived, however, and tolerance and goodwill among
the ethnic communities began to suffer as the Cyprus crises mounted.
The Menderes government, long uninterested in developments relating to
Cypriot demands for self-determination instead of British rule, was dip-
lomatically unprepared when the EOKA[2] established by Grivas started its
underground resistance and the British government decided to convene a
conference on the Cyprus crisis. The conference, which opened in London
on 29 August 1955, was soon deadlocked, and it was clear that it would
be impossible to unite the parties on common ground to work towards a
solution for the future of the island. The parties meeting in London subsequently dispersed without an agreement, ostensibly because of the violent
incidents in Istanbul on 6 and 7 September 1955, which targeted the shops
and places of business of the city's non-Muslims (Akar 2003: 86–93; Alexandris 1983; Demirer 1995; Dosdoğru 1993; Tuncay 1986).

> We were surprised, and very scared, on the 6th and 7th September. ... You
> know that the quarrel started in Thessalonike, there was an explosion.
> They put a bomb at the house of Atatürk. (Interview with R21)

Many analysts of the 6–7 September 1955 incidents have suggested a
well-planned government conspiracy designed to put pressure the ongoing
Cyprus conference in London. Even some diplomatic dispatches by foreign
embassies suggest that the street riots were pre-planned:

> In my unnumbered telegram of the 6th of September I reported that seri-
> ous anti-Greek rioting had broken out in Istanbul that evening. ... The
> immediate cause seems to have been a report received three or four hours
> earlier that Atatürk's birthplace and the Turkish Consulate in Salonika had
> been attacked and blown up by Greek demonstrators. ... It is clear, though
> it is naturally difficult to lay one's hand on conclusive evidence, that the

rioting was well organised in advance ... and I am reliably informed that the Government were aware of and had agreed to an anti-Greek demonstration to be organised under the auspices of the 'Cyprus is Turkish' Association. ... I rather doubt whether, as Greek sources have suggested, the Salonika bomb incident was part of the plot. (F.O. 371/117711/RG 10344/50; Hristidis 2000: 310–315)

They brought a lot of men from Beykoz on the Asian side by ferry-boat. It was clear that everything was planned well ahead. (Interview with T33)

Not only the central commercial district of the city but also suburbs with large concentrations of non-Muslim citizens, such as Arnavutköy, were obviously targeted:

I came back to Arnavutköy with my father, but I could not enter our street. We arrived to the alley. There was a Greek pastry shop called Jonker; it had been ransacked. There was Avram the haberdasher; his shop was broken into and completely destroyed. They had torn rolls of cloth into many pieces. They had brought in a truck full of men from outside, and let them loose. These men have also assaulted women, broken into homes. Towards midnight, martial law was declared, everyone was forced to stay indoors. ... Then, the Greeks started to leave one by one. (Interview with T33)

In March 1964 a United Nations Peacekeeping Force was established on the island of Cyprus after President Makarios refused to recognize the Turkish Cypriots' power sharing in the government of the island. Turkey responded by issuing the Government Decree of 16 March 1964, which forced Orthodox Greeks carrying Greek passports (approximately 30,000 people at that date) either to change their nationality or to leave.[3] This initiated more migrations from the neighbourhood:

More people left in 1964 than they did in 1955. Many Greeks who were citizens of Turkey had to leave, as well, because they were married to Greek citizens who were being evicted with the Decree of 1964. (Interview with T33)

The Samson coup d'état on the island and the invasion of Northern Cyprus by the Turkish Army in July 1974 were the final blow to the Greek residents of Arnavutköy. Today the total figure of Greek residents in Istanbul is estimated around 3,500, while only about 250 Greeks were registered in Arnavutköy in the 1999 election census, making them around 5 per cent of the neighbourhood's population.

You wouldn't understand when they were leaving. They used to disappear very, very quietly. Only my neighbour on the opposite corner, Madame Victoria, she said farewell to everyone, crying all the time. She was very sad. Her son who was doing his military service had deserted and gone to Greece; then refused to return. For this reason, Madame Victoria was forced to leave, as well. She had the nationality of Turkey. (Interview with T31)

Solidarity in the Face of Contentious Politics

A surprising discovery in the oral interviews was that in the face of contentious politics from above, a determined solidarity grew among the members of various ethnic groups at the grass-roots level. A recent study that made use of the Municipal Road Tax Register for the year 1930 at Arnavutköy proved extremely useful for the oral history project of the neighbourhood (Üstün 2003). During the interview the interviewees were shown the register, which included the names of 596 shopkeepers. These names triggered further memories regarding the commercial life of the community, as well as the shops and their owners. To find out that certain professions were traditionally under the monopoly of certain ethnic communities was an unexpected bonus of analysis of the register. Discussion of these findings opened up new avenues of memory and revelations during the interviews. It was obvious that the collective memory of the community was made up of instances of conflict and instances of solidarity. The Municipal Road Tax Register made it easier for the interviewees to talk more comfortably regarding their traumatic experiences. A sampling of these instances of solidarity at Arnavutköy in the face of contentious politics makes a strong case for existence of an essential layer of tolerance cementing the community together.

A typical example of economic solidarity was the case of a local shopkeeper who was unable to pay the wealth tax, which prompted his friends and neighbours to extend him credit:

There were those that had to go to Ashkale. Not many, because they were shopkeepers, and what else can a shopkeeper do, except to try to keep his shop open. Now, I have to speak openly, when the tax we had to pay was declared to be 3,500 lira, my father could only gather around 2,000 to 2,500 lira. Now, I don't want to blame, but when he went to the wholesale merchant to buy sacks of merchandise, he would take me along sometimes, instead of paying the whole price of 200 lira, he would give 50, and pay the rest in installments gradually. But when this Wealth Tax came, the merchant didn't give us even one sack on credit, perhaps thinking we would pay the Tax and not him. But fortunately we had neighbours, Turkish neighbours, who wanted to give what we needed. Not much, small sums, but without asking any surety or interest; they helped, and we paid back in time. That is how we gathered the 3,500 lira. And I would never forget, don't know what happened to those papers, he would always ask for a receipt when he paid back. I asked him why he took those. He said, 'My son, tomorrow when I go back to the wholesale merchant, I can show that I have paid my taxes, so that he would sell me merchandise on credit again.' (Interview with E11)

Humanitarian aid seems to have been a more frequently occurring type of solidarity, particularly during the height of sectarian conflict, as the following examples indicate:

Acrobat Mustafa, our neighbour, he saved us during 6–7 September. He is still alive but aged now, walking with his cane. He and a friend of his barricaded our street, carrying picks and shovels, and he shouted, 'No one enters here, you won't touch any one who lives here.' (Interview with R21)

Trying to save property was perhaps as difficult as trying to save lives:

A retired air-force captain, maybe he was a major, but retired; he used to be my customer; coming around for the special tobacco for his water pipe. Maybe for that reason, when the mad crowd on the evening of 6th September started to bring down my shop-window, he appeared suddenly, with his pistol drawn, and declared, 'I will shoot anyone who tries to enter this place.' He stood there defiantly and he saved my shop. (Interview with E11)

Nostalgia for the peaceful and friendly days of the past also gives clues to instances of solidarity:

Whenever I and my mother went on house visits to our Greek neighbours, they would first serve us chocolate and liqueur, before serving coffee. Then, their white coloured traditional desert with gum mastic [mastika] would be brought, to be eaten with a spoon from the water glass, and its sweet juice to be sipped on top. … During the Easter time, the whole village would be filled with sweet smell of Easter bread. Our [Greek] neighbours would bring us coloured Easter eggs and Easter sweet-bread. The church would be completely full at the midnight mass during the Great feast, with people from every denomination present. (Interview with T31)

Respecting each other's customs during the religious holidays was also an act of solidarity:

> As a result of living alongside with Moslems, we had gotten accustomed to each other's traditional habits. At the Feast of Sacrifice, they used to share with us their meat; we usually got a whole leg of lamb. During Easters, we would exchange our sweet-bread and eggs with our neighbours. The baker Hristo would distribute Easter bread to the poor. We were careful not to eat food openly during the month of Ramadan, when Turks were around fasting. (Interview with E11)

Solidarity sometimes raised the collective consciousness. Another major trauma experienced by the residents of Arnavutköy in 1988, this time instigated by the local municipal authority, perhaps played a key role in the creation of ASG a decade later. The Metropolitan Municipality built the double-lane highway known as the 'pyloned road' over the sea through the coastal strip, starting from the Kurucheshme end of Arnavutköy in the south towards Bebek in the north, without going through the necessary planning consultation procedures. It effectively severed the neighbourhood from its Bosphorus waterside, and as usual in such cases, created a much larger and faster volume of traffic, dangerous to pedestrians. Object-

Figure 8.3. ASG on the march along the 'pyloned road', demanding a rail tunnel under the Bosphorus (instead of a third bridge).

ing citizens' petitions to the appeals court resulted in the court's decision to cancel the road project. The 'pyloned road' was thus declared illegal, but it was a decision that came too late for the residents of Arnavutköy. The project was stopped after Bebek, but the portion already constructed through Arnavutköy would stay.

ASG or the Final Act of Defiance

The proposal to build a third bridge across Arnavutköy posed a major threat to all the neighbourhood's residents, regardless of ethnic or denominational background. Over time, the success of ASG's civil disobedience awakened national and international interest in the movement. The fight turned from a protest against a destructive bridge project into recognition of the civic rights of citizens. The significant steps in ASG's rise to fame can be summarized as follows.

An NGO Champions the Cause of Public Transport for the First Time in Turkey

Transportation experts consistently objected to the construction of the first bridge across the Bosphorus in 1973 and the second bridge in 1988, on the grounds that they would serve only to increase numbers of private cars without presenting a solution to the city's public transport needs. But populist politicians and spokesmen for various governments, supported by automotive sector and car-user lobbies as well as land speculators who had purchased prime properties on either side of the bridge projects, moved to discredit the scientists and experts by claiming that the two bridges were quickly becoming insufficient for the growing traffic and therefore a third, fourth, and even a fifth bridge needed to be constructed. However, when the plan to start work on a third bridge was finally announced in November 1998, this time the objections came from the citizens who were going to be directly affected.

The politicians and bureaucrats were unprepared for this defiance, which took the form of open-air meetings, street demonstrations and other forms of disobedience. ASG immediately began to organize coffeehouse meetings, attended by university professors, representatives of engineering and architectural chambers, and other transport experts, as a series of self-information sessions on Istanbul's traffic problems and their proposed solutions. As members of ASG became more informed, they began to take part in televised discussion forums, attended conferences as participants, wrote letters to local and national politicians, planned sit-ins at the parliament building and circulated petitions, collecting thousands of signatures from the whole city. A very active Internet website was prepared to display arguments against the bridge and explain why alternative projects such as a rail tunnel and increased use of ferries were real solutions for public transport in Istanbul.

As Arnavutköy residents raised their voices louder, the media began to cover news from the neighbourhood more frequently. The traditional Arnavutköy street festivals were re-created, and they turned into jolly occasions of protest in which nationally renowned musicians, actors and artists took part. It became fashionable to show solidarity with the Arnavutköy residents. In the meantime, the residents – having learned from their mistakes during the resistance to the 'pyloned road' – regularly consulted legal experts on the steps the needed to take in order to stop the project before it was too late. Politicians from all parties standing for municipal elections visited Arnavutköy, declaring themselves against the third bridge and for improved public transport systems. Not only the members of ASG, but the majority of the city's population started to demand better forms of public transport. Awareness among the public at large that the motorcar, which had become the sacred cow of the Turkish automotive industry, could not co-exist with a city of more than 2,500 years of history and cultural heritage, forced the bridge lobby onto the defence, whereupon the project was temporarily shelved.

Nevertheless, the global economy still tried to dictate its terms: when opposition arose to plans for constructing a new Japanese automobile factory on very fertile agricultural land, the populist president of the republic hit back at the protestors by stating that he would let the factory be built in the garden of the Presidential Palace, if need be. It was clear that the struggle facing ASG would be long and difficult.

ASG's Strategy Develops to Defend Rail Tunnel as Alternative to Bridge

While the Ministry of Public Works was pushing its pet bridge project, the Ministry of Transportation had completed a thorough proposal for a rail tunnel running underneath the waterway along the top of a natural ridge forty meters below the surface between Scudari in Asia and Sarayburnu at the tip of the walled city.[4] It would accommodate two-way surface metro lines, as well as an international railroad line connecting London with Vladivostok. While the two bridges had the capacity of 10,000 passengers an hour, the rail tunnel would be able to carry 75,000 passengers an hour.

In 1999 representatives of ASG paid a visit to the minister of transport in Ankara, requesting that he send his technical experts to explain the environment-friendly rail tunnel project to the residents of Arnavutköy, and to the rest of Istanbul. The media were quick to give this event wide coverage, which highlighted the noise pollution and the increase in lead-containing exhaust fumes that would be generated by use of the bridge. Arnavutköy citizens, in effect, had assumed the job of public relations to promote the project for the rail tunnel, which was equal in capacity to seven or eight bridges. Additionally, ASG was fighting the third bridge project by proposing a more attractive alternative to meet the public transportation needs of the city – an important advantage compared to the objections raised in the earlier cases of the first and second bridges, which had failed to propose viable alternatives.

Willingness to Share Information (or Not)

In spite of repeated requests from ASG, neither the Ministry of Public Works nor the State Highways Department revealed their detailed plans for the construction of the third bridge. Requests to provide information on preparations for compulsory purchase orders for listed private properties and on the scale of destruction that the neighbourhood's historic fabric would suffer during construction operations were rejected on the grounds that the bridge project was not yet finalized and therefore, could not be revealed to the public. Additionally, ASG's public demonstrations were condemned as unnecessary reactions to a hypothetical project; however, citizens of Istanbul, professional organizations and other NGOs were not impressed. Instigators of the contentious politics of the early 2000s are still trying to push improper engineering projects forward as discreetly as possible without sharing information via planning inquiry processes, and meanwhile are trying to intimidate conscientious objectors to these projects.

ASG, on the other hand, was more than willing to share its experiences and its strategies with other NGOs in the city. Residents of Arnavutköy took active part in open-air demonstrations when Istanbul Municipality wanted to construct a public building in the middle of a park at Kuzguncuk, another multiethnic village on the Asian side of the Bosphorus, and during a protest march they walked arm in arm with residents of the Moda district in Kadıköy, who were trying to stop the concreting of their beaches following the mayor of Istanbul's expressed wish to build a coastal highway. ASG members frequently attend seminars, for example on how to administer an NGO effectively and create sustainability. In return members from other civil organizations in the city have begun to take part regularly in Arnavutköy festivals and open-air meetings. Sharing information means more power to the civil movement.

Future Prospects

There is no doubt that conflict created by contentious politics is increasing solidarity among the residents of the neighbourhood of Arnavutköy, as they become a more effective NGO. ASG members have met weekly since November 1998, regardless of whether there was an imminent threat. Their agenda is no longer solely the third bridge project: they have widened their horizons and begun to discuss possible measures to prevent the environmental disasters likely to be caused by high risk Russian oil tankers passing through the Bosphorus, or to regenerate the traditional fish species through projects such as sponsoring surface cleaning vessels for pollution collection, or to organize civilian disaster management teams and a first-aid fire station in the neighbourhood in anticipation of an eventual big earthquake. Arnavutköy residents are slowly becoming more active in shaping local and national political agendas. What is perhaps more significant for the future is that closer relationships are being cultivated with the former residents of Arnavutköy who have established an association in Athens.

The contentious politics of the proposed third bridge has brought forward two new concepts for the residents of Arnavutköy. One of them is 'subsidiarity', creating administrative solutions and raising financial re-

Figure 8.4. Arnavutköy residents gathered in the neighbourhood plaza to start a protest march against the bridge proposal.

sources to problems at the level where they arise; the other is 'good governance', creating partnership between the decision makers and those to be affected by these decisions at the local level (Uğur 1999). ASG's final victory will come when the central government in Ankara allows the decision for a third bridge project over the Bosphorus to be taken by the citizens and the Municipality of Istanbul.

NOTES

The Oral History Project sponsored by the Arnavutköy's Citizens' Initiative, which forms the basis of field research underlying this chapter, was a partner of the EU project Euromed Heritage II: Mediterranean Voices through the Turkish Economic and Social History Foundation. Funding was provided by the Scientific Research Centre of Boğaziçi University of Istanbul through Project No. 01-HB-902.

1. The coding system for interviewee identification uses capital letters to refer to different ethnic groups: E for Armenian, M for Jewish, R for Greek and T for Turkish. The numbers indicate the sequence of interviewed persons. Full identification of the interviewees, the original taped recordings and the transcriptions of the interviews are available to serious researchers at the Oral History Research Centre of Boğaziçi University, Istanbul.

2. EOKA, Ethniki Organosis Kiprion Agoniston, was the Greek Cypriot military resistance movement against British rule at the time.

3. The decree of 16 March 1964, issued by the Cabinet of Ministers, required Greek citizens resident in Turkey either to change their nationality and to continue to reside and work in Turkey, or to leave the country within six months of the date of this decree.

4. The construction of the rail tunnel began in early 2005, with the first few sections of the metal tunnel being assembled at a nearby shipyard and then floated to their point of submersion by the end of 2006. The project is slated to be completed by the end of 2012.

REFERENCES

Ahmed Cevdet Paşa, 1309/1891. *Tarih-i Cevdet,* Cilt 4: *Der Saadet.* Istanbul.

Akar, R. 2000. *Aşkale Yolcuları: Varlık Vergisi ve Çalışma Kampları,* Istanbul: Belge Yayını.

Akar, R. 2003. 'İki Yıllık Gecikme: 6-7 Eylül 1955', in *Toplumsal Tarih,* Sayi 117, Istanbul: Tarih Vakfı Yayınları, 86–93.

Alexandris, A. 1983. *The Greek Minority of Istanbul and Greek-Turkish Relations: 1918–1974.* Athens: Center for Asia Minor Studies.

Arı, K. 2000. *Büyük Mübadele: Türkiye'ye Zorunlu Göç (1923-1925),* 2. Baski, Istanbul: Tarih Vakfı Yurt Yayınları.

Artan, T. 1993. 'Arnavutköy', in Çağatay Anadol (ed), *Dünden Bugüne İstanbul Ansiklopedisi,* Cilt 1, Istanbul: Kültür Bakanlığı & Tarih Vakfı Ortak Yayını, 172–174.

Çelebi, E. 1971. *Evliya Çelebi Seyyahatnamesi,* Cilt 1, Kitap 2, trans. Z. Danişman. Istanbul.

Constantios, P. 1846. *Constantiniade.* Constantinople.

Danişman, H.H.G. 1999. 'Karakavak Sokak No. 4: A Late Nineteenth Century Town House Within the Historical Background of a Bosporus Neighbourhood' in Ç. Kafesçioğlu and L. Thys-Şenocak (eds), *Essays in Honour of Aptullah Kuran.* Istanbul: Yapı Kredi Publications.

Danişman, H.H.G. and İ. Üstün. 2000. 'Arnavutköy 1900-2000: Urban Transformation at a Multi-ethnic Neighborhood of Istanbul as Evidenced Through Narratives of its Senior Citizens', in J. Wilton, A. Ritchie, M. De Moraes Ferreira and A. Lichtblau (eds), *Crossroads of History: Experience, Memory, Orality.* Istanbul: Boğaziçi University Publication.

Demirer, M.A. 1995. *6 Eylül 1955: Yassıada 6/7Eylül Davası.* Ankara: Bağlam yayınları.

Dosdoğru, M.H. 1993. *6-7 Eylül Olayları.* Ankara: Bağlam Yayınları.

Eyice, S. 1976. *Bizans Devrinde Boğaziçi.* Istanbul: İstanbul Üniversitesi Edebiyat, Fakültesi Yayınları.

Hirschon, R. 2000. *Mübadele Çocukları,* trans. S. Çağlayan. Istanbul: Tarih Vakfı Yurt Yayınları.

Hristidis, H. 2000. *Ta Septembriana.* Athens: Kentro Mikrasiatikon Spudon.

İncicyan, P. G. 1976. *18. Asırda Istanbul,* trans. H. D. Andreasyan. Istanbul.

Keyder, Ç. 1999. 'A Tale of Two Neighborhoods', in Ç. Keyder (ed), *Istanbul: Between the Global and the Local.* New York: Rowman & Littlefield.

Koçu, R. E. 1946. *Istanbul Ansiklopedisi,* Cilt 2. Istanbul.

Kömürcüyan, E. Ç. 1952. *Istanbul Tarihi 17Asırda,* Istanbul: İstanbul Üniversitesi Edebiyat, Fakültesi Yayınları, trans. H. D. Andreasyan.

Ökte, F. 1957. *Varlık Vergisi Faciası.* Istanbul: Nebioğlu Yayınevi.

Pekin, K. and Ç. Turan. 2002. *Mübadele Bibliografyası: Lozan Mübadelesi ile İlgili Yayınlar ve Yayınlanmamış Çalışmalar.* Istanbul: Lozan Mübadelesi Vakfı Yayını.

Tezel, Y.S. 2001. *Cumhuriyet Dönemi İktisat Tarihi,* 3 *baskı.* Istanbul: Tarih Vakfı Yurt Yayınları.

Tuncay, M. 1986. 'Kıbrıs Sorununun Gelişmesi Bağlamında 6-7 Eylül Olayları', in *Tarih ve Toplum,* 33. Istanbul: İletişim Yayınları, 11–26.

Üstün, I. 2003. *Economic Life During Early Republican Period: Professions at Arnavutköy (Example of Road Tax Register and Oral History Interviews),* unpublished M.A. thesis. Mimar Sinan University, Istanbul.

Uğur, A. 1999. *Yerel Siyaset ve Demokrasi, Çoğulculuk, Sivil Toplum. Sivil Toplum için Kent: Yerel Siyaset ve Demokrasi Seminerleri.* Istanbul: Demokrasi Kitaplığı.

Chapter 9

Playing Snakes and Ladders in Ciutat de Mallorca

*An Ethnographic Approach to the Production of the Neighbourhood Scale**

MARC MORELL AND JAUME FRANQUESA

Introduction

The historic centre of Ciutat de Mallorca (from now on Ciutat)[1] is the object of an everlasting urban renewal process that in recent years has involved several public administrations, private companies and organizations belonging to what has come to be called 'civil society'. Although, because of its centrality, this process has become especially important for the whole of the city, its implementation has gone hand in hand with a more minute scale: one that has to do with the 'neighbourhood' question. In other words, the renewal of the whole of the historic centre has been carried out through a series of partial renewals that have taken the neighbourhood as the adequate intervention unit, the 'right' scale for the implementation of urban renewal policies. In this way, the issue of the neighbourhood scale becomes central to understanding the urban restructuring of the historic centre and the whole of Ciutat.

By 'neighbourhood scale' we refer to the encapsulation of the neighbourhood through top-down and bottom-up power processes (Tilly 1999) that parcel the neighbourhood as a coherent, 'natural' spatial unit 'ready' for intervention, thus concealing that it is this intervention that produces such a scale. 'Public powers' (together with private ones) penetrate the affairs that belong to the neighbourhood realm and re-signify its space by extracting certain features that will later contribute to encapsulating it through the downscaling of particular urban policies from the corridors of public power. We refer to these top-down processes as 'snakes'. Parallel with, and also intrinsically linked to this downscaling process, this encapsulation can only take place if it is connected to the strategies of certain agents that use these snakes to put up their 'ladders' and scale positions in the network of public power. We will specifically focus on the part of a renewal intervention that involves the European Union (EU). Although the neighbourhood was already present before the involvement of the EU, we are here interested in focusing on the major shift the EU urban policies take, a shift that we fear is not detached from the specific neoliberal frame adopted across the EU. Therefore, the first part of this chapter will offer a theoretical sketch on what has come to be known as the 'neoliberal turn'.

Our aim is to undertake an analysis of those policies that privilege the downscaling process referred to above, and more particularly the role the EU plays. But it is clear to us that this analysis needs to be 'grounded'. We believe ethnography possesses the capacity to elaborate this 'groundedness' through two clear-cut strongholds: observation and critique (Wolf 1999). While observation, as the prop of the ethnographic method, has the capacity to apprehend the developments at a large scale from the 'flesh and bone' of the field, critique, understood as the unmasking of the naturalized state of things, helps to understand processes that escape observation. In short, this methodological combination makes feasible a social anthropology beyond the strictly local and closer than the strictly global (Hannerz 2003). Having said this, it is by no means our duty to evaluate the results of these renewal policies with regards to their achievement, nor to view how these results adjust or not to the original aims established by the renewal schemes. Such an evaluative operation would only tacitly condone the way in which these policies work out of their abstract formulation. This procedure would lead us to present policies as if external to their practice. On the contrary, the analysis of a specific case, that of the Urban-Temple Project (hereafter Urban-Temple) – an URBAN Community Initiative of the European Union in Ciutat de Mallorca (Balearic Islands, Spain) – allows us to focus on policy practices.

The second part of this essay will be aimed at showing the crux that guides the adoption of this new scale, since policies do not happen in the 'abstract' but are applied in places that have a history of their own. This long process that the places undergo becomes a necessary fact for those areas that become susceptible to renewal. As we will show, the history of the Urban-Temple area of Ciutat fits neatly within the frame of these new policies. Thus, a practical analysis of the neighbourhood's history, of how it came to be the neighbourhood it is, will not only lead us to state that the existence of this very same history is conditioned by the emergence of new political approaches and by the specificity of certain places, but, just as important, it will show the particular correlation of forces that take place and that can shape place. This will be shown both through the particular circumstances that moved the town council of Ciutat to apply for the URBAN Community Initiative[2] (hereafter URBAN) and by the fact that the neighbourhood is not always the integrated 'community' that most literature evokes. In the light of this, we will show how the adoption of the neighbourhood scale affects different groups of people in different ways, and that, parallel to the 'snaking' of policies and 'laddering' of specific agents, some people lose out while others gain.

The Entrepreneurial Turn in Urban Governance: Scaling the Neighbourhood

The New Global Economy (Sassen 2000) obliges cities to compete and precipitates the urban order to adapt or accommodate the diverse urban policies to the specificities dictated by economic pressures, and to find in the perennial projection of urban development the attraction and accumulation of the capital that is necessary for competition (Swyngedouw, Moulaert and Rodriguez 2002).[3] A clear indicator of this accommodation we refer to is the move from local government towards local governance (that is to say, the incorporation of business agents and of the 'third sector' in public governability), signalling the neoliberalization of urban space (Geddes 2006). This implies what Harvey (1989) calls the 'entrepreneurial turn': a shift in the very same public governability that pushes the city to behave as an enterprise, the main aim of which is to promote economic success. This not only implies the maximization of the public environment by the private initiative but also the constant speculation of development and its phases of design, execution and projection. This shift, thus, involves a new emphasis on the production of place to the detriment of those policies of a redistributive kind, based on the territory. We understand that this emphasis on place is defined by the expectation for surplus value that ideally generates from the subordination of the use value to the exchange value (what Lefebvre 2000 [1974] calls 'abstract space').

The emphasis on place rather than on territory is linked to the adoption of the neighbourhood scale, and as we will see, it goes hand in hand with a new political discourse that stresses cultural questions and the idea of participation and citizen involvement. In addition to this, the emphasis on place often reshapes places into landscapes,[4] which – no matter what the 'scape' – are anchored in the 'raw material' (in this case, the neighbourhood) they are built upon. Nevertheless, as we will later show, this raw material that is the neighbourhood is indeed extremely prolific in so far as it is precisely able to produce, reproduce and market landscapes. It is under this focus that we understand the insistence of the entrepreneurial turn in 'localizing' memory (Nora 1997 [1992]) and/or in theming it (Lowenthal 2002; Delgado 2006). Taking into account how this landscaping logic works within the urban system, we argue that the public environments that have been most subject to landscape modelling are the neighbourhoods, and that this is so because of the 'cosy', familiar and romanticized scale they represent.

Likewise, the neighbourhood scale is innovatively exploited at a multiscale level by the 'entrepreneurial turn'. Indeed, it implies the governance of the urban space through the command of 'the organisation and the production of space in order to be able to exercise a major degree of control both in the friction of distance and in the way in which space is appropriated' (Harvey 1989 [1985]: 264). This frontier field of frictions between domination and appropriation that the neighbourhood scale represents, is where the organization and production of scale takes place – and where the several public powers find the urban countenance of their economic policies, since all administrative powers (not only the local and state powers but also the EU itself) seem to need to tailor a scale that is 'nearer' to the average citizen. We herein find that the neighbourhood scale, precisely because of its uneven and 'easy to find' conditions, plays an important role in the idealization of place.

Therefore, we understand that the neighbourhood scale is a threshold that comprises the territory that swings between the ideas of 'neighbourhood', understood as a space merely lived by its inhabitants, and 'neighbourhood unit', understood as a space that comes to existence as embodied in planning strategies (Keller 1975 [1968]).[5] In short, the neighbourhood scale possesses certain attributes that make it tempting to the eyes of the entrepreneurial turn, given its liminal condition and its potential for extracting matter from its environment and its practice in order to fuel future projects (landscapes, experiences, memories, etc). Thus, these neighbourhood attributes have to do mainly with the specific position of the neighbourhood part within the urban whole and with the values about living together that emanate from this part of the whole (Gravano 2005).

In this entrepreneurial turn that seems to legitimate the 'happy' dénouement of the crisis of the municipal power within the crisis of Fordist capitalism (in other words, of the very same 'managerial government model'), such a liminal condition of the neighbourhood opens the door to what Castells (1981) calls 'political brokers', or 'local bosses': those who know how to take advantage of novelties and of the different steps needed to advance from rung to rung on their own particular ladder. Herein lies our interest in paying thorough 'attention to how political agents – leaders and others – enter and influence these processes through their acquisition and manipulation of economic and ideological instruments of power as they pursue political goals' (Kurtz 2001: 120). We understand URBAN and its effective production of the 'neighbourhood scale' as precisely one of these novelties the local bosses will take advantage of in their urban renewal.

Snaking Down the URBAN:
The Case of the Urban-Temple Project

The emphasis of the EU in the neighbourhood scale is part of a more general process in which other transnational organizations (UNESCO, Council of Europe, etc.) have also played an important role by developing certain cultural policies in urban contexts. Hereby, in 1995 Raymond Weber (former director for education, culture and sport of the Council of Europe) tells us, in the preface to the first of five volumes that explore the relation between neighbourhood and culture in Europe, about the importance the Council of Europe concedes to the work of culture within territories, and this strategic importance is further underlined in the genealogy he offers to us. In the 1980s the Council of Europe worked intensely with the public institutions of several cities and regions, since they were territories whose representative institutions were valid for the implementation of social and economic developments within Europe. Weber explains that at the beginning of the 1990s there was a major leap (one that seems to have been voluntary rather than obligatory) in dealing with the smaller pieces of the European urban puzzle: the neighbourhoods. Here, neighbourhoods are understood as territories that contain the complicated relation maintained between the minimum public space of interaction and the minimum public space of social control – in other words, the basic unit of the European cultural policy.

This very same basic cultural policy unit is often explained in terms of regeneration and takes the valuing of the city centres as a cultural regenerative model. In this sense it is interesting to outline the way in which Bianchini (1995), in the same publication, states that the role of the neighbourhoods in the urban policies has gone hand in hand with the development of local cultural policies.[6] Taking the ideas Weber and Bianchini develop, it seems to us that they support the general trend that posits a correspondence between the 'entrepreneurial turn' and the 'cultural turn' (Storper 2001). Although these two shifts do not necessarily need each other to take place, their relation is not a casual one either. However, rather than being the result of a conspiracy concoction, they end up gelling because of the possibilities they discover in each other for the gain of value in their projects and for granting the legitimacy of these. Admittedly, we are facing a general drift with regards to community approaches. Moreover, the demand for boosting the development of 'the culture of the community' will render a different yet also related topic: the participation of the very same community in its cultural and urban programming:

> What is important here is that a central part of the neoliberal agenda is to gain broad-based support for and participation in urban restructuring plans through governmental 'reforms' designed to mobilize urban residents as entrepreneurs, consumers, and neighbourhood citizen-volunteers. With respect to inner city residents, it is precisely through the 'empowerment' of their 'community' that they are now encouraged to be included as active participants in urban governance (Maskovsky 2006: 77).

Bearing in mind this tendency towards a multi-scalar urban governance that champions the neighbourhood scale as the appropriate milieu for cultural development, citizen empowerment and entrepreneurial resurgence, the EU launched URBAN (1994–1999), which today, since there was a second edition, is also known as URBAN I. This initiative was (and still is) financed with structural funds from the European Social Fund (ESF) and the European Regional Development Fund (ERDF). URBAN was the product of a task carried out by several networks and lobbies that sought to achieve the backing of the EU for the urban context by granting it a decisive role in EU governance (Le Galès 2002: 99–108). As we have already noted, this pressure resulted from positive outcomes of recent regional developments.

The aim of URBAN[7] was (and still is, for the current URBAN projects) to improve the quality of life and the habitat of the 'degraded urban areas' of the EU where it operated through an integrated approach. In addition to this, and responding to operative and management needs, these degraded areas would be classified. The type of degraded area we worked in was presented as an 'inner-city' area: a poor central city neighbourhood excluded from the city's centrality and urban life. This degraded neighbourhood had to contain the cause of its degradation, which would be found in 'deprivation', following the very same terminology established by the official guidelines and other related documents of URBAN. Deprivation would be understood as an urban uneasiness characterized by the geographical concentration of social and economic problems as well as other discomforts related to the conditions of the built environment where this uneasiness was to be found. In other words, URBAN formulated a programme of actions that had to positively resolve the deprivation of places and their people. The following extract summarizes the kind of problems URBAN tackled and the type of solutions it put forward:

Poor living conditions aggravate individual problems and distress. In turn, social malaise and the lack of economic opportunity make the individual hostile to his/her environment. This vicious circle is today the cause of growing conflicts and imbalances, particularly evident in the areas where the problems are most acute. The novelty of the approach proposed by URBAN is that it tries to break this vicious circle by revalorising the individual through his/her habitat and not in spite of it.[8]

The existence of 'social malaise' that aggravates and reaffirms deprivation (the 'poor living conditions') is here referred to as a kind of vicious circle caused by and cause of deprivation. Anchored in specific milieus, it has to do with the unevenness of conflicts and imbalances that are seen as problems that affect the environment – that is to say, both the individual and his/her habitat. URBAN promised to break the vicious circle of the 'social malaise', especially in those areas where the problems were most acute. In fact, it proposed to revalue the individual through revaluing his/her habitat. Social malaise fits neatly with the deprivation terminology. Whereas deprivation (a conglomerate of need and marginality) demands a more structural kind of approach often perceived as beyond any practical outcome, since deprivation affects common living conditions and economic opportunities for the whole of society, 'social malaise' can easily become a simile for 'social pathology' that affects 'individuals', no matter how social the pathology may be. Moreover, since it can be regarded as pathology it will need a 'remedy', thus paralleling nineteenth-century hygienist discourses; in this case the remedy is tailored to individuals through the revaluing of their habitat: their neighbourhood.

URBAN's habitat revaluing would consist of the rehabilitation of obsolete infrastructure and the direction of actions for revitalizing the labour market. As a substantial pivot of this combination, and accompanying its implementation, the 'revaluation' adopted measures against the social exclusion considered to be inherent to any degraded zone, improving the quality of the environment and promoting the involvement of organized grass-roots associations in the decision making process – although, as we have already stated, the 'social malaise' seems to affect population in an individual manner. On the whole, the improvement of the quality of the environment depends on breaking the isolation of the 'problematic neighbourhoods' that locally contain and also produce 'social malaise' at the neighbourhood scale.

The breaking of such a 'vicious circle' in the degraded neighbourhood seems to be achievable only by boosting its accessibility to and its communication with the whole of the city, thereby 'opening' its space in order to attract capital in the form of private investment and visitors. This cannot happen without improvement to the quality of the urban environment, which in turn is dependent on the emphasis placed on infrastructure, the economic tissue, the social and cultural facilities, training, etc.

In the case examined here, while the EU offered the methodological and theoretical frame of action and the local entities integrated management, it was the state that decided which operational programmes were or were not to be implemented. The specific circumstances of the time were that the municipality of Ciutat, the Autonomous Community of the Balearics and the government of Spain were governed by the same political party. At the time this correspondence was crucial for URBAN to trickle down to Ciutat, and it does show us the 'contingencies' that plague what is often conceived and analysed as a 'need' (e.g. the 'abstract policies' of supranational agents such as the EU, but also the World Bank, the IMF, etc.).

It happened that the Spanish government, through the Ministry of Economy and Treasury, approved 29 operational programmes, a considerable number since there were only 118 programmes of URBAN (1994–1999) for the whole of the EU at the time. These 118 programmes were activated in two different batches. It was not until the approval of the second batch, that of 1997, that the Ajuntament de Palma (Town Council of Palma) came into the game with its operational Urban-Temple programme, which was presented as the 'culmination of a process' (Ajuntament de Palma 1999). The culmination of the process that Urban-Temple represented has to be understood as a final thrust in a long phase of projects with regards to the eastern margins of the historic centre of Ciutat. Therefore, in order to grasp a better understanding of Urban-Temple we need to contextualize the space of Ciutat, in which URBAN landed, all in all accounting for the origins of this very same space and the several and diversified speculations to which it has been historically subjected.

Contextualization of the Eastern Margins of Ciutat's Historic Centre

The boundaries of the historic centre of Ciutat are defined both by a ring of avenues (where the Renaissance ramparts once stood) that corner it against the seafront and by the complex relation that exists among its commercial activation, its tourist promotion and its heritage protection. The latter, heritage, is the element of the triad that leads enhancement and/or renewal, depending on which particular part of the centre we refer to. Following this, it is no wonder that this dense combination would be boosted by the *Pla General d'Ordenació Urbana* (PGOU, General Scheme for Town Planning) of 1985, a scheme that would make of the whole of the historic centre an 'area' subject to a 'singular regime' and therefore supposedly receiving special treatment because of its heritage, historic and artistic features. Nevertheless, the unevenness within it, which we could also qualify as historical, explains why we speak of margins. Thus, the kernel of the centre has for a long time been the commercial, heritage and cultural tourist zone par excellence of Ciutat while the shell has remained a marginal territory, especially the eastern flank of the centre (see Figure 9.1 below). In order to understand why this particular area was the chosen for URBAN, it is convenient to briefly consider its historic construction as a 'marginal inner-area'.

Since ancient times, the area had been mostly inhabited by the humble and working classes of Ciutat. In addition, it was one of the most important areas for the trade of products and people with the Part Forana, the Ma-

Figure 9.1. Limits of the historic centre within the urban layout of Ciutat. East of the centre lies the Urban-Temple site, including the planning schemes of Sa Calatrava, Sa Gerreria and El Temple.

jorcan hinterland, and as such the agricultural and labour force reservoir of the capital city, Ciutat. Parallel to this, and intrinsically linked to these conditions of commercial bustle, supplies and comings and goings, these eastern margins became the scene of feverish guild activity, where manufacturing maintained a privileged position until the introduction of mercantile capital in the mid nineteenth century, when it started to take shape as an industrial activity. At the end of the nineteenth century the eastern margins were the focus of most of the industrial production of Ciutat and the sphere of reproduction of the necessary labour force (Escartin Bisbal 2001), to the extent that urban renewals were announced in response to denunciations of the dreadful social conditions prevailing in the area. These renewals took shape in territorial reconfigurations of industry, which took recourse to hygienist logic to justify pulling down the ramparts where we nowadays find the avenues, and quartering the centre of Ciutat into sections according to its population density (Estada 2003 [1892]).

With these credentials, the eastern margins of the historic centre of Ciutat passed the twentieth century subject to constant speculation, which meant leaving it 'fallow' (in other words, subject to consecutive rotation) by combining two processes, necessarily interlinked, that would attempt to re-signify the de-industrialized territory of the margins of the historic centre: the urban renewal and the designation of spaces for renewal (Ruiz Viñals 2000). It seems that the successes and failures of these renewal programmes – and to a major extent, especially for the case we are here dealing with, their postponements – had an uneven bearing on the territory, depending on the areas designated for renewal and on the ordering of such places (here it is necessary to understand that these places are neighbourhoods).

Although with the passage of time, and of the projects, these places would vary in content and form as well as in name, the hierarchy of places these projects established would never be completely effaced. It is in this context that we understand the evolution of the urban renewal of the historic centre of Ciutat and, more specifically, the plans that had the most impact on the reformulation of the eastern margins of the centre: (1) the inner renewals of the General Scheme for Town Planning of 1943 (Alomar Esteve 2000 [1950]), which, precisely because of the fact that they never happened, would define in a definitive fashion the marginal condition of these eastern margins; and (2) the *Plans Especials de Reforma Interior* (PERIs, Special Schemes for Inner Renewal) that the PGOU of 1985 triggered. The different PERIs that were defined in this PGOU would come to cover approximately the same area Alomar proposed to quarter and took the neighbourhood scale as their naturalized environment. This is more significant than it may seem at first sight, since these PERIs of the eastern margins of the centre paved the way for the Urban-Temple's access to the neighbourhood scale, the very same one that the EU's URBAN promoted. We could therefore argue that since these PERIs constructed the area on such a scale, that of the neighbourhood, it prepared the field that URBAN would encounter.

The detonator for the design of these PERIs is to be found in the pre-cipitation of 'social malaise' the territory experienced in the mid 1970s and especially in the mid 1980s in terms of degradation and deprivation (and the insecurity and stigma that go along with them). This precipitation is explained by the inflow of drug trafficking, exploited to a large extent by the media but also certainly noticeable at street level. Even so, it would be absurd to think that this by itself motivated the need to project new renew-als; here we ought to underline that degradation and deprivation, which by this point had been present for decades, had mostly to do with the aging of the population and the built environment, and with the impoverished living conditions. We repeat that these circumstances are inseparable from the fact that the land had been left fallow through the non-execution of the Alomar Scheme of 1943 and the deindustrialization of the area due to pro-duction relocating to newly urbanized areas. Furthermore, from the 1950s onwards a new, encompassing conditioning factor would predominate: the tourist industry. The PERIs would try to solve, or at the very least to palli-ate, the unfavourable diagnosis via measures that envisaged equal shares of social work, the arrival of public facilities and the logic of the gentrifying maximization.

The diversity one could find, and that can still be found, in the terri-tory of these margins (the incidence of degradation and deprivation, the presence of strong neighbour networks and of neighbourhood belonging, the intangible heritage resources, etc.) led the PGOU of 1985 to define three distinct PERIs: Sa Calatrava, Sa Gerreria and El Temple. Sa Calatrava, though not exempt from conflict or population exodus, boasted a privi-leged position with regards to real estate, given its heritage-rich housing stock and its location on the seafront, besides housing a dense and socially cohesive community. Prior to the announcement of its PERI, Sa Gerreria was distinguished by its 'rotten' real estate stock,[9] the highest concentration of prostitution and drug trafficking in Ciutat and a nonexistent associated neighbour network. El Temple is the largest single block of buildings in the whole of the centre of Ciutat. It ought to be said that the different nature of each PERI would order their appearance: implementation of the PERI of Sa Calatrava began that very same year (1985), that of Sa Gerreria would not see the light until 1995 and that of El Temple is still pending.

The different PERIs were adjusted to the mentioned specificities, as was noticeable in the effort to protect and promote heritage in Sa Calatrava, which would subject the neighbourhood to a slow gentrification, whereas in Sa Gerreria the emphasis was placed on crowding it out while 'recovering' its memory. El Temple would act as a buffer zone in between the two others and would also give a name to the whole assemblage. Thus the outcomes of these PERIs are extremely varied, and some of their processes have still not even come to an end (if there is an end in fallowing urban land). However, what we should not dismiss as petty is that not only were the PERIs a response to the unevenness of the territory of each area and to the different historical moments in which each of these PERIs took place, but they were also a response to the demands made by citizens of the city as a whole and in some cases by the very inhabitants of the neighbourhoods in question. It is important to realize that the implementation and timing of such plans are not independent of the reaction they arouse among citizens, whether or not they are residents.

In this sense, it is important to stress the emergence of an organized movement of dissent resulting from the joint efforts of 'civil society' organizations such as ARCA and FAVP. ARCA (Associació per la Revitalització de Centres Antics, or Association for the Revitalization of the Old Centres) appeared in 1987 and monitors the preservation and revitalization of heritage (something that the whole of the historic centre is). The FAVP (Federació d'Associacions de Veïns de Palma, or Federation of Neighbours' Associations of Palma) emerged in the first half of the 1970s; as its name indicates, it federates several neighbours' associations with the aim of promoting the citizens' power from a scale that is also perceived to be closer to the citizen. In due time, these organizations became credible, reputable and legitimate agents capable of speaking of heritage salvation and neighbourhood matters in the name of the citizenry. In fact, the pressure these organizations applied on a constant and enduring basis with regards to the dominant values of the 'built environment' and 'good neighbourliness' would influence the urban policies at stake, to the extent that the latter would precisely emphasize the features of places through their heritageable items (and the degradation of the built environment) and their neighbourhood conditions (and the deprivation of the population).

These good intentions, such as we understand them to the present, were suitable for the urban renewal in the course of time, applied here and there depending on the very same unevenness of the margins. However, we may argue that 'place features' – involving, on the one hand, protective and enhancement measures in order to battle against the degradation of the built environment and, on the other, social remedies for deprivation – lengthened and complicated the revision process of the renewal scheme and its cost, impelling the town council of Ciutat to search for new intervention formulas and new financing methods.

Urban-Temple and the Culmination of a Process

The Urban-Temple project not only officially gelled the three areas of the PERIs but also signified the opportunity for a culmination of the PERI of Sa Calatrava, transformed the chances of the PERI of Sa Gerreria, served as an initiation endorsement to the possible future PERI of El Temple and, still more importantly, helped integrate the implementation of the diverse projects and their management. Until that point, the urban infrastructure management of the historic centre fell chiefly on the Pla Mirall-Palma-Centre (known as Pla Mirall), funded by autonomous regional and municipal bodies. With the implementation of URBAN the Pla Mirall would become the Consorci Mirall-Palma-Centre (hereafter Consorci Mirall). The team in charge of the design of Urban-Temple found itself subordinated to the Consorci Mirall, which to a certain extent had inspired it. Furthermore, Urban-Temple gave way to the 'integrated management of the integrated actions' that would become the brand of the Consorci Mirall.

The Consorci Mirall was funded on a fifty-fifty basis by the Town Council of Palma and the Autonomous Community of the Balearic Islands. In Ciutat, it blended those actions the Pla Mirall carried out autonomously but localized in the municipalities, with those undertaken by the local housing authority. While the Pla Mirall was originally a regional development that streamed down to the municipalities, the housing authority was the main entity involved in improvement of the built environment of Ciutat. In addition to this, the Consorci Mirall combined its public agency partnership structure with private agents, who in turn would implement the design and execution phases of the projects by tailoring them to their own needs and profit. Thus, to a certain extent it turned the 'integrated management' into 'integrated entrepreneurship': a shadowy, if not opaque, strategy with regards to accountability to the public.

The aim of Urban-Temple was to revitalize its territory, a depressed zone with an urban problematic of social malaise (the fusion of individual deprivation and environmental degradation), which were the required conditions for accessing funding from URBAN. Nevertheless, this revitalization did not happen equitably among the different PERI zones of Urban-Temple but instead focused rather bitterly on Sa Gerreria, given the serious 'malaise' to be found there. Interestingly, Sa Gerreria was also the area most in need of funding due to the magnitude of the renewal that had been planned for it, since more than a third of the neighbourhood was to be pulled down. In 1997 a total sum of €15,260,000 was dedicated to revitalizing the area, of which €7,630,000 came from structural funds (€6,829,000 from the ERDF and €801,000 from the ESF) and €7,630,000 from the Consorci Mirall.

In 1997 the Urban-Temple area contained approximately 3,000 inhabitants (less than 1 per cent of the municipal population) living in around 900
dwellings. While almost 28 per cent of the population was older than sixty-
five and 46.8 per cent had no formal education, 47.7 per cent of the property
was rented and 48.6 per cent of it was in decay (Ballester and Orte 2001).
Here, it is clear that revitalization of the habitat meant rejuvenating both the
population and the habitat, which would presumably be achieved through
the implementation of innovative actions that would take into account
four different goals: the improvement of infrastructure, the reactivation of
the economic tissue, attention to social integration and training, including subsequent labour insertion.[10] This collection of projects illustrates
the ambition of the team designing Urban-Temple. As the final report on
Urban-Temple project argues, it seems that the operational programme was
a success. Not only does this report (which was presented as a final evaluation of Urban-Temple) avoid any kind of negative valuation, but it goes on
to praise the achievement of centralizing and articulating a space that to
that point had been 'undesirable'. The achievement consisted of recovering
the historic centre for Ciutat, fostering the return of the population to the
centre, treating its marginal pockets and strengthening the quality of tourism thanks to the economic reactivation of the centre. The 'undesirability',
which took shape with 'degradation', consisted of dismantled workshops,
uninhabitable housing, substandard housing, empty plots of land used as
rubbish dumps, the presence of drug sales and usage, prostitution and the
continuous dismissal of plans (Ballester and Orte 2001: 8).

However, far from the triumphalism these very same Urban-Temple
evaluations breathe, there are other elements and value judgements. Thus,
and in the same spirit as the mentioned evaluation, other works appeared
(also financed by the same Consorci Mirall) that, viewing Urban-Temple
with neither a critical eye nor a triumphal attitude, reminded readers that
in 2000, out of the total population (3,005 inhabitants of all age groups),
only 287 people (of working age) approached Urban-Temple offices for information about work or training and that of these only 117 individualized itineraries were produced for training and labour insertion (Salvà et
al 2000). In other words, the project represented less than 4 per cent of the
whole of the population of Urban-Temple neighbourhood unit (or set of
neighbourhood units) and less than 0.04 per cent of the whole of the municipal population. All the while the whole of the enterprise of the PERIs
and Urban-Temple were qualified in the national press as a

> disaster of such a magnitude that it appears in the satellite images. The
> huge and ignored hole at the centre of Palma can be distinguished among
> what used to be the first roofs and the network of populous streets of the

capital city. In silence, they have razed to the ground a thousand years of
life in the old town – Sa Gerreria – to transform them into plots and business. The soul of Palma is quartered, in some stretches cobbled. What is
left of the old nucleus is almost a stage, a piece of furniture, with façades,
pavements and restorer carriageways, a museum of gateways and streets
without open businesses and almost without clients. The rest is demolition and speculation material. (Manresa 2005, translation by authors)

In other words, Urban-Temple promoted training and jobs for the marginal population of the neighbourhood unit while its members were being
expelled – a contradiction in data, to say the least. As one of the social
workers at the local housing authority put it, the Consorci Mirall, together
with the private developers working within it, determined different com-
pensations for each of the numerous displaced tenants and owners (the
majority of the latter lived outside of the neighbourhood unit). Most of the
tenants ended up finding accommodation in areas far from the centre of
Ciutat, places that in due time would also become the object of projection
and planning since they were considered to be the next in the row of decay
and deprivation. Other inhabitants of lesser means were shifted around
within the very same borders of the Urban-Temple area. In short: eliminating degradation meant getting rid of those who were considered to be the
dregs of the neighbourhood.

In general, the methods put into action were, as they usually are, a matter of opinion. Lola, for instance, the owner of a paper shop in the area
for around fifteen years whom we interviewed in 2004 and who was keen
to participate in the cultural and training activities developed by Urban-
Temple and other entities, celebrated the changes brought in by the renewal at the neighbourhood scale, although she did acknowledge the lack
of businesses and tried to understand why this was so through her reflection on gentrifying issues that could only bring business substitution:

Everything they've done is 'fab': Sa Calatrava, Flassaders, the Urban, the
Court, in other words, it's all very well done. There is a lack of things:
there's a lack of business. 'Cause we need it. And I am the first one to
need it. I need somewhere where I can go and buy something. Moreover,
houses are priced as if they were made of gold. They're building houses for
rich people. ... For Germans that come here with their money to exploit it.
Flats: one-hundred million pesetas, here in Sa Calatrava. The fact is that
not just anyone can come and live in the old town now. And it ought to be
said that the old town was the poorest and lowest to be found. That's what
there was here: gypsies, humble people. ... And of course, the majority of
the people owning these expensive houses are foreigners, what do they

do? They go to more expensive places to buy stuff. Even if it costs the same in my shop they'll go to spend their money elsewhere. They don't buy in the neighbourhood. In the neighbourhoods it is us, the normal ones, who buy, in other words, the humblest. (translation by authors)

The material neighbourhood on which the scaling encapsulation took place was a neighbourhood based on its own disappearance, since the scale was used not only to attract new inhabitants but also new businesses. The problem for many, though, as in Lola's case, was that the guidelines for eviction and expulsion turned out to be different from the ones they had presumed would be applied and were, more importantly, quite arguable. Lola praised the 'cleaning' that took place against drug trafficking and the Roma in the late 1990s while she insisted on the cosiness of the neighbourhood and the positive neighbourliness of its people. Beyond this apparent contradiction comes a paradox. She, who praised the 'sweeping', as many residents put it, all of a sudden became the target of the brush:

One day a man came in and told me he was the new owner of the building, he said he had bought the whole of it and that I had to leave. I then told him that I wasn't leaving because I had 11 years of contract left. He then offered me a super-small amount and I told him no, that for that money I wouldn't leave. I was at home, I had 11 years left on my contract and we would carry on there. Since this man saw he couldn't win with me, he started threatening, spilling concrete from above on my car, buckets full of liquid concrete on my car. ... He would come around and call me names and say we were scum; I was a poor devil. ... And ... And he didn't know how to chuck me out. ... He actually sold the premises! Some people came to me asking me if I could show them the paper-shop premises since they were for sale.

Moreover, along with the 'cleaning' and the shuffling of its inhabitants, as well as the pressure exerted by businesses attempting to muscle into the neighbourhood, the whole of the neighbourhood was being promoted as a heritageable past through the image of its 'cosiness' – the very same 'cosiness' Lola seemed to long for. The 'cosy' ideal of the neighbourhood with its 'living together paraphernalia' would become the discursive alibi, and its neighbourly entourage would be localized and promoted as a crafts place while the authorities would ease the establishment of its craftspeople and create an urban tourist itinerary of its own making. A place crafted in such a manner would take advantage of the 'meanings' and the 'own values' of the preceding neighbourhoods, all in all shaping the manageability of the neighbourhood scale and of its projection as a place of memory. It is in this light that we need to understand the use of the neighbourhood scale by the various administrative initiatives at stake. Therefore, what we are interested in is not so much what the evaluations exactly evaluated, and not even whether they are truthful or not. Our real aim is to discern what kind of strategies hide behind these evaluations and what uses the neighbourhood scale was put to in order to attract EU funding down to the very local.

Local Bosses and Strategic Ladders

We have already mentioned how political brokers have adapted to the new entrepreneurial turn that signifies urban governance, developing methodologies and specific techniques for the execution of the command and control of urban space through the division into neighbourhoods. We can find a clear sample of this adaptation in what we call 'integral management of integrated actions'. Behind the obsession with the integrative approach lies a very particular logic that shows how certain local bosses use the neighbourhood scale and the calls for its renewal to make their own business in the neighbourhood, and how they adapt the neighbourhood projects in order to achieve the optimization of their positions in the political ladder. We understand that this example is in agreement with de Certeau's notion of strategy:

> I call *strategy* the calculation (or manipulation) of power relationships that becomes possible as soon as a subject with will and of power (a business, an army, a city, a scientific institution) can be isolated. It postulates a place that can be delimited as its own and serve as the base from which relations with an exteriority composed of targets or threats (customers or competitors, enemies, the country surrounding the city, objectives and objects of research, etc) can be managed. As in management, every 'strategic' rationalization seeks first of all to distinguish its 'own' place, that is, the place of its own power and will, from an 'environment'. (de Certeau 1997 [1980]: 35–36)

In other words, those political brokers who were most involved in the urban renewal calculated and manipulated the integration of their management (in this case that of Urban-Temple), all in all using this urban renewal to make the place from which they would administer the command and the control of the environment they unified and idealized (the whole of the eastern margins of the historic centre of Ciutat). This is the main contribution to the emergence of the neighbourhood scale, from a local elite standpoint. Meanwhile, this production of scale that they developed became for them a doubly gratifying resource, since they laddered positions while also centralizing them. Thus in 1996, in order to present Urban-Temple to the second round of the URBAN bid, the Consorci Mirall, which had integrated the diverse PERIs and their actions, was put under the direct guidance of the Town Planning Department of the town council of Ciutat. This entity, which was responsible for the PERIs, was also indispensable in the Consorci Mirall, which at that moment was led by the former general secretary of the party in both the local and autonomous governments, while the consortium's management fell on the political broker that had instigated its progenitor Pla Mirall. In other words, its management ended up being of an integrated kind.

The narrowness of the definition of social malaise that URBAN dealt with and the integrated palliative remedy it proposed facilitated, by and large, the strategies the local bosses had conceived in order to confront the problematic of the eastern margins. It is in this light that we have to understand the welcome these political brokers gave to what URBAN promoted and qualified as a novelty: the revalorization of the individual through the revalorization of his or her habitat, and not the other way round. We ought to clearly bear this in mind since we believe it is central to the very same logic of the urban renewal. It is not about resolving social problems, from which individuals may be a sample, so much as it is about tidying up the environment where these individuals are to be found – their habitat – in a clear sign of what Garnier (2006) qualifies as the 'ideology of spatialism'. This way of elaborating the remedy (spatialism and individualism) gives way to the detachment of the population from the territory. All in all, it does so by individualizing each case and therefore weakening the unity of the neighbours through the neighbourhood unit – and, more importantly, by leaving aside the action that is intrinsic to the habitat: inhabiting. 'Close-up land-planning', the kind of planning that uses the neighbourhood scale, does not transform the issue of detaching people from territory since, as Urban-Temple shows, it precisely spatializes and individualizes.

> What has come to be named as urbanism is nothing other than a too co-herent set – a system – of stipulations and limitations that maintain this essential activity at strict level of a technical minimum. This has the effect of reducing a situation and an activity, inhabiting, to a brutally material reality, to a function: the habitat. (Lefebvre 1980 [1971]: 20; translation by authors)

It is in this context of tidying up the habitat and of reducing the inhabiting that the 'culmination' of the urban renewal of the historic centre has to be understood. Within the very same logic of renewal endorsed by the ideology of spatialism and following the logic of 'integration', there was an attempt to try to fill in the gaps left by the disappearance of the inhabiting in the habitat. The local authorities would foster the arrival of new businesses that would grant 'activity' to the area in this transitional modelling stage. These businesses would relate to crafts, and the boulevard where they would be located would be named 'Boulevard for Crafts'. It would also involve public offices of various different administrations (most of them municipal), a few 'alternative' shops, bars and restaurants that would give an untamed look and, most importantly, estate agencies selling properties in the area and beyond. Property is nowadays mainly promoted, whether for rent or for sale, by its 'heritageable' qualities, be they of a prosperous kind or even of a more humble one, as the following excerpt shows:

> One bedroom rental apartment, in central Palma de Mallorca available from April of 2008. – €900 Per month Ground floor 55m² 1 bedroom apartment accessed from the private courtyard, of a reformed building in central Palma de Mallorca. This open plan 1 bedroom apartment is part of the modernization of a pottery craftwork shop at the center of the neighborhood, 'Sa Gerreria' the industrial building has been reformed into spacious modern loft style apartments retaining the industrial feel of this unique building. … With a flat screen television, a digital multilingual television package and Wifi connection.[11]

What the area seems to have become is a place with different and even opposed meanings under the logic of spatialism that we have referred to previously: an area sold with an 'authentic' image but adapted to the state of the art in new information technologies, people leaving spaces that other people with other needs and lifestyles will occupy, and all of this done in the name of culture. Thus, we may well argue that 'culturalization', understood as the process by which acquired taste finds its habitat, is strongly linked to the individualization spatialism implies. It is no wonder that this educated taste the neighbourhood scale offers under the cultural turn is only for the few – and, as we have seen in Lola's case, it is a taste set upon very high standards, standards beyond the 'normal people' that invite real estate businesses, cultural services agencies and bars and restaurants to settle in the area.

That is to say, 'social malaise' in this case was not solved through provision of 'structural solutions' that ascertain the origins of exclusion, but only palliative measures that ended up dissolving the unity of the social malaise and went on to tackle space as a problem – the habitat instead of the social problem – since the social contents had come to define the location and the conception of these parts of the urban agglomeration in the neighbourhood scale, which URBAN calls neighbourhood. It was precisely in this gap between people and space that the local bosses saw the chances to implement the new entrepreneurial turn in order to carry out what was publicly demanded of them while finding the proper rungs for their own laddering.

The two examples given of the local political brokers that packaged UR-BAN thanks to their multi-scalar tandem work quite graphically express this laddering we mention, which needs to snake down funds. The first case was that of the general secretary who also became the vice-mayor of Ciutat between 1991 and 1999, and was directly in charge of the municipal land planning department. His good connections with those in control of the government of the state and his control of the local and regional structures of the party he belonged to, paved the way for including Urban-Temple in the Spanish wish list for URBAN. He was one of the main proponents of the creation of the Consorci Mirall and therefore one of the main players in the implementation of Urban-Temple. After his municipal activity he was a member of the European Parliament until 2004. There, he unsuccessfully continued to try to direct more EU structural funds to the Balearic archipelago. In 2004 he became a Spanish senator for the Balearics. Rumour has it that close family of his acquired property in the area of Urban-Temple by using privileged information before the PERI of Sa Gerreria was approved.[12]

The second case involves a civil engineer who was the minister for Works and Land Planning of the Balearic Autonomous Government in three different administrations between 1983 and 1993. He left his post two years before the elections in 1995, presumably due to his involvement in a corruption affair that forced the dismissal of the then regional president. He then descended to the municipal level and became the manager of the Pla Mirall and, therefore, the most visible head of the Urban-Temple project. When the Consorci Mirall ended at the beginning of the millennium (to be replaced by another consortium of similar characteristics for other PERIs elsewhere in Ciutat), he left in order to become an advisor to the municipal company in charge of water and sewage issues. Although his career seems to have taken a downward turn, he was nevertheless the necessary counterpiece for the first political broker mentioned above, since he was the one to integrate the 'tops' with the 'downs' in Urban-Temple. After Urban-Temple he tried to bring other planning EU programmes in line with the successful 'integration approach' but never succeeded again. He retired in September 2006, although over drinks he would admit to friends in a joyful manner that this only had to do with his 'official job' since he was still working on his 'other' matters. His good connections within the different local and regional institutions and his knowledge of the field (and the business of what went on under this field) made Urban-Temple possible.

Thus Urban-Temple proved a springboard for both local bosses: while the first became an elected European deputy for the Balearic Islands and therefore used his parliamentary interventions to attract more European projects towards the Balearics, the second retired after consolidating the Consorci Mirall with Urban-Temple and achieving the managerial integration of the different renewal schemes – the different neighbourhood units or 'neighbourhoods', as the Consorci Mirall would call them – that were subsequently announced. In short, while one of the political brokers ended up climbing up the ladder all the way to the European scale, the other one ended up descending towards the neighbourhood scale, both of them collaborating in order to maintain their position as local bosses.

What is clear, then, is that the political brokers explored and exploited not only the built environment of the urban territory but also its population. And both things were made possible by focusing on the neighbourhood scale, with all of its landscapes and with all of its problems and illnesses. In defending the neighbourhood units they proposed they did nothing more than lay ground for the enterprise that would benefit the calculation and the manipulation of the surpluses brought about by the abstract space they programmed – calculations and manipulations that at the end of the day affected neighbourhoods peopled by citizens.

Conclusion: On the Neighbourhood Realm and Entrepreneurial Governance

As a starting point for this chapter, we pointed out the correspondence between the rise of the entrepreneurial character of urban governance and the reinforcement of the use of the neighbourhood scale. The entrepreneurial focus supposes the reinforcement of the commoditization of the urban space and of the social relations of all kind that take place within it, in such a manner that the adoption of the neighbourhood scale as a privileged field of action can be read as an attempt for penetrating into new regions of social reality. We thus find ourselves looking at a mechanism by which entrepreneurial governance snakes down towards what we usually understand as being proper to the neighbourhood realm: propinquity relations, use values associated to space, confidence, informal relation networks, etc. Only as a last resort is the neighbourhood realm characterized by the strong correspondence between a space and the social relations that take place within it.

In this chapter we have focused on the long road to effecting the strategy that cut out a neighbourhood unit from a particular area that was traditionally marginal within the historic centre of Ciutat. The analysis of this case allows us to suggest some general considerations. The first block of conclusions has to do with the relevance of the political field and its specific manifestations in times that seem dominated by undisguised market forces. The building process of Urban-Temple as a neighbourhood unit was borne of a long bureaucratic process in which many administrative levels intervened, mostly in a changing ideological context. Such a circumstance shows us that far from withdrawing, the state (at its different levels of administration, including the supra-state ones) has strategic importance in the mobilization of urban space for profit. This process has shown us three relevant ideas: (1) the transnational transfer of policies is an important factor in understanding what has come to be called globalization, an aspect usually neglected by the specialized literature; (2) neighbourhood planning not only serves public and market powers snaking down their strategies, but also offers opportunities for particular local leaders to put up the ladders that allow them to consolidate their power; and (3) we err if we understand the production of space as only an immediate reflex of the exigencies of the accumulation system.

Among other reasons that make this simple reflex impossible is the relative autonomy that the 'political sphere' possesses, even in the times of entrepreneurial governance, something shown in our case by the importance of the changing political circumstances of the city and the bureaucratic complexity of the process described above. The most evident manifestation of this relative autonomy of the political sphere is the fact that the political brokers find space for their ladders in the interstices created by the very same bureaucratic apparatus and thus obtain positions of power. Moreover, these positions of power and the ladder on which they support themselves depend on political networks and reciprocities that, although they already are activities aimed at favouring the market, act repeatedly with a certain autonomy to benefit that same market.

In another order of things, we find a series of conclusions on the relation between neighbourhood and neighbourhood scale. Our case shows that the creation of the neighbourhood scale has as much to do with direct intervention as it does with non-intervention. In other words, the fact that the municipality decides not to intervene in a delimited area where it has projected a renewal (what we here have called 'fallowing') has to be understood as a form of intervention, in so far as it builds a marginal area whose exceptionality constructs the propitious conditions for establishing a programme of exceptional actions, that is to say, limited to the neighbourhood scale. In this fashion, whereas the neighbourhood can be read as a way of naming what has been left on the margin, the neighbourhood scale appears as a way of dealing with the anomic or degraded.

The reinforcement of the neighbourhood scale has to do with an attempt to achieve the aims of entrepreneurial governance: deepening the reaches of social control and simultaneously putting into the service of the market elements formerly ruled by logics largely alien to the very same neighbourhood. But this hardly means that the framing of the neighbourhood scale works absolutely beyond the neighbourhood as a pure top-down encapsulation process. What it actually means is that the top-down encapsulation feeds upon bottom-up synergies brought up by the entrepreneurship of those local bosses seeking to climb up the ladder..

The fallacy on which the construction of the neighbourhood scale relies – at least in the case we have analysed here – is made clear in the methodology of the proposed urban intervention. Thus, while the neighbourhood realm comes to be defined by the relations between close people, the proposed solutions are based on an individualized approach to the 'neighbourhood problem'. Simultaneously, the rooted belief in spatialism – that is to say, in the idea that the habitat creates the inhabiting; and singularly the idea that certain spaces are 'pathogen' and/or 'criminogen' (that is, conducive to crime or encouraging criminal tendencies) – allows power to justify some interventions centred on the renewal of space, something that moves farther away from communitarian intervention and takes the emphasis on entrepreneurial governance nearer to the place (in contrast to the territory).

The idea of the neighbourhood is presented as 'near' to the citizen. But what it actually provokes and proffers (willingly or not) is its adoption by the neoliberal frame in order to create a good business climate, meanwhile dealing with the population and its wellbeing, and any planning in redistributive terms, as a matter of second order. In other words, while the power relations internal to the neighbourhood are hidden, the very same notion of neighbourhood, managed in the top-down production of the neighbourhood scale, tends to promote power inequalities.

This series of considerations leads us to reconsider the way in which we understand the relation between the neighbourhood and the neighbourhood scale. The main distinction between the neighbourhood as the space of the neighbourliness relations and the neighbourhood as a scale of management is becoming blurred. Moreover, the emergence of neighbourhood planning requires a neighbourhood problematic so it can legitimize itself and carry on. Thus, the important thing is to understand the position of the neighbourhood slice within the urban whole – which particulars signify one as a neighbourhood and which do not.

NOTES

We want to thank both the Programa de Beques Doctorals (Conselleria d'Economia, Hisenda i Innovació – Govern de les Illes Balears) and the Programa Beatriu de Pinós (Comissionat per a Universitats i Recerca del Departament d'Innovació, Universitats i Empresa – Generalitat de Catalunya) for giving support to Marc Morell and Jaume Franquesa respectively.

1. The city where we have carried out our research, known both as Ciutat (de Mallorca) and Palma, is the capital city of the Balearic Islands. Although both names are correct, throughout this research we have used 'Ciutat' [city] because of its wide connotations.
2. URBAN, URBAN1 (1994-1999) and URBAN2 (2000-2006) were all Community Initiatives of the European Regional Development Fund (ERDF).
3. Ciutat has its own specificities in the competition among cities triggered by the new global economy, fundamentally its specialization in tourism, which is often tightly bound to the real estate business.
4. Our understanding of this term is based on Williams (2001 [1973]), who stresses that 'landscapes' imply specific vantage points, that is to say, viewpoints that ease the consumption of the place and justify its production.
5. An earlier account of ours on the URBAN (Franquesa and Morell 2005) is complementary to this one. While here the neighbourhood scale is approached through a top-down lens that focuses on the 'neighbourhood unit', the former stressed a bottom-up approach.
6. Within this relation, Bianchini (1995) establishes three stages he considers substantial when bringing together common tendencies: (1) The stage of reconstruction (the end of the 1940s to the end of the 1960s), (2) the stage of participation (the 1970s to the beginning of the 1980s), and (3) the stage of urban regeneration (the mid 1980s to the beginning of the 1990s). We are interested in focusing on this latter stage, which, following Bianchini, will emphasize the 'investment' instead of the 'subsidy' and will also show the urban centres as showcases of the local economy within the competition among cities we have previously acknowledged.
7. There is abundant official information with regards to the different URBAN programmes at http://ec.europa.eu/regional_policy/urban2/index_en.html.
8. See: http://ec.europa.eu/regional_policy/urban2/urban/initiative/src/frame1 .html.
9. The fact that this real estate stock was rotten does not mean that it was not heritageable; in fact it would become heritage in an odd combination of industrial heritage and craft commemoration.
10. In order to attain an optimum result when combining these goals, the operational programme of Urban-Temple presented a series of programmes of its own that, in keeping with the philosophy of URBAN, would: (1) improve the urban environment through the provision of services; (2) develop the economic tissue by incentivizing commercial and craft activity via the creation of the Passeig per l'Artesania (Boulevard for Crafts), including a tourist itinerary, and pushing for the computerization of the social and economic agents of the neighbourhood; (3) establish social facilities of all kinds in and for the neighbourhood but 'open to the rest of the city'; (4) do the same with regard to training and labour insertion facilities; (5) carry out follow-up, evaluation and dissemination of the operational programme; 6) provide social programmes for the general public but also for specific profiles (aging population, prostitutes, drug users, children etc.); and (7) carry out training and labour insertion

that would refer to particular facilities, especially the School for Craft Works (Consorci Mirall-Palma-Centre 1999).

11. See http://encasa2007.com/ezrealty/detail/one-bedroom-rental-apartment-in-central-palma-de-mallorca-available-from-april-of-2008.html.

12. See http://bayona.balearweb.net/post/19530

REFERENCES

Ajuntament de Palma. 1985. *Plan General de Ordenación Urbana.* Palma de Mallorca: Ajuntament de Palma.

Ajuntament de Palma. 1999. *El centre històric de Palma: De la rehabilitació monumental a la rehabilitació integral. Història d'un procés.* Palma de Mallorca: Ajuntament de Palma.

Alomar Esteve, G. 2000 [1950]. *La reforma de Palma: Hacia la renovación de una ciudad a través de un proceso de evolución creativa.* Palma de Mallorca: Collegi Oficial d'Arquitectes de Balears.

Ballester, L. and C. Orte. 2001. 'Informe sobre la situación social: Evaluación final', in L.Ballester and C. Orte, *La iniciativa Urban-El Temple: Medio urbano y contexto social.* Palma: Fundació Universitat-Empresa.

Bianchini, F. 1995. 'Cultural Considerations in Inner City Regeneration', in E. Delgado (ed.), *Culture and Neighbourhoods. Vol. 1: Concepts and References.* Strasbourg: Council of Europe Publishing.

Castells, M. 1981. 'Crisis urbana, cambio social y poder municipal', in M.Castells, *Crisis urbana y cambio social.* Madrid: Siglo XXI de España Editores.

Consorci Mirall-Palma-Centre. 1999. *Iniciativa comunitaria URBAN El Temple* (information leaflet). Palma de Mallorca: Consorci Mirall-Palma-Centre.

de Certeau, M. 1997 [1980]. *The Practice of Everyday Life.* Berkeley: University of California Press.

Delgado, M. 2006. 'Ciudades de mentira: El turismo cultural como estrategia de desactivación urbana', *Archipiélago* 68: 17–28.

Escartín Bisbal, J.M. 2001. *La ciutat amuntegada: Indústria del calçat, desenvolupament urbà i condicions de vida en la Palma contemporània (1840–1940).* Palma: Documenta Balear.

Estada, E. 2003 (1892). *La Ciudad de Palma: Su industria, sus fortificaciones, sus condiciones sanitarias y su ensanche, con un apéndice sobre las condiciones que han de reunir las viviendas para ser salubres.* Palma: Conselleria d'Innovació i Energia – Govern de les Illes Balears.

Franquesa, J. and M. Morell. 2005. 'Heritage Deviations in Relation to Town Planning in Ciutat de Mallorca', *Journal of Mediterranean Studies* 15(2): 427–462.

Garnier, J.-P. 2006. 'Un espacio indefendible: La reordenación urbana en la hora securitaria', in J.P.Garnier, *Contra los territorios del poder.* Barcelona: Virus.

Geddes, M. 2006. 'Partnership and the Limits to Local Governance in England: Institutionalist Analysis and Neoliberalism', *International Journal of Urban and Regional Research* 30(1): 76–97.

Gravano, A. 2005. *El barrio en la teoría social.* Buenos Aires: Espacio Editorial.

Hannerz, U. 2003. 'Macro-scenarios: Anthropology and the Debate over Contemporary and Future Worlds', *Social Anthropology* 11(2): 169–187.
Harvey, D. 1989 (1985). 'Flexible Accumulation through Urbanization', in D. Harvey, *The Urban Experience*, Oxford: Basil Blackwell.
Harvey, D. 1989. 'From Managerialism to Entrepreneurialism: The Transformation of Governance in Late Capitalism', *Geografiska Annaler*, 71B: 3–17.
Keller, S. 1975 [1968]. 'Reconsideración de la unidad vecinal', in S. Keller, *El vecindario urbano: Una perspectiva sociológica*. Madrid: Siglo XXI de España Editores S.A..
Kurtz, D. 2001. *Political Anthropology: Paradigms and Power.* Boulder: Westview Press.
Le Galès, P. 2002. *European Cities: Social Conflict and Governance.* New York: Oxford University Press.
Lefebvre, H. 1980 [1971]. *Hacia el cibernantropo: Una crítica de la tecnocracia.* Barcelona: Gedisa.
Lefebvre, H. 2000 [1974]. *La production de l'espace.* Paris: Ed. Anthropos.
Lowenthal, D. 2002. 'The Past as a Theme Park', in T. Young and R. Riley (eds), *Theme Park Landscapes: Antecedents and Variations.* Washington, D.C.: Dumbarton Oaks Research Library and Collection.
Manresa, A. 2005. 'El cràter i el seu negoci', in A. Manresa and F. Montserrat, *Paratges i personatges de Balears S.A.* Palma: Edicions Hiperdimensional.
Maskovsky, J. 2006. 'Governing the 'New Hometowns': Race, Power, and Neighborhood in the Inner City', *Identities: Global Studies in Culture and Power*, 13(1): 73–100.
Nora, P. 1997 [1992]. 'L'ére de la commémoration', in P. Nora (ed.), *Les lieux de mémoire*, vol. 3. Paris: Éditions Gallimard.
Ruiz Viñals, C. 2000. *L'urbanisme de la Ciutat de Palma.* Palma: El Far de les Crestes.
Salvà, F. et al. 2000. 'Urban-El Temple: Inserción sociolaboral en una zona urbana degradada en rehabilitación', in F. Salvà, *Proyectos de inserción sociolaboral y economía social: Descripción, análisis y propuestas para la intervención.* Madrid: Editorial Popular.
Sassen, S. 2000. *Cities in a World Economy.* London: Pine Forge Press.
Storper, M. 2001. 'The Poverty of Radical Theory Today: From the False Promises of Marxism to the Mirage of the Cultural Turn', *International Journal of Urban and Regional Research* 25(1): 155–179.
Swyngedouw, E., F. Moulaert and A. Rodriguez. 2002. 'Neoliberal Urbanization in Europe: Large-scale Urban Development Projects and the New Urban Policy', *Antipode* 34(3): 542–577.
Tilly, C. 1999. 'Power: Top Down and Bottom Up', *The Journal of Political Philosophy* 7(3): 330–352.
Weber, R. 1995. 'Preface', in E. Delgado (ed.), *Culture and Neighbourhoods. Vol. 1: Concepts and References.* Strasbourg: Council of Europe Publishing.
Williams, R. 2001 [1973]. *El campo y la ciudad.* Barcelona: Ediciones Paidós Ibérica.
Wolf, E. 1999. 'Anthropology among the Powers', *Social Anthropology* 7(2): 121–134.

Part 4

⤙ ◆ ⤚

Transforming Identities:
Imagination and Representations

❧ Chapter 10 ❧

Ethnicized Interreligious Conflicts in Contemporary Granada, Spain

JAVIER ROSÓN LORENTE AND GUNTHER DIETZ

Over the past few years in the city of Granada in Andalusia (Spain), formerly the cradle of the Nazarí (Nazarite) dynasty and a symbol of a peaceful and harmonious interreligious community, there has been a perceived 'return of Islam', possibly as the result of the convergence of two different processes. On the one hand, as has occurred in the rest of Spain, the city has been experiencing a marked increase in the immigrant population, amongst which there is a large and significant percentage of Muslims from the Maghreb. On the other hand, parallel to this increased immigration and as of the end of the Franco regime, there has been a growing trend, in Andalusian cities such as Córdoba and Granada, for the local population to convert to Islam, plus a steady increase in the number of foreign immigrants setting up residence in Granada for religious reasons. Both of these phenomena have given rise to attendant anti-Muslim and anti-Moor movements that reflect the varying dimensions of discrimination widely prevalent in broad-ranging sectors of the Spanish public.

An ethnographic study of the old 'Arab quarter', El Albayzín, and of the various areas of interrelations bringing Muslims and non-Muslims together has allowed us to analyse the formation of Muslim and neo-Muslim communities in the light of the regionalist policies of local elites, set on generating an 'Andalusí' identity of multi-mix religions. Such multifaceted identity can then be exploited to good effect for cultural tourism, above all targeting the significant numbers of 'Oriental' tourists who visit the city. The current context of generalized 'Islamophobia' has only served to exacerbate an existing grievance provoked by the growing visibility of the Granada Muslims, which has not only produced reactions of repulsion on the part of the local Catholics and the ecclesiastical institutions, but is also categorically rejected by such sectors as are fighting to establish lay, nonreligious communal spaces. In the process, the local school of Islam, its communities and its representatives become 'ethnicized', symbols and markers of an 'otherness' that is, hypothetically, incommensurate with the modernization and 'Europeanization' of the Andalusian culture. This creates serious challenges for the management of religious diversity, one of the great outstanding tasks still to be tackled by Spanish society, in itself increasingly multicultural and multi-religious.

Introduction: The Return of Islam

Spain, which for many centuries was a country of emigration, became a country of immigrants as of 1986 and the entry into what was then known as the European Economic Community, with growing numbers of foreigners moving into the country to stay, of which Muslims from the Maghreb represent a significant percentage (Izquierdo Escribano 1992; Cornelius 2004). The history of migration and exile for the Muslim population dates back to 1492, the time of the re-conquest of Granada by the Catholic monarchs. This wave of expulsion lasted through to the years between 1601 and 1617, when the Moriscos were finally thrown out of Spain, marking the beginning of the Andalusian and Sephardic diasporas throughout the Mediterranean basin (Viñes Millet, 1995). History, however, has changed this situation radically. Spain, like most other countries in the European Union, is now a country of immigrants. Although the proportion of immigrants is low in comparison to neighbouring countries, and indeed in comparison with classic countries for immigration such as Australia, Canada or the United States, the increase in migratory flow in recent years has been very marked. This has led to concern amongst some people, who go as far as to suggest that such immigration has now acquired the dimensions of a national problem, despite the fact that the proportion of foreigners in Spain is still under 2.5 per cent of the total population (Gil Araujo 2004). Moving away from the well-worn 'mono-directional' perspective of migratory processes and analysing the data qualitatively, we can observe that we are witnessing a very heterogeneous model of migration with at least four different strands that at times interweave, and with different sources and target destinations (Dietz 2004). These migratory processes are the following.

In the first place are the children of Spanish emigrants to the North. This whole new generation of sons and daughters of Spaniards living and working in Northern Europe wish to return in order to seek out their Mediterranean roots and those of their ancestors (Ruiz Garzon 2001). Then there are the Spanish workers who migrated legally to Northern Europe, but did not manage to fully integrate into the host society. When they retire, they try to return to their roots, thereby establishing a second migratory process. Third are the people from the North of Europe, mainly pensioners or retired, who decide to migrate to Spain, attracted by the climate, the tourist services and the cost of living. And finally there are non-European immigrants, who increasingly choose Spain as their target destination; the flows from North Africa and Latin American countries are of particular significance. Immigration from Latin America is a clear reflection of the postcolonial ties that still exist between the mainland of Spain and Latin America, favoured, in part, by the Spanish state policies for regulating and contracting workers in their country of origin through special work permits (Izquierdo Escribano 2002; Gil Araujo 2003). Immigration from Latin America, at present, represents almost 40 per cent of all immigration to Spain. For the first time in many years, Morocco does not top the list of source countries of migrants to the peninsula.

However, to all intents and purposes, the perception and visibility of the Muslims who are settling in various regions of Spain is, for a large part of the 'local' population, far superior to any other migratory process – much more than the aforementioned Latin American influx, for example. A large part of the immigrant population that gets to Spain in general, and to the region of Andalusia in particular (García Castaño 2001; Martín Muñoz, 2003), is made up of Muslims, most of whom are Arabs. They form part of a heterogeneous process of migratory flows, generated directly by the demand for labour (Gil Araujo 2004) in sectors characterized by high seasonality and lack of regulation. Therefore, we have to distinguish between, on the one hand, Arab Muslims who have residence permits or are in the process of getting their papers sorted out and, on the other hand, the 'unknown number' who are, at present, 'illegal' immigrants in Spain. Likewise, we have to add to the total the Moroccan students who decide to study in Spain rather than in their traditional 'alma mater', France. The number of these is on the rise, with almost sixty thousand qualified students/immigrants living temporarily in Granada who have begun to generate their own transnational migratory process (González Barea and Dietz 1999). On top of this, there is the Muslim population that resides permanently in Ceuta and Melilla, the Spanish 'enclaves' in the North of Morocco.

Nevertheless, the visibility of the 'Muslim immigrant population' is not the only factor that has contributed towards the upsurge of ethno-religious communities in cities like Granada. A whole series of other factors of a completely different order have intervened in these circumstances, such as the appearance of neo-Muslim Spaniards and 'Muslimophile' activists, which are essential factors to be taken into account when analysing the various spaces of interrelationship that are opening up between the Muslim communities and the 'natives' at the local, regional and national levels.

The First Communities of 'Converts': Somewhere between Sub-national Regionalism and Provincial Localism

The Spanish Constitution of 1978 is a decisive reference point in the process of the growing presence of Muslim communities in Spain, and in various regions such as Andalusia. It establishes the first system of relations between the state and non-Catholic religions, which had not been acknowledged up until then. Under article 16, the constitution guarantees 'freedom of religion and devotion for all persons and communities'. The process was completed in June 1989 with the declaration of the well-known roots of the Islamic religion. Meanwhile, by opening the possibility of subnationalization and the federalization of the Spanish nation-state, a whole process was created for subnational policies of identity, often clearly distinct from the hegemony of the national identity. This led to unique historical circumstances being emphasized to maintain the apparent distance between 'national and regional identities, distinguishing two political forms of access to autonomy, via the fast lane or the slow' (Verlot and Dietz, 2001). Catalonia, Galicia and the Basque Country embraced immediate access to full devolution and autonomy, since they were able to 'prove' their historical, cultural and linguistic past, apart from the fact that they had already passed their statutes by referendum and had provisional autonomous regimes.

However, in Andalusia there was no such clearly differentiated identity, no different language nor a distinctive past. Its own history had been 'manipulated', both during the dictatorship of Franco and years before, by the very history of the nation-state and the pro-Spanish doctrine, which refused to recognize the historical existence of the Andalusians as a differentiated ethnic group. Without a different language, 'history' or 'differentiated doctrine', the Andalusian identity 'invented' by the pro-Andalusians had little clout with respect to the overpowering identity of the nation state, Spain. After a referendum in 1980 Andalusia was finally able to take advantage of the fast lane, but then the elites and the political leaders, in dogged pursuit of what they perceived as the needed justification of the unique history of Andalusia, exploited the stereotypes of popular Andalusian culture such as bullfighting, flamenco and religious celebrations. As a result of the creation of these autonomous communities, regionalist movements became consolidated, both in the 'historical communities' and in Andalusia, taking advantage of what Hobsbawm (1992) called 'the invention of tradition'.

At this point there emerged two separate groups that considered 'conversion to Islam' a potentially effective means by which to establish a distinct self-identity for the region, grounded in a flourishing history of cultural pluralism and tolerance based on religious precepts in the Iberian peninsula

(Al-Andalus). Initially, the first Spanish converts, or neo-Muslims, appeared as a direct consequence of their lack of satisfaction with the sociopolitical situation of the day. 'Men and women who, then, were between 20 and 30, belonged to the middle class, with a high academic level, and who generally had militated in left-wing parties or flirted with Oriental philosophies, took up Islam' (Tarrés 1999). Second, there were 'movements', generally of minority groups of left-wing academics, poets, artists and singers from Granada, Córdoba and Seville, etc. who did not embrace Islam de facto but recognized, in it, differentiating and identifying characteristics that had vanished centuries back from the 'history of the Andalusian region'. They advocated re-adoption of these values and Islamic norms in order to reconstruct Andalusian identity.

Parallel to this, political and social movements arose in Andalusia whose differentiating nature consisted in a special 'religious feeling' of proximity to Islam, which gave rise to the political party Liberación Andaluza (LA), the 'first and only political proposal of Islam in Andalusia or, for that matter, in Spain, up until the present time' (Del Olmo Garrudo 1997). The advocacy role of the political movements articulating Islam in the region began to lose steam, and they soon changed their former process of local visibility for a certain form of internal involution. These groups of Muslim and neo-Muslim converts began to make reference to a process of population that was a thing of the past, holding that 'Islamic Andalusia' transcended the values of Al-Andalus and offering an alternative that was more cultural than political. It was then that the Spanish Federation of Islamic Religious Entities (la Federación Española de Entidades Religiosas Islámicas, FEERI) appeared on the scene to offer cohesion for most of the 'Neo-Muslim communities'.

Around the 1990s this type of movement began to grow, thanks to the international impact of migration.[1] As of that moment, mosques, schools of the Koran, organizations, etc. began to appear, generating the first meeting place for the Spanish converts to Islam and the immigrant Moroccan workers. The search for identity that can be observed in this process is intimately linked to the social construction of a common shared space, forging 'characteristics and identifying signs' that brought similar groups together and, at the same time, marked their external differences.

Together with these phenomena, anti-Islamic and anti-Arab attitudes prevailed in broad sectors of Spanish society, mixing ethnic discrimination, religious bias and nationalism (ASEP 1998) to varying degrees. These attitudes are, in fact, deeply rooted and manifested in historical stigmatizations of the 'other'. As Stallaert has shown (1998), since 1492 and the first Spanish project of a nation state, the latter has been based on a mixture of 'Arab-phobia' and Islamophobia, legitimized in 'laws of purity of race' that constantly switch among supposedly biological, ethnic and religious discourses, giving rise to what we will hereafter call 'Muslim-phobia.'

The Dynamics and Emerging Impact of the Ethno-religious Communities

The upsurge of new ethno-religious communities, together with migratory processes, created international diasporas with a common imagery and cultural code of what had been lost. This also produced a constant tension between the sense of belonging to a nation state and of belonging to a locality or community (Elbaz and Helly 1996). These processes triggered in local populations a widespread localist movement that sought desperately and constantly for an identity to oppose to the 'other', to what was strange and/or foreign in the urban context and at odds with the social and political movements of a regionalist nature. The confrontations that arose as a result, far from expressing themselves frontally and radically in all the Spanish cities (barring a few exceptional cases), were met with constantly growing social and institutional alarm, which had the effect of reproducing existing prejudices and the historical stereotypes of the Muslim community of Al-Andalus. The 'hypothetical' rebirth of the process of Islamic re-conquest was confronted with the hypothetical Christian roots of the local community in ways that would permanently affect day-to-day life in the city and the various neighbourhoods, producing a constant process of daily negotiation based on difference.

It was the irruption on the scene of the immigrant population, this 'new actor', that would destructure the bases of centralist and localist philosophy and 'gum up the works' of the already intricate political structures that, over time, had been appearing in the region. The Morisco legacy, which in its day had served to differentiate the historical identity of the Andalusian from the rest of the Spanish people, clashed head-on with the ethnicizing localist groups, whose idea was to create a multi-religious Andalusian identity to play to the significant gallery of 'Oriental-type' tourists they were receiving (Said 1978) in the city. As a result, the contemporary processes of ethnogenesis and ethnic reaffirmation via cultural reappropriation or re-invention necessarily generated 'hybrid cultures' (García Canclini 1989). These cultures have seen their practices and representations profoundly transformed by the modification and reinterpretation of intracultural relationships, and by the incorporation of intercultural elements that have been submitted to a process of 'ethnic retouching' to be assimilated, later, as their own (Dietz 2003). These hybrid figures have created, in the city of

Granada and in the neighbourhood of El Albayzin, an awareness of an identity that we can analyse and describe from various different perspectives.

First, the social alarm was sounded when the Muslim communities who had settled in several of the different neighbourhoods no longer were merely anecdotal, a handful of invisible persons, but had become a visible force in both the public and the private sphere. This growing visibility of the 'other' awakened the slumbering but deeply rooted, historical 'Muslim-phobia' that is growing in strength, and palpably so, in broad sectors of Granada society. The new communities of converts, together with the Moroccan immigration, are basically being used, initially, to arouse the old stereotype of the return of the 'Moors to our shores' – which at present, as a result of the terrorist attacks of 11 March (Madrid), 11 September (New York and Washington, D.C.) and 7 July (London), merely bolsters the 'essential stigmatisation of the Muslim world' (Martín Muñoz 2003). Overnight, the immigrant population in the neighbourhood was converted into the 'lurking terrorist', producing something of a national psychosis and, therefrom, the repulsion shown towards these communities, and to everything relating to Islam.

Second, the appearance of communities of converts has added more fuel to the fire of the historical movement against Islam and has only increased the sense of frustration, which has led to locals regarding the new converts, who are 'dissidents' from the perspective of the Christian world, as 'deserters' or 'outlaws'. Third and last, immigration from the Maghreb is of growing importance in the process of consolidation of the 'Muslimophiles' mentioned previously, celebrated by the Andalusian intellectuals as the seeds of the 'rediscovery' and 'reinvention' of the Muslim roots of the Al-Andalus region.

'Muslim-phobia' is met with 'Muslimophilia'. The 'problem' that arises between the new Diaspora communities and the 'locals' is mainly a political problem of recognition and historical memory. This historical memory is evoked whenever community groups attempting to integrate into the social structure of life in Granada have a significant need to protest against the people who wish to exclude them from national identity and culture (Elbaz and Helly 1996). In Granada society this is exemplified by new social actors who emerged in the process of political transition during the final hours of the Franco regime. The new Spanish Muslims, Spaniards 'converted' to Islam, have shaped the roots of a new Islam at a local level and laid the foundations for future organizations and federations of Muslims at the level of the state, as a whole. In this conflict, both the neo-Muslim community and the immigrants have been exposed to a process of external ascription, with both the Muslimophiles and the Muslim-phobes subjecting them to ethnic discrimination.

We are going to examine the case of El Albayzin, where the stage is being fought over by three different actors: the Muslim community, sectors of the population with leanings towards the Muslim community, and those actors who are completely opposed to the Muslim community. This will enable us to analyse the political-migratory framework of the 'ethnicizing' of this neighbourhood, and the foreseeable radicalization of ethnic trends in Granada. All of this is reflected in the cultural dynamics of the present society, through their constant struggle to consolidate an identity that will unify the group from within whilst clearly manifesting their external differences with others.

Muslimophilia vs. Muslim-phobia: Ethnic-religious Conflicts in the Neighbourhood of El Albayzín

In the present context of generalized Islamophobia, not only has the growing visibility of Islam met with rejection on the part of the local Catholics and ecclesiastical institutions in Granada, but this is now also accompanied by protests from lay groups seeking to create true 'open' public spaces. Throughout this process, local Islam, its communities and its representatives have ended up being 'ethnicized' as symbols and markers of a hypothetically limitless 'otherness', in opposition to the modernization and 'Europeanization' of Andalusian culture. This has created serious challenges for the management of religious diversity, one of the great outstanding items on the agenda of an ever more multi-religious and multicultural Spanish society.

In the course of the process of construction of the Muslim communities, both immigrants and converts began to concentrate themselves in the neighbourhoods in the centre of the city, such as the neighbourhood of El Albayzin, which before this had been largely abandoned in the process of middle-class suburbanization. As of the early 1990s, these neighbourhoods, having submitted to processes of gentrification and exploitation of cultural tourism in the city, began to regain population (Latiesa Rodríguez 2000). The neighbourhood of El Albayzín is well known for its characteristic Arab architecture and its Moorish legacy. It is now beginning to be rediscovered and reused by an emerging elite of Moroccan immigrants and the 'great minds' of the community of Muslim converts, activists and intellectuals (Rosón Lorente 2001). Paradoxically, both of the opposed groups – Muslimophiles and Muslim-phobes – focus habitually on the 'oriental' legacy to defend the unique nature of their neighbourhood, and to claim for it the common roots of the Al-Andalus culture. The Muslim-phobes, however, perceive the 'return of Islam' to the neighbourhood as a constant threat, not only to their own religious identity but also to the 'quality of life' in the neighbourhood, although at heart they too make constant and reiterative use of the 'myth of the Past'.

With the initial process of religious-cultural ethnogenesis partly vindicating a reinvention of Al-Andalus, these factions of Andalusian regionalism are running full face into anti-regionalist centralism as well as the other factions of Andalusian regionalism that are opposed to Islam as an 'ethnic marker' of the Andalusian culture (Eriksen 1993). Thus, the dialectic that has arisen between Muslim-phobia and Muslimophilia is not merely a microcosm of the conflict between the centralized nation state and subnational regionalism: at least in Granada and the neighbourhood of El Albayzín, it represents a strange and ill-defined 'coalition of interests' between the centralist Conservative nationalists on the one hand, and localist movements on the other.

The empirical study of the conflict between nationalist, regionalist and localist ideologies, in the context of migration, affords us an interesting analysis of the structural similarities of nationalism and ethnogenesis. Both use similar strategies of territorialization, temporization and substantiation to legitimize their demands (Dietz 2000).

Strategies of Territorialization

Strategies of territorialization transform space into territory, converting peripheral areas of interaction between groups into clearly defined frontiers of separation. The spatial expansion of the nation state clashes with previously established local and regional entities, upon which the nationalist argument of the indivisible 'sovereignty' of an emerging 'nation' is appropriately deployed, and is returned by the counter-hegemonic ethnic movements. The group that is responsible for the national project thereafter defines the centre as the nation, and the periphery as the sub-nation.

Various examples demonstrate the strategies of territorialization in action in the neighbourhood of El Albayzín, where the 'local' people are facing an accelerated process of 'gentrification' and the Muslim population is beginning to develop the necessary infrastructure for the progress of their community. Amongst many other protests, we should perhaps highlight the permanent grievance on the part of the neighbourhood association in respect to what they consider to be an abusive occupancy of the streets in some areas of the neighbourhood. In particular, they mention the street of Calderería Vieja y Nueva, where the tables, stalls and merchandise of street vendors, whom they define as 'immigrants and Spanish converts', invade the streets, terraces and pavements. This gives the impression of a souk, projecting a negative image of the city to the visiting tourists and requiring locals to skilfully manoeuvre their passage through the stalls of the 'Moors'. They protest against not only this occupancy or misappropriation of public space, transformed into territory, but also the lack of public safety, associated with the Muslim community and all of its attendant stereotypes – thieves, criminals, illegal immigrants, etc. (Tarrés 1999).

The Muslim community, together with the centre for immigrant youth, the Bermúdez de Castro, is blamed for all the problems relating to public safety and robbery in the neighbourhood. The localist forces in the neighbourhood have even gone so far as to declare in official institutions such as the town council, and over and over again in the neighbourhood association, that 'to set up a centre for immigrant youth in the Cuesta de Chapiz, in the centre of the Albayzín, is putting temptation in harm's way' (*Diario La Opinión de Granada,* 2 October 2005). These problems, which may appear to be momentary and passing, can be observed with all their force in the process of construction of the first Mezquita Mayor, the Grand Mosque of Granada, and the celebration of the return of Islam to El Albayzín, five centuries after the Catholic monarchs defeated the 'Nazarís' and took possession of the kingdom in 1492.

The Mezquita Mayor of Granada

Granada's Grand Mosque, which was recently inaugurated in the neighbourhood of El Albayzín, where the heritage space is hypothetically shared, has inflamed a whole series of cultural prejudices of the local people of the neighbourhood in defence of what is 'traditional' and 'really theirs'. On the one hand, the Islamic community and the Muslimophiles, reacting to the cultural rejection to which they are being subjected locally, have accused the neighbours of xenophobia and racism. The Muslim-phobes, on the other hand, that is, the residents who represent the Catholic parishes and various neighbourhood associations, have presented various measures to local politicians, calling upon them to block the creation of the mosque, which they consider to be more a problem of visual and heritage contamination than one of 'culture clash'. The 'schism' now appearing in the localist control mechanisms that were successfully used in the past to paralyse new construction, has given rise to a political problem of substantial dimensions, with decisions being taken as to whether or not to give building licences.

This phase can be clearly observed in the 'public analysis' (Modood 1999) of the re-vindications of both sides, where it is evident that a majority have assimilated the process of construction and the creation of infrastructure for the Islamic community, and have established a clear timeline for the process. This has led to a series of attitudes and protests, spread out over time and space, by both the neighbours and associations who are opposed to the construction of the mosque, and the Islamic community.

Since the mosque's inauguration on 10 July 2003, a decade after the land had been purchased by the Islamic Community of Spain, far from representing a place of worship and devotion for the Muslims of Granada and a place of encounter (Lacomba Vázquez, 2001), it has rather become a place of mis-encounter. This is felt to be the case by both the 'sensitized' neighbours and the rest of the Muslim-phobes, as well as the local Muslims themselves.

Temporization Strategies

Territorialization is closely linked to temporization, with the 'nation state' imposing one sole interpretation on 'invented tradition'. Or rather, the nation state reinterprets tradition in order to achieve its national project. In the subnational ethnic discourses, this metaphorical 'possession' of a given territory is based on the 'invention of tradition', which uses the justification of the age of the counter-hegemonic ethnic actor as opposed to the dominant national actor. The politics of 'local roots' is projected as born of a remote and mythical past, as is demonstrated by its many witnesses, authors of multiple strands of discourse (Estefermann 1998; Strubell 1998).

The Conquest of Granada and the Celebration of the Fifth Centenary of the Death of Isabel la Católica, the Catholic Monarch

Parallel to the debate that arose over the construction of the Mezquita Mayor in Granada, serious ill feeling began to be made manifest with respect to the professed historical roots and the identity of Granada. The commemoration of the last Muslim dynasty in 1492 has proved to be a bone of contention between those in favour, the Muslimophiles,[2] and those against, the Muslim-phobes.

Countless political attempts have been made over the last decade to modify the Commemoration of the Conquest of Granada by making explicit mention of the legacy of the 'three cultures' of Spain. However, the Nationalist Union of Spain and various local forces, such as the fraternities of the Catholic parishes, have always defended the single, non-modifiable version of the commemoration, considering it to be a static element, a 'traditional' tradition, without any type of possible evolution.

At present, there are various chinks to be seen in the traditional armour. The celebration of music and poetry called the Festival de las Culturas, or

Day of Reconciliation, is celebrated in the Mezquita Mayor on the second of January. In addition, activities are organized, in conjunction with the Association in Defence of Human Rights in Morocco, by the citizens' platform called Granada for Tolerance (Granada por la Tolerancia[3]) as a counter and alternative to the commemoration ceremony.

These celebrations, with their divergent interpretations of the past in the light of a constructed present, will be accompanied this year by the Commemoration of the Fifth Centenary of the Death of Isabel La Católica. Parallel to the re-vindications with respect to the celebration of la Toma, the conquest, these and other 'traditional celebrations' are confronting two radically opposed groups. On one side are 'Muslimophiles' representing Andalusian nationalism and regionalism, the Nación Andaluza, who consider that 'there is nothing to celebrate and a lot to regret' in the whole process of the re-conquest of the kingdom together with the consolidation of 'Spanish Imperialism', led by Isabel la Católica. On the other side are groups in favour of the commemoration – Democracia Nacional, España 2000, etc. – who have articulated a totally opposite discourse, highlighting the value of 'differential tradition', and consider that the celebration of the historic event to be vital for the formation of a strong and united Spain.

The aforementioned Fiesta de la Toma, or its counterpart, the Día de la Reconciliación, are more and more becoming not so much events where 'civilisations clash', to quote Huntington (1996), but rather a process of formation of antagonistic groups, differentiated in time, that are shaping civil society in Granada. These groups allude to both the past and the living present of the presumed traditions of the city, using different strategies of invention and reinvention of time and space, attempting thereby to reinforce their control over history and historical memory. This will allow them, in turn, to construct their own identity, which will be culturally and socially differentiated from that of the other. Given the point of 'intransigence' reached, the celebrations are progressively losing their hypothetical 'tradition', to become an unbeatable and novelty showcase of the protests against the Muslim population.

Such events, which form part of the cultural and identity construct of any given population, are gradually becoming, to an ever greater extent if such is possible, the object of the rejection and negation of the public space of the other, and have begun to divide the civil society of Granada in two. Both the citizens who celebrate the Toma de Granada in the Plaza del Carmen, and those who celebrate its counterpart, 'sin Toma', stigmatize the Muslim population that is resident in Granada and in the neighbourhood of El Albayzín. Both groups construct themselves as differentiated segments that desire 'to maintain a certain distance with respect to those others with whom they must share the same social space, and with whom'

(Delgado Ruiz 2000: 88) they do not wish to mix, although daily life obliges them to do so.

Likewise, this process of struggle for a collective cultural identity has been confounded by the recent appearance and growing presence of the immigrant population. The importance of the migratory process from South to North and the recent 'return of Islam' in Spain are increasingly perceived in Andalusia as a threat to the growing 'contest' for autonomous identity and decentralization. The immigration, which is basically from Morocco, and recent events that have affected national security, such as the terrorist attacks in Madrid, New York and London, have awoken the old stereotypes and converted them into a pretext for the evident and growing xenophobia, whose seeds were planted over five centuries back.

Substantiation Strategies: Institutions and Organizations

Finally, a third strategy, that of the substantiation of difference, reinterprets social relations from a biological perspective in order to confer solidity on the project of the nation state. This process can be observed in the creation of institutions and organizations that channel Muslim-phobia and Muslimophilia in the city of Granada. The institutionalization and centralization of the nation state is challenged by the persistence, reinvention and revitalization of 'communities', 'regions' and regional units, increasingly substantiated at a subnational level (Stavenhagen 1989). Often these emerging entities take advantage of the impact of globalization, generating supranational alliances with similar actors to produce 'self-empowerment' in the face of hegemonic nationalism (Dietz 2003; Squires 1999).

In this vein are institutions such as the Catholic parish fraternities, brotherhoods, etc., who joined forces with local organizations to defend the Christian faith and their distinctive traditions. Similarly, neo-Muslim groups have begun to approach the recently established migrant communities to promote a common identity. One example of this was the creation of the Islamic Council of Granada, formed by both representatives of the immigrant community and Spanish neo-Muslims. At present, various associations and institutions associated with the University of Granada are trying to bring together the local antagonistic forces and encourage a public debate between them, thereby challenging and channelling the strategies of temporization and territorialization articulated by the various contesting groups.

Likewise, the 'Mezquita de Granada' foundation, set up by the Islamic Community of Spain, the United Arab Emirates and the Arab Emirate of Sharjah in 2002, is attempting to spread information about the Islamic culture and religion, as well as attending to the religious life and spiritual needs of all Muslims living Spain and in Granada in particular.

Conclusions

Since the 1970s, with the arrival of the first Spanish Muslims in the neighbourhood of El Albayzín, together with the increased visibility of an immigrant population in the lower part of the district in the Calle Calderería and Calle Elvira, the presumed conflict between Islamic tradition and the values of Spanish society has become more and more apparent. This confrontation between the 'traditional values' of local residents and those of newcomers to Granada is one of the great challenges faced by so-called multicultural societies. This is especially so in a place that has been historically acknowledged by some as the paradigm of peaceful and harmonious community life, of three cultures living side by side: the Jews, the Christians and the Muslims.

The 'idyllic' vision of a multi-cultured society presupposes that goodwill and tolerance are basic ingredients of harmonious life for different cultural communities sharing social space and common politics. However, the concern caused by the increase in immigration has generated contradictory responses in Andalusia. Such responses include the commemoration of the events of la Toma and its counter-celebration, the sin Toma, as well as the current celebration of the Fifth Centenary of the Death of Isabel la Católica. All these are factors of great importance in understanding both the demand for religious rights by minority groups and the reactions of the dominant group, whether it be Muslimophile or Muslim-phobe (Del Olmo Garrudo 1997).

In conclusion, the essentialization of the 'other', practised both through policies of identity promoted by groups of Muslim-phobes and through movements in favour of Islam, seem to come together to produce a potentially risky attitude. The 'time policy' (the invocation of the historical memory of conflict) and the 'politics of space' (the territorial dimension of cultures) converge in their efforts to generate a collective identity. The relationship established between ethnicity and culture, through contact with various groups – communities anchored in local Catholicism, migrant workers and neo-Muslims, etc. – is to be observed through the selective use of intangible cultural heritages marking difference between locals and outsiders.

Perhaps this is not a 'reinvention' of historical roots, as affirmed by Stallaert (1999), but rather a reproduction of historical baggage, i.e. the opinions and prejudices that led to the Granada Moriscos being expelled from the city over 500 years ago. This and other potential conflicts that are appearing in the urban context of the neighbourhood of El Albayzín are an object of dispute between three different actors: the Muslim community, the Muslimophile sector of local society and the local Muslim-phobes. In the course of this conflict, centred round the mosque as a symbol, and not only a religious one, Islam is instrumentalized by each of the groups to forge its own respective collective identity.

Thus, far from the hypothetical ideal of harmonious community life among different residents, where shared values predominate and means of integration are actively sought out, the neighbourhood has shattered into two 'ethnic communities' at loggerheads, who share the same urban space but who, at a symbolic level, challenge and question their respective essentialist definitions of this space. In the broader context of the conflicts over historical heritage, the example of El Albayzín does not appear to open new perspectives upon the multicultural life of a shared past for Christians and Muslims in Granada. On the contrary, the dividing line of religion, which structures the emerging ethnic communities at the local level, eradicates all possibilities of the social actors contributing towards an inclusive reinterpretation of two powerful historical myths, that of the 'harmonious life in Al-Andalus' and that of the 'glorious Christian re-conquest'.

NOTES

1. At that moment, the Unión de Comunidades Islámicas (UCIDE) appeared, on the 10th April, 1990. Both UCIDE and FEERI would fight for control of the representation of Muslim communities in Spain, though not before going through a process of criticism and self-evaluation, which continues to this day. For more details, see Rosón Lorente (2001).
2. Years back, Muslimophile intellectuals grouped together in an organization called Asamblea Civil, which demanded the transformation of this event into a 'multi-cultural festivity'.
3. The platform is made up of different local associations and political parties: Izquierda Unida, Human Rights, SOS Racismo, ASPA, Granada Laica (the Lay Society of Granada), Centro de Estudios Históricos de Andalucía, Manifesto 2 de enero (the 2nd January Manifesto – 2 January is the date of the commemoration ceremony) and Granada Acoge.

REFERENCES

ASEP (Análisis Sociológicos, Económicos y Políticos). 1998. *Actitudes hacia los inmigrantes.* Madrid: Ministerio de Trabajo y Asuntos Sociales.
Cornelius, W.A. 1994. 'Spain: the uneasy transition from labor exporter to labor importer', in W.A. Cornelius , P.L. Martin and J.F. Hollifield (eds.) *Controlling*

Immigration: a global perspective, Stanford, CA: Stanford University Press, 331–369.

Del Olmo Garrudo, A. 1997. 'Liberación Andaluza: un proyecto musulmán para Andalucía', *AWRĀQ: Estudios Sobre el Mundo Árabe e Islámico Contemporáneo* 18: 157–170.

Delgado Ruiz, M. 2000. 'La ciudad y la fiesta: afirmación y disolución de la identidad', in J. García Casdtaño (ed.), *Fiesta, tradición y cambio*. Granada: Proyecto Sur Ediciones.

Dietz, G. 2000. *El desafío de la interculturalidad: el voluntariado y las ONG ante el reto de la inmigración: el caso de la ciudad de Granada*. Barcelona and Granada: Fundación la Caixa and Laboratorio de Estudios Interculturales.

Dietz, G. 2003. *Multiculturalismo, interculturalidad y educación: una aproximación antropológica*. Granada and México, D.F.: Editorial Universidad de Granada and CIESAS.

Dietz, G. 2004. 'Frontier Hybridization or Culture Clash? Trans-national Migrant Communities and Sub-national Identity Politics in Andalusia, Spain', *Journal of Ethnic and Migration Studies* 30(6): 1087–1112.

Elbaz, M. and D. Helly. 1996. 'Modernidad y postmodernidad de las identidades nacionales', *Revista Internacional de Filosofía Política* 7: 72–92.

Eriksen, T. 1993. *Ethnicity and Nationalism: Anthropological Perspectives*. London and Boulder: Pluto.

Estefermann, J. 1998. *Filosofía andina: estudio intercultural de la sabiduría autóctona andina*. Quito: Abya-Yala.

García Canclini, N. 1989. *Culturas híbridas: estrategias para entrar y salir de la modernidad*. México: CNCA.

García Castaño, F.J. 2001. 'Algunos datos aproximativos a la presencia de extranjeros en España, Andalucía y Granada', in F.J. García Castaño et al.(eds.) *Inmigración extranjera en Granada*, Granada: Ayuntamiento de Granada, 41–56.

Gil Araujo, S. 2002. *Inmigración y Gestión de la Diversidad en el Contexto Europeo: informe comparado sobre las políticas migratorias en los Países Bajos y el Estado Español*. Madrid and Amsterdam: IECAH and Transnational Institute.

Gil Araujo, S. 2003. 'Las migraciones en las políticas de la Fortaleza. Sobre las múltiples fronteras de la Europa comunitaria', in Gil Araujo, S. and M. Dahiri (eds.): *Movimientos migratorios en el Mediterráneo occidental. ¿Un fenómeno o un problema?* Córdoba: Ayuntamiento de Córdoba.

Gil Araujo, S. 2004. *Documento de trabajo: Inmigración latinoamericana en España: Estado de la cuestión*. Alcalá de Henares and Miami: Instituto Universitario de Estudios Norteamericanos de la Universidad de Alcalá and International Florida University.

González Barea, E. and G. Dietz. 1999. 'Eine grenzüberschreitende Bildungselite: Studierende aus Marokko an der Universität Granada', *Der Überblick* 35(4): 26–28.

Hobsbawm, E.J. 1992. 'Introduction: Inventing Traditions', in E. Hobsbawm and T. Ranger (eds), *The Invention of Tradition*. Cambridge: Cambridge University Press.

Huntington, S. 1996. *The Clash of Civilizations and the Remaking of the World Order.* New York: Simon & Schuster.

Izquierdo Escribano, A. 1992. *La inmigración en España 1980–1990.* Madrid: Trotta.

Izquierdo Escribano, A. et al. 2002. 'Los preferidos del siglo XXI: la inmigración latinoamericana en España', in García Castaño, F. J. and Muriel López, C. (eds.) *La inmigración en España. Contextos y alternativas, vol. 2, Actas del III Congreso sobre la inmigración en España (ponencias),* Granada: Laboratorio de Estudios Interculturales.

Lacomba Vázquez, 2001. *El Islam inmigrado. Transformaciones y adaptaciones de las prácticas culturales y religiosas.* Bilbao: Ministerio de Educación, Cultura y Deporte.

Latiesa Rodríguez, M. 2000. *Granada y el turismo: análisis sociológico, planificación y desarrollo del proyecto europeo Pass-Enger.* Granada: Universidad de Granada – Diputación Provincial - Ayuntamiento de Granada.

Martín Muñoz, G. (ed.) 2003. *Marroquíes en España. Estudio sobre su integración.* Madrid: Repsol YPF.

Modood, T. 1999. *The Place of Muslims in British Secular Multiculturalism.* Bristol: University of Bristol.

Ruiz Garzon, F. 2001. *De la Primera a la Segunda Generación: Identidad, Cultura y Mundo de Vida de los Emigrantes Españoles en Hamburgo, Alemania.* Granada: Ager.

Rosón Lorente, J. 2001. *¿El Retorno de Tariq? Las Comunidades Musulmanas en la Cuidad de Granada.* Granada: Universidad de Granada.

Said, E. 1978. *Orientalism: Western Conceptions of the Orient.* New York: Pantheon.

Squires, J. 1999. 'Catalonia, Spain and the European Union: a Tale of a Region's Empowerment', *International Journal of Iberian Studies* 12 (1): 34–42.

Stallaert, C. 1998. *Etnogénesis y etnicidad.* Barcelona: Proyecto a Ediciones.

Stallaert, C. 1999. 'El multiculturalismo en el entrecruce de la convivencia 'nacional' y 'extranjera'', in M.J. Escartín Caparrós and M.D. Vargas Llovera (eds), *La inmigración en la sociedad actual: Una visión desde las ciencias sociales.* Alicante: Librería Compas.

Stavenhagen, R. 1989. 'Comunidades étnicas en estados modernos', *América Indígena* vol. 49 (1): 11–33.

Strubell, M. 1998. 'Language, Democracy and Devolution in Catalonia', *Language and Society* 5 (3): 146–180.

Tarrés, S. 1999. 'Islamización de la vida cotidiana: el Tablig en Sevilla', in F. Checa and E. Soriano (eds), *Inmigrantes entre nosotros.* Barcelona: Icaria Editorial.

Verlot, M. and G. Dietz. 2001. *Dual Tracking in Identity Policies: Interrogating 'Territorialization' through the Case of Belgium/Flanders and Spain/Andalusia.* Ghent: Universiteit Ghent.

Viñes Millet, C. (ed.) 1995. *Granada y Marruecos. Arabismo y africanismo en la cultura granadina.* Granada: Proyecto Sur de Ediciones.

◁ Chapter 11 ▷

Governance, Alliance and Resistance

Jewish Museums in Italy

DAVID CLARK

Clifford (1997) developed the notion of contact zones to denote the manner in which contemporary museums are drawn into a set of relationships with other social groups around them, arising partly out of previously unequal power relationships, such as between colonized and colonizers. Bennett (1998) saw such interplay in terms of institutions of governance and community groups, whilst Witcomb (2003) introduces a further note of caution by pointing out that even within the community group camp there are a number of different and competing voices. This chapter outlines the special kind of mosaic represented by the contact zone associated with two Jewish museums in Italy.

In order to examine this issue in greater depth, the chapter will also make reference to the six dimensions outlined in the introduction of this book, namely politics, capital and expressions or representations of identity on the one hand, and the interplay between region, state and neighbourhood on the other. Thus, for instance, enabling legislation at the Italian national level has devolved responsibility for maintaining Jewish material culture at the local level. This chapter explores what this has meant in practice, in the case of Jewish museums in Bologna and Ferrara, and the manner in which different state agencies pursuing a variety of policies might coalesce and come together in support of setting up a Jewish museum. Nevertheless, such a venture also requires the active support of local Jewish communities and activists, not all of them, by any means, speaking with one voice. Hence, the analysis also focuses on discourse formation (Foucault 1972), on rules of appropriation, institutional settings and policy agendas. Finally, the chapter examines the role of controversy and resistance and so also incorporates Foucault's notions on power as being diffuse and integral to all social interactions (Foucault 1980).

Politics: Museums as Contact Zones

Museums have long been seen as seats of learning, disseminating knowledge and understanding to a scholarly and learned audience as well as helping to provide opportunities for self-improvement for the masses (Hooper-Greenhill 1992). Yet museums have also been regarded as agencies of social control, shaping and reproducing knowledge in such a manner as to reproduce existing social relationships and inequalities of power (Bennett 1995). Since the 1970s, however, there has been an increasing and highly vocal barrage of criticism directed at museums (Simpson 1996). This was particularly the case when members of ethnic minorities or indigenous groups felt aggrieved by the tone and content of certain exhibitions, or by the disrespect shown to articles on display, including body parts, which should have been handled more appropriately, buried or repatriated.

It is in the light of such controversies that Clifford (1997) coined the term contact zone, to denote the kind of relationship in which museum management and community groups are increasingly finding themselves. Clifford argues that contemporary museums are drawn into a set of relationships with other social groups and institutions around them that arise partly out of previously unequal power relationships, such as between colonized and colonizers, and partly as a result of contemporary power struggles that are constantly changing and evolving. Clifford notes that such relationships involve 'an ongoing historical, political, moral relationship – a power-charged set of exchanges, of push and pull' (Clifford 1997: 192). In the context of the Americas, the history of colonial contact, together with the appropriation of land and objects, provides a powerful backdrop for disputes concerning both museum objects and museum interpretation, shaping and reshaping current practices and relationships.

Protagonists in the Struggle within Contact Zones

Clifford (1997) refers to the contact zone as consisting essentially of two interest groups, the colonized and the colonizers, or the dominant and the minority group. Bennett (1998) tends to regard the contact zone as involving institutions of governance seeking to implement various social policies, and community groups. Witcomb (2003) begins to unpack these terms and to discuss internal differentiation within the community or minority group, so that several voices from within the minority or community group need to be taken into account. Moreover, whilst Clifford and Bennett stress the distinction between cultures of governance and community cultures, and the extent to which these cultures clash or converge, Witcomb introduces the notion of a tripartite struggle within the contact zone, with the curator representing a third party and a third culture. Hence, this chapter takes as broad a view of the contact zone as possible, so that the museum can be seen to involve a wide range of protagonists, interests and objectives, more akin to a mosaic than to two or three separate camps.

Discourse Theory

This chapter also incorporates discourse theory within the discussion on contact zones. In particular, Foucault (1972) singled out three key elements in discourse formation that seem to be particularly germane here. These are: (1) who is allowed to speak, (2) the importance of institutional settings and (3) the functions of discourse within a pragmatic policy-oriented field. These three elements are moreover interlinked, though in complicated ways that in turn is related to issues of power relationships. Here it should be pointed out that Foucault does not regard power as simply emanating from the top downwards; power is rather seen as infusing all social relationships. In this formulation, power is regarded as both productive and diffuse, with all parties concerned having some measure of power to consent or resist (Foucault 1980). In order to exert power more effectively, discourses are constructed and alliances are forged, which in turn create resistance and struggles, leading to the creation of new alliances and struggles.

Finally, this chapter moves away from a focus on the museum in the colonial and postcolonial context, whether in the Americas or Australia, to one that entails shifting dominant-minority relations within the European context. Thus, this chapter focuses on Jewish museums in Italy, and within Italy on just two such museums, one in Bologna and the other in Ferrara.

Research Methods

The inspiration for my research came from a reading of Clifford's article on four Canadian north-coast museums devoted to Native Canadian culture (Clifford 1997). Two of these museums were set up within mainstream institutions, whilst Native Canadian communities established the other two museums. Yet they all represented very contrasting perspectives on Native Canadian culture.

I had attended a Jewish studies conference in 1998, at which I met the curator designate of the Jewish museum in Bologna, due to be launched in 1999. As a result, I began to formulate a research design that would focus on four museums in Italy, the Bologna museum and three other Jewish museums (previously outlined in Clark 2004b and 2007). I chose Florence and Ferrara as they are within easy train journey of Bologna, and Venice is not much farther away.

Over the three-year period from 1999 to 2002, I visited Bologna six times, for short visits ranging from one to three weeks. I was able to 'hang out' in various settings within Bologna's Jewish community, which comprises about 200 members. On the day of my arrival in Bologna I contacted the Jewish community to find out the times of the evening service. After the service that evening I spoke to a number of people in the congregation and was immediately asked by the rabbi to attend the service the following morning at 7.30 A.M., as I would help to make up the required quorum (minyan) of ten men; subsequently I was to attend a funeral. This gave me a role in the community and also allowed me to meet and talk to members of the congregation. My willingness to be part of a group of 'extras', to make up a quorum of ten men as and when required, gave me an opportunity to simply be there, in the field, and observe.

My status as a student also put me in that category of potential volunteers to be drafted into community service for helping out in the office, stuffing envelopes and the like. On subsequent visits to Bologna I continued my stints as volunteer in the community office and gradually was able to join in some social events as well. In addition to such participant observation I was able to conduct more formal interviews with key personnel of the Jewish museum, including the director, the curator and the educational officer, both before the launch of the museum and thereafter. During my stays in Bologna I was also able to visit Ferrara on a number of occasions, interviewing leading members of the Jewish community there, including the rabbi and the president of the community, as well as leading proponents of the Jewish museum. I was shown round the museum a few times, sometimes joining the regular guided tours of the museum.

Politics: The National Framework

There are currently approximately 35,000 Jews in Italy and until recently official ties between the state and Italian Jewry was accorded a low profile. However, this was to change in the 1980s, when a general trend in Europe and North America increased awareness and willingness to acknowledge the Jewish presence, especially in relation to the events of the Holocaust (Clark 2007).

In Italy three further factors gave impetus to such acknowledgement. Firstly, there were the initial steps taken towards reconciliation between the Catholic Church and the Jewish people. This was enshrined in a Vatican encyclical of 1965 that rejected previous charges against the Jewish people of deicide. Such rapprochement was given a further boost by the visit of Pope Paul II to the Great Synagogue in Rome in 1986 and to Israel in the year 2000.

Secondly, there were moves to place relationships between the Italian state and Italian Jewry on a more formal basis. One of the reasons for this was the concern expressed by the authorities at the flight of material cultural heritage to Israel since the early 1950s, particularly of ritual objects and synagogue interiors. Such flight of material culture represented a potential loss to Italy of an important cultural asset, especially in view of Italy's growing reliance on cultural tourism and the relative decline of seaside resorts. This led to an agreement for active collaboration between the Italian state and the Italian Jewish communities on a number of issues. Section 1 of article 17 of Law 101, March 1989, made specific reference to cultural heritage. It specified that the state (at central, regional and local levels), the Unione delle Comunità Ebraiche Italiane (Union of Italian Jewish Communities) and the individual Jewish communities should collaborate in the stewardship and maintenance of all historic, artistic, architectural, archaeological, archival and cultural heritage of Italian Jewry (Tedeschi 1996).

Thirdly, there was renewed European interest in minorities and regional groups at the time, which was evident in Italy as well. Thus, the increased visibility of ethnic minorities in the country was beginning to have an effect, as was the political mobilization of regional sentiment in Northern Italy (Rossi 2002). The central government was becoming increasingly concerned about the need to combat racism and anti-alien sentiments, and to provide educational programmes that would address these issues (Feldman 2002). Nevertheless, the precise manner in which this collaboration between state and Italian Jewry was to take place was not clearly specified, though it was envisaged that a joint commission would be set up to oversee such collaboration. In the absence of clear guidelines, negotiations at the local level have been crucial in determining the manner in which such collaboration would unfold.

To give just two examples of collaboration from neighbouring regions, we can point to the restoration of the disused baroque synagogue in Pesaro, just north of Ancona. There is no Jewish community left in Pesaro, and the building now belongs to the Jewish community in Ancona instead. The synagogue was renovated under the aegis of the local authorities and then leased free of charge to the city of Pesaro, to be used for cultural activities (Tedeschi 1996). By contrast, in Ferrara, where there is still a small congregation, the synagogue premises have been renovated with state and regional funds, while use of the building is retained for Jewish communal and religious purposes. A small museum has now been added under the auspices of the Ferrara Jewish community (Ravenna 1998). The Jewish community in Ferrara remains firmly in control of the building, the synagogue and the museum.

Politics at Regional and Local Level:
The Contact Zone in Bologna and Ferrara

A multiplicity of agencies, institutions, communities and indeed personalities were involved in setting up and running the two museums under investigation. Thus, for instance, the following institutions were involved in setting up the Jewish Museum in Bologna.

1. The regional institute for cultural heritage, the Istituto per I Beni Culturali, played a leading role in setting up the museum.
2. The municipality and province of Bologna, as well as the region of Emilia Romagna, joined the steering committee (the Jewish Culture Program).
3. Consultations were held with the local Jewish communities in the region, within the framework of legislation stipulating that responsibility for preserving Jewish cultural heritage is shared jointly between the Italian state and Italian Jewry.
4. Members of the committee of experts in charge of writing up the museum narrative were drawn from a number of universities and university departments; they represent a third block, between governance and Jewish community, though within this block, too, views and opinions differed widely.

Yet collaboration between these various institutions and groups was a matter of negotiation involving power relationships and differing agendas. Local authority agencies sought to implement a variety of policy objectives, from urban regeneration to tourism promotion and educational initiatives. Also, within the committee of experts there were lively discussions as to the overall objectives of the museum.

Other external agencies could also become involved in the contact zone. In the case of the Jewish Museum in Ferrara, the initiative to set up the museum received support from the municipal and provincial authorities, but also from a leading voluntary heritage organization, Italia Nostra, as well as local corporate sponsorship. In Venice and in Florence the local Jewish communities found themselves forced to enlist the help of outside agencies, such as cooperatives specializing in managing leisure and tourist attractions, in order to run their museums on a day-to-day basis (see Clark 2004a for more detailed discussion of issues concerning the day-to-day running of these museums).

In both Bologna and Ferrara there was also a considerable degree of debate from within the Jewish communities themselves over whether to have a Jewish museum or what kind of museum it should be. Resistance to the museum was partly a struggle over who should best represent the Jewish community to the outside world, but also partly over what kind of community should be portrayed and who should be included or excluded from such notions of community. In addition, there was considerable apprehension, particularly on the part of the rabbinical authorities, concerning the possibility that a Jewish museum might divert resources and attention from more pressing needs of the Jewish community.

The contact zone is thus characterized both by collaboration and struggle, collaboration and struggle *between* groups and *within* groups, between different agencies of governance, museum personnel and advisors, and the local Jewish communities. Such collaboration is undertaken within a framework of unequal power relationships and, as a result, leads to struggle and resistance.

Setting up the Jewish Museum in Bologna

Institutional settings and institutional power bases are certainly of paramount importance in connection with the kind of arrangements to be found in contact zones. One organization in particular played a leading role in setting up a Jewish museum in Bologna, namely the Istituto per I Beni Culturali (IBC), the regional institute for cultural heritage. First set up in 1974, its mission was to safeguard as much cultural heritage as possible in situ, on the spot, but at the same time take into account the present needs of the local residents and local stakeholders, including business and local government. Consultation with local groups and interests was seen as a crucial and vital part of the process of maintaining cultural heritage; hence the IBC initially included a consultative council comprised of seventy individuals representing a whole range of local interests, community groups and stakeholders. Indeed, such consultations proved so successful that soon the IBC took on additional statutory responsibilities, such as coordinating museum services in the region and coordinating regional policies over the built environment (Regional Legislation N. 20 of 1990).

As part of this process of research and consultation, the IBC undertook a survey of Jewish material heritage in the area between 1984 and 1989 and began actively to seek a coordinating role for itself in preserving and maintaining such heritage. In 1988 the IBC, in collaboration with the municipality of Ferrara and the Jewish communities in the region, mounted an exhibition on the Marvels of the Ghetto (Mann 1989).

National legislation (Law 101 of March 1989, mentioned previously) had already provided a framework for collaborative efforts between local government and local Jewish communities to preserve and maintain Jewish cultural heritage. This enabling legislation, together with the IBC's new responsibilities for regional museum coordination, led the IBC to build upon its work on local Jewish cultural heritage by seeking to coordinate the various museological projects concerning Jewish heritage that were already in progress and, in addition, to set up a Jewish museum in Bologna.

It is important to note that right from the start, the Jewish museum in Bologna was never intended to be a 'traditional' museum housing a collection of material objects but was meant to fulfil other functions. Its main function was to support the co-ordination function of the IBC and to be a link in the chain of Jewish heritage sites scattered across the region. Some of these sites were museums; others were synagogues, ghettos and cemeteries, while yet other sites were libraries and archives. In order to fulfil this support function, the Jewish museum in Bologna was also meant to have a research and documentation centre.

The first major step towards a Jewish museum in Bologna was the formation in 1991 of the Jewish Culture Program, consisting initially of representatives of the IBC, the city of Bologna and the Jewish community in Bologna. The province of Bologna later also joined the steering committee. By 1994, the city had designated a suitable site for the museum, within the old ghetto area of Bologna.

Why Set Up a Museum in the Ghetto?

This section examines three separate and distinct factors that together account for the choice of museum site in Bologna. Firstly, there was strong support from within the Jewish community to site the museum within the ghetto. Here we are very much in the realm of expressing ethnic and community identity. Secondly, the city administration was engaged in urban regeneration of the city centre at the time, including the ghetto area. Here is where capital and politics merge or clash, in a manner explored in other chapters in this book focusing on neighbourhoods, such as the chapter on Cuitat de Mallorca by Morell and Franquesa, or that on the Bosphorus neighbourhood by Danişman and Üstün. Thirdly, the siting of a museum in that particular area also happened to fit quite neatly into the cultural zoning policy for the city.

Expressions of Identity

In actual fact, the ghetto itself had long ceased to function as a Jewish residential area. The ghetto in Bologna operated as a designated and enforced segregated area of Jewish residence for the very short period of time from 1556 to 1593, when Jews were expelled from the city. Jews gradually trickled back into the city but were no longer compelled to reside in any particular area. It was only in the 1980s that the ghetto was designated for revival as a distinct area of the city centre.

Two events highlighted the Jewish community's renewed interest in the ghetto area. A commemorative plaque was mounted on the wall of one of the houses in the ghetto, commemorating Jewish deportees who were rounded up in 1943 and sent to death camps. The Jewish community put up the plaque in 1988, fifty years after the enactment of racial legislation in Italy. Such a plaque should be seen in the context of a much wider phenomenon of Holocaust memorialization in Europe and elsewhere at the time (Clark 1999 and 2007). Yet the erection of the plaque in the Bologna ghetto was also the first step in marking out the ghetto space as symbolically being a Jewish space. It was a reminder to the rest of Bologna's residents not only of a Jewish past in the city, but also of a Jewish presence in the present and a reclaiming of the area as a symbolic Jewish space, even if it was no longer a 'lived' Jewish space. This symbolic claim for Jewish space was further reinforced by a photographic exhibition, also held in 1988, consisting of large colour photographs of the ghetto, alternating with panels of text explaining the history of Jewish settlement in Bologna. This exhibition was jointly sponsored by the city of Bologna, the regional cultural heritage board and the city's chamber of commerce (Feldman 2002).

One of the leading lights behind the exhibition was Lucio Pardo, who became the vice-president of the Bologna Jewish community in the 1990s and then its president, shortly after the launch of the museum in 1999. Pardo himself was never asked to join the steering committee of the Jewish Museum (the Jewish Culture Program). Nevertheless, the sole Jewish representative on that committee, Eugenio Heiman, a former president of the Bologna Jewish community, became a keen supporter of the idea of siting the museum in the ghetto area and indeed championed the idea within that committee. Nevertheless, it is unlikely that the city of Bologna would have been quite so generous about providing suitable premises in the ghetto and refurbishing such premises, were it not for the fact that this also happened to coincide with other city policies at the time.

Politics and Urban Renewal

Urban regeneration and reconstruction of the city's historic centre had been an issue ever since the end of the Second World War. The city had seen extensive war damage, and initial efforts in the 1950s and early 1960s had been directed at restoring the fabric of residential areas. The 1980s saw a period of intense property speculation in the areas immediately surrounding the city centre, leading to poorer tenants being forced out of the area whilst much of the housing stock remained neglected. The city's planning authorities intervened, setting up an agency to oversee the development of the commercial centre of the city, involving simultaneously an upgrading of the physical environment and an attempt to attract small-scale craft industries and studios, shops and neighbourhood-based arts facilities (Forlay 1993; Bianchini 1993). The ghetto area itself became the focus of one such redevelopment scheme, and between 1993 and 1996 the ghetto streets, pavements and lighting were given a suitable facelift, while landlords and homeowners were given generous grants for building improvements (Palmieri 1996).

The siting of a Jewish museum in the ghetto area therefore fit neatly into the aspirations to create small-scale cultural facilities in the area. Moreover, it also fit into the cultural zoning policy for the wider area immediately adjacent to the ghetto. Indeed, the museum, although located in Via Valdonica in the ghetto, is actually adjacent to Via Zamboni, which leads directly to the university quarter and is lined by a number of museums, art galleries, churches and building of historic interest. The Via Zamboni is recognized as one of the city's leading cultural 'arteries' and in 2002 was featured as one of the city's main cultural attractions, with banners and posters proclaiming Via Zamboni as the 'Strada delle Arti: spetttacoli, concerti, mostre, emozioni' (the street of the arts: spectacles, concerts, exhibitions, events).

Finally, it should be added that the launching of a Jewish museum in the ghetto in May 1999 also coincided with plans for Bologna 2000, when the city would become one of the European cities of culture for that year. Designation as one of Europe's cities of culture increasingly requires some evidence of activities or facilities addressing the issue of cultural diversity within the city – how better to demonstrate this than by establishing a Jewish museum in the city?

Issues of Governance: Collaboration and Conflict

I have outlined a number of policy issues that contributed to the setting up of the Jewish museum in Bologna. In addition, however, it was necessary to consult and involve various representatives of the Jewish communities in the region. It is this process of consultation and collaboration that really begins to flesh out some of the complexities and intricacies of the process summarized by the term contact zone. A number of key areas provide focal points for interaction within the context of such contact zones. These areas include formal representation on committees and management boards,

more informal consultations, issues of authorship and curatorship, and issues of interpretation of the site and guiding.

In terms of formal representation of the Jewish community on committees, there was one Jewish representative on the steering committee (Jewish Culture Program) right up till the launch of the museum. The steering
committee has now been replaced by a management board that includes
four Jewish representatives. During the preparation stage, three Jewish representatives sat on the eleven-member committee of experts that drew up
the museum narrative and textual information. At a more informal level,
the chief rabbi of Bologna was consulted on religious matters and on the
Hebrew language, whilst other members of the Jewish community of Bologna were also consulted during the research stage or, on several occasions,
were used as guides once the museum was launched.

Yet such a process of consultation and collaboration is far from straight-
forward. Who gets to represent the community is a thorny question. In
many respects, whoever represents the community will determine what
kind of community is portrayed and represented in the museum. Witcomb
boldly suggests that 'we need to reject the idea of an "authentic" representation, including the belief that the community groups must only represent themselves ... as many community gallery curators have argued, the
representations that result in community galleries are those of particular
sections of the community' (Witcomb 2003: 101).

The number of Jewish individuals who were involved in helping to set up
the museum in Bologna ranged from the chair of the steering committee
to the chief rabbi of Bologna and other members of the Jewish community
who were consulted. The issue in such a case is that those who are formally
recognized as having a position of authority within the Jewish community
– whether in the religious field, such as the chief rabbi of Bologna, or in the
lay sphere, such as the president and board of management of the community – may indeed face some internal dissent and opposition.

Feldman (2002) notes some tensions between the chief rabbi and his
congregation in Bologna, particularly concerning which tunes and traditions would be followed in the liturgy. No doubt some of these tensions
spilled out into other areas of communal life. In the specific case of the
Jewish museum in Bologna, however, internal dissent became most apparent after the launch of the museum. Within weeks of the launch, a letter of
protest severely criticizing the museum exhibits was circulated within the
Bologna Jewish community and also sent to a number of external Jewish
agencies and institutions. The letter was signed by four individuals, only
one of whom is formally a member of the Jewish community in Bologna;
the other three are associated or linked to the Jewish community through

membership of the Israel-Italian Friendship Society (open to Jews and gen-
tiles alike) or through marriage. It should be noted that while the letter of
protest was ostensibly aimed at criticizing the museum exhibits, it was also
implicitly a direct attack against the leadership of the community, especially the lay leadership. This becomes even clearer in subsequent letters
of protest, in which the leadership was attacked for its left-wing bias, being
allegedly in cahoots with the former left-wing city administration responsible for launching the museum.

However, the vociferous and strident manner in which such dissent was
expressed only alienated the rest of the Jewish community, and in the subsequent elections for the board of management of the Jewish community
many of the people who were elected to office were actually supporters
of the museum project. More recent elections to office, however, show a
more ambivalent attitude to the museum, and plans are now afoot either
to set up a rival Jewish museum within the synagogue premises or else to
insist on Jewish majority representation on the current museum's board
of management. Since the city, the province of Bologna and the region of
Emilia Romagna are currently funding the running expenses of the museum, whilst the city owns the premises on which the museum is located,
they are unlikely to accede to such demands.

Yet another stream of dissent came from outside the formal Jewish
community in Bologna altogether, namely from a group of Israeli students
studying in Bologna who complained that the museum focused too much
on religious issues and failed to note the tremendous contribution made
by Jews to society, and to the arts and sciences more generally. The point
here is that this involves yet another definition of what a Jewish community
entails. These students were defining themselves in terms of world Jewry,
as an ethnic group rather than a religious group. They wished to speak on
behalf of all secular Jews, noting that even in Israel secular Jews are in the
majority, and thus deserve to be represented as such.

Setting up the Jewish Museum in Ferrara: Expressing Identity

The impetus to set up the Ferrara museum came from within the Jewish
community, while funding for the renovation and refurbishment of the
exhibition area came from the city and province of Ferrara, the region of
Emilia Romagna and the local savings bank in Ferrara (Ravenna 1998). Collaboration between the Ferrara Jewish community and the local authorities
was much closer than in Bologna, but there was also much greater internal
dissension over whether to have a museum in the first place.

Thus, in an interview with Rabbi Caro, Ferrara's part-time rabbi, I was told that he was not particularly well disposed towards the museum. He said that Ferrara has such a small Jewish community, fewer than 100 members, and has so many other calls on its resources, that such a museum can hardly be justified. Moreover, he feared that slowly, slowly, the community itself would be transformed into a museum. He wished the community to be a testimony to living Judaism, not simply a window on the past. If it has any function at all, he stated, the museum ought to serve a Jewish audience, but in fact the majority of visitors to the museum were non-Jews.

Like many of the rabbis I talked to in Italy, Rabbi Caro had misgivings about a Jewish museum. Other rabbis were unsure about whether Jewish ritual objects ought to be displayed in museums at all and would prefer that such objects should continue to be used in ritual and in worship. Rabbi Caro, however, bitterly opposed the very establishment of the museum, so much so that the Unione delle Comunità Ebraiche Italiane, the overall umbrella organization for Italian Jews, had to be asked to intervene in the dispute. Dr Bassi, who had been instrumental in setting up the Jewish Museum in Venice, was amongst those called in to help resolve the dispute. Eventually, the museum project was allowed to proceed.

By contrast, the local authorities were much more receptive to the idea of a Jewish museum in the city. This was partly due to the efforts of a local Jewish enthusiast, Paolo Ravenna, who managed to straddle both Jewish and non-Jewish concerns, in part by becoming an active member of Italia Nostra, one of the main voluntary associations involved in campaigning for preservation of cultural heritage in Italy. For many years he led a personal campaign to renovate and rehabilitate a large part of the city walls of Ferrara. By 1984 Ravenna had become chairman of the local branch of Italia Nostra. At the same time, he became increasingly interested in maintaining and preserving Jewish sites in Ferrara and sought to interest others in such matters. His vision encompassed not only the renovation of the synagogue complex, but also the restoration of the ghetto streets and of the two Jewish cemeteries as well.

The local authorities subsequently enthusiastically supported the idea of a Jewish heritage trail in Ferrara. Thus, by the time I visited Ferrara in 1999, the local tourist information office was issuing various leaflets on Jewish itineraries in Ferrara. It should also be noted that some of these information leaflets allude to the fact that in December 1995, Ferrara was entered in the UNESCO World Heritage list as an outstanding example of a Renaissance city. Such international recognition might also have had some impact on the city's willingness to support the renovation of Jewish sites and to promote a Jewish heritage trail within the city.

Taking on the Role of a Local 'Broker'

Ravenna also had plans for a Jewish museum and, in 1984, delivered a paper on the subject (Ravenna 1986). At this stage, the plans for the museum were still somewhat vague. In his interview with me in 1999, Ravenna stressed that the Jewish community did not have sufficient resources to develop a museum on its own. Hence, he felt that the participation of both Jews and non-Jews was required in order to get the project off the ground.

Ravenna was well placed to enlist the support of others within both the Jewish community and the wider community. His position in Italia Nostra and his active involvement in preserving local heritage meant that he had already established networks and relationships with city, provincial and regional officials. Indeed, he also had close contacts with the regional Institute for Cultural Heritage (the IBC).

Meanwhile, Ravenna's family had long been closely involved with the affairs of the Jewish community. A plaque in the synagogue building commemorates Leone Ravenna, 1837–1920. Another plaque commemorates Felice di Leone Ravenna, 1869–1937, president of the Jewish community in Ferrara between 1920 and 1930. Thus, Paolo Ravenna's long-established connections within the Jewish community would stand him in good stead when it came to seeking support for his proposal for a Jewish museum.

It could also be argued that Paolo Ravenna's close association with the museum project enabled him to further reinscribe his family's history into the history of Ferrara Jewry by exhibiting copies of his family's marriage certificates (dated 1908), the correspondence of Felice Ravenna concerning the World Zionist Congress, and so forth. Nevertheless, it is clear that his family had played a crucial role in the history of the local community over the last century or so.

Further Internal Controversy: What Storyline to Present

Whereas Paolo Ravenna was able to successfully promote the museum project and to ensure that his family's history was firmly inscribed in the museum narrative, he nevertheless ended up parting ways with the museum management. Having successfully negotiated the opening of the museum, he fell out with other leading members of the museum management over plans for expansion. By the time I visited the museum in April 1999, a further exhibition room had been opened up to the public. The new exhibits focus on post-emancipation events, increased economic diversification within the city, the rise of Zionism as a movement and the rise of Fascism in Italy.

Paolo Ravenna had hoped that the new exhibition room would focus on the manner in which Italian Jewry took advantage of emancipation to join fully and vigorously in all aspects of Italian society. In particular he was keen to emphasize the leading role local Jews had taken in the city's affairs, rising to prominence in city politics, in the professions and in the arts. This would probably have spotlighted the roles played by Leone and Felice Ravenna within the legal profession, as well as in municipal politics: Felice Ravenna also served as mayor of the city for a while.

In addition, Paolo Ravenna was also very keen to highlight the role played by artists and writers, such as Bassani, for instance, whose novels focused on the life of the town and whose novel, *The Garden of the Finzi-Contini*, was turned into a highly acclaimed film. Ravenna's ambitions, however, were overruled, and the new exhibition room ended up exploring various aspects of 'difference', such as Zionism, Fascism and anti-Semitism, rather than focusing on post-emancipation achievements within the framework of the new nation state. One of the reasons given for rejecting Ravenna's plans for the new extension, according to an informal conversation with a member of the Ferrara community, was the feeling that the focus on post-emancipation local history would have given too much prominence to the history of the Ravenna family.

It is also worth pointing out that the decision to focus on Ferrara's close connections with the early days of the World Zionist Congress, in which Felice Ravenna had played a role, as well as the rise of Fascism in Italy, was closely connected with the needs of the Italian school curriculum. Feldman (2002) notes the manner in which the new anti-racism in Italy offers some form of contrition at the treatment of Jews under Fascism, leading to a renewed interest in Jewish culture. This focus on Jewish history is also meant to provide an object lesson for greater tolerance in society, particularly at a time when Italy is facing increasing waves of immigration from the Balkans, from sub-Saharan Africa and further afield.

Thus, the education officer for the Jewish Museum in Bologna, Katia Pedretti, explained to me that more and more schools are now coming to visit the museum in order to learn about the Holocaust. This is partly a result of the emphasis placed on thematic issues within the school curriculum, including issues of tolerance and intolerance.

Family Positioning, Community Positioning and Controversy

It could be argued that Ravenna's brokerage role between the Jewish community and the wider community was crucial in enabling the museum to be set up in the first place. Ravenna was a key player in setting up the museum and in deciding what went into the museum. This in turn is reflected in the museum narrative and in the prominence given to the history of the Ravenna family within the narrative.

The museum narrative is thus intimately bound up with claims for subject positioning within the history of the local community, both in the past and, by implication, in the present. Yet such prominence also caused controversy, resentment and resistance – so much so that further expansion of the museum led to the ousting of Ravenna from the museum management and the attempt to introduce other narratives and other 'voices'. Thus, while Ravenna had hoped to emphasize 'sameness' – the extent of Italian Jewry's full integration into Italian society and its values, at the level of the local state – the new room in the museum ended up focusing on issues of 'difference', such as Zionism, Fascism and anti-Semitism. Such issues may well fit into concerns stemming from Italy's new curriculum focus on multiculturalism and the need to instil greater levels of tolerance towards other peoples and cultures.

Discussion: Combining Notions of Contact Zone with Discourse Theory

This chapter has outlined the special kind of mosaic represented by the contact zone associated with Jewish museums in Italy. Enabling legislation at the national level has devolved responsibility for maintaining Jewish material culture to the local level. In practice this involves collaboration between different levels of government, regional, provincial and municipal, with formally organized local Jewish communities. Collaboration, however, is easier said than done. Not only are there a large number of protagonists entering this contact zone, each with their own set of agendas and interests, but there is a great deal of push and pull involved, entailing struggles both within and between different groups.

Moreover, this chapter has sought to reformulate the notion of contact zone by incorporating some of Foucault's concepts concerning discourse formation (Foucault 1972). These involve the rules of appropriation of discourse, in terms of who is allowed to speak, the importance of institutional settings and the function such discourse is expected to carry out within a pragmatic policy-oriented field. Foucault also views power as being both productive and diffuse, with all parties concerned having some measure of power to consent or resist (Foucault 1980).

In Bologna, the ghetto area initially held no special significance to any particular group. This attitude changed in the 1980s, when the Bologna Jewish community attempted to reclaim the ghetto as a symbolic space, thereby seeking simultaneously to give expression to ethnic identity and to receive recognition for being an integral part of the city's social fabric. The erection of a plaque commemorating those who died in the Holocaust was part of a wider contemporary discourse concerning Holocaust memorialization, yet the inauguration of the plaque marked the fiftieth anniversary of the enactment of Italy's racial laws in 1938. This in turn can be linked to issues of practical policy, as the theme of tolerance and intolerance is one that would be taken up later on, in the twenty-first century, by the Italian educational system as part of its campaign to combat racism.

Yet within the Jewish community of Bologna, the theme of the ghetto as a symbolic Jewish space denoting a long-standing Jewish presence in the area received a further boost from the photographic exhibition on the ghetto also held in 1988. Lucio Pardo, the initiator of the exhibition and an enthusiastic amateur historian, was able to obtain funding and support from the local authorities and from the city's chamber of commerce. At that stage he was not yet an office holder within the Jewish community, but subsequently he rose to be vice-president and then president of the Bologna Jewish community.

Nevertheless, when it came to nominating a Jewish representative to the steering committee of the proposed Jewish museum in 1991, the Jewish community did not choose Pardo, but instead opted for Heiman. The latter was well respected within the Jewish community, had previously served as president of the community for some twenty years and also had informal links with the IBC. Hence, the voice chosen to be the community's representative was closely linked to the formal organizational structure of the Jewish community. But even as Heiman was chosen over Pardo to speak on behalf of the Jewish community, the discourse initiated by Pardo concerning the symbolic importance of the ghetto was not forgotten. Thus, Heiman began insisting that the proposed Jewish museum should be located in the ghetto area, in order to reinforce the message that Bologna's Jews had been settled in the city for some time and were to be considered an integral part of the city's past and present. By 1994 the city had agreed to locate the museum in the ghetto and set aside premises for that purpose.

Yet the symbolic dimension was not sufficient to carry the project forward. Pragmatic policy issues also had a role to play. Indeed, I have argued that the city might not have agreed so readily were it not for the coincidence of a number of policy objectives that supported such a move. Issues of urban regeneration, cultural zoning and the designation of Bologna as one of the European cities of culture for the year 2000 all seemed to favour such an approach. Nevertheless, collaboration between municipal, provincial and regional levels of government, as well as between different departments within the city administration, was not always easy. This resulted in repeated delays in sorting out funding for the refurbishment of the building and determining which department would ultimately be responsible for the running costs of the museum. The museum was finally launched in May 1999, amidst much fanfare and the presence of assorted dignitaries from both central and local governments.

Whereas the Bologna museum was initiated by the regional institute for cultural heritage (the IBC), the Ferrara museum was initiated by the Jewish community itself. Like the ghetto exhibition in Bologna, the project was driven by a local enthusiast, Paolo Ravenna, an influential member of the Ferrara Jewish community who was also active in local heritage issues and local affairs. Moreover, the Jewish community was well placed to sponsor such a project, in that the synagogue complex had ample space to house the proposed museum.

Yet matters did not run smoothly here either. There was dissension within the Ferrara Jewish community from the outset; a reminder, if need be, of Witcomb's assertion that all communities are internally differentiated and that any communal 'voice' is likely to be a partial voice representing a particular segment of that community (Witcomb 2003). In Ferrara's case, there was strong disagreement between the religious and lay leadership, disagreement that could be resolved only by recourse to the intermediary of a third party, the higher-level organizational structure of the Unione delle Comunità Ebraiche Italiane, the umbrella organization for Italian Jewry.

Once the dispute was resolved, Ravenna was free to approach the various institutions of government and corporate sponsors in search of funding and further support. Ravenna's standing within the Jewish community, as well as his work within the local branch of the heritage association Italia Nostra, which provided him with contacts both within the city's administration and the IBC, all stood him in good stead, and the museum was successfully launched in 1997. Here we have a coincidence of a credible voice together with the apt use of institutional settings.

Still, the launch of the museum brought not an end to the controversy but rather its continuance, though the conflict and struggle persisted under a different guise. Only a few years after the opening of the Ferrara museum in 1997, Ravenna was ousted from its board of management. The vision that had propelled him to establish the museum was only partially fulfilled. Ravenna had hoped to further showcase the great contribution Italian Jewry had made to the city and to the nation, but the new wing of the museum was instead modified to take into account some of the concerns and needs of the Italian school curriculum, focusing on anti-Semitism, racial legislation and the need for tolerance in contemporary society.

The point about the contact zone is that it is an ongoing process and series of relationships, with ever shifting alliances and collaborative efforts partly counterbalanced by resistance and struggles – a series of pushes and pulls, as Clifford notes (1997). I have extended Clifford's original formulation of the contact zone beyond the relationship between colonizers and colonized, to include minority/mainstream relationships as well. Indeed, this chapter has sought to illustrate some of the dynamics and power relationships involved in two specific instances, namely the setting up of Jewish museums in Bologna and in Ferrara. Thus, the protagonists involved local authorities at different levels of government and different departments within these local authorities, usually pursuing different agendas. The process also involved the participation of formally constituted local Jewish communities, within which different opinions and voices were heard, and occasionally the intervention of organizational bodies at the national level to iron out disputes at the local level. It involved the participation of local heritage associations, local chambers of commerce and corporate sponsors, as well as the very committed involvement of the regional institute for cultural heritage. These were the active participants in the contact zone.

To understand, however, how these different protagonists interacted together and eventually came to some sort of understanding and joint agreement to set up a museum, I have found Foucault's notion of discourse formation particularly helpful. Who is given the right to speak on behalf of the Jewish community and who takes on such a role, the uses of relevant institutional settings and the kinds of pragmatic policy agendas that are being pursued are all issues explored in this chapter. This investigation has illustrated some of the dynamics involved in setting up a Jewish museum. Yet not least of the lessons to be learnt from all of this, is that all such efforts at reaching a compromise and an agreement are but temporary and transient, and that the launching of a new museum is a beginning, not an end. The contact zone is a field of interaction that does not stand still but creates its own dynamics, requiring the continued support and involvement of key players, continual attempts to create new alliances and partnerships, and the constant challenge of facing new criticism, opposition and resistance.

REFERENCES

Bennett, T. 1995. *The Birth of the Museum*. London: Routledge.
Bennett, T. 1998. *Culture: A Reformer's Science*. London: Sage Publications.
Bianchini, F. 1993. 'Culture, Conflict and Cities: Issues and Prospects for the 1990s', in F. Bianchini and M. Parkinson (eds), *Cultural Policy and Regeneration: The West European Experience*. Manchester: Manchester University Press.
Clark, D. 1999. 'Creating Jewish Spaces: Amnesia and Collective Memory', in Judit Targarona Borras and Angel Saenz-Badillos (eds), *Jewish Studies at the Turn of the 20th Century*. Leyden: Brill.
Clark, D. 2004a. 'Managing Jewish Museums in a Multi-faith Society: Notes from Italy', *Journal of Management, Spirituality and Religion* 1(1): 93–113.

Clark, D. 2004b. 'The Field as "Habitus": Reflections on Inner and Outer Dialogue', *Anthropology Matters* 6(2), htpp://www.anthropologymatters.com.

Clark, D. 2007. 'Sites of Memory or Aids to Multiculturalism? Conflicting Uses of Jewish Heritage Sites', *Sociological Research Online*, March 2007.

Clifford, J. 1997. *Routes: Travel and Translation in the Late Twentieth Century.* Cambridge, MA: Harvard University Press.

Feldman, J.D. 2002. 'Museum without a Collection: Jewish Culture in the New Italian Multiculturalism', unpublished Ph.D. dissertation. Charlottesville, Department of Anthropology, University of Virginia.

Forlay, F. 1993. 'Prefigurazione "Ghetto" progetto e identita storica', in S. Vincenzi (ed.), *Il Ghetto: Bologna: Storia e rinascita di un luogo.* Bologna: Grafis Edizioni.

Foucault, M. 1972. *The Archaeology of Knowledge.* London: Tavistock Publications.

Foucault, M. 1980. *Power/Knowledge.* Hemel Hempstead: Harvester Wheatsheaf.

Hooper-Greenhill, E. 1992. *Museums and the Shaping of Knowledge.* London: Routledge.

Mann, V.B. 1989. *Gardens and Ghettos: The Art of Jewish Life in Italy.* Berkeley: University of California Press.

Palmieri, D. 1996. 'Rinascita del ghetto ebraico: opere eseguite e prospettive di sviluppo', in, *Il Ghetto riscoperto: Bologna: Recupero e rinascita di un luogo.* Bologna: Grafis Edizioni.

Ravenna, P. 1986. 'Il museo della comunità Israelitica, un patrimonio della città', in F. Pesarini, *Musei ferraresi: Proposte di un sistema.* Ferrara: Gabriele Corbo.

Ravenna, P. 1998. 'Il museo ebraico di Ferrara', in F. Bonilauri and V. Maugeri (eds), *Musei ebraici in Europa: Jewish Museums in Europe.* Milan: Electa.

Rossi, C. 2002. 'The Venetian Independent Political Movement between Ethnic Localism and European Identity', paper delivered at the Conference on 'Nationalities, Identities and Regional Co-operation: Compatibilities and Incompatibilities', University of Bologna at Forli, 6 June.

Simpson, M.G. 1996. *Making Representations: Museums in the Post-Colonial Era.* London: Routledge.

Tedeschi, D. 1996. 'Problemi giuridici della tutela dei beni culturali ebraici', in F. Bonilauri and V. Maugeri (eds), *La Tutela dei Beni Culturali Ebraici in Italia.* Bologna: Istituto per I Beni Culturali.

Witcomb, A. 2003. *Re-Imagining the Museum: Beyond the Mausoleum.* London: Routledge.

៩ Chapter 12 ៩

The Making of Home Away from Home

The Role of Ethno-cultural Festivals in Contesting Local Spaces

ELIA VARDAKI

Introduction

The focus of this chapter is on the Ethno-Cultural Festival of Chania, in Crete. The main goal of the event was to make visible a number of foreigners who were living and working in the town of Chania, to acquaint locals with the history and culture of the working migrants and to contest ignorance and xenophobia as a result. The organizing committee made the effort to reposition new working migrants in the social and cultural scene of the town not as economic actors but as social subjects.

The significance of the festival was that it tried to challenge nationalistic stereotypes of what constitutes home, exile, territories, boundaries and inclusive or exclusive practices. It created an informed space for various cultural actors to create a 'niche of home' away from 'home'. It remains to be assessed whether it succeeded in its purpose.

In the process of cultural representation of the Other, the festival generated a series of conceptual contradictions. These contradictions resulted from the tension between cultural homologies of the nation state, still prevalent at the grass-roots level, and the high-level official discourse on multiculturalism that emerged in Greece in the post-EU integration era, which has influenced local officials in Chania. The shift towards the EU politics of belonging and the promotion of a multicultural agenda in Greece resulted in the emergence of the 'Other' as an analytical category to promote local, ethnic and cultural diversity instead of cultural homogeneity (Yiakoumaki 2006).

Although multiculturalism encourages cultural pluralism and tolerance of religious, linguistic or ethnic difference, it is not counter-hegemonic to the nation state but rather presupposes the existence of a dominant form of political power (Glick Schiller and Wimmer 2002; Gupta and Ferguson 1997). Multiculturalism re-creates fixed categories of people, bounding them with physical territories and thereby helping them to construct a sense of belonging to a particular place. The nation state provides the structures and the locus for the development of multicultural and hybrid cultures. Therefore, the exploration of the cultural representation of the ethnic Other highlights the issue of the specificity of place in the construction of multiple identities. Place thus does not dissolve but becomes a meaningful and ideologically significant space, the locus for the (de)construction of national ideologies.

In this theoretical framework the chapter examines cultural practices that validate the place as an organizational authority, which in turn allows different and sometimes opposed dynamics to flourish. These dynamics involve local people, immigrants and authorities, all interrelated in constructing and negotiating a new set of power relations.

Common Places, Different Cultures

The rise of global communication and human mobility led scholars to re-evaluate the spatial relativity of cultures and the social mechanics that constitute place. The territorial entity of culture – a product of modernity – was challenged as an ideological construction with clearly nationalistic roots (Olwig and Hastrup 1997; Glick Schiller and Wimmer 2002; Dawson and Johnson 2001; Gupta and Ferguson 1997). Concepts such as national boundaries, 'home', belongingness and cultural homogeneity were reviewed in the light of mobility. The reconsideration of these concepts points to the flexibility of the relationships developed by mobile populations that feel at home in exile and feel exiled while at home. This new geopolitical reality has led to cultural entities being disconnected from their spatial boundaries.

The locality dissolves when one considers that 'home' is constituted on an everyday level where sensual and bodily practices are taking place and meaningful habitats are produced. Accordingly, boundaries and identity are viewed as contingent terms, subject to transformation. Borders artificially divide territories and cultural groups, whereas boundaries are constructed in order for individuals to arrange a perceived social space in an orderly fashion. Whereas territorial borders are a clear-cut category, boundaries dividing cultural groups are more elusive and imaginative. The recognition of the plurality of conceptual construction of boundaries has led scholars to look at identity construction processes on an experiential base. A place becomes meaningful once it is connected with human experiences, senses and emotions, and animated by memories (de Certau1984). Hence, the division between those who are 'emplaced' and those who are 'out-of-place' is contested. Dawson and Johnson have suggested that 'place and identity are rarely made or inhabited in a singular manner but are most often constructed and experienced as a variety of both literal and metaphorical roots and routes' (2001: 320).

In the light of this discussion, the notion of community and belonging shifts in relation to place-making. In any cultural and social group, people want to belong to collectivities, either real or imagined. People mobilize different resources to construct their sense of belonging through social locations, emotional attachment or political value systems (Yuval-Davis 2006: 199). Especially in cultural practices, these varied resources of belonging are mutually interrelated and mobilized to create meaningful existence for the participants and to solidify their sense of belonging to a group. Therefore, they produce narratives, experiences and performances that situate them in a cultural setting. Each group perceives 'home' differently, depending on the position he/she holds in the locality. Thus, legitimation claims over place arise among people who share the same space but mobilize different resources. It follows that 'emplaced' populations mobilize cultural resources, i.e. common history, language and ancestry, while the claims of 'displaced' populations, by contrast, lie in the position they hold within the economic structures of the community. Additionally, such cultural practices generate power relations between groups who do not share the same sense of belonging, thereby magnifying differences. In other words, these cultural performances provide the context in which strategies for belonging and struggles for power are played out.

The Ethno-Cultural Festival in Chania can be viewed as a cultural performance that produces different sociocultural positioning. Hence, it provides the ground for the construction of a sense of belonging in the local community for varied ethnic, linguistic and religious groups. Here I will try to review the varied narratives of belonging that different groups of people have produced.

With the influx of many working migrants in Chania, a newly emerged social reality has led intellectuals, public officers and NGOs to contest cultural territoriality as this is constructed along the lines of a modernist tradition of homogeneous cultural wholes. In response to this challenge, local authorities have employed cultural practices that underline the de-territorialization of culture in order to incorporate varied groups.[1] In other words, they sought to stretch conceptual and ideological borders to include people from diverse ethno-cultural backgrounds. However, the process of de-territorializing culture to challenge conceptual borders gave rise to a counter process of cultural re-territorialization by other ethno-cultural groups via the construction of a sense of belonging. Since the sense of belonging and the making of home is a reflective activity constructed on an experiential basis, the same place might be viewed as 'home' for people from various ethno-cultural locations.

However, tensions and power relations are generated when a dominant cultural group tends to construct other groups' identity, situating them in certain social locations vis-à-vis ethnicity and ignoring other, i.e. religious, political, gender, social or racial, differences. The form of the Ethno-Cultural Festival of Chania, which highlighted the ethnic elements of each cultural group, reflects these ambiguities and incorporates a series of contradictions. Such ambiguities and contradictions are characteristic of postmodern places: even as cultural homogenization dissolves, there is a growing tendency for people to identify themselves with a place, to belong to a place. However, before turning to the discussion on its form and the effects that the Ethno-Cultural Festival had in town, I will include a brief discussion of the political complexities of immigration in Greece.

Migration in the Greek Context

With the fall of the Iron Curtain and the expansion of the European Union, many people from the ex-Soviet bloc sought a better living in the countries of the EU, including Southern Europe. At the beginning of the 1990s, many people – mainly from the Balkans and the ex-Soviet countries – came to Greece to work (Cavounidis 2002). Unlike countries with long experience of migration, Greece lacked migration policies and laws to control the flow of the non-EU immigrants into the country. The Greek state, characterized by an informal and unregulated public sector, and by a lack of civil society to protect human rights and provide the infrastructures for immigrants' integration, was unprepared to take in large numbers of migrants or to regulate their entry visas and working permits (Mousouri 1991; Petrinioti 1993; Petrakou 2001).

Notwithstanding, public and private actors' interests clashed. There were heated discussions vis-à-vis the threat that immigrants posed to the state and national sovereignty. Such perceptions were also promoted and exaggerated by the media (Petrinioti 1993; Kourtovick 2001). As a result, Greek governments employed tighter control of the country's borders and expulsions as measures to prevent immigrants from entering Greece. Meanwhile, though, many farmers and entrepreneurs in the private sector fostered illegal forms of migration, since they needed cheap labour for heavy tasks that Greeks refused to perform (Petrinioti 1993; Petrakou 2001). This contrast between public and private sector encouraged illegal operations in which immigrants found themselves trapped and the ensuing black labour market.

In such political and socioeconomic contexts, the police appeared to be the only regulating mechanism, posing as the guardian of the nation against newcomers. A significant proportion of the population accepted the repressive mechanisms that the police employed (Petrakou 2001). Xenophobic incidents intensified, often resulting in psychological and physical abuse of immigrants by the police, or even by civilians (Kourtovick 2001).

During this period, Greeks were living a contradiction between perceived threats to the homogeneity of the nation and the real needs of a globally competitive market. Immigrants embodied this contradiction, experiencing forms of inclusion and exclusion: inclusion in the economic sector on the one hand, exclusion from the cultural, political and social sectors on the other. There was no legal platform to regularize employment, health care or welfare system (Petrinioti 1993; Mousouri 1991). In 1998, with a large number of unregistered migrants living and working in Greece under harsh and difficult conditions, the Greek government made the first serious attempt to acknowledge their existence by enforcing a law that granted working permits to a large number of immigrants (Cavounidis 2002).

The problem was more acute in local communities, which faced difficulties accepting different ethno-cultural identities. Within such communities membership of a social group depends on identification with a family group as well cultural and economic affinity to this group. Greek political and economic structures are characterized by a strong clientism, making it even harder for any newcomer, let alone an immigrant, to be admitted to the group. Cultural and social difficulties hindering the integration of the 'Other' were reinforced by national discourses of a homogeneous ethnic identity, cultural continuity from ancient Greece until the present, and resistance to perceived cultural threats from foreign cultures. Such perceptions were accentuated by the religious conservatism of the Greek Orthodox Church (for an extensive discussion see Christopoulos 2001; Pettifer 1996).

This new social reality and the 'newly found' cultural diversity led to the emergence of the 'Other' as an analytical category. In the context of migration in particular, researchers have attempted to understand the challenges that migration poses to the nation state and to the structures of the welfare and health care system, as well as the economic and social problems that immigrants face in Greece (Maratou-Alipranti and Gazon 2005; Christopoulos 2001; Marvakis, Parsanolglou and Pavlou 2001). Institutes and researchers alike explore the relationship between immigration and development, the cultural activities of migrants, the emergence of multicultural discourse and its impact on the integration or assimilation process (Veikou 2001; Psimmenos 2001). In such a rich context the present undertaking adds to the existing literature by placing the focus on a place-orientated approach, in order to illustrate the ambiguity and inherent contradiction of the dialectical relationship between place and identity.

Methodology

This chapter is the outcome of my short-term collaboration with the European-funded Mediterranean Voices project. Med-Voices focused on the oral history and cultural practices of different Mediterranean cities expanding from the east to the west and from the north to the south shores of the basin. The context of the study was different neighbourhoods within each urban centre. The aim was the elicitation of oral history in an attempt to illuminate the multicultural character of different cities and the historic ties that connect Mediterranean cities.

In Greece the target city was Chania on Crete. In many ways the Ethno-Cultural Festival seemed an ideal setting for examining the political implementation of a multicultural agenda promoted by the EU. However, given the non-systematic character of the festival's organization, funded by local resources, what transpired reflected more the political 'culture' of the festival's organizing committee than any systematic attempt by the official state to align itself to an EU multicultural agenda or a wish to integrate immigrants into the local cultural setting.

The members of the organizing committee belonged to the left and socialist government (Synaspismos and Pasok accordingly) of the time. The unsystematic character of the event is underlined by the fact that its staging ceased when the municipal authority changed upon the liberals' accession to power (Nea Dimokratia). Having said this, though, I only wish to underline the lack of a uniform national policy towards immigrants: in no way is this account meant to indicate the views or aspirations of any particular political party. Identifying the festival with political parties would underestimate the complexities of the event by illuminating only one side of an event that managed to reach out to people from various sociopolitical contexts and crossed political parties. The reason for its termination, which coincided with a change in the political scene of the municipality, lay more in the new government's financial priorities of than in its cultural ones.

The material on which this chapter is based was collected between December 2005 and March 2006. It derives from fieldwork research conducted in Chania and was collected through structured and unstructured interviews. The groups I interviewed were migrants from Syria, Palestine, Georgia and Albania who had lived in Chania for more than a decade; their ages were between thirty and fifty, and they had various levels of education. All of them had actively participated in organizing the festival. I also interviewed the organizer of the festival, who was then acting as a member of the local council. I conducted archival work in two major local newspapers published during the period of the first festival, *Agonas tis Kritis* and *Chaniotika Nea*, in order to understand how the festival was received by the press.

In the next section, I first present the structures of the festival and the effect it had in town, including a short discussion on the ways working migrants perceived and experienced the festival. Through their narratives, it will become clear that immigrants felt themselves to be part of the cultural life and history of Chania, if only for a short while. People who felt displaced were 'in place' even away from 'home'. In the second part I analyse the effects the festival had on the negotiation of social and cultural boundaries, and on various people's identity construction processes. It aims to shed light on the ambiguities and contradictions that the festival generated in the process of dissolving cultural boundaries.

The Multicultural Festival

A considerable number of Greece's immigrants reside on Crete.[2] On Crete, 5.8 per cent of immigrants have a green card, while 5.7 per cent have a white card. According to the census of 2001, 7,075 foreigners were recorded as residing in the prefecture (Koumandraki 2005: 5). However, it is speculated that the number of undocumented migrants is higher (Vice-Mayor personal communication). According to the same census, the foreigners who live in Chania originally come from eighty-three countries in the Balkans, Eastern Europe, Asia, Africa, North and South America and the European Union (Koumandraki 2005: 6). Albania is the source of the highest number of immigrants in Chania (2,474), followed by Bulgaria (880), Georgia (679), the U.S. (637), Romania (441), Syria (280), the Russian Federation (246), Ukraine (191) and Yugoslavia (178) (Koumandraki 2005: 6).

In such a diverse and rich context, the Ethno-Cultural Festival presented an opportunity for a number of foreigners to integrate into the sociocultural structures of the town. In 1997, the local administration of Chania attempted to institutionalize the festival by organizing it on a regular basis, first annually and then biennially. However, the lack of economic and political support from wider state institutions to promote such cultural activities as part of a national policy brought about the end of the festival in 2002, when a new local administration came to power. Nevertheless, the importance of the festival at local, regional and national levels should be highlighted, since it was the first attempt by a regional-level administration to institutionalize practices for the cultural and social integration of its foreign residents. Hence the festival acknowledged and dealt with cultural, social and political issues of different cultural groups residing in the country at a time when the Greek federal government wore blinders.

The Festival

The Ethno-Cultural Festival, organized by the municipality of Chania from 1997 to 2001, can be regarded as a kind of metaphorical 'roots and routes' event. For seven days an 'ethnic plural niche' was created in the space of the Municipal Garden. The festival gave a number of ethnic groups that were living and working in Chania an opportunity to create their own space of activity, as well as to accustom locals to the cultural history of each participant country. Through the medium of cultural expression people sought recognition and acceptance; the unknown became the familiar. The distance between 'the centre', belonging to locals, and 'the periphery', pertaining to foreigners, was reduced, violence and xenophobic incidents were minimized, and the working migrants became familiar faces identified with the history and culture of their own countries.

Each festival was organized in July in the Municipal Garden in the centre of the town. Twenty different nationalities participated in the first festival in 1997, while in subsequent festivals the number increased to include as many as twenty-eight. This number was considered a success, reflecting its wider acceptance by both locals and foreigners. On the first day there was a parade of people dressed in their national costumes. Each national contingent flew its flag, and at the end of the parade the flags were hoisted. In the Municipal Garden were stalls for each nationality displaying ethnic handicrafts, pictures, photographs and tourist information about each country, or providing information on the immigrants' political agenda and political networks, e.g. in the case of the Kurds. Every day the festival began around seven in the evening, and finished at one in the morning. There were playgrounds for children, dancing and theatre performances, as well as ethnic cuisine nights organized by different ethnic groups each day. The festival also included football games, speeches and discussion groups that addressed key political issues regarding immigration. Sometimes dancing groups were invited over from counties such as Serbia, Georgia or Romania. Although inviting dancing groups from non-European countries was among the aims of the organizers, it proved to be very expensive and failed due to bureaucracy. Financial difficulties and specific political decisions proved major hindrances, leading the festival to a final closure four years later.

Short extracts from interviews with immigrants who participated show the longing for such cultural events to reposition immigrants as cultural subjects. An extract of the interview with the president of the organizing committee illuminates the problems they had to deal with but also sheds light on the positive and negative effects it had on subject populations. Hatem from Syria, aged 47, a resident of Chania for twenty years, is a building contractor:

> The idea of the festival was very good; people in Chania got to know us so they did not fear us anymore. People in Chania really fear us (*fovountai*). The festival made us come closer. Locals really liked it. A lot of people visited the Garden; they came to the dancing, music and ethnic cuisine nights. Especially in the ethnic cuisine there was a lot of people every night. There was so many of them that sometimes food was finishing within an hour. Two or three different groups each day prepared the food for the night. We all helped to organize the festival. I personally participated in all four of them. I am looking forward to the next one. ... My mother was in Chania one time so we built an oven made out of clay like the traditional ones in Syria, and we baked the bread in the evening of the festival, it was a sort of a happening. People liked it a lot, I took a lot of pictures. (Translated by the author, field notes 2005)

Amin from Palestine, aged 40, married to an Ukrainian, came to Chania to study:

> I have lived in Chania for 20 years, I feel like home here, if not my homeland but definitely I feel Chania as my second home. The festival did good for us. A lot of people came; they got to know our culture more. If you know something you are not afraid of it. There is xenophobia in Chania and this sort of events, of this scale was really important. It was like a celebration. Relative to the size of the town it was the major event of the summer. A lot of people, both locals and *xeni* [foreigners], were waiting for it. Many foreigners participated in the organization. It was something that we did for the town. Thousands of local people came every night to the theatre of the Municipal Garden. Even until today a lot of people ask me when the next festival is going to be. (Translated by the author, field notes 2006)

Alkis from Albania, aged 40, married to a Greek, is a building contractor:

I believe that cultural events can bring the two people (*laous*) closer. The Ethno-Cultural Festival was very good. It helped the people (*laous*) to get to know each other well. The people do not have anything to share. The television does bad to us. We should organize cultural events to bring people from Albania here and to send Greeks there [to Albania]. To learn each other's culture better. It is the only way to coexist, because as a matter of fact we do not want to leave Greece. Here is our life, our children. (Translated by the author, field notes 2005)

Gazis, a Greek, aged 61, was the president of the organizing committee:

The idea came to me in Vienna. While on a business trip. I noticed that at a central Viennese square people were dismantling stalls. When I asked my local friends what these stalls were for, they informed me that it was an ethnic cuisine festival, of the different communities living in Vienna. So, I thought that it would be a good idea to organize it in Chania too. I brought the idea to my colleagues in the municipal committee and we thought of an event that would also include food, performances, discussions and presentation of the history of each country.

After we had worked and planned everything out we had to look for representatives of the different ethnic groups to help us in the organizing. We knew a few people from the construction business and these few knew some others. We also put an ad in the local newspapers asking people from the different communities to help us. The representatives of each group were in charge of their community, to organize its members, to design their stall, to cook food for the ethnic cuisine night, to invite groups from their countries. We sought their active participation since it was a festival for them, so, it should have been organized by them. The bureaucracy for these events was enormous and we had to deal with it as well. We had to issue visas literally at the last minute, to make long-distance phone calls, to find sponsors for the festivals. All these were very expensive. Moreover, we had to ask the police not to prosecute any immigrant who participated during that week. It was a period when most of the immigrants had no papers, they were illegal. We then reassured immigrants that they should feel safe.

Solidarity was one of the aims of the festival so we took great care to place ethnic groups in dispute one next to the other. The Palestinians were next to the Israelis; the Serbs were next to the Albanians from Kosovo. Not that there were not any tensions, I remember one day Serbs and Albanians started to fight but when the president of the Albanian association in Chania intervened they stopped. ... Apart from such minor incidents we managed to succeed in our purpose. Each ethnic group helped the other. One evening in particular, Albanians were building the stage for the Serbs to dance on, it was a symbolic act ... However, we faced a lot of troubles and we had a lot of voices of discontent, especially during the parades. One year in particular the former Yugoslavia Republic of Macedonia dressed in their national costumes and paraded across town holding their flag, like the rest of the national groups. After the parade we hoisted the flags, an act that marked the commencement of the festival. The same night some locals tore it down. It was such a shame. It cost the savings of those people who had sewn it especially for the occasion. (Translated by the author, field notes 2005)

Analysis

Two main points arise from this short presentation: diversity as a political option, and solidarity as a social condition. For a week during the festival, immigrants created a melting pot of different ethnicities with clearly demarcated cultural boundaries. Each stall represented a small cultural site (Olwig and Hastrup 1997) that promoted issues of the country's political agenda, its tourist development and knowledge of the history and culture of each ethno-cultural group. In that respect, each group reinforced its community consciousness and solidarity in respect to its ethnic background.

Additionally, cultural classification of immigrants into one single category was avoided. Classification based on generic categories deprives people of their history and cultural heritage, victimizes them and even encourages intolerance and offensive behaviour. The emphasis on diversity and cultural pluralism not only showed that different communities are able to coexist, respecting each other's identities and enriching each other's cultural history, but also underlined the flexibility of territorial and ideological boundaries. 'Locals' and 'foreigners' felt part of a larger whole, of a cosmopolitan culture exchanging ideas and communicating to each other the values, history and tastes of different countries. The festival forced people to reevaluate oppositional pairings such as locals/immigrants, displaced/emplaced, home/exile, rootedness/uprootedness.

These small cultural enclaves made immigrants feel at 'home'. Working migrants became 'local', even for a few days, in the ethnic diverse space that they had created. Immigrants introduced exotic places, dances, artworks, foods – weaving thus a multicultural folklore patchwork. On the other hand, locals were transformed into 'foreigners', becoming visitors to this celebration. The Garden was transformed into a liminal space,[3] dislocated from the rest of the town to become a transborder or cross-bounded space.

In that respect, the festival challenged the container model of a homogeneous culture with claims on a common cultural heritage on a bounded territory. It de-territorialized dominant culture, while at the same time each group re-territorialized the place by creating small cultural enclaves within the de-territorialized space. This re-territorialization process is best reflected in Amin's words. He feels Chania is his home, 'if not my first, definitely my second'. Natali, a young woman from Georgia, also thought the same of Chania – or at least she wants to feel part of Chania, because she likes the town: 'I have friends here, I live so many years, and I want to become part of Chania. But sometimes I feel like a stranger in both Chania and my hometown' (field notes 2006).

Developing a sense of belonging is a far more complex process, especially for people whose mobility is an integral part of their lives. For those people, identification with a place or culture is more elusive and abstract. They constantly reposition themselves within cultural settings according to their social location, emotional attachment and the political conditions of the places they live in and between.

On the other hand, from the 'local' perspective, the notion of cultural entities is still pervasive. The connection between culture and places has not dissolved; rather, it is solidified and positioned in an alternative context, that of *difference.* Hence, many local people mobilize cultural resources to lay claim to a place by connecting 'home' with arguments of cultural continuity, common language and heritage. They prefer to imagine a more fixed world where East and West, Us and Other, Home and Exile are fixed categories. Immigrants would always be *xeni* (the word recently has acquired a negative meaning, a diminishing connotation, something that it is outside the natural order); they are the outsiders to locals' own cultural space and bounded world. As one wrote in the local newspaper, 'we should be more concerned with *our own language* which is in danger rather than with the customs, fiestas and parades of *other nationalities* which are manipulated by multiethnic capitals and the New Social Order' (Alifierakis 1997: 8) (emphasis is mine). Or it was felt that the concern should lie with the social and welfare problems that the *Greek* working class was also facing (*Chaniotika Nea* 12 July 1997: 8) The incident with the flag from the Former Yugoslav Republic of Macedonia also shows the limits of cultural tolerance towards the Other, especially when this Other challenges the political and symbolic integrity of the nation state. Hence, the festival created a dynamic multilayered discourse extending in a number of directions, one of which was to highlight the notion of 'Us' by exaggerating the difference from the 'Other'.

Accordingly, the folkloric form of the festival reproduced the hegemony of a dominant culture over others and provided a controlled space for the negotiation of cultural difference. Clearly the pursuit of the organizing committee was to focus on multiculturalism and emphasize the possibility of sharing a common place. However, the form of the performances and the way each ethnic group was represented emphasized its folkloric elements.

Folklore is closely connected with ethnicity and disseminates meaning to a broader audience through intelligible forms of representation. The use of folklore to accept difference is a process of naturalization of the ethnic Other, placing him/her in recognizable cultural categories. In the nation-building process, folklore became integral to the formation of territorial and cultural entities. In a similar vein, in late modernity folklore is used to construct different ethnic subjectivities in the framework of a dominant culture. In the festival in particular, there was an exoticization of the 'Other' via the parade of national costumes, the ethnic cuisine nights, or the musical performances, which precluded presenting the immigrants as people whose identity is influenced by their sex, race, class and mobility. It limited the discourse of diversity to intelligible forms of representation. The festival provided an opportunity to promote each ethnicity's culture and history, but this occurred in the context of a hegemonic discourse that conceals tensions and inequalities within cultures. Instead of bringing out and playing out the multiplicities of the social reality immigrants live in, either in their country of origin or in the receiving country, the folklore performances emphasized cultural homogeneity, which was influenced by the national discourse of both the countries of origin and the receiving one.

Setting the festival in the broader context of the celebration of a long history of multiculturalism in Chania, this endeavour also points in another direction: it attempts to naturalize a complicated political reality in Chania and present it as one instance in a long tradition of multiculturalism that forms part and parcel of the town's history. In other words, it reinvents a multicultural landscape as part of the historic tradition of the town. Historically Chania was at the crossroads of different cultures, whose presence is apparent in the historic monuments of the town. Reinventing a multicultural landscape caused these new ethnic groups to seem to blend into a long historic tradition of the town itself, as historic subjects. This was apparent in the reception of the festival by the local press, which praised the event as one that promoted the multicultural character of Chania, reconnecting the town with its cultural history (*Chaniotika Nea* 3–11 July 1997). However, as radical as such notion might appear to be, it actually points to an insider/outsider view of history. Whereas outsiders were in a constant motion, changing places according to historic circumstances, insiders remained loyal to their ancestral connections to the place.

In any case, the festival helped residents, both locals and foreigners, to solidify their sense of belonging, influenced by their cultural positionality. As a result, the festival reproduced a fixed notion of cultural identities, essentializing national identity and naturalizing the notion of cultural boundaries and entities based on claims to common ancestry and cultural continuity. The term *xeni,* employed by locals and immigrants alike, reinforced mutually exclusive practices.

These contradictions are particularly apparent in the immigrants' narratives. As the interviews showed, immigrants felt part of two countries: their own and that of their hosts. In that respect, they were influenced by and engaged in the economic, social and political processes of both countries. They were influenced by the local and national discourses on the issue of migration and in response to the nation-building processes of both the host country and the country of origin.

Migrants broadly use words such as 'foreigners', 'fear' and 'second home' to describe the experiential aspect of identity formation – i.e. formation of an identity that is influenced by the political, emotional and social conditions of the transborder crossing. In this sense, the festival provided people with venue and opportunity to express their identities, although in the framework of broader national discourses. Therefore, the festival appears to have been less a celebration of multiculturalism than of multi-nationalisms.

Final remark

This chapter explored the ways in which the Ethno-Cultural Festival attempted to construct a sense of inclusivity/exclusivity and to reshape various kinds of borders, contesting the idea of cultural homogeneity within national territories. It de-territorialized the dominant culture, only to substitute for it other different cultural wholes, solidifying community identity and constructing a sense of belonging in the light of ethnicity. In that respect, the festival provided the locus for the deconstruction of a homologous national ideology, only to reconstruct it on the basis of many different ones.

NOTES

1. The notion of deterritorialization and reterritorialization is taken from Deleuze and Guattari 2009 (1972).
2. The numbers and percentages given measure only those who applied for white and green cards in 1998 (Cavounidis 2002: 190–191, 215–216, 233, 247–248, 386, 401, 411, 421).

3. In liminal spaces the everyday life is turned upside down. In these spaces the taboo and the fantastic are made possible and dreams can be more easily expressed (Featherstone 1991: 22).

REFERENCES

Alifierakis, M. 1997. 'Our Cultural Heritage', *Chaniotika Nea* 20 June 1997, 8.

Cavounidis, J. 2002. *Migrants' Characteristics: The Greek Project of Legalisation in 1998.* Athens: Sakkoula.

Christopoulos, D. 2001. 'The End of National Homogeneity: Traditional and New Forms of Alterity in Greece', in A. Marvakis, D. Parsanoglou and M. Pavlou (eds), *Migrants in Greece.* Athens: Ellinika Grammata.

Dawson, A. and Mark Johnson. 2001. "Migration, Exile and Landscapes of Imagination", in B.Bender and M.Winer (eds), *Contested Landscapes, Movements, Exile and Place.* London: Berg, 319–331.

de Certeau, M. 1984. *The practice of Everyday Life,* Berkeley: University of California Press.

Deleuze G. and F. Guattari. 2009 (1972). *Capitalism and Schizophrenia, Anti-Oedipus.* London: Penguin Classics (translators: Hurley, Seem and Lane).

Featherstone, M. 1991. *Consumer Culture and Postmodernism.* London: Sage.

Glick Schiller, N. and P. Levitt. 2006. *Haven't We Heard this Somewhere Before? A Substantive View of Transnational Migration by Way of a Reply to Waldinger and Fitzgerald,* CMD Working Paper 06-01, Princeton, NJ: the Center for Migration and Development, Princeton University.

Glick Schiller, N. and A. Wimmer. 2002. 'Methodological Nationalism and Beyond: Nation-State Building, Migration and the Social Sciences', *Global Networks* 2(4): 301–334.

Gupta, A. and J. Ferguson. 1997. 'Culture, Power, Place: Ethnography at the End of an Era', in A. Gupta, and J. Ferguson (eds), *Culture, Power, Place: Explorations in Critical Anthropology.* London: Duke University Press.

Koumandraki, M. 2005. *Old and New Migration Flows and Cultural Heritages of Chanea: The Cases of Asia Minors, Pontics, Bulgarians, Georgians, Americans.* Rethymno: Department of Sociology, University of Crete, unpublished report.

Kourtovick, I. 2001. 'Migrants: Between Justice and Legalisation', in A. Marvakis, D. Parsanoglou and M. Pavlou (eds), *Migrants in Greece.* Athens: Ellinika Grammata.

Maratou-Alipranti, L. and E. Gazon. 2005. *Immigration and Health-Care System.* Athens: National Center for Social Research.

Marvakis, A., D. Parsanoglou, and M. Pavlou. 2001. '*Migrants in Greece*: Problems, Social Phenomenon and Subjects', in A. Marvakis, D. Parsanoglou and M. Pavlou (eds), *Migrants in Greece.* Athens: Ellinika Grammata.

Mousouri, L. 1991. *Migration and Migration Politics in Greece and in Europe.* Athens: Gutenberg.

Olwig, K.F. and K. Hastrup. 1997. 'Introduction', in K.F. Olwig and K. Hastrup (eds), *Siting Culture: The Shifting Anthropological Object.* London: Routledge.

Petrakou, I. 2001. 'Constructing Migration in the Greek Society', in A. Marvakis, D. Parsanoglou and M. Pavlou (eds), *Migrants in Greece.* Athens: Ellinika Grammata.

Petrinioti, X. 1993. *Migration towards Greece.* Athens: Odysseus.

Pettifer, J. 1996. 'Greece in a Changing Europe', in K. Featherstone and C. Ifantis (eds), *Greece in a Changing Europe: Between European Integration and Balkan Disintegration.* Manchester: Manchester University Press.

Psimmenos, I. 2001. 'New Forms of Employment and Illegal Migrants in Athens', in A. Marvakis, D. Parsanoglou and M. Pavlou (eds), *Migrants in Greece.* Athens: Ellinika Grammata.

Yiakoumaki, V. 2006. '"Local", "Ethnic" and "Rural" Food: On the Emergence of "Cultural Diversity" in Post-EU-Accession Greece', *Journal of Modern Greek Studies* 24: 415–445.

Yuval-Davis, N. 2006. 'Belonging and the Politics of Belonging', *Patterns of Prejudice* 40(3): 197–214.

Veikou, M. 2001. 'The Performativity of Ethnic Identity: Greek-Albanian Migrants and their Everyday Living in a Greek Neighbourhood', in A. Marvakis, D. Parsanoglou and M. Pavlou (eds), *Migrants in Greece.* Athens: Ellinika Grammata.

Chapter 13

Tears on the Border

The Case of Rachel's Tomb, Bethlehem, Palestine

TOM SELWYN

Introduction

This chapter is concerned with the fate of a small religious building in Bethlehem commonly known as Rachel's Tomb[1] named after the biblical matriarch Rachel, daughter of Laban, wife of Jacob and mother of Joseph and Benjamin, two founding ancestors of the twelve tribes of Israel. Located in one of the most contentious sites of the Mediterranean, namely the borderlands of Palestine/Israel, the story of Rachel's Tomb may be read as a microcosm of larger structures and processes in the region, which the present chapter holds in mind throughout.

The aim of this chapter is to describe the present state of both the tomb and its surrounding neighbourhood and then to use this ethnographic setting to reflect on how this case and the story of Rachel herself intersect with aspects of the broader conflict in the region. Finally, I offer several preliminary thoughts about how narratives about Rachel and her tomb might be 'reframed', to use Halper's (2004) auspicious phrase, and how such a reframing might contribute to looking at the conflict itself in a new way. To these ends the chapter is in three parts. First of all there is a description of Rachel's Tomb and its immediate neighbourhood. This includes discussion about the Wall[2] or, rather, the multiple walls that now surround the tomb. Second, an indication is given of some of the terms in which Rachel's Tomb is contested. As will be seen, part of this discussion concerns the way that Rachel herself is interpreted and symbolically deployed by those arguing for her tomb to be walled up and removed from Bethlehem. The section concludes with a brief reflection on how the site takes part in the formation of Israeli ideas about the relationship between 'security' and ethno-religious segregation in the area. The third part responds to the 'settler'[3] interpretation of Rachel and her (commonly assumed) tomb by suggesting the basis for a possible alternative interpretation.

For several hundred years Rachel's Tomb was situated in the Palestinian city of Bethlehem. The neighbourhood around the tomb, known today as Qubbet Rahil, comprised 11 per cent of the area of metropolitan Bethlehem and was, until fairly recently, one of the economic hubs of the city. The ancient highway between Jerusalem and Hebron ran through it. It boasted a number of fashionable restaurants, cafés, grocery stores and a high-class pharmacy. Residential property was sought-after and pricey. In 2005, however, the Israeli authorities expropriated Rachel's Tomb, built multiple walls and armed watchtowers around and near it and declared it part of the Israeli municipality of Jerusalem. In the process the neighbourhood was effectively destroyed. Although recently there has been a modicum of post-Wall revival within what amounts to a fragmented enclave hemmed in by walls, the majority of the neighbourhood's population have left the area, and its former businesses have nearly all closed down.

The story of the tomb and its neighbourhood grows out of its setting, namely the bleak borderland areas that mark the contentious spaces that divide Palestinians and Israelis. Like the tomb itself, there is much in these areas – this particular site in particular – that speak of death, the pain of exile, the impossibility of recognition and the inevitability of separation. And yet, if the story of the tomb and Rachel herself were to be approached imaginatively, a narrative might emerge that could become part of a reframing of the way that the relationship is conceived not only between Israelis and Palestinians but also, more generally, between Muslims, Christians and Jews. The present chapter seeks very lightly to sketch ways of achieving such a reframing, one that is grounded in the very nature of borderlands. Thus, as we proceed, we might keep in mind that whilst borders are routinely associated with danger (of the 'other' who lies beyond), defence and (social, cultural, political) endings, they are often also actual and potential creative and productive spaces across which goods, ideas, travellers and other objects and persons flow. In these senses borderlands are ambivalent spaces in which various imagined transformations can take place.

The field research on which the chapter is based was carried out during an association with Bethlehem that the author has had for nearly two decades, most recently during the course of two programmes of academic work and institutional development partly funded by the European Commission under the aegis of their Tempus and Med-Heritage programmes.[4]

Part I: Abduction, 'Separation' and Dispersal: The Case of Rachel's Tomb

Piecing together the story of Rachel's Tomb involves drawing on a variety of sources. I start here by following recent work about the site by my research associate for this chapter, Carol Sansour Dabdoub, and then move on to report on various written and oral sources, including historical accounts located in the École Biblique in Jerusalem, the University of Bethlehem and elsewhere.

Oral Sources

Sansour Dabdoub has recently researched the history of the tomb by talking to a number of sources in contemporary Bethlehem, including elderly Bethlehem residents, the mufti of Bethlehem, Abdel Majeed Atta Amarneh, and members of the Bethlehem *Waqf.* Her interlocutors maintain that the present structure known as Rachel's Tomb is of Ottoman origin, having been used throughout most of its history as a mosque. The site is said to have consisted throughout this period of two rooms, one the site of a tomb, the other the mosque. Both rooms had Islamic crescents inscribed on them, and in order to reach the tomb visitors needed to pass through the mosque. The crescents were removed at some time following the 1967 war. Adjacent to the building is an Islamic cemetery.

During the Ottoman period the majority of visitors to the site are said to have been Muslim. During the British Mandate (1918–1948) both Muslim and Jewish visitors are reported to have visited the tomb. The latter are said to have visited the room with the sepulchre, which was looked after by a Jewish religious specialist. Throughout the Mandate period Muslims not only prayed in the mosque but also used the cemetery, which was the main Muslim cemetery in the Bethlehem area. The dead were washed at the site, and the last prayers before burial were recited there. There were routinely two Islamic keepers of the shrine, the last being Hassan Salem Khaliel and Mohammed Yousef Batah.

Jewish and Muslim visitors to the site are said to have respected each other's beliefs and made space for their rituals. There was, it is insisted, a culture of mutual tolerance. At Muslim prayer times Jews are said to have stayed voluntarily within the tomb room. The cleaning and maintenance of the site was said to have been the responsibility of Muslims. No incidents of friction are recorded, and a small but steady stream of tourists visited the site.

During the Jordanian period from 1948 to 1967 Israelis did not visit the tomb, as they did not openly visit Jordan itself. Israel and Jordan were, after all, only in a state of armistice. Foreign Jewish visitors, however, continued to visit the site. In 1967, like the West Bank as a whole, the area was occupied by the Israeli army and placed under Israeli military administration. It is claimed that Muslims were prevented from using the mosque, although access to the cemetery remained possible for a while. In 1993, however, Muslims were barred from using the cemetery – although the *waqf* did manage to purchase land behind the mosque/tomb that continued to be used as a burial ground for a few more years.

Written Sources

The Franciscan writer Petrozzi (1975) reported that the earliest documents referring to the spot where Rachel died speak of a simple pyramid of eleven (or twelve) stones in the open air. As for a building on the site of what is now known as Rachel's Tomb in Bethlehem he quotes sources that claim that by the tenth century the site had become known as 'Rachel's Church', having been consecrated between the fifth and eighth centuries. At some point a sepulchre was placed on the site, over which a convex roof supported by stone arches was built in the fourteenth century. In 1560 the Ottoman Pasha, Mohammed of Jerusalem, enclosed the open spaces between these arches and added a cupola. In 1632 (P. 176) Sandys reported "The sepulchre of Rachel ... is mounted on a square ... within which another sepulchre is used for a place of prayer by the Mohometans". In 1841 the British Jewish philanthropist Sir Moses Montefiore bought the building and built a small square prayer room containing a *mihrab* (a niche in the wall pointing towards Mecca) adjacent to the room in which the sepulchre rested.

Petrozzi observed that the building as a whole looked less like a tomb than a *weli*, a Muslim funerary monument commemorating a saint or person of distinction. This comment raises several questions, including the fairly fundamental one of whether or not Rachel herself was actually buried on or near the site on which the building named after her now stands. Several authors, including another Franciscan, Lombardi, have concluded that Rachel was actually buried near Himzeh, north rather than south of Jerusalem, where there are other stone monuments known as the 'tombs of the sons of Israel'.

The most authoritative voice on the topography of Rachel's Tomb is that of the archaeologist R.A.S Macalister (1912) who wrote that biblical references to Rachel's Tomb being located in Ephrath, Bethlehem, are the result of a copyist's mistake. Macalister claims that in the earliest versions of Genesis it is written (in chapter 35) that Rachel was buried in Ephrathah, not Ephrath, and that this name refers to the village of Ramah, now er-Ram, near Himzeh to the north of Jerusalem. He quotes verse 15 of Jeremiah 31: 'A voice was heard in Ramah, lamentation and bitter weeping. Rachel weeping for her children refused to be comforted'.

Summary of Oral and Written Sources

The point of all this is not so much to establish exactly what 'Rachel's Tomb' was throughout its history, or even exactly where Rachel herself was buried, but to stress what the building was not. There is overwhelming evidence that what is now known as Rachel's Tomb and its site in Bethlehem has been subject over the years to various kinds of practices, interventions and accretions over the past two millennia by Muslims, Christians and Jews. It is highly probable, for example, that a structure that began life open to the elements was enclosed during the early part of the Ottoman period. All the sources agree that Montefiore built the Muslim prayer room in the mid nineteenth century. Photographic evidence from the British period confirms that the two pillars that stood for a while at either side of the entrance to the tomb and which now stand in the interior of the tomb building were brought from the British police station in Manger Square. A contemporary descendent from the distinguished Bandak family of Bethlehem tells how one of his uncles, a master stonemason, was commissioned by the British to carve the pillars. Following the 1967 war the Israelis transferred these pillars from the police station to the tomb.

The cumulative evidence thus suggests that the site was never the exclusive domain of any one of the three religions, that the structure may well have started life as something other than what is thought now to be, and that anyway it is unlikely to mark the site of Rachel's actual death. In all these respects it shares qualities and characteristics that are fairly typical of comparable shrines in the region. But whatever a complete historical record would tell us it is likely that throughout its career, Rachel's Tomb has been associated with varying and overlapping narratives (Strickert, 2007). All of these, it seems, have been accommodated with a minimum of physical contention and a maximum of cooperation between followers of the three religions. Raheb (2000: 73) thus rightly observes that 'such co-operation [was] especially appropriate considering the role of Rachel as a matriarch respected in all three monotheistic religions'.

Towards the Present

Coming to its more recent history, the site underwent very considerable change in the 1990s following the first Intifada. The Israeli authorities built walls around the tomb and placed a large menorah on the roof. By 1998 a high wall had been built in front of and around the tomb, not only obscuring any remaining view of the tomb itself but also jutting out into what the old north-south road linking Jerusalem and other northern cities with Hebron and the south. The tomb area became an army encampment. More recently still, as the tomb interior became a yeshiva (centre for religious study), the entire area around the tomb was walled up, the Jerusalem-Hebron road on which it had been located for hundreds of years being completely blockaded at both the north and south ends of the tomb area.

The walling up of the tomb and the areas adjacent to and opposite the tomb, is part of the much more extensive wall building project stretching from the north to the south of Palestine – much of it being to the east of the 'Green Line'.[5] This consists of what is referred in this chapter as the Wall, as well as numerous subsidiary walls, many of which completely surround Palestinian towns, including Bethlehem. The Wall and its associated walls are themselves part of a landscape of bypass roads (Selwyn 2001), tunnels, armed checkpoints, boulders blocking road entrances and other technologies of obstruction and surveillance throughout the West Bank.

Spokespersons for the Israeli government are apt to argue that the walling up of Rachel's Tomb was, and is, done for 'security' reasons. There are routine claims that the tomb area has witnessed confrontations between Palestinians and the Israeli army. Whilst it is true that confrontations have indeed taken place in the vicinity – this is where an army encampment came to be located, after all – it is wholly doubtful that the tomb itself was ever targeted, and I am not aware of a single hostile act by Bethlehemites or anyone else towards Jewish or any other pilgrims or visitors to the tomb in the several hundred years of its existence. On a wider plane it seems impossibly far-fetched to think that the sculpting of the Palestinian landscape, in which Rachel's Tomb is one out of many exemplary sites, into its present fractured and disjointed state was not present in the minds of planning authorities for many years before even the first Intifada, let alone the second.

Qubbet Rahil

As already noted, Rachel's Tomb is in the neighbourhood of Qubbet Rahil,[6] a once prosperous and economically active part of Bethlehem. Processions at Christmas and Easter from Jerusalem to the Church of the Nativity in central Bethlehem have wended their way through the area for hundreds of years. Property was mostly Christian-owned. From the late 1980s through the 1990s, the area slowly declined. There was periodic shooting between the Israeli army and residents of the A'ida camp, not far from Rachel's Tomb. The presence of the army generally in the neighbourhood became more noticeable. Following the beginning of the second Intifada in 2000, however, the neighbourhood underwent even more radical change. The Israeli army entered the area and progressively took over buildings. From 2002 on, land and property were confiscated on grounds of 'security'. Families and businesses dispersed and, in 2003, the notice that the Wall was to be built in the area was posted. Construction began in 2004, accompanied by the huge programme of road blockages and diversions already referred to.

Not surprisingly, many families formerly resident in Qubbet Rahil have moved out of the area. Those who stayed have all suffered. An architect, who has lived in the neighbourhood since 1974 and raised three children there, had a thriving practice that employed fifteen people and was involved in construction of university and hospital buildings in Palestine and abroad until 2001. By 2006 the practice was down to four employees.

A 63-year-old shopkeeper has owned a grocery store in Qubbet Rahil since 1966, a livelihood that supported a family of seven. In 2001 his business grossed $100 (U.S.) per day. By 2006 the shop, being surrounded on all four sides and inserted into a corridor between the two walls enclosing Rachel's Tomb, grosses $2.50 daily from renting seats to taxi drivers. The family is effectively dependent on charity.

A 56-year-old Christian and a father of nine, bought the Karawan restaurant in the area (a prime location at the time) in 1974 with the proceeds of two businesses elsewhere in Bethlehem. In 2001 there was a staff of ten; by 2006 it was down to two. He himself was injured when he was shot whilst driving a car near the restaurant. The business was closed for four years but reopened in 2005. The Wall and entry tower are now 100 feet away from the entrance to the restaurant. Business has almost completely dried up, having declined by 90 per cent between 2001 and 2006. He is badly in debt.

Two brothers returned from working in Saudi Arabia and opened a large grocery and pharmacy in the neighbourhood, both of which prospered in the 1990s, being patronized by the generally well-off residents of not only the immediate neighbourhood around the tomb but also the wider area. By 2006 there was little business except from a few former patrons with a personal loyalty to the business. And so on.

The demise of Qubbet Rahil and the abduction of the tomb was the subject of an Early Day Motion[7] in the British parliament. Roger Berry MP (2006) tabled a motion as follows:

> That this House calls attention to the completion of the section of the 8-metre high concrete wall separating Bethlehem from Jerusalem; notes that around 40 Bethlehem families will be cut off from schools and medical facilities; recalls the ruling of the International Court of Justice in July 2004 that the building of the wall on occupied Palestinian territory is unlawful; further notes that the shrine of Rachel's Tomb, sacred to the three major religions, has been purposefully enveloped by the route of the walls and is therefore barred to Palestinians, whether Christian or Muslim; takes heed of widespread anxiety that new Israeli settlement building on the confiscated land around the Tomb may be about to begin with the consequence that Bethlehem may follow the example of Hebron, where recent Israeli settlements are embedded in the midst of the local Palestinian population, causing great provocation; and further notes the warn-

ing of Bethlehem's mayor, Dr Victor Batarseh, that 'the ghettoization of Bethlehem is not only destroying ancient communities, but is destroying the prospects of peace in the Middle East and the whole concept of international law'.

The Site and the Terms of its Contestation

Rachel's Tomb is a classically 'contested site'. Although I will spend more time here on particular Jewish/Israeli institutional voices, a brief re-statement of (what I believe to be) a fairly standard Bethlehemite view of the present status of the tomb and its neighbourhood is needed first. Thus, taking the reports on the history of the site by Sansour Dabdoub's interlocutors, literary sources and various types of written, photographic and oral testimony by participants of the EU projects referred to earlier, a common view of Rachel's Tomb in Bethlehem combines a general outrage at the Israeli occupation and military domination of a sizeable area of the city with a very clear commitment to return the tomb to its status as a site shared by the three monotheistic religions. The position of the participants in the Tempus project (see note four), for example, is that Rachel's Tomb needs to be integrated back into Bethlehem's tourism/pilgrimage offer as a site historically founded on the shared religious traditions of Palestine and as a symbol of what could and should constitute the religious and political foundations of a just settlement in the region more generally.

The Jewish/Israeli voices[8] which we will explore now contrast sharply in tone and content with these. Two closely linked organizations that are distinguished from each other by slightly different names but that seem to have identical-looking projects (to such an extent that a casual observer might assume that they are, in fact, one) are the Committee for Rachel's Tomb and the Kever Rachel Foundation.[9] These organizations post information, including political and historical 'updates', as well as links to affiliated sites on the web. A selection of the outputs they produce provides an outline of the position(s) they adopt.

In 2005 the foundation posted a short 'history' of Rachel's Tomb. It opens with the announcement that the tomb is 'Judaism's third holiest site, having been the scene of prayer and pilgrimage for more than three thousand years'. The death of Rachel 'on the road to Efrat – now Bethlehem' and the setting up by her husband Ya'acov of a pillar – 'the pillar at Rachel's grave to this day'[10] is quoted from the book of Genesis (35:16–21). We are told that Ya'acov buried Rachel at this spot, rather than the family burial plot at the Cave of the Patriarchs in Hebron, 'because he foresaw that his descendents would pass this site during their forced exile to Babylon in 423 BCE'. There follows the famous quotation from the prophet Jeremiah (3:15–17): 'Rachel weeping for her children refused to be comforted for her children who are gone' together with the promise by *Ha Shem* (literally 'the name', i.e. God) that 'your children shall return to their own country'.

According to 'ancient writings' the grave was originally marked by twelve stones, but, the foundation informs us, 'from the Byzantine period until the 1800s Rachel's Tomb consisted of a tiny domed structure'. Sir Moses Montefiore renovated the tomb. According to the foundation he 'added on an anteroom and enclosed the grave marker so that pilgrims could find shelter from the elements'. We then learn that the town of Bethlehem has expanded over the years so that the tomb now stands 'in the centre of one of the town's main streets' rather than in the open area in which it once stood. Moreover, '[s]ince 1948 Muslims have created their own cemetery surrounding the building' and 'for political purposes Muslims claim that Rachel's Tomb is one of their burial plots and that it contains a Muslim notable rather than Rachel'. 'Our own generation', the foundation claims, remembers the 'rustic charm' of the tomb 'before the State of Israel agreed to give Bethlehem to the Palestinian Authority. ... Now the State of Israel's Ministry of Religion renovated the site once again, and this time it has been enlarged many times its original size. This new Rachel's Tomb consists of the previous structure housed within the expanded and reinforced edifice. New editions include 2 guard towers [making] the new complex into a modern and stately building that has been designed to protect the tomb and those inside. ... Rachel's Tomb', the foundation concludes, 'is a living symbol of *Ha Shem's* promise to Rachel that her children will return to the Land of Israel'.

Readers of this narrative would not necessarily be aware of the political and military processes that preceded the erection and settlement of the 'modern and stately building' described by the foundation. Scrolling back to the news and views posted by the Committee for Rachel's Tomb helps fill in this version of the picture. In 2001, for example, several months into the second Intifada, the committee reports firefights between the Israeli Defence Force (IDF) and the 'Arab machine gun fire [directed] at Rachel's Tomb'. Bombardments by the IDF of PLO positions are reported, and the tomb is reported to have been in danger. A camp is reported to have been set up by Women in Green at the intersection of the Gilo tunnel[11] for activities surrounding the tomb. Readers are directed towards this latter site so that they might consider how best 'to show your support and conviction to keep *Kever Rachel* open to Jews and in Jewish hands!'

There then follow a series of 'updates' tracing the nature of the conflict over the tomb.[12] The root of the problem is traced back to the 1993 Oslo Accords, in which a 'Peace Process was agreed on the White House lawn under the auspices of President Bill Clinton between the Nobel Prize Laureates, the late Israeli Prime Minister Rabin and Yassir Arafat.' 'At that time,' the committee tells us, 'many regarded this signing as if it would usher in a new secular era, a secular-messianic era of peace and good-will between the Children of Israel and the Children of Ishmael. The secular, politically liberal and in Israel the anti-religious, took boastful credit for the monumental work of burying the hatchet between Jews and Arabs.' But 'unfortunately, all that was reversed when the Arabs unleashed a deadly wave of violence in November 2000 because they were miffed at PM Ariel Sharon daring to set foot on their turf – the Temple Mount, Judaism's holiest religious site.' Then, '[a]bout the beginning of July 2002 the IDF was sent back into the territories that Arafat and Co. hold.' Things quieted down, but 'the Arabs and their mentality will persist and terrorism will return so long as the heart of the Arab-on-the-street supports the calls of their leaders to terrorism and the annihilation of the Jews.'

References to 'areas where terrorists are trained and outfitted for mass-murder' are made in various forms, and it is observed that 'there is a very strong possibility that the only means that the State of Israel can defend herself from thousands of such morally repugnant people is to expel every Arab that has ever raised a finger or voiced a word hostile to the Children of Israel. For even if hostilities stop, Jews will live next to an Arab culture that continues to promote mass-death to Jews, and certainly no one can be expected to live with neighbours of that calibre'. Meanwhile, '[a]s far as Rachel's Tomb goes, so long as the IDF keeps control of Bethlehem her grave is safe. But politicians, especially those remnants on the secular-messianic-Left [sic], still have great influence in the affairs of the State of Israel, and appear to fall back into their old ways and mentality'.

Having laid the ground in the above fashion, the committee's 'updates', issued over the next two years or so, maintain the pressure. Dale Baranowski, one of the committee's spokespersons, reports in 2002 the decision of the government to build the '350 kilometer long fence [sic] along the entire Green Line' but observes that 'one difficulty with this plan is that this Green Line runs about 200 meters away from Rachel's Tomb and at this time the government has no plans to include the Tomb within the safety of the fence.' This is despite the fact that Rachel's Tomb is the Jewish people's third most important religious site while not at all revered by the Muslims'. Eventually Ehud Olmert (then mayor of Jerusalem) prevailed on the IDF to include the tomb within the boundary of the 'fence'.

At this point there is reference to the 'public relations disaster' that a Defence Ministry source predicted, should the 'fence' come indeed to encircle the tomb. According to a senior IDF officer, including the tomb within the 'fence' would involve the demolition of between thirty and forty Palestinian houses. Reference is made to a possible solution consisting of the building of a tunnel from the Israeli side of the 'fence' to the tomb. But the committee leaves readers reasonably clear that it would be disastrous for Rachel's Tomb to remain outside the 'fence'. Whilst this argument is being made there is an interesting reference to what Baranowski terms 'the Jerusalem Fence'. According to him, this relatively simple construction is to be 'little more than coils of barbed wire sometimes inserted in ditches about three meters wide'.

The upshot of the political struggle to include Rachel's Tomb on the Jerusalem side of the 'fence' is finalized following the news, reported by the Arutz Sheva News Service[13] and posted by the committee that 'the Security Cabinet approved Prime Minister Sharon's "Jerusalem envelope plan" including his recommendation to incorporate the tomb of Rachel the Matriarch within the capital's jurisdiction'. During the intervening months the committee posted cartoons of Arafat with a pickaxe breaking down Joseph's Tomb in Nablus, references to 'jihad' against the Jewish people and exhortations such as the following: 'Be alert and treat Joseph's Tomb and Rachel's Tomb as parcels of Palestinian land which must be liberated'.

By May 2004 Wall building was proceeding at high speed. The committee reported that 'in addition to the Bnei Rachel yeshiva and Beit Midrash (study hall) located on the premises two stores adjacent to the property are in the process of being converted into a visitors' centre. Two families are scheduled to move in to the apartments upstairs within a few weeks'. Additionally readers are informed that the Torah scroll at the site, dedicated by the Rachel's Children Reclamation Foundation, is kept in a Holy Ark with a curtain memorializing Rabbi Dr David Appelbaum and his daughter Nava. The curtain is made of 'material from the wedding gown of Nava, who was murdered by terrorists in Jerusalem last September on the night before she was to be married'.

During the process of the walling up of the tomb the committee directed readers to other websites. Some of these referred to political and/or business initiatives likely to be of interest of readers of the committee's website. Before the 'withdrawal' from Gaza, for example, Rachel watchers were linked to the website of Gush Katif where articles were to be found concerning the history of Jewish occupation in Gaza. The *katif* site also contained information about 'Gush Katif's On-Line Store' where readers could purchase a wide variety of goods possessing religious, nationalistic and/or security connotations (or all three combined). The Committee for Rachel's Tomb itself also became involved in business ventures. In 2004, for example, it launched a 'new campaign called *Standing Together*'. This involved sending 'good wishes and treats to our soldiers guarding the borders of Israel [sic]' courtesy of a Minnesota company, Lil Orbits, 'that manufactures a unique mobile trailer that is especially equipped to produce fresh doughnuts on a daily basis – perfect for our project which is aimed at distributing free fresh doughnuts and drinks to the soldiers while they are on active duty'. Around the same time another initiative was launched distributing pizza to the soldiers.

The fashion for linking the mobilization of popular support for Rachel's Tomb to business enterprises of various kinds seems to have grown during and following 2004. Temple Models, for example, offered models of the tomb at $99.[14] The same company also marketed a 'hand painted desktop charity box model depicting Rachel's Tomb, which is located in Bethlehem, Israel'. Their online brochure comes with explanatory historical pictures of the tomb in the past and in its contemporary manifestation 'after an extensive fortress was built for security'. In the same year the Lucky String company[15] offered 'Rachel's Red String', which is reported to have encircled the tomb seven times and which has especially protective powers ('Our Red Strings are 100 per cent authentic'). Potential customers are enjoined to 'Send the red string to those who you care about – protect them and yourself from the "Evil Eye"'.

Walls and 'Security'

Without claiming that the few words earlier on in this chapter about the terminal decline of the neighbourhood of Qubbet Rahil amount to sustained ethnographic description,[16] the outline does help to give some indication of what 'security' through 'separation' by way of the Wall and associated walls actually means on the ground.

Rachel's Tomb and the landscape in and around Bethlehem District, as in the Palestinian West Bank more generally, is now part of a patchwork of fragmented territory sculpted by ubiquitous bulldozers into a world of walls, barriers and checkpoints, tunnels, flyovers, military and bypass roads, watchtowers, settlements and settlement blocks (Halper 2004: 12–21). Halper himself describes the West Bank, including the Bethlehem district, in terms of a 'matrix of control' that oversees a series of Bantustans. The two narratives sketched out above – those generated by a collection of Bethlehemite voices, on the one hand, and by the Committee for Rachel's Tomb and its sister institutions, on the other – clearly legitimate radically different approaches towards Rachel's Tomb and its history. These alternative narratives, in turn, lay the foundations for the imagining of two differing futures for Bethlehem and the region. Whilst the former leads to a view that the 'security' of the Tomb, its neighbourhood and the region is to be found within frameworks of historical cooperation between the three religions and the possibility of the recovery of that co-operation (Selwyn, 2009) the latter leads to the promotion of the view that 'security' generally may only be achieved as a result of the militarily enforced ethnic and religious 'separation' that the Wall and its watchtowers[17] seek to achieve.

Part II: Re-Framing the Narrative

If we propose any kind of re-framed narrative, there is no better way to start than with Rachel herself.

Rachel

Rachel was born into a clan of sheep, goat and cattle herders. The name Rachel means ewe in Aramaic, and biblical scholars (e.g. van der Toorn, Becking and van der Horst 1995) have suggested that the ewe could have been her clan's totemic emblem. This seems a reasonable enough guess in a cultural and religious landscape of clan totems alongside household and ancestral gods that mingled with ideas about a single god. Rachel's clan lived in the eastern valleys of Padanaram, Mesopotamia, not far from the birthplace of Abraham. She was the youngest daughter of Laban and sister to Leah.

The book of Genesis tells us that Jacob, her cousin, journeyed east from Canaan to find a wife. Arriving at Padanaram he caught sight of Rachel, instantly fell in love, and kissed her. He asked her father for her hand in marriage. Laban agreed, but on condition that Jacob would work for him for seven years first. Jacob did this, but Laban tricked him into marrying Rachel's elder sister Leah. Jacob objected, and Laban agreed that he should marry Rachel as well as Leah – provided he worked for Laban for another seven years. During this period Jacob also had relations with two women servants, Zilpah and Bilah, who each bore him two sons. At the end of his fourteen-year stay Jacob had ten sons: six from Leah, four from Zilpah and Bilah, and none from Rachel, who was barren.

Rachel sought out whatever remedies were available at the time to deal with her infertility, eventually finding some magical formulas that worked, after which she gave birth to Jacob's eleventh son, Joseph. By now the family was large, and Jacob decided to return to Canaan. Before she left, Rachel took a number of household godlings, *teraphim,* from her father's house and put them in her baggage. Scholars have reported that these were objects of human form with pronounced sexual organs clearly associated with fertility. Nearing the end of their journey, on the road to Ephrathah, Rachel gave birth to her second son, Benjamin, and died in the process. To mark the spot Jacob placed eleven or twelve stones in a column.

This story has caught the imagination of a variety of European artists, writers and commentators. Scenes of Rachel and Jacob were painted by the Dutch and Italian Renaissance painters Hugo Van Der Goes (1440–1482), Raphael (1483–1520) and Palma Il Vecchio (1515–1525). Then there is a sparkling literary reference to Rachel in an anonymous text written in 1787 entitled 'A dissertation wherein the meaning, duty, and happiness of kissing are explained from Genesis 29:11'. The author's intention is to consider the meaning of the words 'Jacob kissed Rachel' and to enquire into the very important duty of kissing in an endeavour to represent the pleasure that always attends the true performance of this duty. The lively author of this piece makes high claims for this kiss, asking rhetorically of his readers at one point: 'Would you not embrace the happy moment, and without remorse, snatch nectar and ambrosia from her balmy lips?'

The references to Rachel's tears come from two sources, the Old Testament book of Jeremiah the prophet and the New Testament gospel of St Matthew. In the former Jeremiah speaks of Rachel watching and weeping as the children of Israel are exiled by the Babylonians. In the latter her tears are linked to the birth of Jesus, after whose birth the wise men asked Herod to direct them the King of the Jews. Herod advised them to follow the star to Bethlehem and directed them to report back to him once they had found the child. However, fearing for Jesus' life they did not come back to him. Having been thus tricked, Herod (to quote from the 1611 Kings James translation of the Bible) 'was exceeding wrath' and 'slew all the children that were in Bethlehem from two years old and under ... Then was fulfilled that which was spoken by Jeremy the prophet, saying, In Rama was there a voice heard, lamentation and weeping, and great mourning, Rachel weeping for her children, and would not be comforted, because they are no more'. The Slaughter of the Innocents, as the Christian calendar has it, and Rachel's sorrow place her within the Christian as well as the Jewish traditions.

Before coming to the question of what the story and personality of Rachel herself might have to tell us, we might state explicitly what has already been made clear implicitly, namely that Rachel is presently being used by voices and institutions, some of whom claim to speak for the Israeli state, together with various commercial pizza, doughnut and model making corporations, red string manufacturers, 'Women in Green' and assorted others – notably, of course, the arms and 'security' industries, to legitimate a series of social and political ideas and practices that link (at the very least) notions of 'security', 'separation' and military occupation.

In these circumstances the question becomes quite precise: is there an alternative way of interpreting Rachel's life history that might lead to an alternative set of dispositions?

Rachel: The First Cosmopolitan

Rachel's story begins near Abraham's birthplace – near what we now know as the Persian Gulf; thus her travels encompassed a wide geographical region, covering a lot of what is now Arabia. In this respect Rachel appears as a person associated with a vast area of open space unconstrained by borders and border guards and populated by clans and tribes in many respects like her own. As such she appears much closer to the ideal of a citizen of a modern global world than one trapped in between the alleys and tunnels that presently surround her tomb. Her life speaks of the potential of an open society and economy, both of which seem worlds away from the system of the minutely managed 'matrix of control' in which she is presently embedded.

The geographical aspects of her story imply a sense of openness and possibility of movement between and beside others. If it is possible that the Aramaic language was known throughout the region (a reminder, if one is needed, of the common ancestry of Hebrew and Arabic and the common kinship that it implies), it is more than probable that common cultural practices – such as those governing rules of hospitality or the practices at family shrines – were widely known and shared.

The sense of kinship and potential kinship that the sharing of a common language evokes is itself strengthened by one of the most famous aspects of Rachel's story – her espousal and use of the *teraphim*. As already noted, these were figures, commonly said, as their form implies, to be associated with fertility and infertility. Historical evidence indicates that such objects were used widely in the region. Together with household and ancestral gods themselves, they are examples of a category of religious objects that later became subject to sustained repudiation by those attracted to the idea of a single deity. Indeed, they are arguably examples of the sort of 'secondary' objects typically used by people of all faiths and none for particular purposes – such as warding off evil spirits and aiding fertility. Comparable objects in the contemporary world might include the ritual five fingered hand, made normally of brass or pottery, used by Christians, Jews and Muslims (with alternative names and designations to match) to guard against the evil eye, which is found dangling in cars and taxis in towns throughout the Mediterranean from Alexandria to Istanbul, Tel-Aviv, Bethlehem and beyond. The 'eye' itself is another example. Frequently a blue pendant in the shape of an eye, this is also found throughout the region. Even candles might qualify, under certain circumstances, as secondary objects. Thus, for example, not far south of Rachel's Tomb is the church of Saint George, known to Muslim and Christian women alike as a site at which candles may be lit to good effect for the saint's intercession to aid childbirth.

According to the bible and those European painters who have been inspired by her story, Rachel was a beautiful woman. The point here is part philosophical and part sociological. Like the notion of person itself, beauty is part universal and part culturally coded, part physical and part social. It is an attribute belonging to an individual that, in order to be itself, needs recognition by another.

Finally, what may we make of Rachel's tears? One interpretation might wish to emphasize her distress over 'her' children, the children of Israel, being exiled to Babylon. A second, encompassing the New Testament reference to the infants of pre-Christian Bethlehem, might choose to emphasize her compassion for both exile and untimely death. A third has a more contemporary edge to it: her tears today may be understood as expressions of grief at the pain of dislocation, dispersal and exile that the walling up of her tomb has caused those who until recently have lived and worked in its vicinity.

In summary, Rachel herself may be read as symbolizing suffering (her early barrenness), spiritual pragmatism (her use of the *teraphim*), compassion for exiles (both ancient and modern) and even (by way of what has become an iconic kiss between her and Jacob) pleasure. As woman, lover and mother Rachel seems naturally to attract and deserve a recognition and identification that is more universal than partial. Socially and geographically, moreover, the routine capacities of members of her clan and tribe to move amongst all the other tribes and clans of the desert (all of whom might have recognized the *teraphim* and comparable objects as versions of family deities of their own) make Rachel one of the earliest examples of the global cosmopolitan.

Some Lessons from Rachel on Reframing the Border Itself

So far it has been argued that Rachel's Tomb is presently being used by particular voices to construct a border landscape that is legitimated by, and helps both symbolically and practically to constitute, powerfully persuasive ethno-nationalist associations between 'security', the walling up of the frontier and the exclusive use of a previously shared religious site – resulting in the dislocation of those living on the other side. Such an interpretation fits well with corporate agendas, including American ones, present in the area operating in various fields including fast food, religious tokens (such as red strings) and the armaments industry.

But it has also been argued that Rachel's story is open to a more inclusive interpretation. Thus the final section of this chapter seeks to use her story to take the first steps towards imagining how the borderland around her tomb might be transformed from its present closed, defensive and empty state to one more in keeping with the open and borderless spaces, inhabited by people with whom Rachel and her family were themselves associated.

Donnan and Wilson (1999) have argued that borders are by nature ambivalent places. On the one hand, a border or boundary is an essential part of any human relationship and can play a role in productive exchanges between people and groups who recognize both their similarities and differences. On the other hand, borders can and do routinely articulate forced division and coercive separation between people. The borderlands around Rachel's Tomb today are being used by powerful voices, encouraged by corporate interests of various kinds to ensure that they are placed in the latter category: marginal spaces on the periphery of established national territory governed by an unremitting ethno-nationalist ideology. As such they are subject to processes of uneven development, underdevelopment and de-development. This is the fate of the borderlands around Rachel's Tomb.

Reframing can counter such assumptions by conceiving the possibilities for economic interconnectedness and social and cultural exchange. Such interchange was precisely the basis of the rapid economic growth of Qubbet Rahil in parts of the 1970s and 1980s and between 1992 and 2000, for it was along the old Jerusalem-Hebron road near Rachel's Tomb that visitors, including many Israelis, entered Bethlehem, using the retail and service facilities in the process. It was no accident that this was the site chosen to establish the Bethlehem Intercontinental Hotel, very briefly held (in late 1999 and early 2000) to be the 'best' hotel in the Middle East.[18] During this period one could briefly glimpse the possibility of reintegrating Bethlehem and Jerusalem, Palestine and Israel, within a reintegrated Mediterranean. Here we can perceive shades of the *Geniza*, that great body of work, assembled by Goitein (1967–1988), documenting Jewish life in the medieval in the Introduction of which we read that the region '[t]eemed with people, their quarrels, their wedding contracts, their dowries, their house furnishings and also their dreams and visions, their religion, and their most intimate feelings'. A contemporary writer, Amitav Ghosh (1994), used the *Geniza* to tell the story of Abraham Ben Yiju, a Jewish merchant originally from Tunisia, as he journeyed in the late fifteenth century through Egypt to Aden and thence to Mangalore on the Malabar Coast of India. He described Ben Yiju's various cultural and literary accomplishments, as well as his flair for business. Ben Yiju moved across the region unencumbered by borders and checkpoints, spending time, for example, in Aden, which at the time was a thriving centre of business and cultural activity, there being several gifted Hebrew poets resident in the city.

By the early sixteenth century, however, the world had changed completely and 'the remains of the civilization that had brought Ben Yiju to Mangalore were devoured by that unquenchable, demonic thirst that has raged ever since, for almost five hundred years, over the Indian Ocean, the Arabian Sea and the Persian Gulf' (and, we may add, over the lands to the immediate west of this region). Keeping in mind those living and working in contemporary Bethlehem, in particular the citizens of Qubbet Rahil who, even as this paragraph is being read, are being cleared ('cleansed' is a rougher but more accurate word) and displaced from their homes by the terrifying aggression of the Wall and its works, we are challenged by Ghosh's reflections to ask whether this 'demonic thirst' has any prospects, even in the twenty-first century, of being quenched.

In the present discussion of Rachel's Tomb and the walls and surveillance points around it today, the combination of the *Geniza* and Ghosh's commentary points towards a concluding thought. This is that the tradition of Rachel and her family in the mists of biblical history seems to join seamlessly to a medieval Jewish tradition in the Mediterranean world relatively free from the violence of essentially colonial structures and processes. The thought is that the present fate of Rachel's Tomb represents a radical departure, a dismembering even, of a historical – and fundamentally Jewish – tradition of cosmopolitan coexistence that has as much relevance for the present and future as it has it has for the understanding and appreciation of the past.

NOTES

1. The building is also known by Muslims as the Bilal Ibn Rabah mosque.
2. Rather than refer to this structure as the 'Security Wall', 'Security Fence' or 'Separation Wall' – some of the alternative terms used by official Israeli government spokespersons – or the 'Apartheid Wall', favoured by opposition Israeli circles and many Palestinians, the convention is adopted here of simply referring to it as the Wall. It needs emphasizing, however, that the Wall around Rachel's Tomb, as in many other parts of Palestine, amounts in fact to multiple walls associated in turn with multiple barriers, watchtowers, tunnels and other examples of military engineering that are designed very precisely to separate Israelis from Palestinians and Palestinians from each other. The enormity of this extraordinary project may be approached by consulting www.arij.org.
3. This is shorthand for the collection of voices and political forces and processes that, in the present context, are represented by the Committee for Rachel's Tomb and more widely by the West Bank 'settler' movement. Thanks to Jackie Feldman for giving me the idea for this epithet during the EASA conference in Bristol in September 2006.
4. The overall aim of the EC's Tempus (Trans-European Mobility Programme for University Studies) Programme is to encourage co-operation between universities from member states with universities beyond the borders of the EU. In the present case, the project, which ran from 2005–2008, thereafter gaining

a life of its own, involved a consortium of universities in the UK, Finland, and Malta, working with the University of Bethlehem to set up a Master's Degree, with associated research, in Pilgrimage and Tourism. Overlapping with the Tempus project the present writer also co-directed another programme of EU funded research work in the Mediterranean region, namely the Med-Voices project, of which the Centre for Cultural Heritage Preservation (CCHP) in Bethlehem was a partner. This three year project was part of the EU's Euromed Programme and has been described in the preface to the present volume. The views and approaches adopted in this chapter are the author's own and do not represent the views of the Tempus and/or Euromed authorities.

5. This refers to the Armistice Line agreed by the UN in 1949, marking the conclusion of hostilities that followed the declaration of Israeli independence. After the occupation of the West Bank by Israel following the 1967 war, the Green Line became, for a majority of Israelis, Palestinians and outsiders, the notional boundary between Israel and Palestine.

6. Once again I acknowledge the assistance of Carol Sansour for the following paragraphs on the neighbourhood.

7. EDM 1803. 2006.

8. It should be made clear that the voices and views reported here are those made by a limited number of organizations and institutions. It is not implied or assumed that they represent Jewish/Israeli voices in general. Indeed, it is assumed that there are views held by many Jews and Israelis that are diametrically opposed to those expressed here. Nevertheless, in so far as the views outlined here have clearly succeeded in mobilizing Israeli governmental and military institutions in the abduction of Rachel's Tomb and its neighbourhood into Israeli territory, it is assumed that these voices are representative of powerful and politically persuasive strands of thought in contemporary Israel.

9. The Committee for Rachel's Tomb (www.Rachelstomb.org) and the Kever Rachel Foundation (www.rachelstomb.com).

10. There is no discernible 'pillar' in Rachel's Tomb today. Two pillars that the visitor will find, which have already been mentioned earlier in the main body of the present text, come from the former police station in Bethlehem's Manger Square.

11. The Women in Green website is www.womeningreen. The route from Jerusalem to Hebron via the old established road running through Bethlehem to which references have been made in the text was (for Israeli drivers) superseded in the 1990s by the completion of Route 60 – effectively a main bypass road from Jerusalem to Hebron and settlements south of Bethlehem. Just south of Jerusalem Route 60 consists of a tunnel running under Beit Jala on its way southwards.

12. For example, www.rachelstomb.org.

13. www.IsraelNationalNews.com

14. www.templemodels.com/rachel

15. support@rachelsredstring.com

16. See the website of the Applied Research Institute of Jerusalem (Arij) <www .Arij.org > for more extensive description and analysis.

17. There would be those who might point to the building around each new Jewish settlement in the early years of the *yishuv* (pre-state Jewish settlement of Palestine from the end of the nineteenth century) of a stockade and watchtower (*choma ve migdal*). They might argue, with some justification, that although the Wall and watchtowers of twenty-first–century Palestine are on a far bigger scale, nothing essentially has changed in the disposition of settlers who regard 'security' (from potentially dangerous 'Arabs') as deriving from walls and the technologies of ethnic 'separation'. For many reasons (which need arguing through in a full and separate analysis), such simplistic structuralism, neat though it may appear, would be misleading.
18. Clearly this is a subjective and possibly hyperbolic judgement. But in the spring of 2000 the hotel was booked out for the rest of that year.

References

Anonymous. 1787. *A Dissertation wherein the meaning, duty, and happiness of kissing are explained from Genesis 29:11 'Jacob Kissed Rachel',* ms, British Library.

Berry, R. 2006. Early Day Motion 1803. London: House of Commons.

Donnan, H. and T.M. Wilson. 1999. *Borders: Frontiers of Identity, Nation and State.* Oxford: Berg.

Halper, J. 2004. *Obstacles to Peace: A Re-framing of the Palestinian-Israeli Conflict.* Jerusalem: Palmap.

Goitein, S.D. 1967–1988, *A Mediterranean Society: The Jewish communities of the Arab world as portrayed in the documents of the Cairo Geniza: Vols 1-6,* Berkeley, University of California Press and Cambridge University Press.

Ghosh, A. 1994. *In An Antique Land.* New York: Vintage Books.

Macalister, R.A.S. 1912. 'The Topography of Rachel's Tomb', Jerusalem and London, *Journal of the Palestine Exploration Fund,* April, 74–82.

Petrozzi, M.T. 1975. *Bethléem.* Jerusalem: Franciscan Printing Press.

Raheb, M. 2000. *Bethlehem 2000.* Heidelberg: Palmyra.

Sandys, G. 1632. *A Relation of a Journey Begun in 1610 to the Holy Land.* London: Ro Allot.

Selwyn, T. 2001. 'Landscapes of Separation: Reflections on the Symbolism of Bypass roads in Palestine', in B. Bender and M. Winer (eds), *Contested Landscapes: Movement, Exile and Place.* Oxford: Berg.

Selwyn, T. 2009. 'Ghettoizing a Matriarch and a City', *Journal of Borderland Studies,* 24: 39–59.

Strickert, F. 2007. *Rachel Weeping: Jews, Christians and Muslims at the Fortress Tomb.* Collegeville, Minnesota: Liturgical Press.

van der Toorn, K., B. Becking and P.W. van der Horst (eds). 1995. *Dictionary of Deities and Demons in the Bible.* Leiden: Brill.

Websites

www.arij.org (Final Retrieval in 2.2011)
http://katif.net (Final Retrieval in 6.2005)

IsraelNationalNews.com (Final Retrieval in 7.2006)
medvoices.org (Final Retrieval in 10.2005)
rachelstomb.com (Final Retrieval in 2.2011)
Rachelstomb.org (Final Retrieval in 2.2011)
rachelstomb.org/update (Final Retrieval in 2.2011)
templemodels.com/Rachel (Final Retrieval in 2.2011)
womeningreen.org (Final Retrieval in 2.2011)

♂ NOTES ON CONTRIBUTORS ♃

JEREMY BOISSEVAIN is Emeritus Professor of Social Anthropology, University of Amsterdam. His field research in Malta, Sicily, Montreal and Amsterdam has included local politics, ethnic relations, small entrepreneurs, ritual change and, currently, the impact of tourism and civic reaction to environmental degradation. His books include *Saints and Fireworks: Religion and Politics in Rural Malta* (London, 1965; Malta, 1993), *The Italians of Montreal: Social Adjustment in a Plural Society* (Ottawa, 1970), *Friends of Friends: Networks, Manipulators and Coalitions* (Oxford, 1974), *A Village in Malta* (New York 1980), *Hal Kirkop* (Malta, 2006) and the following edited collections: (with John Friedl) *Beyond the Community: Social Process in Europe* (The Hague, 1975), (with Hans Vermeulen) *Ethnic Challenge: The Politics of Ethnicity in Europe* (Göttingen, 1985), (with Jojada Verrips) *Dutch Dilemmas: Anthropologists Look at the Netherlands* (Assen, 1989), *Revitalizing European Rituals* (London, 1992), *Coping with Tourists: European Reactions to Mass Tourism* (Oxford, 1996), (with Tom Selwyn) *Contesting the Foreshore: Tourism, Society and Politics on the Coast* (Amsterdam, 2004). Translations of his work have appeared in Dutch, French, Italian, Spanish, Hungarian, Japanese and Polish.

DAVID CLARK studied anthropology in Canada, Uganda, the United States and Britain. He completed his doctoral work at London Metropolitan University and has undertaken research on community organization in Nairobi, housing and employment of ethnic minorities in Britain and Jewish museums in Europe. His current research interests include a study of European expatriates in Crete. He is also on the editorial committees of the cultural magazine *Jewish Renaissance* and of *Exiled Writers Ink*, a magazine devoted to the writings of refugee writers currently living in Britain and elsewhere in Europe.

H.H. GÜNHAN DANIŞMAN was, until his untimely death (on 17 January 2009), Professor of History at the Department of History of the Faculty of Arts and Sciences of Boğaziçi University in Istanbul. He acted as the academic adviser to the Arnavutköy Citizens Initiative during their fight against the third bridge planned to be constructed across the Bosphorus and organized an oral history project with the citizens during this period. He published the results of this research in several articles co-authored with İsmail Üstün.

GUNTHER DIETZ studied anthropology, Hispanic studies, philosophy and sociology at the Universities of Granada (Spain) and Göttingen and at Hamburg University, where he received his PhD in anthropology. He has taught at the Universities of Hamburg, Ghent (Belgium), Aalborg (Denmark) and Granada (Spain) and is currently Research Professor at Universidad Veracruzana (Mexico). He has undertaken ethnographic fieldwork on handicraft and *indigenismo* policy as well as on indigenous communities and ethnic movements in Michoacán (Mexico) and on migrant communities, nongovernmental organizations and 'multiculturalist' social movements in Hamburg (Germany) and Andalusia (Spain). Selected publications: *Multiculturalismo, interculturalidad y educación* (Mexico and Granada, 2003); *Muslim Women in Southern Spain: Stepdaughters of Al-Andalus* (San Diego, 2005); *Patrimonio Inmaterial y Diversidad Cultural* (ed.) (Seville, 2005); *Cultural Diversity: A Guide through the Debate, Journal 'Zeitschrift für Erziehungswissenschaft'* (Berlin, 2007); *Diccionario de Relaciones Interculturales: diversidad y globalización* (co-authored) (Madrid, 2007).

JAUME FRANQUESA received his PhD in social anthropology from the Universitat de Barcelona in 2006 and is currently assistant professor at SUNY Buffalo. His research is concerned with urban governance and place commodification, with a special focus on the relationship between processes of value creation and divergent forms of citizenship. He has carried out field research in Catalonia, Mallorca and Toronto.

CAROLINE GATT has been doing anthropology research and working with environmental nongovernmental organizations and environmental politics since 2000. From 2001 to 2005 she also worked as a theatre practitioner with two research theatre groups, in Malta and in Italy, as well as carrying out anthropological fieldwork. She is now a doctoral candidate in anthropology at the University of Aberdeen, having done fieldwork with Friends of the Earth.

SUNE HAUGBOLLE is Assistant Professor in Modern Islam and Middle East Studies at the Department for Cross-Cultural and Regional Studies, University of Copenhagen. He holds MSt and D.Phil. degrees in Middle East Studies from the University of Oxford, and BA and MA degrees in Arabic from the University of Copenhagen. He has published several articles on the politics and culture of war memory in Lebanon, Syria and the wider Middle East, and is editor of *The Politics of Violence, Truth and Reconciliation in the Arab Middle East* (Routledge, 2009). He is a member of the New Islamic Public Sphere.

ELENI KALLIMOPOULOU is lecturer in ethnomusicology at the University of Macedonia in Thessaloniki, Greece. She completed her PhD in ethnomusicology at the School of Oriental and African Studies (SOAS), University of London, and has taught in the Faculty of Music at the University of Cambridge and at the SOAS Music Department. She is author of the book *Paradosiaká: Music, Meaning and Identity in Modern Greece* (Ashgate, 2009); other forthcoming contributions include an article in *The World of Music* and entries in *The Continuum Encyclopedia of Popular Music of the World.* Her present research interests comprise music, meaning and ideology; music performance; ethnography; cultural production and institutions; and the world music market. She is also active as a composer and performer.

MARIA KOUSIS is Professor and Vice Director of the MSc in Bioethics at the University of Crete and Resource Editor of *Annals of Tourism Research* and *R: Revista de Estudios de Comunicacion.* She has co-edited a volume (with Charles Tilly) on *Economic and Political Contention in Comparative Perspective* (Paradigm Publishers, 2005), a special issue (with Charles Tilly) on 'Contentious Politics and Social Change' (*Theory and Society,* 2004) and a volume (with Klaus Eder) on *Environmental Politics in Southern Europe: Actors, Institutions and Discourses in a Europeanizing Society* (Kluwer, 2001). She has coordinated or participated as partner in European Commission projects including EuroMed Heritage II, Environment and Climate Research Programme, and the 6th EU Framework Programme for Research and Technology. With interests in Mediterranean environmental and contentious politics, as well as sustainability and social change, she has published articles in journals including *Mobilization, Environmental Politics, Annals of Tourism Research, Theory and Society* and *Sociologia Ruralis.*

MARC MORELL is currently completing his PhD thesis in Social Anthropology at the Universitat de Barcelona and is based at the Politics, Labour and Sustainability research team at the Universitat de les Illes Balears. Drawing on political anthropology, he inquires into urban and tourism issues by focusing on the production of space in market society. He has conducted field research in Mallorca and Malta. For more information please visit http://www.uib.es/depart/dfl/pts/morell_eng.htm.

KATERINA PSARIKIDOU is Doctoral Researcher and Teaching Assistant at the Department of Sociology, Lancaster University, UK. Her research interests cover the fields of environmental sociology, rural sociology, sociology of science, political economy of environment and agriculture. She has also worked as a researcher for EU projects (http://www.faanweb. eu/; http://www.univie.ac.at/life-science-governance/paganini). Her MA thesis in Bioethics was entitled 'Bioethics and Biodiversity: The *Caretta caretta* Case in Greece'. Related publications include 'Environmental Ethics and Biodiversity Policy in Tourism: the *Caretta caretta* case in Greece' (*TOURISMOS*, 2008) and 'Tourism, the Environmental Habitats Directive and *Carreta carreta* in Greece', in O. Iakobidou (ed.), *Mediterranean Tourism Beyond The Coastline: New Trends in Tourism and the Social Organisation of Space* (Ziti, 2005). She is currently working on the constituencies of Alternative Agro-food Networks (AAFNs) and their relationship with the Knowledge-based Bio-economic (KBBE) narrative.

JAVIER ROSÓN LORENTE holds a BA in pedagogy and a PhD in Anthropology (Universidad de Granada, Spain). His main research areas include religion, ethnicity, migrant communities and Spanish Islam. He is currently working as a postdoctoral researcher at the Laboratorio de Estudios Interculturales (Granada) in the FP6 project 'Religion in Education: A Contribution to Dialogue or a Factor of Conflict Transforming Societies of European Countries' (REDCo; cf. www.redco.uni-hamburg.de).

MINAS SAMATAS, currently Associate Professor of Political Sociology in the Sociology Department at the University of Crete, has a PhD from the Graduate Faculty of New School for Social Research (New York). He has published in international and Greek journals on such issues as 'Greek Bureaucratism', 'Greek McCarthyism', 'Greece in "Schengenland"' and 'Security and Surveillance in Athens 2004 Olympics'. He is co-editor with Kevin Haggerty of a volume on *Surveillance and Democracy* (Routledge, 2010). Based on his book *Surveillance in Greece: From Anticommunist to Consumer Surveillance* (Pella, NY, 2004) he is a participant in various international surveillance study groups.

CAROL SANSOUR DABDOUB has been involved since 1994 with local and international NGOs and initiatives related to community mobilization, local economic development, events, tourism and public awareness. In 1999 she was appointed Head of the Tourism and Private Sector Department in the Bethlehem 2000 Project, preparing the ground for the turn of the millennium. She also served at the International Centre of Bethlehem, where she assisted in establishing the Bethlehem Media Centre. In 2004 Ms Sansour Dabdoub cofounded *Open Bethlehem,* an international campaign to save the city of Bethlehem. In 2006 she served as Public Relations Director at Bethlehem University. Today Carol leads a national award-winning public health awareness campaign against diabetes in the United Arab Emirates.

TOM SELWYN is Professorial Research Associate and Director of Studies of the Masters Degree in Travel, Tourism, and Pilgrimage in the Department of Anthropology and Sociology at the School of Oriental and African Studies (SOAS), University of London. Following field research in India, Palestine/Israel, and the Mediterranean region he is widely published in the fields of tourism, pilgrimage, hospitality, landscape and nationalism, post-conflict development, and the caste system in rural India. Recent edited books/special journal issues include *The Tourist Image* (Wiley, 1996), *Contesting the Foreshore* (with Jeremy Boissevain) (University of Amsterdam, 2004), *Turning Back to the Mediterranean* (with Rachel Radmilli) (special issue of Journal of Mediterranean Studies, 2005), *Pilgrimage and Religious Tourism* (with Nelson Graburn and Amos Ron) (special issue of Journal of Management and Spirituality, 2009), *Thinking Through Tourism* (with Julie Scott) (Berg, 2010). Since 1995 he has directed/co-directed programmes of research and development for the EC and several governments and international agencies in the Mediterranean, Bosnia-Herzegovina, and Palestine in the fields of tourism and development. He is Honorary Librarian and Council member of the Royal Anthropological Institute (RAI) and was awarded the RAI's Lucy Mair medal in 2009.

İSMAİL ÜSTÜN is Lecturer at the Department of Tourism and Hotel Management at the Vocational School of Yildiz Technical University and is completing his PhD studies at the Department of *Principles of Kemalism and Modern Turkish History* at the same university. After receiving his BA in sociology at the Aegean University in İzmir, he obtained an MA in sociology at the Mimar Sinan Fine Arts University in Istanbul. His MA thesis, based on an archival research of a 1930s road-tax register for the neighbourhood of Arnavutköy, served as the basis for this chapter in this book.

ELIA VARDAKI received her PhD in cultural anthropology from Oxford University. She holds an MSt in anthropological archaeology from Oxford and a BA in archaeology and history of art from the University of Crete. She taught at the University of Crete (Department of Sociology) and at the University of Ioannina (Department of Art Sciences). She is Visiting Scholar at UC Berkeley. She has conducted anthropological research in the island of

Kythera and has published in internationally acclaimed journals and edited books, as well as acted as a reviewer for the *Journal of South European Society and Politics.* Her research interests include anthropology of material culture, anthropology of food consumption, social memory, gender relations and identity formation. Her current research focuses on violence and criminality from a bio-political perspective.

VASSILIKI YIAKOUMAKI (PhD, New School for Social Research) is Lecturer in Social Anthropology at the University of Thessaly (Volos), Greece. Her area of research is ethnic groups, minorities and multiculturalist politics in Europe, and she has written on topics such as Mediterranean cultures, Jewish identities and cultural politics of food. Besides conducting research for the European Programme Mediterranean Voices/Euromed Heritage II, she has published in journals (*South European Society & Politics, Journal of Modern Greek Studies*) and in the edited volumes *Visual Interventions* (ed. S. Pink, 2007) and *Thinking Through Tourism* (eds. J. Scott and T. Selwyn, 2010).

CAROL ZOUGHBI-JANINEH has recently served at Bethlehem University – Institute for Community Partnership as Project Manager in charge of the Media Education and Blended-Learning Centres. With a background in business administration, she worked for three years coordinating cultural heritage projects through her previous position at the Centre for Cultural Heritage Preservation in Bethlehem. She also worked as a researcher in the field of oral history in the Bethlehem area through Mediterranean Voices, a Euro-Med Heritage II Project that ended in March 2006. She received her master's degree in pilgrimage and tourism from London Metropolitan University in 2007 through the Tempus Programme in Palestine. Currently involved in a family-owned graphic designs and printing business, Creative Ad Design and Print Co. Ltd., Ms Zoughbi-Janineh aims to work in the field of tourism and cultural development.

⊰ INDEX ⊱

Berghahn Books

BERLIN, ALEXANDERPLATZ
Transforming Place in a Unified Germany
Gisa Weszkalnys

. . . presents multiple perspectives with a clear focus, enabling the reader to apprehend a complex, consequential, and always transforming site as the nexus of multiple views, values, experiences, and hopes. Smart, deeply researched, interpretively sophisticated without being overburdened by theory, this is a real contribution to an anthropology of urban sites and life.　　**Don Brenneis,** University of California, Santa Cruz

A benchmark study in the changing field of urban anthropology, Berlin, Alexanderplatz is an ethnographic examination of the rapid transformation of the unified Berlin. Through a captivating account of the controversy around this symbolic public square in East Berlin, the book raises acute questions about expertise, citizenship, government and belonging. Based on ethnographic fieldwork in the city administration bureaus, developers' offices, citizen groups and in Alexanderplatz itself, the author advances a richly innovative analysis of the multiplicity of place. She reveals how Alexanderplatz is assembled through the encounters between planners, citizen activists, social workers, artists and ordinary Berliners, in processes of popular participation and personal narratives, in plans, timetables, documents and files, and in the distribution of pipes, tram tracks and street lights. Alexanderplatz emerges as a socialist spatial exemplar, a 'future' under construction, an object of grievance, and a vision of robust public space. This book is both a critical contribution to the anthropology of contemporary modernity and a radical intervention in current cross-disciplinary debates on the city.

Gisa Weszkalnys studied in Berlin and Cambridge and received her PhD in Social Anthropology from the University of Cambridge. She is a Lecturer in Anthropology at the University of Exeter and is conducting new research on oil developments in West Africa.

Space and Place, volume 1
224 pages, 17 ills, bibliog., index
ISBN 978-1-84545-723-5 Hardback

CULTURAL DIVERSITY IN RUSSIAN CITIES
The Urban Landscape in the post-Soviet Era
Edited by Cordula Gdaniec

Cultural diversity – the multitude of different lifestyles that are not necessarily based on ethnic culture – is a catchphrase increasingly used in place of multiculturalism and in conjunction with globalization. Even though it is often used as a slogan it does capture a widespread phenomenon that cities must contend with in dealing with their increasingly diverse populations. The contributors examine how Russian cities are responding and through case studies from Moscow, St. Petersburg, Novosibirsk, and Sochi explore the ways in which different cultures are inscribed into urban spaces, when and where they are present in public space, and where and how they carve out their private spaces. Through its unique exploration of the Russian example, this volume addresses the implications of the fragmented urban landscape on cultural practices and discourses, ethnicity, lifestyles and subcultures, and economic practices, and in doing so provides important insights applicable to a global context.

Cordula Gdaniec is currently an independent researcher. From 2003–2008, she was a Research Fellow and Lecturer at the Department of European Ethnology at Humboldt University in Berlin, involved in the project "Urban culture and ethnic representation - Berlin and Moscow as emerging world cities?" Her publications include Kommunalka und Penthouse. Stadt und Stadtgesellschaft im postsowjetischen Moskau (LIT Verlag, 2005).

Space and Place, volume 2
196 pages, 21 ills, bibliog, index
ISBN 978-1-84545-665-8 Hardback

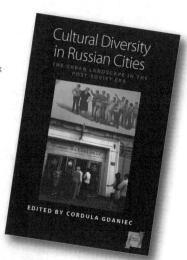

Berghahn Books

SETTLING FOR LESS
The Planned Resettlement of Israel's Negev Bedouin
Steven C. Dinero

This is an excellent study of an important and timely topic that is of relevance not only for the people involved but for the wider areas of Israel and the Arab world. It is a comprehensive detailed description and analysis of a process of change and transformation that started in 1948 and continues until the present.
Donald AbdAllah Cole, The American University in Cairo

The author is a geographer interested in town planning, who also has a solid grounding in anthropology. Two things make the book very attractive: that it is totally focused on town planning, and that the fieldwork was spread out over a decade which permitted the author to concentrate on the frequent changes in the plans and in their implementation. **Emanuel Marx,** Tel Aviv University

The resettlement of the Negev Bedouin (Israel) has been wrought with controversy since its inception in the 1960s. Presenting evidence from a two-decade period, the author addresses how the changes that took place over the past sixty to seventy years have served the needs and interests of the State rather than those of Bedouin community at large. While town living fostered improvements in social and economic development, numerous unintended consequences jeopardized the success of this planning initiative. As a result, the Bedouin community endured excessive hardship and rapid change, abandoning its nomadic lifestyle and traditions in response to the economic, political, and social pressure from the State—and received very little in return.

Steven C. Dinero is Associate Professor of Human Geography at Philadelphia University. He has published extensively on such topics as community planning and development, gender, identity formation, religion, education, and tourism in post-nomadic environments. His recent work addresses the impacts of globalization and climate change upon indigenous peoples, and the role of new technologies in helping such communities respond and adapt to these environmental challenges.

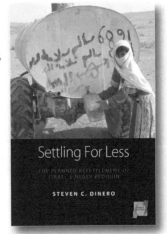

Space and Place, volume 3
248 pages, 20 photos, 16 figures, 10 tables, bibliog., index
ISBN 978-1-84545-762-4 Hardback

IRON IN THE SOUL

Displacement, Livelihood and Health in Cyprus

Peter Loizos

There are few if any longitudinal accounts of how long-term forcibly displaced populations survive and adapt. Providing a unique and intricate account of a lifetime in exile represented through the experiences of the refugees from Argaki, the book is an innovative contribution to the literature . . . A richly metaphorical style adds to the engaging content.   Journal of Refugee Studies

This is an important book, not only in the very particular context of Cyprus, but also in the longitudinal study of displacement . . . Loizos quietly and clearly exhorts us to consider the profound and long-term effects of displacement, and Iron in the Soul cannot be recommended highly enough for anyone interested in the experience of refugees over time, the impact on health of forced migration, or the lived history of Cyprus over the past several decades.   JRAI

What this work represents is the culmination of 40 years of engagement with the same community, a community that the author knew in his youth and with which he himself has grown and matured. This in itself makes the work a type of landmark in anthropology, and one that is best read in relation to his earlier work.
                    South European Society & Politics **Jason Hart** is a Senior Research Officer
                    at the Refugee Studies Centre, University of Oxford.

Peter Loizos, Professor Emeritus in Anthropology, London School of Economics, was born in London, studied at Cambridge, Harvard and L.S.E., where he taught Social Anthropology for thirty-three years. As a photographer and documentary filmmaker, Peter Loïzos has written a textbook on ethnographic films, and carried out development consultancies in Sudan, Sri Lanka, Nepal and Bangladesh for organisations including Oxfam, Save the Children and DFID. His latest work is an attempt to refine the concept of 'generation' in forced migration studies.

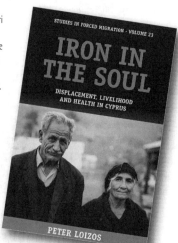

224 pages, 18 photos, 6 figs, 2 maps, bibliog., index
ISBN 978-1-84545-444-9 Hardback
ISBN 978-1-84545-484-5 Paperback

Berghahn Books

EUROPE AT THE SEASIDE

The Economic History of Mass Tourism in the Mediterranean

Edited by Luciano Segreto, Carles Manera and Manfred Pohl

The essays in this book investigate aspects directly related to tourism, such as hotel entrepreneurs, travel agencies, charter companies and firms developing advertising networks. The outcome is an extensively documented and successful collage of information on mass tourism as an alternative or complementary source of income for the population residing around the Mediterranean.

Journal of Contemporary European Studies

Mass tourism is one of the most striking developments in postwar western societies, involving economic, social, cultural, and anthropological factors. For many countries it has become a significant, if not the primary, source of income for the resident population. The Mediterranean basin, which has long been a very popular destination, is explored here in the first study to scrutinize the region as a whole and over a long period of time. In particular, it investigates the area's economic and social networks directly involved in tourism, which includes examining the most popular spots that attract tourists and the crucial actors, such as hotel entrepreneurs, travel agencies, charter companies, and companies developing seaside resort networks. This important volume presents a fascinating picture of the economics of tourism in one of the world's most visited destinations.

Luciano Segreto is Professor of Economic History and the History of International Economic Relations at the University of Florence. Chairman of the Cultural Memory Council of the ICCA, he is a member of the Scientific Committee of the Maison des Sciences de l'Homme d'Aquitaine and of many international journals.

Carles Manera has a PhD in history and one in economics. He has been awarded several prizes for his research, including the Prize of Economics in Catalonia (2003). Currently, he is director of the research group on economic history and the researcher in charge of the project "Economic History of Mass Tourism in Spain, 1940-2000: the Balearic Islands and the Mediterranean Contrasts," financed by the Ministry of Science and Education of Spain.

Manfred Pohl is founder and chairman of the International Centre for Corporate Culture and History (ICCCH), which consists of the European Association for Banking and Financial History (EABH), the Institute for Corporate Culture Affairs (ICCA) as well as the Frankfurter Kultur Komitee. He is also founder of the Gesellschaft für Unternehmensgeschichte and co-founder of the Konvent für Deutschland. After forty years with Deutsche Bank, he officially retired in May of this year. Since 1997 he has been Honorary Professor at the University of Frankfurt.

304 pages, 68 tables, 16 ills, 2 maps, bibliog., index
ISBN 978-1-84545-323-7 Hardback